AMERICAN

SHAME

AMERICAN
SHAME

STIGMA AND THE BODY POLITIC

EDITED BY
MYRA MENDIBLE

INDIANA UNIVERSITY PRESS
Bloomington & Indianapolis

This book is a publication of

Indiana University Press
Office of Scholarly Publishing
Herman B Wells Library 350
1320 East 10th Street
Bloomington, Indiana 47405 USA

iupress.indiana.edu

∞ The paper used in this publication meets the minimum requirements of the American National Standard for Information Sciences—Permanence of Paper for Printed Library Materials, ANSI Z39.48-1992.

Manufactured in the United States of America

Cataloging information is available from the Library of Congress.

ISBN 978-0-253-01979-0 (cloth)
ISBN 978-0-253-01982-0 (paperback)
ISBN 978-0-253-01986-8 (ebook)

1 2 3 4 5 21 20 19 18 17 16

To Ernesto, for always believing in me.

And as long as you are in any way ashamed before yourself, you do not yet belong with us.

—Friedrich Nietzsche, *The Gay Science*

CONTENTS

ACKNOWLEDGMENTS

I owe a debt of gratitude to Evelin Gerda Lindner for her tireless efforts on behalf of human dignity. A "public intellectual," global citizen, and genuinely kind human being, Lindner's fieldwork and writing have produced remarkable insights, given rise to related efforts among a community of activists and scholars around the world, and inspired a journey that led to this book. I also wish to acknowledge my friend and colleague, Delphine Gras, for her encouragement, feedback, and generosity of spirit. Thank you.

AMERICAN
SHAME

American Shame and the Boundaries of Belonging

Myra Mendible

Shame as Spectacle: Bodies That Matter

The spectacle is the acme of ideology, for in its full flower it exposes and manifests . . . the impoverishment, enslavement and negation of real life.
—Guy Debord, *Society of the Spectacle*[1]

On any given day in America's twenty-four-hour news cycle, shame is a hot commodity. Stories and images of disgraced politicians and celebrities solicit our moral indignation, their misdeeds fueling a lucrative economy of shame and scandal. Nothing fosters the illusion of solidarity like shared condemnation: joining the chorus of outrage that follows the exposure of the rich and famous, we play out a fantasy of community that otherwise eludes us. Here is the stuff of cultural belonging today—a bonding ritual that fills in for the spectacles that once were town square stocks and pillories. Righteous rants about the latest breach in conduct circulate via chat rooms, blogs, and social media; civic interactivity plays out in tweets, hashtags, and posts. Duly disciplined, the exposed offender, egotist, or fool bolsters our faith in the notion that, in America, personal responsibility accounts for failures and everyone—even the rich and famous—get what they deserve.

But of course this is a comforting fiction. We watch as the disgraced politician goes on to profit from memoirs and reality show appearances; the chastened celebrity is rehabilitated and rebranded. Whereas the experience of shame prompts a desire to hide and conceal, shame spectacles generate publicity, increasing marketability and "trending" stats. They garner photo-ops, TV appearances, feature stories, press releases, and—most enthralling—staged mea culpas. As spectators, we play our part in these charades, expressing our outrage in shrill tirades, all Sturm und Drang and grand gestures. Commodified and converted into spectacle, shame is more entertaining than disciplinary, more akin to a system of sociality than morality. It produces tabloid fodder for mass consumption—a carnival of moral outrage that channels a people's discontent but ultimately deflects attention from the embodied conditions where shame does its work. Instead, we are induced to speak of shame as an absence, to behold it in its undoing. Performing a trifling dance in public, shame becomes form emptied of content, a kind of holographic image projected on bodies that matter enough to be singled out for media attention.

We are so acculturated to shame as spectacle that its power is often overshadowed by its trivialization. In the logic of abstract exchange that dominates market cultures, spectacle reflects the commodity's complete "colonization of social life."[2] Commodification transfers the intersubjective nature of the shame dynamic into the realm of "pseudo-events" in which social relations are enacted via images rather than persons. After all, most of us have no actual relationship with the celebrities and power brokers whom we excoriate with glee; we relate to them as we do to familiar product brands—to their function as "mediating frames" rather than individuals.[3] They are "known" to us not for what they *are* but for what they *have* (money, power, fame). In a society of spectacle, an event or person becomes meaningful only when it appears as image. Guy Debord theorizes spectacle as a tool of pacification that distracts and stupefies social subjects, but new technologies such as online chat rooms, call-in radio, and social media add a more interactive dimension. Although this facilitates an active role for the subject, it also signals the subject's eclipse and the "growing power of the object."[4] Relevant here is how these interactions deflect attention from the self and toward its objects: shame in this context has nothing to do with our own behaviors or flaws. It remains safely detached—a story *we* tell about *them*.

As I write this, the internet is alight with another celebrity shame spectacle—the so-called "slut shaming" prompted by Miley Cyrus's lewd onstage "twerking" at the MTV 2013 Music Video Awards. Moral indignation at Miley's behavior is the flavor of the month: "Shame on you, Miley" videos have popped up on YouTube, the online magazine *Celebuzz* has declared it "the twerk heard round the world," and there have been numerous complaints to the FCC (which does not have the authority to sanction cable networks). Twitter has announced that Miley's performance set a record on the social networking site, garnering 306,100 tweets per minute.[5] The online tirades have spilled into newspaper editorials and television news shows. On MSNBC's *Morning Joe*, Mika Brzezinski expressed indignation at Miley's "really, really disturbing performance," which she called "disgusting and embarrassing." She suggested that Miley's behavior shows that the twenty-year-old diva is "obviously deeply troubled, deeply disturbed" and probably has an "eating disorder." Moral outrage then turned to concern: "She is a mess. Someone needs to take care of her," Brzezinski opined. The furor has gone on to produce more spectacular "pseudo-events" for our consumption, as other celebrities and even politicians have weighed in on the Miley affair. An infusion of race and politics has intensified the fury, with several commentators outraged by the image of the White former Disney star "twerking" with an all-Black cast of dancers. The popular blog "Defend the Modern World" posted a commentary on June 21, 2013, decrying Miley's behavior as a badge of shame for "American Caucasians" and a victory for "Blacks, Hispanics and Asians" who were presumably "delighted, triumphant even" at "the decline of White society." *Politico*'s Keith Koffler opined that Miley's performance heralded "our culture's destruction," an imminent collapse he attributes to President Obama for "abetting our moral disintegration."[6]

Shame as commodity spectacle is most productive (and profitable) when projected on media-worthy objects, on bodies that matter enough to merit attention. In an American society where the *success ethic* predominates, achievement measures our "intrinsic worth."[7] Being famous or "powerful" imbues certain bodies with "intrinsic worth" that makes them worthy of recognition, rehabilitation, or concern. Their shame matters. Marveling at the viral nature of moral indignation in the wake of the Miley scandal, I wonder at the day-to-day indignities suffered by bodies that do not seem to matter at all. Driving to work, I catch a brief report on NPR about elderly Americans who depend on supplementary food programs for their next meal; dwindling funds led one community agency to recommend that "its seniors stretch the food they already have—by watering down milk and soup."[8] Where is the flurry of outraged tweets at this shameful "solution" to hunger in the world's richest nation? Where are the outcries of moral indignation at the incarceration of a generation of young Black men, the demonization of immigrants, the injustices committed in our name on "foreign" or "alien" bodies? This is the unacknowledged shame that binds us in silent resignation, the shame whose name we dare not speak; the shame that is a condition of American life for those who have the "wrong" bodies or the "wrong" desires. Distracted and preoccupied by shame as spectacle, an increasingly polarized American citizenry disavows the shame that can spur moral action, the shame of our complicity, the shame born of recognition that is, in Paul Gilroy's words, "complicated by a sense of responsibility." Gilroy expresses the need "to answer the corrosive allure of absolute sameness and purity" by invoking the "political, ethical, and educational potential of human *shame*."[9] This involves, in part, attention to the ways that human dignity is eroded by biopolitical processes that are naturalized and familiarized to the point that they are made invisible.

Shame calls out for a witness. The elderly woman who must water down her soup may be socialized to endure her shame in private, but its public disclosure bears acknowledgment, registers what Sara Ahmed has called the "sociality of pain." As witnesses to another's experience of shame, we grant it the status of an event, endowing it with "a life outside the fragile borders of [the other's] body."[10] Our proximity to another's psychological and/or physical anguish makes their pain more difficult to ignore or justify. It offers a kind of knowledge that has the potential to disrupt our epistemological moorings; the more direct this knowledge is, the greater the potential for an emotional corrective to occur. In *Totality and Infinity*, Emmanuel Levinas argues that the face does more than request ethical treatment: its vulnerability and "nakedness" demand it. To hear the other's cries for justice, Levinas insists, "is not to represent an image to oneself, but is to posit oneself as responsible. . . . For the face summons me to my obligations and judges me."[11] But when the face is absent, ethical foundations become less stable. Denying the other's longing for recognition and place, we deny his very existence. The other's shame—written in her facial features and body language, signals her self-consciousness: a testament to their humanity. Although this affirmation may not be authorized or acknowledged on the structural level—through institutions and social practices—it nonetheless registers at the level of affect. This is one reason that prejudice and hostility between different groups tend to decrease when groups interact often and why political leaders who aim to incite violence between rivals first segregate target groups, denigrating and humiliating them out of sight, erecting walls between them (literal and symbolic) so as to avoid reminders of their humanity. Jews were restricted to ghettoes; Blacks, to separate schools and neighborhoods; Native Americans, to reservations. These were locations where their shame and humiliation—even extinction—could remain on the periphery of social consciousness. It is one thing to ignore another's suffering when it occurs out of sight or is deferred through representation so that it remains *elsewhere*; it is quite another when the other jolts us into a sensory knowledge— where emotional pain has a smell, a sound, an embodied presence. This knowledge provides the basis on which to build affective bonds born of identification. But in the logic of abstract exchange that characterizes a society of spectacle, we place blame but disclaim obligation. We claim membership in a moral order while remaining morally oblivious.

Shame Revivalism and the Politics of Virtue

In the stories we tell ourselves, we are nearly always too good: too soft on criminals, too easy on terrorists, too lenient with immigrants, too kind to animals. In the stories told by our numbers, we imprison, we drone, we deport, and we euthanize with an easy conscience and an avenging zeal.
—Tom Junod, "The State of the American Dog"[12]

Conveying otherwise "private" or localized events into the public sphere, shame spectacles privilege and make visible certain events and people, displacing everyday experiences with the singular, the exceptional, and the sensational. We might easily discount the importance of these pseudo-events given their ephemeral nature—as Janet Jackson's so-called wardrobe malfunctions or Miley Cyrus's twerks invariably give way to freshly minted moral scandals (and American neologisms).[13] Working in conjunction with certain ideological frameworks, however, shame spectacles also play a political role as "meaning machines," to use Murray Edelman's term, generating points of view and "perceptions, anxieties, aspirations, and strategies."[14] As tropes for cultural and moral decline, shame narratives reify and reproduce beliefs about the state of the nation and its people. Scaffolding that which must be expelled, restrained, or purified, they serve as moral provocations by feeding on collective narcissism. Invoking threats against an in-group's idealized self-image, reputation, or moral status, this strategy of misattribution involves both a disavowal of and an investment in shame: "our" image is contaminated and sullied by "their" behavior. Shame becomes a crucial weapon in efforts to divest and dissociate others in a strategy that political philosopher Jean Bethke Elshtain calls the "politics of displacement," a strategy that uses shame to draw boundaries between full and partial citizenship.[15] Stage-managed and circulated, images of "shameful" identities translate into political capital: behold the wages of shamelessness, our self-appointed Paul Reveres warn, looking for convenient culprits and villains.

Not surprisingly, most recent discussions about shame in contemporary America bemoan its absence. In particular, American shame is said to have gone soft or gone missing, a casualty of declining moral values, rampant secularism, or vulgar commercialism. This reputed erosion of shame has inspired a kind of shame revivalism among politicians, pundits, and critics, who posit the need to "rehabilitate" American shame. Blaming "liberals," feminists, gays and lesbians, or, more broadly, "secular humanists," contemporary jeremiads urge a resurgence of shame and intolerance, which, according to *Newsweek*, have "gotten a bad rap in recent years."[16] Examples are ubiquitous, but a few should suffice here: An emeritus professor presents the case in his local newspaper that American culture is on the decline because of too little shame;[17] a blogger opines that in shame's absence, too much "tolerance" is "lowering our standards"[18]; a Facebook page invites visitors to join their "bring back shame" community.[19] Shame brokers voice their concern in print and on the air, warning of dire consequences. Sonny Bunch of the *Washington Free Beacon* and Michael Goodwin of the *New York Post* each contributed recent op-eds exhorting Americans to "bring back shame."[20]

The laments extend beyond blogs, op-eds, and media commentaries. Engaging in what historian David Lowenthal calls the "age-old American need to deny sin and escape history,"[21] Diana West's *The Death of the Grown-Up* eulogizes the "good old days" in America when shame kept bad behaviors in check (or in the closet). West rails against the death of American shame, which she sees as the "toxic fallout" of the culture wars. Arguing that shame once fostered "the kind of self-control that became a hallmark of Western civilization," she sees its demise in

American culture as the explanation for everything from the "exponential rise in crime . . . to the ever-rising flood of obscenity, to the breakdown of the family."[22] Academics also contribute to shame revivalism, as exemplified by James B. Twitchell's *For Shame: The Loss of Common Decency in American Culture*, which offers an English professor's take on these "shameless times."[23] Twitchell acknowledges the rise of shaming displays in television talk shows, tabloid news, and even criminal justice—what he calls the "merchandising of shaming and shamelessness"—and rightfully points to the loss of civility in public life. But his gripe is not with the surfeit of shame but with its effacement. He argues that Americans have removed stigmas that once controlled behavior: "Why don't we reprimand the able-bodied drunk, addict, or panhandler?" he asks. "Why do we not excoriate the unwed teenage mother? Why do we not locate, hector, and shun her reprobate companion?" Twitchell insists that we "admit that using shame is nothing to be ashamed of; rather, it shows an understanding that feeling bad often has a central purpose."[24] In this latest salvo in an ongoing culture war, Twitchell calls shame the "electric fence" that has long kept American culture from devolving into barbarism.[25]

But shame has always been a capricious mistress, ruling over some and eluding others. This fickleness is reflected in some of shame's most prominent advocates and spokesmen. For whose behavior is characterized as shameful, who is deemed redeemable, and who is forgiven and welcomed back to the fold varies by context and subject position. Historically the moral force of shame has tended to serve power rather than to challenge it. Thus we should ask who the targets of these admonitions are. This is an important question at a time when shame purveyors are marketing their wares and shame is making a comeback. Consider the wages of sin in cases involving a few of our most ardent moral arbiters: Governor Mark Sanford repents for conducting an adulterous affair while on the taxpayer's dime, then wins reelection to Congress and is hailed as "a consistent, principled, and courageous conservative"[26]; anti-gay crusader Reverend Ted Haggard is "outed" by a male prostitute, then stages a series of "repentance broadcasts" and earns a spot on *Time* magazine's "most influential evangelicals in America" list; and Bill Bennett (also known as "the virtue magnate," who made millions on moral outrage with books such as *Book of Virtues* and *The Death of Outrage*), the moralist who vehemently crusaded against gays, drinking, and drugs, fesses up to losing millions to his gambling habit. He gets his own TV show and is named the "leading spokesman of the Traditional Values wing of the Republican Party" by the *New York Times*. This is the same Bill Bennett who once told a caller on his radio show that though an "impossible" and "morally reprehensible" thing to do, aborting African American babies would be a sure way to reduce the crime rate.[27] It would appear that these men pose no threat to "American"—or, in particular—"Anglo-Protestant" culture.[28]

That power is reserved for the usual suspects—people of color, women, gays and lesbians, foreigners, and of course the poor—those "takers" responsible for what Nicholas Eberstadt diagnoses as *America's Entitlement Epidemic*. Like West and Twitchell, Eberstadt argues for restoration of America's historical stigma against "dependency on government largesse."[29] Proposing "market-based solutions" to poverty and calling for more "personal responsibility" (often a way of chiding—and shaming—the poor and the needy for their predicament), these moral arbiters present a Manichean view of America's inhabitants: self-reliant "job creators" and do-nothing "takers" (Mitt Romney's 47%). Similarly, columnist Christopher Freind urges Americans to "bring back shame" so that people will stop relying on welfare and disability programs and America can once again pull itself up by its own bootstraps.[30] Appeals such as these construct a mythologized cultural past in order to contrast it with the diminished present; these retreats tend to reenact a regressive national story intended "to mobilize 'the people' to purify their ranks, to expel the 'others' who threaten their identity."[31] They conceal the complex historical, economic, and social sources of inequality and conflict. Just as important, "bring back shame" narratives often serve as a pretext for the restoration of "traditional" social structures or the implementation of reactionary policies. We should note that much of the outcry over the erosion of shame stems in part from the heightened visibility and tenacity of America's internal others: gay pride parades, "undocumented and unashamed" immigrant protests, the election of a Black president with a "Muslim" middle name, the increasing voting power of African American and Latino constituencies, and even the popularity of soccer in America—all reflect cultural changes that challenge the status quo.[32] Invoked in this clamor for order is an idealized American past in which marriage was a "sacred" institution, women knew their place, and immigrants spoke English.[33] National decline is here imagined as the loss of control over those who now refuse to bow their heads in shame.

Whereas pride acts as the public face of the nation—the emotion most often invoked and celebrated—the politics of shame draws from the same rhetorical wellspring to negotiate competing stories of who "we" are and who "we" aspire be: the language of patriotism, morality, and cultural belonging. The stakes involved in these articulations intensify during periods of cultural instability or disunity, giving shame a prominent role in the discursive production of difference. Shaming narratives—with their righteous protagonists and disruptive, morally flawed others—intersect with a constellation of beliefs about citizenship, capitalism, moral authority, accountability, and responsibility. They take root at the intersection where cultural myths, social capital, and economics meet, relying on convenient fictions about who we are as a people or what defines the "American character." Archetypes of American self-reliance and resourcefulness play their part, as does a history of internal colonization dependent on hierarchies of class, race, and ethnicity. The politics of shame thus articulates an ideological divide that has fueled tensions and moral anxieties throughout America's history as exclusionary, xenophobic, and racist strands strain against an inclusive "civic nationalism" committed to equal protections under the law.[34] The politics of shame consistently registers these ideological tensions in America's political culture.

We have heard these morality tales before, and they rarely have a happy ending for those who reject their moral certitudes, market fundamentalisms, or amnesiac views of American history. Shame—or, as Twitchell puts it, "feeling bad"—works to align certain subjects with or against others, to articulate literal and figurative boundaries. Stoking economic discontent or social anxieties, those calling for the revival of shame, often wrapped in the American flag, warn of encroaching hoards: Close the borders! Build more fences! Circle the wagons! In this context, tolerance becomes a dirty word, a gateway to anarchy or an instrument of "multiculturalists" bent on undermining American values. Economic and social problems are transformed into narratives of moral decline, and the hunt is on for people to blame and pillory. Buttressed by claims of moral certitude and cultural supremacy, shame revivalism intensifies its political clout by exaggerating threats. In particular, racialized shaming thrives when the dominant culture buys into the idea that it is under attack. From Lothrop Stoddard's *The Rising Tide of Color Against White World-Supremacy*, published in 1920, to Pat Buchanan's 2001 book, *The Death of the West*, to the 2009 *Atlantic* headline proclaiming the "end of white America," the dread of waning "white power" or that White U.S.-born citizens are an "oppressed majority" (in Rush Limbaugh's words) fuels reactionary impulses and deepens the nation's racial and political fault lines.

In recent years, the alleged erosion of White privilege—particularly White male privilege—has earned considerable media attention and invoked elegiac rants from conservative pundits. Obama's presidency, combined with the psychological and economic effects of the great recession, add weight to the notion that Whites are no longer in control. In this context, shame entrepreneurs offer a panacea for what ails an anxious hierarchy: a means to tighten the reins on designated others and a way to assuage bruised egos and "restore psychological comfort for the group."[35] Against this backdrop, the essays collected in this volume represent a kind of intervention, a timely reminder that shame's currency remains vital in interpellating a sociopolitical order, often in its more reactionary guises. Transacted and felt in the pinch and pull of everyday encounters, shame, we hope to show, is also on occasion thrust into the national spotlight, hailed into being as an instrument of power.

The Shame That Binds: Stigma and the Politics of Us

[A] "culture" is the ensemble of stigmata one group bears in the eyes of the other group (and vice versa).
    —Fredric Jameson, "On 'Cultural Studies'"[36]

American Shame was born out of the conviction that shame discourses and practices inform significant aspects of the American habitus, the dispositions and judgments that shape our identity as citizens, consumers, and moral actors. Our eclectic selection of topics reveals shame's handiwork in a range of settings, affirming that it is indeed "difficult to understand most issues that dominate the political and cultural landscape in the United States without reference to shame."[37] We argue for the central, mostly unacknowledged role that shame and stigma play in positioning bodies within cultural narratives of inclusion and exclusion, prominence and invisibility. Drawn from a variety of disciplinary perspectives, our essays explore the ways that subjects challenge, negotiate, or internalize shaming practices and effects; how shame works to maintain fundamental social divisions and antagonisms; how it *ideologically* encodes and regulates diverse bodies. Veering from a traditional focus on emotions as "internal" or psychobiological events, we highlight shame's contingent role as *cultural practice*—that is, as part of the complex body of forces that produce and express shared meanings. Our analyses stress the ontological and temporal priority of the public sphere, situating shame and stigma within a discursive arena of interrelations in American culture. It is in this realm, we contend, that shame is politicized, routinized, and naturalized—attached to some bodies and disavowed by others.

Examining shame through the prism of race, sexuality, class, and gender, the chapters that follow showcase its roles in configuring and policing the terms of cultural membership. Our task assumes that shame cues function differently in different systems of meaning and that one culture's emotional lexicon does not translate neatly into another's. The representational power of shame relies on a network of categories, dispositions, and meanings—what Michel Foucault calls "notions"—to endorse hierarchies of bodies, values, and relationships.[38] Thus, although many scholars relegate emotion to the realm of individual psychology, our interest is in the cultural labor it performs, especially in attempts to mark and contain the fluid boundaries of national identity. Our approach is aligned with Stuart Hall's view of culture as a discourse that shapes our collective self-image and encourages us to act in certain ways. As Hall puts it, discursive strategies are "how a national culture functions as a source of cultural meaning, a focus of identification, and a system of representation."[39] Theorizing culture as an ongoing process underscores the participatory, interactive meaning making transactions involved in privileging certain behaviors, identities, or events. Just as important, however, it recognizes that the invocation and management of affect work to inscribe categories of affiliation and difference in American culture.

Culture is the lens through which we locate our place in the world and affirm or discredit a variety of beliefs and values, but emotions produce the "affective economies" through which we negotiate our relationships with others. They mediate the boundaries between bodily and social space, identifying, segregating, and containing social and cultural differences and inscribing borders between groups. As Sara Ahmed argues, emotions are neither "in" the individual nor "in" the social; rather, they are culturally inscribed *effects* that allow us to distinguish an "inside" and an "outside" in the first place, to "produce the very surfaces and boundaries that allow the individual and the social to be delineated as if they are objects."[40] The slide from "I" to "we" involves "both adherence (sticking to the nation) and coherence (sticking together)."[41] That is, shared emotional responses align us with and against others, dissolving the boundaries between private and public spaces. As the essays in this volume attest, to "feel" shame is to participate in a cultural economy of prescribed behaviors and expectations, cued responses and decodings; it is also to participate in the formation of that economy—to interpret, produce, and transact meaning.

Drawing from Erving Goffman's seminal work on stigma, we contend that stigmatizing shame undermines other claims to normality and cultural citizenship. Goffman identifies three types of stigma: that associated with bodily "defect," that associated with immoral character, and that associated with membership in a reviled or outcast social group. He contends that a stigma linked to an attribute is more difficult to change than is one linked to behavior.[42] As several subjects examined in this volume exemplify, one can also be falsely accused or discredited because of what one is rather than what one has done, as is the case when "deviance" is tied to race, disability, body type, or disease. Deviance in these cases is not the result of doing something "wrong," for the "normal and the stigmatized are not persons but rather perspectives."[43] This is the critical distinction between reintegrative shaming and stigmatization shaming. The former focuses on the disapproval of the deed; the shamed subject can make amends, show proper deference to the judgments and expectations of the group, and maintain the social and cultural bonds of belonging.[44] The spectacular shaming rituals alluded to in my earlier discussion showcase these common interactive processes of judgment, denunciation, and forgiveness—emotional transactions animated by the thrill of watching the mighty stumble. In contrast, stigmatizing shame casts its object into an underclass or even subclass group that is irredeemable. This is a literal and figurative expulsion—the realm of the outcast, the criminal, the alien. The stigmatized body does not elicit concern; it is not entitled to respect or even dignity. This condition represents the ontological insecurity experienced by those whose very being is the basis of their rejection or marginalization.

Stigmas attached to certain ethnic or racial groups, which Goffman calls "tribal stigmas," shape social attitudes that "filter into" political policy making and play an integral role in cultural identity formations. One of the aims of this book is to theorize tribal stigmas as products of historical and cultural interactions that foster attitudes grounded not in deviant behavior but in deviant identities that can remain "spoiled" regardless of behavior. Examining the experiential, ideological, and juridical ramifications of stigma is particularly important because they can become an enduring feature of the target identity.[45] For example, despite proclamations of a "post-racial" America in the wake of Barack Obama's election, members of the nation's two largest minority groups, African Americans and Latinos, are still subject to subtle (and sometimes overt) stigmatization. In a 2012 Associated Press survey, 51 percent of Americans expressed explicit anti-Black attitudes and 57 percent expressed anti-Hispanic attitudes.[46] More than half of respondents associated words such as "violent" and "lazy" with African Americans and Latinos. These attitudes bolster recent moves to undermine or eliminate affirmative action or other minority "entitlements." Stigmatizing political narratives endow their cultural protagonists with moral authority and just causes. They arouse feelings of helplessness, anger, or fear in the citizenry, feelings that can be exploited and fetishized through an erasure or denial of the circumstances of their production and circulation. Exploiting negative predispositions toward stigmatized groups, leaders can deflect blame and accountability, instead casting these on target groups who are held responsible not only for their own but for the nation's problems. In recent years, this tactic has helped raise support for cuts to food stamps, unemployment benefits, Temporary Assistance for Needy Families (TANF), the Children's Health Insurance Program (CHIP), Medicaid, and other "entitlements."[47]

Shaming rituals express and signal distance between persons; they make social hierarchies visible. Rather than being "gradually subsumed" within national identity, ethnic and racial difference entails "the binding and marking of symbolic boundaries, the production of 'frontier effects.'"[48] Participation in collective shaming enculturates individuals into certain kinds of relationships: it turns a body into a "body-for-others."[49] The shamed body stands as testament to the authority of the group, the law, the social order. It manifests the self's recognition of itself as deficient, flawed, inadequate. Although shame and humiliation are often conflated in both academic and popular usage, we differentiate them in at least one important way: the experience of humiliation typically elicits a primitive response directed at an external object, a need to lash out and avenge. Shame, on the other hand, arouses extreme self-consciousness and self-directed contempt; thus it is "the affect of indignity, of defeat, of transgression, of inferiority, and of alienation."[50] The experience of shame—especially stigmatizing shame—turns the self against the self. In other words, we believe we deserve our shame because of some moral failing or lapse in judgment, but we never believe we deserve our humiliation.

Stigmatizing shame further complicates this judgment. Our sense of injury increases the more we presume ourselves worthy of dignity regardless of race, gender, or other variables. However, when stigmatized persons internalize the negative qualities ascribed to them and do not recognize these as cultural constructs, their capacity for self-respect, social agency, and community is compromised. Furthermore, refusing to recognize the stigmatizing effects that still plague our "others"—we ("the normals" in Goffman's terms) deflect the shame that arises when we fail to meet up to our positive national and individual self-image. For stigmatized groups, shame is thus often experienced as "a pervasive affective attunement to the social environment . . . a profound mode of disclosure both of self and situation."[51] Identified with a flawed and indelible set of traits, stigmatized groups are relegated to the margins of society, bound to an attributive relation in which identity is a static construct devoid of agency. Sedgwick notes that shame makes a "double movement . . . toward painful individuation, toward uncontrollable relationality."[52] Our collective effort in this book illustrates that stigmatized groups are *desubjectified*—forced to recognize themselves in a distorted view of their own identity—and also *subjectified*—identified in their singularity or at least in their distinction from other groups and most especially from "us."

American Shame maps some of the political and institutional contours of group stigmatization. Stigmatizing shame is a complex social process linked to competition for power and tied into existing mechanisms of dominance and exclusion. Stigmatized bodies serve as emblems of what a society rejects. Witch burnings, public executions, lynching, homophobia, the treatment of immigrants, and the abuse of "enemy combatants" all share a dependence on stigmatized identities. Caroline Howarth points out that "stigmatizing representations . . . are more than ways of seeing or cognitive maps: they filter into, and so construct, the institutionalized practices of differentiation, division and discrimination."[53] They motivate and inspire, mobilize and constitute political subjects, framing "the attitudinal and behavioral matrix within which the political system is located."[54] The racializing and gendering of poverty ("welfare queens," "anchor babies," "baby mamas") may express a reactionary bent in America's political culture, but it can also channel Americans' own anger, frustrations, or unacknowledged personal shame. Negative feelings aroused by economic woes, security concerns, and the perceived loss of personal or national power can be harnessed to "bring publics into being, organizing diffuse, sometimes inchoate beliefs and moralities into political action."[55] In this role, the politics of stigmatization predisposes citizens to accept more punitive public policies and practices meant to reduce social threats, instability, or anxiety.

Several essays in this volume examine the alignment of shame and stigma with a biopolitics of containment and exposure. We see evidence of this in American law and criminal justice practices. Consider, for example, the criminalization of homelessness, which is occurring in numerous cities across America even as funding cuts force many shelters to close; or consider emergent trends in the American penal system, such as the renewed use of public shaming tactics including chain gangs, boot camps, surveillance technologies, and so-called red-letter punishment.[56] A number of judges—especially in the South—have resorted to shaming penalties as a cheap alternative to incarceration in the United States, which has 5% of the world's population but almost a quarter of the world's prisoners.[57] In some ways, these practices hark back to nineteenth-century stigmatizing crusades against "idleness" or colonial-era public shaming rituals. Legal scholar Chad Flanders notes the twofold moral effects suggested by the return of public shaming penalties: they "manifest an objective disrespect for the offender by shaming him, *and* they incite subjective attitudes of disrespect in the public, by making individual citizens instruments of the offender's punishment."[58] Stigmatizing shame also feeds racial disparity in the criminal justice system, where 1 in every 15 African American men and 1 in every 36 Latino men are incarcerated in comparison to 1 in every 106 White men. Moreover, African Americans and Latinos are more likely to be searched during a traffic stop and to receive longer sentences.[59] The darker the skin, the more stigmatized the identity, as recent studies show: dark-skinned Blacks in the United States have lower socioeconomic status, more punitive relationships with the criminal justice system, less prestige, and less likelihood of holding elective office than their lighter counterparts do.[60] What pardon, rehabilitation, or reintegration is possible when a shamed identity rests not on what you *do* but on the color of your skin?

An important incentive for this book stems from the effects that stigmatizing tactics have on the embodied experiences of women and minorities in the United States. We hope to show that stigmatizing shame remains pivotal in policing target groups and in legitimizing policies for their containment. We believe that this concern is especially warranted as the surveillance and control of bodies reaches unprecedented levels in the wake of the terrorist attack of September 11, 2001(9/11), the "war on terror," and the militarization of police—all of which disproportionately affect communities of color. Suzanne Oboler has identified "blatant attacks on rights and human dignity in US society" particularly, but certainly not only, against Latinos: among these are the enactment of Arizona's SB 1070, officially promoting racial profiling; the establishment of officially endorsed censorship through HB 2281, which bans ethnic studies classes and textbooks in

Arizona's public schools; the official condoning of the removal of teachers who speak English with heavy accents from Arizona's classrooms; the ongoing abuses of power through immigration raids and in detention and deportation centers.[61] Immigration-related media spectacles construct knowledge about Latinos generally and about immigration, citizenship, and national belonging. They often draw on what Leo Chavez calls the "Latino Threat Narrative," which posits that Latinos are somehow "different" from other immigrant groups and that they are unwilling or incapable of assimilating.[62] In a 2004 issue of *Foreign Policy*, Samuel Huntington goes as far as to identify Latino immigration—which he refers to as an "invasion" in other contexts—as the "single most immediate and most serious challenge to America's traditional identity."[63] Despite their growing numbers and economic clout, Latinos remain "alien citizens" in the United States. Consider the outraged tweets and commentaries when Marc Anthony, born and raised in New York, sang "God Bless America" at the 2013 MLB All-Star game.[64]

This affective matrix of suspicion and resentment underlies attitudes toward Latinos and thus shapes policy preferences. Research shows that Whites overwhelmingly oppose policies regarding increases in immigration, affirmative action, bilingual education, and welfare / public benefits; many regard Latinos as both perpetual foreigners and an inferior race. Thus Tom Tancredo, a former Republican representative, can rail during a Tea Party convention that "People who could not even spell the word 'vote' or say it in English put a committed socialist in the White House."[65] Blaming Obama's election on what he calls "the cult of multiculturalism," Tancredo evokes fears identified with non-English-speaking voters (namely, a growing Latino constituency) while echoing the kind of discourse that justified literacy tests meant to suppress the Black vote under Jim Crow. "We are committing cultural suicide," Tancredo warns, as "the barbarians at the gate will only need to give us a slight push, and the emaciated body of Western civilization will collapse in a heap"[66]

Although not exclusively focused on racial stigma, the analyses we offer here call specific attention to the body politics that undergirds a range of American shaming practices. In the wake of Obama's election, for example, many commentators proclaimed America a "post-race" society, an idea that legitimizes so-called color-blind initiatives in college admissions and scholarship selection practices. Disavowed, race is shoved into the closet, as it were, and stigma takes over the house. Who needs to utter the word "Black" when words such as "welfare recipient" or "thug" have been so effectively racialized? Encoding that which cannot be said directly, racial or "tribal" stigmas function as a kind of indexical sign system that registers correlations between a set of negative traits and a given body or "type." They activate attitudes that inform America's political culture. Gilroy argues that today's racism "has taken a necessary distance from crude ideas of biological inferiority and superiority"; instead, race is now aligned "with nationhood, patriotism and nationalism" to construct the image of a precarious national culture that is "perpetually vulnerable to attack from enemies within and without."[67] This tactic has been useful in strategically positioning America's first African American president "outside" the parameters of what is legitimately "American" and thus a threat to the nation's imagined cultural integrity. A Harris poll conducted in March of 2010 showed that 67 percent of Republicans believed that President Obama was a socialist; another 57 percent, that he was a Muslim; and 45 percent, that he was not born in the United States and was therefore ineligible for the presidency.[68] Dinesh D'Souza's recent bestseller, *Obama's America: Unmaking the American Dream* goes well beyond the antagonism and vitriol that characterize negative political rhetoric: not only is Obama driven by a "Third World, anti-American ideology that he got from his Kenyan father," Dinesh warns. The nation's first Black president is "single-handedly" responsible for "America's decline and fall."

The conflation of poverty with race further buttresses the political efficacy of stigmatizing shame. During the 2012 presidential campaign, Newt Gingrich echoed his 1994 Contract with America, which targeted federal food stamp entitlement programs for elimination, this time culling associations between the Black president and entitlement programs. At a debate in South Carolina jointly sponsored by Fox News and the *Wall Street Journal*, he referred to President Obama as "the best food stamp president in history," exploiting racist stereotypes that attribute Blacks' economic status to laziness or lack of willpower. Gingrich signaled the difference between "them" (Obama and the 95% of Blacks who supported him in the first election) and "us" (a majority White Republican audience and, by extension, "real"—that is, "hard-working"—Americans): "We believe in work. We believe people should learn to work and that we're opposed to dependency."[69] Despite the fact that most recipients of federal food aid are children, the elderly, and the severely disabled and that only 22% of all food stamp recipients are Black, Gingrich was able to draw on a stigmatized vision of Black identity to elicit a standing ovation. As a socially coded language, racialized stigma allowed him to tap racist sentiments without ever uttering the word "Black"—a rhetorical sleight of hand that clearly pays political dividends.

Locating shame at the forefront of our concerns, our project participates in feminist efforts to politicize the emotions as sites of resistance, intervention, and transformation. In *Femininity and Domination*, Sandra Bartky stresses the need for a political phenomenology of the emotions, calling for feminist research that examines the emotions of self-assessment to theorize their role "both in the constitution of subjectivity and in the perpetuation of subjection."[70] Shame is a crucial component in techniques of social control and in the formation, maintenance, and management of any systematic process of subjection. Historically, as Erica

Johnson and Patricia Moran explain, "women have been defined as corporeal in a way that men are not, and the female body is thus a critical locus for discourses and representations that link femininity with shame."[71] As several essays in this book attest, the coercive power of shame consistently works its magic on the bodies of women, especially where sexuality is concerned. We should note that the term "slut shaming" has only recently entered our lexicon and that "shame revivalism" has been accompanied by various policies and initiatives meant to control women's bodies and curtail their rights.[72] Our analyses of shame and stigma offer important insights for understanding widespread attitudes and behaviors that produce what Bartky refers to as "socially inferiorized" bodies.[73] As we show here, an economy of shame is central in efforts to inscribe, manage, and enforce certain versions of gendered identity; it is crucial in sustaining disciplinary processes aimed at "correcting" bodies deemed fundamentally flawed, problematic, or lacking. Shame inheres in traditional notions of femininity, a construct that demands restraint, discretion, and modesty. It works to withhold and police female pleasure, to rein in our desires and our bodies. Shame reminds us to measure our delights, to temper our exuberance in everything from having sex to eating chocolate. It is the punishment endured by women who fail to control their unruly desires and bodies, who, in Judith Butler's words, "fail to do their gender right," a doing that is always already shaped by race and class. Black women have long borne stigmas associated with excessive or aberrant sexuality, a dehumanizing tactic evident in racially coded comments about Michelle Obama's body. In a shame economy of exchange and valuation, gendered shame produces an ontological deficit—a deficiency that inheres and endures despite women's economic gains.

Our book is organized into three parts, each exploring the politics and culture of shame and stigma on different bodies, groups, and identities. Part 1, "Scarlet Letters: Gender, Race, and Stigma," opens with Karen Weingarten's critical examination of abortion discourse and its stigmatizing effects. Weingarten contends that shame works in anti-choice rhetoric as a perfected technology of disciplinary and regulative control over women's bodies. Just as important, however, she argues that abortion shaming also works in conjunction with a racialized biopolitics of state control and management. Daniel McNeil turns our attention to Philippa Schuyler, a child prodigy who renounced her African American culture and thus the stigmatized identity associated with Blackness in mid-twentieth century America. McNeil draws on Franz Fanon's body of work to read Schuyler's choices in the context of Cold War sexual politics, the transnational liberation struggles of non-White cultures, and neocolonialism. In "Neoliberal Crimmigration: The 'Common Sense' Shaming of the Undocumented," Leah Perry considers the criminalization of immigrants through the neoliberal discourse of contemporary America, showing how gendered and racialized stigmatization and shaming bolster exploitive economic policies and labor practices. Frances Negrón-Muntaner interrogates the relationship between stigma and ethnic sovereignty. She focuses on the Young Lords of New York, a grassroots political movement that seized a site of shame and subordination—the Puerto Rican body—and restyled it to maximize its potential as a mobile political sign intended to counter its stigmatic associations with sickness, ignorance, dirtiness, and poverty.

Part 2, "Disciplining the Body Politic," focuses on a variety of ways that shame works to produce "docile bodies" both in domestic and foreign policies and practices. Renee Lee Gardner's essay examines unacknowledged shame in post-9/11 American culture through an analysis of Mohsin Hamid's novel *The Reluctant Fundamentalist*. Gardner interprets the work as an allegorical commentary on America's response to 9/11, focusing particular attention on its female protagonist, Erica, to show how her character invokes and responds to the nation's unacknowledged shame. Our exploration of shame's disciplinary role in American culture then turns to examine public health policy. Meghan Griffin draws attention to some of the forces shaping Americans' relation to food, eating, and health, showing the ways that a network of shame is activated, maintained, and promoted, often to the detriment of public health. Part 2 concludes with Noel Glover's thoughtful discussion of shame as a widely felt though minimally understood experience for both students and teachers in school settings. Focusing his analysis on physical disability, Glover examines shame's implications for educational policy as well as its potential in fostering an interdependent notion of citizenship in America.

Part 3, "Bodies on Display: Performing Shame in Visual Arts," explores ways that shame is represented, exploited, or subverted as an aesthetic device. The focus here is primarily—though not exclusively—on Hollywood films. Madeline Walker draws on Freud to consider cinematic depictions of female defecation, reading films such as *The Back-up Plan* and *Bridesmaids* in the context of post-feminism to suggest how these reinscribe women's bodies as shamelessly, dangerously out of control. Mike Rancourt traces a history of films that mobilize shame to critique American foreign policies, particularly America's intervention in Vietnam. He examines how national shame is redirected through Iraq War films, which in his view employ "distancing maneuvers" that expose the deceptive justifications for war while sparing the individual soldier the kind of blame and stigma that haunted Vietnam veterans. Anthony Carlton Cooke confronts mental illness as stigma in America, situating his analysis in relation to the deinstitutionalization movement initiated in the 1970s. Cooke mines the "slasher" genre to show how these films reflect popular misconceptions and lingering anxieties about the dangers posed by the mentally ill in the wake of these policies. Our glance at Hollywood film representations culminates with Megan Tagle Adams's essay on the gendering of masturbation in American films. Adams examines the ways that female bodies are both duly disciplined and empowered by representations of female masturbation in films such as *Black Swan*, *American Pie*, and *The 40-Year-Old Virgin*. We conclude with Emily Newman's exploration of the ways that female performance artists Eleanor Antin, Rachel Rosenthal, and Faith Ringgold use their bodies as canvases in ways that both subvert and confirm the disciplinary power of shame over women's sexual identity and expression. Newman shows how these works push viewers to consider their own complicity in the shaming of women's bodies.

In a post-9/11 environment, Americans are confronting both internal and external challenges. On the one hand, our national self-image is grounded in the ideals of individual freedom, inalienable rights, and tolerance. On the other, 9/11 exposed the permeability of our borders, arousing nativist sentiments and testing our commitment to the ideals of an inclusive, open society. Clashes over "American values" or what it means to be a "real American" are most salient following national crises or economic downturns, both of which have characterized much of the nation's introduction to the twenty-first century and fueled opposing views about how best to respond to threats or deal with internal differences.[74] The essays that follow offer a glimpse behind Americans' motley masks of shame and stigma to consider the pleasures and perils of our collective finger wagging. Most of all, they remind us that a shame economy works to enculturate us in ways big and small: in the glare of the media spotlight and in the privacy of our bedrooms, in the storm and stress of political spectacles, and in the nooks and crannies of our daily lives. As an instrument of power, stigmatizing shame legitimizes and facilitates the dehumanization or devaluing of certain bodies, setting the stage for a range of punitive policies, discriminatory gestures, and even violent confrontations. We hope that *American Shame* compels a more critical and sustained reflection on the residual effects left in shame's wake.

Notes

1. Guy Debord, *Society of the Spectacle*, trans. Donald Nicholson-Smith (New York: Zone Books, 1995), para. 215.

2. Ibid., para. 42.

3. Philip Drake and Andy Miah, "The Cultural Politics of Celebrity," *Cultural Politics* 6, no. 1 (2010): 51.

4. Steven Best and Douglas Kellner, "Debord and the Postmodern Turn: New Stages of the Spectacle," *Illuminations,* available at http://www.uta.edu/huma/illuminations/kell17 .htm. Best and Kellner argue that the "interactive spectacle" allows for a subversive politics that appropriates the tools of the spectacle as a means to counter and mobilize. In my view, the SlutWalk movement and Gay Pride parades reflect such tactics. But these, too, may be read as spectacles of conformity rather than defiance because they rely on and reproduce

dominant representations for their effect, offering an illusory image of democratic action without actually disrupting the means or terms of exchange.

5. Helen Popkin, "Miley Cyrus Twerks Her Way to the Top of Twitter," *NBC News*, August 26, 2013, available at http://sys03-public.nbcnews.com/today/money/miley-cyrus-twerks-her-way-top-twitter-300-000-tweets-8C11006754.

6. Keith Koffler, "Miley Cyrus, the Decline of Western Civilization, and the Obamas," *White House Dossier*, August 27, 2013, available at http://www.whitehousedossier.com/2013/08/27/miley-cyrus-decline-western-civilization-obamas.

7. Gershon Kaufman and Lev Raphael, "Shame as Taboo in American Culture," in *Forbidden Fruits: Taboos and Tabooism in Culture*, ed. Ray B. Browne (Bowling Green, OH: Bowling Green State University Popular Press, 1984), 57.

8. Patrick Center, "Shutdown Leaves Some Seniors Worried about Their Next Meal," *NPR Online*, October 11, 2013, available at http://www.npr.org/blogs/thesalt/2013/10/11/232159777/shutdown-leaves-some-seniors-worried-about-their-next-meal.

9. Paul Gilroy, *Darker Than Blue: On the Moral Economies of Black Atlantic Culture* (Cambridge, MA: Harvard University Press, 2010), 75.

10. Sara Ahmed, *The Cultural Politics of Emotion* (New York: Routledge, 2004), 30.

11. Emmanual Levinas, *Totality and Infinity*, trans. Alphonso Lingis (Pittsburgh: Duquesne University Press, 1969), 215.

12. Tom Junod, "The State of the American Dog," *Esquire*, July 14, 2014, http://www.esquire.com/news-politics/a23731/american-dog-0814/.

13. "Wardrobe malfunction" entered the nation's vocabulary after Janet Jackson's breast was exposed during her halftime performance at the 2004 Super Bowl, causing so much moral outrage that the FCC tried to impose a record $550,000 fine on CBS. The term is now included in most standard dictionaries, including the venerable *Oxford English Dictionary*.

14. Murry Edelman, *Constructing the Political Spectacle* (Chicago: University of Chicago Press, 1988), 10.

15. Jean Bethke Elshtain, *Democracy on Trial* (New York: Basic Books, 1995). See especially "The Politics of Displacement," chap. 2, 37–63.

16. Pat Wingert, "The Return of Shame," *Newsweek*, February 5, 1995.

17. Bob Martin, "Guest Column: Bring Back Shame," *Central Kentucky News*, February 27, 2009, available at http://articles.centralkynews.com/2009-02-27/opinion/24850605_1_earmarks-criminal-behavior-shame.

18. Ann888, "Bring Back Shame and Humiliation," *WomenExplode.com*, September 26 2013, available at http://blog.womenexplode.com/2013/09/bring-back-shame-and-humiliation/.

19. Bring Back Shame Community, *Facebook*, available at https://www.facebook.com/pages/Bring-Back-Shame/162661542471?sk=info>.

20. Sonny Bunch, "Bring Back the Stocks," *Washington Free Beacon*, January 31, 2014. See also Michael Goodwin, "Bring Back Shame!" *New York Post*, March 10, 2013.

21. David Lowenthal, "Nostalgia Tells It Like It Wasn't," in *The Imagined Past: History and Nostalgia*, ed. Christopher Shaw and Malcolm Chasem (New York: Manchester University Press, 1989), 26.

22. Diana West, *The Death of the Grown-Up: How America's Arrested Development Is Bringing Down Western Civilization* (New York: St. Martin's Press, 2007), 96.

23. James Twitchell, *For Shame: The Loss of Common Decency in American Culture* (New York: St. Martin's Press, 1997), 2.

24. Ibid., 212.

25. Ibid., 23.

26. Star Parker, "Mark Sanford: Welcome Back to Washington," *The Christian Post*, May 10, 2013. *The Christian Post* describes itself as America's most comprehensive Christian news source on the web.

27. Bill Bennett, *Bill Bennett's Morning in America*, Salem Radio Network, September 28, 2005, available at http://mediamatters.org/mmtv/200509280006.

28. Samuel Huntington identifies Anglo-Protestant culture as the distinguishing characteristic of "American identity," which in his view is threatened by multiculturalism and the spread of Spanish as a second national language. See Huntington, *Who Are We: The Challenges of America's National Identity* (New York: Simon and Schuster, 2004), xvi.

29. Nicholas Eberstadt, *A Nation of Takers: America's Entitlement Epidemic* (West Conshohocken, PA: Templeton Press, 2012), 52.

30. Christopher Freind, "Have Americans Become Too Comfortable Receiving Government Assistance?" *Philadelphia*, October 16, 2013. In another essay he calls for shaming tactics to reduce obesity, arguing that "in genuflecting to political correctness, America shuns shame. It has become a nation so afraid to offend that it turns a blind eye to its *biggest* problems, such as obesity." See Friend, "Solve America's Obesity Problem with Shame," *Philadelphia*, October 12, 2012, available at http://www.phillymag.com/news/2012/10/12/solve-americas-obesity-problem-shame/.

31. Stuart Hall, "The Question of Identity," in *Modernity: An Introduction to Modern Societies*, ed. Stuart Hall, David Held, Don Hubert, and Kenneth Thompson (London: Wiley-Blackwell, 1996), 615.

32. During the 2014 World Cup, conservative pundit Anne Coulter published a piece blaming the popularity of soccer on immigrants and the liberal media. She opined that "any growing interest in soccer can only be a sign of the nation's moral decay" and that "no American whose great grandfather was born in the United States" is watching soccer. Her syndicated column on this topic can be accessed at http://www.clarionledger.com/story/opinion/columnists/2014/06/25/coulter-growing-interest-soccer-sign-nations-moral-decay/11372137/.

33. Contrary to the claim that Latino immigrants refuse to learn English, a study of second-generation Latino students in South Florida and Southern California (where Spanish is still widely spoken) found that English language proficiency is near universal. See Alejandro Portes and Lingxin Hao, "E Pluribus Unum: Bilingualism and Language Loss in the Second Generation," *Social Science Research Network*, available at http://papers.ssrn.com/sol3/papers.cfm?abstract_id=121374.

34. George Gerstle, *American Crucible: Race and Nation in the Twentieth Century* (Princeton, NJ: Princeton University Press, 2002).

35. Gwen Adshead, "Till We Have Faces: On Humiliation," *Journal of the American Academy of Psychiatry and the Law* 38, no. 2 (2010): 206.

36. Fredric Jameson, "On 'Cultural Studies,'" *Social Text* 34 (1993): 33.

37. Dov Cohen, "The American National Conversation about (Everything but) Shame," *Social Research* 79, no. 4 (2003): 1075.

38. Michel Foucault, *Discipline and Punish: The Birth of the Prison*, trans. Alan Sheridan (London: Allen Lane, 1977), 21.

39. Stuart Hall, "The Question of Cultural Identity," in *Modernity: An Introduction to Modern Societies*, ed. Stuart Hall et al. (London: Wiley-Blackwell, 1996), 615.

40. Ibid., 10.

41. Ibid., 111.

42. Erving Goffman, *Stigma: Notes on the Management of Spoiled Identity* (New York: Prentice Hall, 1963), 42.

43. Ibid., 137–138.

44. John Braithwaite, *Crime, Shame, and Reintegration* (New York: Cambridge University Press, 1993), 1.

45. This is painfully brought to the foreground by recent incidents: the killings of three unarmed Black teenagers, Trayvon Martin, Jordan Davis, and Michael Brown. These young men did not know each other, but in each case they were "profiled" by White men (and by the community of voices that came to the White men's defense) as threatening "thugs." Wearing a hoodie, listening to loud rap music, or walking in the street while Black is dangerous when a stigmatized identity makes you suspect.

46. Josh Pasek, Arthur Krosnick, and Trevor Tompson, "The Impact of Anti-Black Racism on Approval of Barack Obama's Job Performance and on Voting in the 2012 Presidential Election," October, 2012, available at http://web.stanford.edu/dept/communication/faculty/krosnick/docs/2012/2012%20Voting%20and%20Racism.pdf.

47. In generating support for these measures, leaders invariably turn to stigmatizing the poor—a tactic that works better than relying on facts. Consider, for example, the USDA study that found that $1 in Supplemental Nutrition Assistance Program (SNAP) benefits generates $1.84 in gross domestic product (GDP). See Michel Nischan, "The Economic Case for Food Stamps," *The Atlantic*, July 18, 2012, available at http://www.theatlantic.com/health/archive/2012/07/the-economic-case-for-food-stamps/260015/.

48. Stuart Hall, "Introduction: Who Needs Identity?" In *Questions of Cultural Identity*, ed. Stuart Hall and Paul Du Gay (London: Sage, 1996), 2.

49. Jean-Paul Sartre describes objectification in terms of the Other's gaze, which evokes self-consciousness and the realization that as a body-for-others I cannot control the other's gaze or how s/he sees me. See *Being and Nothingness*, trans. H. E. Barnes (London: Methuen, 1969), 344, 351, 353.

50. Hersgen Kaufman, *Shame: The Power of Caring* (Rochester, VT: Schenkman Books, 1999), vii.

51. Sandra Lee Bartky, *Femininity and Domination: Studies in the Phenomenology of Oppression* (New York and London: Routledge), 85.

52. Eve Sedgwick, *Touching Feeling: Affect, Pedagogy, Performativity* (Durham, NC: Duke University Press, 2003), 37.

53. Caroline Howarth, "Race as Stigma: Positioning the Stigmatized as Agents, Not Objects," *Journal of Community and Applied Social Psychology* 16, no. 6 (2006): 45.

54. Stephen White, *Political Culture and Soviet Politics* (London: Macmillan, 1979), 1.

55. Janice Irvine, "Transient Feelings: Sex Panics and the Politics of Emotions," *GLQ* 14, no. 1 (2007): 11.

56. Xander Landen, "More Cities across the U.S. Consider Homelessness a Crime." *PBS Newshour,* July 19, 2014.

57. According to a report by Adam Liptak published April 23, 2008, in the *New York Times*, there are 751 people in American prisons or jails for every 100,000 in the population. See Liptak, "U.S. Prison Population Dwarfs That of Other Nations," *New York Times,* April 23, 2008, available at http://www.nytimes.com/2008/04/23/world/americas/23iht-23prison.12253738.html.

58. Chad Flanders, "Shame and the Meanings of Punishment," *Cleveland State Law Review* 54 (2006): 610.

59. See Sophia Kerby, "The Top 10 Most Startling Facts about People of Color and Criminal Justice in the United States," *Center for American Progress*, available at http://www.americanprogress.org/issues/race/news/2012/03/13/11351/the-top-10-most-startling-facts-about-people-of-color-and-criminal-justice-in-the-united-states/.

60. Jennifer Hochschild and Vesla Weaver, "The Skin Color Paradox and the American Racial Order," *Social Forces* 86, no. 2 (2007): 643.

61. Suzanne Oboler, "The Dismantling of our Future," *Latino Studies* 8, no. 3 (2010): 299–303.

62. Leo Chavez, *The Latino Threat: Constructing Immigrants, Citizens, and the Nation* (Stanford, CA: Stanford University Press, 2008).

63. Samuel Huntington, "The Hispanic Challenge," *Foreign Policy,* March 1, 2004, 30–45.

64. Baseball fans expressed everything from disappointment to fury that a "Mexican" had been chosen to sing "God Bless America" (Anthony's heritage is Puerto Rican). See Jacquellena Carrero, "Baseball Fans Take to Twitter to Protest Marc Anthony Singing God Bless America," *NBCLatino,* July 17, 2013, available at http://nbclatino.com/2013/07/17/baseball-fans-take-to-twitter-to-protest-marc-anthony-singing-god-bless-america/.

65. Quoted in Kevin Hechtkopf, "Tom Tancredo Tea Party Speech Slams 'Cult of Multiculturalism.'" *CBS News.* February 5, 2010, available at http://www.cbsnews.com/8301-503544_162-6177125-503544.html.

66. Quoted in Tony Horwitz, "Immigration and the Curse of the Black Legend," editorial, *New York Times,* July 9, 2006.

67. Paul Gilroy, "The End of Antiracism." In *Race Culture and Difference*, eds. James Donald and Ali Rattansi. (London: Sage, 1992), 53.

68. Harris Interactive, "'Wingnuts' and President Obama," available at http://www.harrisinteractive.com/vault/Harris-Interactive-Poll-Research-Politics-Wingnuts-2010-03.pdf.

69. "Gingrich Swipes at Food Stamps," *Miami Herald,* January 23, 2012, available at http://www.miamiherald.com/2012/01/23/2604256/gingrichs-swipes-at-food-stamps.html.

70. Sandra Lee Bartky, *Femininity and Domination: Studies in the Phenomenology of Oppression* (New York: Routledge), 98.

71. Erica Johnson and Patricia Moran, eds. *The Female Face of Shame* (Bloomington: Indiana University Press, 2013), 10.

72. Two examples are the abortion sonogram bill, which in some cases requires doctors to perform a transvaginal ultrasound on women seeking abortions, and the Supreme Court's ruling that private corporations can deny their female employees insurance coverage for contraceptives.

73. Sandra Bartky, ibid., 9.

74. This may help explain the citizenry's troubling response to degrading "anti-terror" measures or civil rights infringements. Recent polls indicate, for instance, that a majority of Americans believe that using torture as a means of extracting information from suspected terrorists is morally justified.

PART 1

Scarlet Letters:
Gender, Race, and Stigma

ONE

Shame before the Law:
Affects of Abortion Regulation

Karen Weingarten

> Self-possession [did not] liberate the former slave from his or her bonds but rather sought to replace the whip with the guilty contract and the collar with the guilty conscience.
> —Saidiya Hartman, *Scenes of Subjection: Terror, Slavery, and Self-Making in Nineteenth-Century America*[1]

With each passing year, anti-abortion activists have managed to institute new laws further restricting women's access to abortion. In March 2013, North Dakota's governor signed the most far-reaching anti-abortion law yet. He decreed that once a fetal heartbeat is detectable then an abortion is no longer legal. Considering that in most cases a fetal heartbeat can be heard in the sixth week of pregnancy, which is often only a week or two after women discover their pregnancies, the law effectively bans abortion. Arkansas has similarly passed a law that prohibits abortion after the twelfth week of pregnancy, or when a fetal heartbeat can be detected via an abdominal ultrasound. Although these laws will most likely be declared unconstitutional in federal court, they represent anti-abortion activists' attempt to overturn Planned Parenthood v. Casey, the 1992 Supreme Court case that ruled that states could not curtail abortion rights if they placed an "undue burden" on women seeking abortions, and Roe v. Wade, the 1973 case that prohibited states from outlawing abortion before twenty-four weeks of pregnancy. In the meantime, these laws, while continuing to limit women's access to abortion through the legal effects they institute, also work through the shaming rhetoric they produce in order to justify their measures. Not only do these laws claim to save "unborn children," they are also defended as protecting women from themselves. In other words, anti-abortion lobbyists and legislators argue that if women only understood that they were taking a human life, they would be repelled by their decision to abort. This position patronizes women but also shames them by suggesting that a "real" woman would never be able to abort once she visibly or audibly witnessed the life inside her.[2]

Although abortion has been legal in the United States since 1973, it is still steeped in shame, in ways that affect how it is both regulated and limited. Almost all relevant Supreme Court cases since Roe v. Wade have made it more difficult for women to obtain abortions. Laws requiring parental notification, waiting periods of twenty-four to seventy-two hours, mandatory counseling, or viewing the fetal ultrasound all work to shame women who choose to have an abortion. Furthermore, although many feminists and women's organizations hold Roe v. Wade to be sacrosanct, worrying over its potential loss with the Supreme Court headed by Chief Justice Roberts and the replacement of the pro-abortion Sandra Day O'Connor with Samuel Alito, they elide the problem with the underlying arguments of the case, which actually allow for the limiting of reproductive rights, particularly through their foundations in American legal discourse on the right to privacy. This essay examines how the affect of shame in current abortion discourse places the burden of choice on the individual woman while still making her accountable to societal expectations. The privacy foundation of this pivotal Supreme Court case actually limits women's access to abortion and other reproductive rights by creating the perfect conditions for shaming, an individualizing and alienating affect.[3] In the latter half of this essay, I expand this argument to look at how shame also regulates bodies as populations, and I show how shame is ultimately not only an affect of individualism but also a regulative measure of life *en masse*, particularly as it works to harden racial classifications. Shame, I suggest, is a perfected technology of control because it invisibly captures the individual in a larger system of disciplinary and regulatory measures.

In the years following World War II, access to abortion was dramatically curtailed for most women across the United States. Although abortion had been illegal in the majority of states since the 1880s, prior to the 1950s government officials rarely prosecuted abortion providers unless death occurred.[4] However, as the post-war cultural climate shifted, it became more difficult to obtain abortions because of witch hunts that targeted women abortion providers in particular. Many women seeking abortions had to leave the country, if money was available, or risk aborting pregnancies through their own means or in unsanitary conditions. A woman's only legal option was to testify before a board of doctors that her physical and/or mental health would be severely impaired if she carried the fetus to term. Many women refused to go through this process, finding it shameful to discuss their reproductive health and personal lives in front of strangers, who were almost always male. Instead, they opted for procedures that risked their lives or their ability to reproduce again.

In Mike Leigh's 2004 film *Vera Drake*, Vera, a happily married mother of two and a housekeeper for wealthy women, secretly performs illegal abortions, or what she calls "helping young girls out."[5] The film, set in England in the 1950s, chronicles several abortion scenes between Vera and these girls, and though we see the girls as scared, lonely, or disdainful, none of them express shame for their choice to transgress the law. In a secondary narrative of the film, Susan, the daughter of one of Vera's wealthy employers, after being raped by a prospective husband, seeks a legal abortion through the help of a therapist who charges more than £100 and permits the procedure after hearing Susan's story. Susan, however, is barely able to articulate what happened to her and what she desires. She answers questions through half-finished sentences and pained expressions. She obtains her abortion under sanitary conditions and the auspices of a caring staff of nurses, but she is the only character who has an abortion during the film who is so shamed by her experience that she can barely speak. She is shamed by having to tell her story once to a family friend who she seems to believe will connect her to an abortionist, then again to a gynecologist, and then once again to a therapist. She is asked intimate questions about her sex life, her love life, and her family life in a cold and clinical way. And yet she answers, even though the experience shames her, because it is the only way she can have the legal abortion that will save her life.

Barbara Ehrenreich, in a July 2004 column in *The New York Times* entitled "Owning Up to Abortion," challenges the shame Americans associate with abortions,[6] pointing out that a Viacom-run channel refused to run an episode of a teen soap opera because a character had an abortion, and the popular HBO series *Six Feet Under*, usually known for its honest depiction of sexual issues, aired a show about abortion that shamed the character choosing to have one. However, the media is not solely to blame, according to Ehrenreich. She cites a website, "A Heartbreaking Choice," which provides emotional support to women who have aborted fetuses with potential birth defects, that quotes a woman complaining that she had to sit next to "all these girls that did not want their babies." Ehrenreich critiques women who claim their abortions were "necessary" because through these claims women attempt to position themselves on a higher moral plane, suggesting that their abortions were not really by choice and thus relegating only so-called ordinary abortions to the realm of the shameful. Ehrenreich warns that this position silences over a million American women a year who choose to have an abortion for a variety of personal reasons and not because of the fetus's potential birth defects; she therefore concludes that this silencing may one day cause all women to lose their right to a legal and safe abortion:

> Choice can be easy, as it was in my case, or truly agonizing. But assuming the fetal position is not an appropriate response. Sartre called this "bad faith," meaning something worse than duplicity: a fundamental denial of freedom and the responsibility that it entails. Time to take your thumbs out of your mouths, ladies, and speak up for

your rights. The freedoms that we exercise but do not acknowledge are easily taken away.[7]

Similarly, and perhaps more surprisingly, in the field of English/American literary criticism, there are few articles and books that discuss abortion post–Roe vs. Wade without the shadow of shame. Some critics looking at the trope of abortion relegate it to the confines of symbolism and metaphor, arguing that abortion *represents* loss or lack, or they justify their investigations through language that equivocates between recognizing the necessity of legal abortion and asserting the implicit shame of choosing to abort. For example, in one of two book-length studies of abortion narratives in American literature, Judith Wilt prefaces her work by explaining, "As a feminist and a Catholic, I believe a woman's freedom to abort a fetus is a monstrous, a tyrannous, but a *necessary* freedom in a fallen world."[8] The rest of her study examines the ways in which abortion works as a trope for the resistance of male control. Wilt's argument is infused with precisely the kind of shame that Ehrenreich critiques. Even as Wilt clearly states her position as a pro-choice feminist, she frames her discussion in terms that might make many women faced with the decision to abort cringe. Wilt seems unable to view abortion outside of Catholicism and its categorization of abortion as "monstrous" and "tyrannous." She chooses what Ehrenreich calls the "fetal position" and what Sartre calls "bad faith" because, even as she proclaims the necessity of a pro-choice position, which she sees as liberatory, she ascribes to that position the very affect that makes it impossible for women to act without feeling shame.

Although I sympathize with Ehrenreich's stance, I don't think that simply acknowledging that we have exercised our freedom to abort will guarantee that freedom. Ehrenreich falls into the trap she warns against if she assumes that speaking out, demanding access to abortion under any circumstances, and admitting to having had an abortion is enough to combat the shame associated with it. Instead, as the epigraph to this essay hints, the shame inherent in contemporary American abortion discourse is rooted in the liberal law that claims to protect our right to abortion—rooted in what Saidiya Hartman describes as the "liberal notions of responsibility modeled on contractual obligation."[9] Hartman's example of slavery may seem to have little relevance to the more contemporary conflict surrounding abortion, but using it as an analogy, I hope to reveal how emancipatory laws may actually create new ways to oppress and repress the newly emancipated subject. To elaborate, Hartman's work explores how the laws that emancipated slaves after the American Civil War worked to keep former slaves and other African Americans in subservient positions. She examines how emancipated African Americans were made to internalize their subordinated class position through legal discourse that granted their freedom but demanded their second-class status. She turns from looking at how the whip and the collar enslaved Blacks to how the ruling White class maintained that enslavement through psychological and disciplinary means.

Similarly, the turn I make looks past the laws that protect our freedom of choice to how shame ensures that women feel alienated and alone if abortion is what they choose. And, as Hartman suggests, this individualized discipline leads to the regulation of entire populations that must be contained and managed to ensure the maintenance of the status quo.

The 2007 film *Juno* models how the disciplining force of shame curtails access to abortion.[10] Juno is a sixteen-year-old White girl from a middle-class family, and she seems to have a bright future ahead of her. She's intelligent, funny, and creative, but she still gets pregnant the first time she has sex with her equally charming boyfriend. Juno considers an abortion, and she even visits an abortion clinic. But once there she encounters her anti-abortion schoolmate chanting outside the door, "All babies want to get borned [*sic*]," and she tells Juno, "Your baby probably has a beating heart, you know. It can feel pain. And it has fingernails!" Juno walks away from her looking dejected, but she is moved by her friend's words, and she's particularly struck by the thought that the fetus inside her might have fingernails. Juno's reception inside the clinic does nothing to reassure. The young receptionist appears bored and unsympathetic, and the thought of her fetus with fingernails obviously haunts Juno. Heather Latimer has noted that the film's depiction of an abortion clinic doesn't match up with reality. "In Minnesota, where Juno lives, pregnant teenagers under the age of 18 need parental consent for an abortion. It also ignores the fact that abortion clinics are actually staffed with trained personnel who often risk their own safety for their jobs, not with glib teenagers who tell patients about their own sexual exploits,"[11] Latimer explains. The film does portray, however glibly, the shaming ritual many women are subjected to by anti-abortion protesters who often stand outside abortion clinic doors. As Juno sits in the clinic attempting to fill out paperwork the camera zooms in on her to emphasize her alienation. She always sits alone in the frame, even though the clinic is obviously full of people, and anyone else the camera shows us is only seen in parts—a hand, an arm, a face. Juno is alone to ponder her friend's shaming rhetoric, and by the end of the scene she decides she can't face an abortion. She runs out of the clinic and decides to pursue adoption instead.

Shame and the Construction of Subjectivity

Shame is felt as an inner torment, a sickness of the soul. It does not matter whether the humiliated one has been shamed by derisive laughter or

whether he mocks himself. In either event, he feels himself naked, defeated, alienated, lacking in dignity or worth.

—Silvan Tomkins, *Shame and Its Sisters*[12]

When Joyce Johnson, in her 1962 memoir *Minor Characters*, tries to obtain
a legal abortion she first resorts to measures similar to those Susan attempted
in *Vera Drake*.[13] She seeks to obtain what was called in the pre-Roe v. Wade era
a therapeutic abortion, pleading to a therapist that she "would rather die" than
carry the pregnancy to term. The narrative suggests that Johnson would not
"rather die" because she feels shamed but rather because having a child at a young
age and without the support of another adult would be a burden that would prevent her from writing and living the independent lifestyle she sought by running
away from her parents.[14] When the therapist refuses, Johnson ends up connecting
to a network of women with names and addresses of people willing to perform
an illegal abortion. Like Juno and Susan in that she is disciplined by the regulating
mechanisms of her society when she chooses to abort, Johnson is ultimately able
to resist that discipline but at the price of an illegal and potentially life-threatening
procedure. In the therapist's office, she is an individual seeking an individual but
legal exemption; to obtain this exemption she must expose herself and play along
with the limits of the law, as Susan does. Because Johnson's narrative is free from
any shame concerning her unintended pregnancy, she prefers to obtain her abortion where no questions are asked and no disciplining judgment is passed. Ironically, Johnson discovers that in the 1950s the legal route to abortion would expose
her to shame, but by choosing to abort illegally she is able to find the support of
women who legitimize her decision.

Silvan Tomkin's definition of shame, which I cite in the epigraph to this
section, strikingly explains how shame can be such an effective means of social
control because it produces loneliness, aloneness, and alienation—a kind of control that Johnson seems to be ultimately able to resist. I am interested in how
shame can therefore be used as an affect of individualism by limiting the subject's
identification with a "we," thus causing that subject's isolation, as Juno experiences. Sedgwick writes that "shame and identity remain in a very dynamic relation to one another, at once deconstituting and foundational, because shame is
peculiarly contagious and peculiarly individuating."[15] In other words, the shame
of abortion works to make the subject feel alone, banished, neglected, and yet to
be shamed one must be in the presence of real or imagined others, like the board
of doctors Johnson would have needed to see in order to obtain a therapeutic abortion. Johnson is able to escape being shamed because she succeeded in connecting
to a network of women who made her feel that her desire to abort was common
and quotidian. Thus, although Johnson has to individually face having an abortion

her experience connected her to a community of women. Mary Poovey similarly argues that abortion should be viewed as a community-based decision rather than as an individual act that places the burden of choice on women. If Poovey's recommendation were to be realized, the power of shaming women for choosing abortion could be minimized. Women would choose abortion with the help of a network of people who supported her position because it was an openly accepted option.[16]

The pregnant woman, and especially the pregnant woman who wants to abort, is subjected to the same regulatory discourses and their paradoxes because they interpellate her as a subject identified by her reproductive body. Once Johnson is pregnant, she can no longer live on the margins of her society as she did as a beatnik. Her body becomes subject to the law and to its terms and conditions in ways that she was able to escape before her body was marked as reproductive. As Rosalind Petchesky argues, laws that monitor women's reproductive abilities are meant to mold them into citizens that are productive within the intelligibility of the state.[17] Johnson rebels against the norms of a 1950s America because she chooses a writing career over marriage and motherhood. Pregnancy, however, almost successfully disciplines her because at first she is forced to abide by biopolitical rules that demand that she expose her body to a group of medical professionals who have the power to decide whether to grant her an abortion. Johnson is lucky because she finds a way to escape this hold, and thus she also escapes being shamed for choosing a path that rejects reproduction.

Bad Girls and Biopolitics

Sexuality exists at the point where body and population meet. And so it is a matter for discipline, but also a matter for regularization.
—Michel Foucault, *Society Must Be Defended: Lectures at the College de France 1975–1976*[18]

What is the relationship between the individual who experiences shame, who is disciplined by the law, and the law, which governs through regulating populations? This question is at the heart of Karl Marx's observation of the liberal shift from the emphasis on the "we" to one on a central "I," and of Wendy Brown's argument, which uses this shift to examine how certain non-normative populations are regulated.[19] The connection between the individual—the disciplined and regulated individual—and populations also underpins an understanding of biopolitics,[20] particularly as it relates to abortion. In other words, how is the disciplining of the individual body through shame part of a larger mechanism of controlling populations? And perhaps there is a larger question: Why is there a need for this control?[21] In this next section, I argue that, although shaming is individuated, it always works to regulate abortion within the larger framework of state control but more specifically through the dispersed technologies of biopolitics, which is ultimately never concerned with the individual but with the management of life along racial lines.

Is shame experienced as part of the process of bourgeois subjectification?[22] Does Susan in *Vera Drake* experience shame because she is White and bourgeois? Perhaps another way of answering this question is to ask what the relationship is between the affects produced through law and their abilities to call forth the processes of racial and class-based subjectification. More important, how does shame work to demarcate populations along racial and class lines? How does that demarcation work by always negotiating between disciplining individuals and yet, at the same time, controlling its populations? And finally, how does exposing these connections force us to reevaluate the language of choice and rights, which feminist activists currently use to fight for abortion?

The politics of abortion in the early twentieth century not only reveals the tension between individuation and the population, which is present in all of the texts discussed previously; it also provides a crucial piece of history necessary for understanding how shame comes to affectively regulate access to abortion through racial discourse. One episode of abortion regulation exposes the workings of biopolitics in the American judicial system and sheds lights on why abortion is such a central issue in American politics. In October of 1916, Margaret Sanger and her sister Ethel Byrne, both licensed nurses, opened the first birth control clinic in Brownsville, Brooklyn. The clinic advertised itself as an advocate for family planning that explicitly opposed abortion. The handbill that circulated around Brownsville, a predominantly poor Jewish and Italian neighborhood at the time, read:

> MOTHERS! Can you afford to have a large family? Do you want any more children? If not, why do you have them? DO NOT KILL, DO NOT TAKE LIFE, BUT PREVENT.[23]

Because no doctor was present, the clinic was supposedly handing out information only about sex and contraceptives. It charged ten cents for consultations and distributed flyers about various methods of birth control. The most common contraceptive at the time was the Mitzpah Pessary, a device conventionally prescribed for women with uterine problems but also proven to work to prevent pregnancy. Boxes of this device were found at the clinic, although Byrne and Sanger were ostensibly only recommending that women obtain the device through their local pharmacies and with a doctor's prescription. Ten days after opening, the clinic was raided by the police and shut down. Margaret Sanger, Fania Mindell, and Ethel Byrne were arrested. Byrne was tried first on January 4, 1917; she was sentenced to one month in jail for violating the Comstock statutes that prohibited the distribution of birth control information.[24] Her trial and subsequent imprisonment made headlines in several prominent newspapers at the time. When she went on a hunger strike in jail and was force-fed through her esophagus, the *New York Times* published cover stories about her case for four straight days.[25]

The Sanger and Byrne case was sensational and brought immediate media attention to the controversy over access to birth control. However, it also extricated the issue of birth control from abortion, which was often seen as synonymous with birth control in the nineteenth century. Instead, Sanger made explicit that abortion was a murderous act—"Do not kill," she warned—while preventing pregnancy was a charitable and responsible act—"Can you afford this?" she asked. Sanger's involvement in the eugenics movement has now been documented extensively,[26] and her language here is obviously implicated in attempting to prevent "overpopulation." Brownsville, the community where she distributed the flyers and where the clinic opened, was in the early twentieth century predominantly Jewish and Irish, two groups which at the time would have been "raced" as outsiders. However, why did she so determinedly see the need to shame women into not aborting? Why did she see the need to promote birth control at the cost of stigmatizing abortion? Abortion had already been villainized by the mid-nineteenth century when doctors in the American Medical Association, led by the vocal member Horatio Storer, began a campaign to outlaw abortion state by state. This movement gained much of its strength after the Civil War, in the late 1860s and the 1870s, when not coincidentally the United States, now a nation without sanctioned slavery, had to redefine its approach to sovereignty and rethink the constitution of its people. In the late nineteenth and the early twentieth century, the United States went through an enormous shift that redefined the makeup of its population; because of an influx of immigrants from Eastern Europe, Ireland, and Italy, and a population of emancipated African Americans, the citizens of the United States could no longer be classified as typically Anglo-Saxon. This new population gave rise to regulatory measures that worked to maintain the status quo, the most obvious being the technologies that emerged out of eugenics and its practices. Thus this shift emphasized the management of bodies as masses, and this kind of management is always implicated in the regulation of reproduction, fertility, and birth rates, particularly as they are organized by race.[27] Alys Eve Weinbaum explains how miscegenation laws beginning in the Jim Crow era and beyond worked to imbue White blood with value, as something that needed to be carefully controlled through laws that prohibited acts of reproduction seen as threatening that value.[28] Anti-abortion laws worked in much the same way; by prohibiting abortion and shaming White women who sought it, the purity of "White blood" could be maintained. White women were encouraged to reproduce with White men and to view their reproduction as precious and in need of protection from vile, contaminating acts like abortion, which were described as something only women from lower classes would do.

As Foucault points to in the epigraph to this section, sexuality was granted such a privileged position in the nineteenth century precisely because it flowed between disciplining the individual organism and regulating the population. Similarly, shame becomes a "neater" mechanism for regulating bodies than the disciplining technologies of site-specific locations, such as school and church. Therefore, even though shame is, as I argued previously, an affect experienced by the individual, its capacity for movement, its circulation through human bodies, and its ability to be transferred "affectively" allows it to be a regulating mechanism for controlling populations. It works by circulating between the body and the population. Sanger's investment in eugenics and birth control bridges the ways in which her ideologies worked to regulate the individual (using abortion is wrong; use birth control) and the ways in which those ideologies always had more generalized and *relational* implications. By disciplining the body into normative behaviors, entire populations can be managed and produced through difference (*I am not them; I* do not do as *they* do). Shame guarantees that even if abortion is legal or accessible, it will be regulated; more important, shame will regulate those very populations that seek abortion.

In addition to the attention Sanger brought to reproductive rights and abortion, the early twentieth century saw the emergence of American novels that dealt with abortion, often in ways that reflected how shame worked to curtail access to it. In each of the texts I discuss, abortion's illegality did little to deter women from seeking abortion or from feeling as though they had transgressed.[29] Ultimately, it was the experience of being shamed that haunted these characters, and as I will demonstrate, that shame is often tinged with racial and class anxieties. To quote Floyd Dell's wealthy, White, and astute protagonist in the eponymous novel *Janet March*, "Why weren't there things like [abortions] in novels—oh yes, there were dreadful things enough in novels, but they only happened to poor girls—ignorant and reckless girls—."[30]

Lewis Sinclair's 1933 *Ann Vickers* echoes Janet's sentiment. The eponymous Ann, an accomplished, independent career woman becomes pregnant in an affair that she soon realizes will never end in marriage. At the same time, Tessie, one of the Jewish, working-class women at the settlement house where Ann works, also becomes pregnant and seeks an abortion. Ann visits an abortionist for her, but when he mistakenly assumes that Ann wants the abortion, she insists, "I tell you, it's *not* myself! How could you! Ridiculous! I tell you, it's a Jewish girl who's one of my charges."[31] Even though Ann does indeed need an abortion, she revolts against the abortionist's perception of her as an "ignorant and reckless girl," to use Janet March's terms. What Ann wants to convey is that educated Anglo-Saxon women don't need abortions, and in fact a moment later the abortionist apologizes and explicitly reinscribes the classist and racist lines that Ann draws. He reassures her, "You're a fine educated young lady—I could tell, the minute you come in—I was just joking about thinking it was you and not the Yid."[32] In this scene, the novel articulates how shame manages the reproductive lives of women through race. Abortion is not only just something ignorant and reckless girls do, as Janet's novels informed her; it draws racial lines because White women like Ann would never be so irresponsible as to need one. Thus Ann's shame about her accidental pregnancy silences her and prevents her from admitting both to Tessie and the abortionist that even smart, wealthy White women make mistakes and need abortions.

In Viña Delmar's 1928 novel *Bad Girl*[33] an abortion is avoided precisely for the reasons that shame Janet and Ann.[34] The novel tells the story of a young couple's aspiration to rise in class position when an unintended pregnancy brings crisis to their household because they don't yet have the financial resources to have a child. Dot, the young woman, thinks she should have an abortion because she doesn't want to interrupt her husband's plans, but the most respected figures in her life effectively shame her from successfully pursuing one. Her close friend Edna tells her that women who have abortions are "dames who'd shoot their fingers off to evade going to war if they were men."[35] Later, Dr. Stewart, the trustworthy doctor recommended to Dot by her friend and clearly a figure of authority in the novel, tells her during her first visit, "I hope you're not thinking of an abortion. . . . A nasty corrupt practice which has a bad effect on the woman who uses it."[36] Both conversations shame Dot, who doesn't admit that she did indeed visit an abortionist who molested her and made her feel like an irresponsible, naïve child. The novel's narrative suggests that Dot's decision to follow both Edna and Dr. Stewart's advice rescues her from the "bad effects" of abortion and helps secure her family's rise in class position.

Dot eventually decides to carry her pregnancy to term, and her husband saves money so that she can birth and recuperate for two weeks in a sanatorium, which they are told is the new modern standard for childbirth. In the ward she has a conversation with a new mother who serves as a reminder that she made the correct choice. The woman tells her about her "Jewess" sister-in-law "who had had eleven abortions," and she informs Dot that when this woman came to visit, Dot "would know her by the big diamond ring she wore."[37] The sister-in-law visits Dot's roommate with two other women, and while there "they talked loud and laughed frequently."[38] Their behavior echoes an earlier description in the novel of "gossiping uncorseted Jewesses" who populate less desirable neighborhoods with their "squalling, dirty-faced babies" and make "noisy, ill-bred families."[39] Dot, the novel narrates with what almost seems like relief, manages to escape becoming like them because she had been shamed from having an abortion. Instead, she chose the respectable route that supports her husband's climb up the social ladder.

The scenes just described all accept the disciplining force of shame as a mechanism to regulate abortion. Langston Hughes's 1936 "Cora Unashamed," explicitly addresses the intersection of abortion, race, and shame and levels a powerful critique in attempting to deconstruct it. Jessie, a young White woman, becomes pregnant after a love affair with a young Greek man in her town. When her mother, one of the town's wealthiest women and a socialite, learns of her daughter's pregnancy she takes her to Kansas City for an abortion. Publically, however, she declares the journey a shopping trip, and when her daughter dies a month later because of the illegal abortion, her illness is talked of as a bad case of indigestion. Cora, the family's African American "maid of all work,"[40] is the only one who refuses to shame Jesse and feel ashamed. Cora's daughter was born the same year as Jessie, and so she nursed Jesse as well, and when Cora's daughter dies of whooping cough, she becomes even more attached to her. Therefore, when Jessie realizes she is pregnant, she asks Cora to break the news to her mother, which Cora does "humbly and shamelessly."[41] However, Jessie's mother feels desperately ashamed. Her daughter's pregnancy, abortion, and then death motivate her to begin what the narrative calls a "campaign of purity" aiming "to rid the town of the objectionable tradespeople and questionable characters."[42] Greeks, including Jessie's lover, are of course included, and Willie Matsoulos, the young man, is banished from the small town.

Jessie, as Cora explains to her mother, would have happily married Willie, but both his immigrant and class status make him not White enough for the family to accept. Unlike Cora, who is "humble and shameless before the fact of the child" because "There were no Negroes in Melton to gossip, and she didn't care what the White people said,"[43] Jessie and her mother are subject to the affective pressures of their community. Jessie's mother isn't shamed because of the abortion, but she forces her daughter to have an abortion because she feels shamed by the illegitimate pregnancy and its exposure of her daughter's love affair with a man not viewed as White. Cora is unashamed because she has little relationality with the other inhabitants of Melton. Jessie's mother, on the other hand, is shaped by her shame, or her potential to be shamed. Her identity is in fact delineated by that shame through what Sedgwick describes as "the place where the *question* of identity arises most originally and most relationally."[44] Jessie's mother's shame identifies her as a wealthy White woman who fears for her position because it rests so precariously in definition against the immigrant working-class inhabitants of the town. Her shame exposes that precariousness and exposes the dependence of her identity on others. She is alone in her shame, but she is shamed because she imagines what others might say. Ultimately, she needs her daughter to have an abortion to hide that shame, even at the risk of her daughter's life. The workings of shame, as Hughes's story demonstrates, momentarily reveal how populations are demarcated from each other to maintain racial hierarchies.

"Cora Unashamed" presents another perspective on the link between abortion and shame. Although Jessie's mother is ashamed of her daughter's abortion, she is even more ashamed by the conditions that led to it. Not only does she consider her daughter's behavior inappropriate for a woman of her class; but if a child were to be born it would challenge the racial lines that divide the community. Early twenty-first-century women are by no means free of such disciplining shame, but premarital sex and inter-racial relations are more accepted. For example, in an early episode of the popular and sometimes controversial HBO series *Girls*, Jessa, one of main characters, discovers her pregnancy and immediately decides she needs an abortion. The show, which deals with sex in daring and at times transgressive ways, attaches little shame to Jessa's decision and the actions that preceded it. However, when she misses her appointment and instead miscarries while making out with an anonymous stranger in the bathroom, she feels an enormous sense of relief. Even Jessa, the sexually promiscuous woman who seems immune to shame, dreads exposing herself in the abortion clinic. *Girls* manages to present abortion with less stigma than most contemporary TV shows and movies. Even so, it shows that we still have a far way to go before abortion has little to do with shame. In the meantime, as anti-abortion activists slowly chip away at Roe v. Wade, shame follows abortion as its specter. And as long as abortion is framed through the rhetoric of individuated choice, it will remain the most powerful tool those activists have.

Notes

1. Saidiya Hartman, *Scenes of Subjection: Terror, Slavery, and Self-Making in Nineteenth-Century America* (New York: Oxford University Press, 1997), 6.

2. One example of this rhetoric is Justice Kennedy's explanation for why the Supreme Court upheld the ban on the late-term abortion procedure called intact dilation and extraction in the 2007 ruling on Gonzales v. Carhart (the procedure was also politicized by the pro-life movement with the label "partial-birth" abortion.) Kennedy, in his decision, wrote, "It is self-evident that a mother who comes to regret her choice to abort must struggle with grief more anguished and sorrow more profound, when she learns, only after the event, what she once did not know: that she allowed a doctor to pierce the skull and vacuum the fast developing brain of her unborn child, a child assuming the human form." Alberto R. Gonzales, Attorney General, Petitioner 05-1382 v. Planned Parenthood Federation of America, Inc. et al. (April 18, 2007), Legal Information Institute, https://www.law.cornell.edu/supct/html/05-380.ZO.html.

3. For other work on the privacy foundation of Roe v. Wade see Rosalind Petchesky, *Abortion and Women's Choice: The State, Sexuality, and Reproductive Freedom* (Boston: North-

eastern University Press, 1990); Drucilla Cornell, *The Imaginary Domain: Abortion, Pornography, and Sexual Harassment* (New York: Routledge, 1995); Dorothy Roberts, *Killing the Black Body: Race, Reproduction, and the Meaning of Liberty* (New York: Vintage, 1997); Mary Poovey, "The Abortion Question and the Death of Man," in *Feminists Theorize the Political,* ed. Judith Butler and Joan W. Scott (New York: Routledge, 1992), 239–256; and Ricki Solinger, *Beggars and Choosers: How the Politics of Choice Shapes Adoption, Abortion, and Welfare in the United States* (New York: Hill and Wang, 2001). Interestingly, Solinger's argument works intently to differentiate between the discourses of rights and choice. Solinger believes that rights are necessary for ensuring access to abortion, at the same time calling choice "rights lite," or a diluted and ineffectual version of rights. I see them as similar versions of the same issue: The rhetorics of both rights and choice is grounded in a liberal and individuated understanding of law—both assume a universal, ahistoricized subject with no attention to particularities that often make the access to right or choice impossible or even more oppressive. Finally, see Karen Newman, *Fetal Positions: Individualism, Science, and Visuality* (Stanford: Stanford University Press, 1996), which does interesting work in linking the discourses of privacy and individualism to fetal imagery and abortion.

4. See Leslie J. Reagan, *When Abortion Was a Crime: Women, Medicine, and the Law, 1867–1973* (Berkeley: University of California Press, 1997) for more details about abortion in the 1950s.

5. *Vera Drake,* directed by Mike Leigh (Burbank, CA: Warner Bros. Pictures, 2004).

6. Barbara Ehrenreich, "Owning Up to Abortion," *The New York Times,* July 22, 2004, A21. Ehrenreich actually uses the word "guilt" rather than shame in her essay. However, I think that shame is a more accurate description of the affect she delineates. In *Touching Feeling: Affect, Pedagogy, Performativity* (Durham: Duke University Press, 2003), Eve Sedgwick offers a succinct distinction between the two. She writes, "The conventional way of distinguishing shame from guilt is that shame attaches to and sharpens the sense of what one is, whereas guilt attaches to what one does" (p. 37). Because women who choose to abort are often described as reckless, irresponsible, unfeeling—and because many women who choose to abort end up viewing themselves in these terms because of such descriptions—abortion has the effect of making women feel as though they *are* "less than," which is exactly the phenomenon that Ehrenreich describes in her essay. As Sedgwick emphasizes, "One *is something* in experiencing shame" (ibid., 37). I discuss this effect in more detail later in this essay.

7. Ehrenreich, "Owning Up to Abortion."

8. Judith Wilt, *Abortion, Choice, and Contemporary Fiction: The Armageddon of the Maternal Instinct* (Chicago: University of Chicago Press, 1990), xii. The other book-length study of abortion in American fiction is Jeff Koloze and Anne Barbeau's pro-life work, *An Ethical Analysis of the Portrayal of Abortion in American Fiction: Dreiser, Hemingway, Faulkner, Dos Passos, Brautigan, and Irving* (Lewiston, NY: Mellen, 2005). Also see Barbara Johnson, "Apostrophe, Animation, and Abortion," in *Contemporary Literary Criticism: Literary and Cultural Studies,* ed. Robert Davis and Ronald Schleifer (New York: Longman, 1998), 215–231.

9. Saidiya V. Hartman, *Scenes of Subjection: Terror, Slavery, and Self-Making in Nineteenth Century America* (New York: Oxford University Press, 1997), 9.

10. *Juno,* directed by Jason Reitman (Los Angeles: Fox Searchlight Pictures, 2007).

11. Heather Latimer, "Popular Culture and Reproductive Politics: *Juno, Knocked Up*, and the Enduring Legacy of the *Handmaid's Tale*," *Feminist Theory* 10, no. 2 (2009): 218.

12. Silvan Tomkins, *Shame and Its Sisters: A Silvan Tomkins Reader*, ed. Eve Kosofsky Sedwick and Adam Frank. (Durham: Duke University Press, 1995), 133.

13. Joyce Johnson, *Minor Characters: A Beat Memoir* (New York: Penguin Books, 1999). Johnson is regarded as one of the few well-known beat woman writers, but she is probably most famous for her love affair with Jack Kerouac, which came after her pregnancy and subsequent abortion.

14. Another reading of Johnson's plea that "she would rather die" is more straightforward: because a therapeutic abortion was only granted if the patient seemed to have a medical condition, either physical or mental, Johnson was hoping to demonstrate that she was psychologically unbalanced and suicidal so that the therapist would grant her request.

15. Sedgwick, *Touching Feeling*, 36.

16. Alison Piepmeier's recent fieldwork with women who decided not to have an abortion after learning their fetus had Down syndrome echoes Poovey's theoretical conclusion. Piepmeier heard over and over from the women she interviewed that they resented the pressure of being told that their decision was their individual choice. Instead, she found that most women wanted "guidance, information, real options, meaningful support." The women who had those things seemed most happy with their decisions—whether or not they decided to abort. See Piepmeier's essay, "The Inadequacy of 'Choice': Disability and What's Wrong with Feminist Framings of Reproduction, *Feminist Studies* 39, no.1 (2013): 173.

17. See Petchesky's *Abortion and Women's Choice*, 10–11.

18. Michel Foucault, *Society Must be Defended: Lectures at the College de France 1975–1976*, Trans. David Macey (New York: Picador, 1976), 251–252.

19. Wendy Brown, *States of Injury: Power and Freedom in Late Modernity* (New Jersey: Princeton University Press, 1995).

20. Biopolitics is first defined by Foucault as "the emergence of something that is no longer an anatomo-politics of the human body, but what I would call a 'biopolitics' of the human race." In other words, a shift where power is no longer directed at the individual but at the mass—what he calls "man-as-species." Michel Foucault, *Society Must Be Defended: Lectures at the Collège de France, 1975–1976*, trans. David Macey (New York: Picador, 2003), 243.

21. I am consciously using the language of control, rather than discipline, to emphasize Gilles Deleuze's reading of biopolitics, where he argues that in the late twentieth century (and I would argue even before) discipline was no longer sufficient for understanding the regulation of bodies because it didn't occur in site-specific locations (such as the school or the factory) but in more dispersed, delocalized places, as in the way capital flows in our contemporary economy. For more see Deleuze, "Postscript on Control Societies" in *Negotiations*, trans. Martin Joughin (New York: Columbia University Press, 1995).

22. The process through which a subject becomes (a subject). See Gilles Deleuze, *Foucault*, trans. Sean Hand (Minneapolis: University of Minnesota Press, 1986).

23. Ellen Chesler, *Woman of Valor: Margaret Sanger and the Birth Control Movement in America* (New York: Simon and Schuster, 1992), 150.

24. The Comstock Statutes were officially called the Act of Suppression of Trade in and Circulation of Obscene Literature and Articles of Immoral Use. For a more complete discussion, see Janet Brodie's *Contraception and Abortion in Nineteenth-Century America* (Ithaca, NY: Cornell University Press, 1994).

25. Brodie, *Contraception and Abortion in Nineteenth-Century America*, 150–160.

26. See Angela Franks, *Margaret Sanger's Eugenic Legacy: The Control of Female Fertility* (Jefferson, NC: McFarland Press, 2005). Also see Margaret Sanger's periodical *The Birth Control Review*, published from 1917 to 1940, which often made explicit its connection to the eugenics movement. Serial Archives Listings for *The Birth Control Review*, last modified January 1, 2015, http://onlinebooks.library.upenn.edu/webbin/serial?id=birthcontrolrev.

27. See Daylanne English's provocative reading of eugenics in post–World War II America, *Unnatural Selections: Eugenics in American Modernism and the Harlem Renaissance* (Chapel Hill: University of North Carolina Press, 2004).

28. Alys Eve Weinbaum, *Wayward Reproductions: Genealogies of Race and Nation in Transatlantic Modern Thought* (Durham, NC: Duke University Press, 2004), 20.

29. My book, *Abortion in the American Imagination: Before Life and Choice: 1880–1940* (New Brunswick, NJ: Rutgers University Press, 2014), discusses these texts in more detail and outside the context of shame.

30. Floyd Dell, *Janet March* (New York: Knopf, 1933), 211.

31. Sinclair Lewis, *Ann Vickers* (New York: Doubleday, Doran, 1993), 199.

32. Ibid., 199.

33. Delmar's novel, although currently out of print, was a huge bestseller when it was first published. In 1938 it was the fifth bestselling novel of the year. That same year, it was also made into a play and an Oscar-nominated film. I have chosen to focus on this novel because it nicely demonstrates the way shame and sexuality encompass both the individual and the population and because it was "the book everybody read, whether he admitted it or not" (Vernon Rice, "Viña Delmar is Mr. and Mrs. Delmar," *New York Post*, January 14, 1953, 58). For more details, see Meg Gillette's "Making Modern Parents in Ernest Hemingway's 'Hills like White Elephants' and Viña Delmar's *Bad Girl*," *Modern Fiction Studies* 53, no. 1 (2007): 50–69. Gillette carefully documents the novel's reception in its time.

34. I am particularly referring here to the eugenics movement that gained strength after World War I and encouraged the ideology that intelligence was inherited, that class and race position were genetically coded, and thus that certain populations needed to be managed through limiting their ability to reproduce, often through forced sterilization. A 1927 Supreme Court case, Buck v. Bell, provides an infamous example of these policies; Carrie Buck was sterilized without her consent because, according to the Court, her "lower intelligence" made her an unsuitable candidate for reproduction. See Buck v. Bell, 774 U.S. 200 (1927) and Buck v. Bell, 130 S.E. 516, 518 (Supreme Court of Appeals of Virginia 1925).

35. Viña Delmar, *Bad Girl* (New York: Harcourt, 1928), 119.

36. Ibid., 131.

37. Ibid., 233.

38. Ibid., 242.

39. Ibid., 34.

40. Langston Hughes, "Cora Unashamed," in *The Ways of White Folk* (New York: Vintage, 1990), 34.

41. Ibid., 40.

42. Ibid., 42.

43. Ibid., 36.

44. Sedgwick, *Touching Feeling*, 37. Shame is tied to identity, Sedgwick writes, but she emphasizes that it is not "the place where identity is most securely attached to essences" (p. 36). Instead, as the quotation in the text notes, it is the place where identity is formed through its questioning.

TWO

Sex, Shame, and the Single Life:
Bond and the "Black Shirley Temple"

Daniel McNeil

Almost four score and seven years ago, Philippa Schuyler was conceived under a cloud of romantic fancy and racist paranoia. Her mother was Josephine Cogdell Schuyler, a White artist from a wealthy background in Texas, who believed that the "white race" was spiritually depleted and that her daughter and other racially mixed children were needed to save America's soul.[1] Her father was George Schuyler, one of the most prominent African American journalists and authors of the early twentieth century, who thought that his daughter's genius would confound Nazis in Europe as well as right-wing anthropologists in America invested in pseudo-scientific ideas about Black intellectual inferiority.[2] Yet many Americans did not share the hopes and dreams of the Schuylers and their friends in a New York avant-garde. During a time in which the Schuylers were unable to marry in Texas and many other states of the union, mainstream journalists expressed their shock and concern for a blue-blooded "blonde Texan" who fell in love with a "coal black Negro." They also filed the prodigious talents of Philippa Schuyler in newspaper reports about a "strange curiosity" or a "Black Shirley Temple."[3]

After being marketed as a child prodigy in America and then touring the globe as a peripatetic concert pianist sponsored by the U.S. State Department, Schuyler lamented the lack of cultural opportunities available for her in America.[4] She expressed hatred for her home and native land, and drew on a wide range of cultural materials to create a new identity for herself as Felipa Monterro, a woman from the Iberian Peninsula who could find gainful employment as a writer of Catholic hagiographies or "sexy novels." Yet whether she wrote under the name Philippa Schuyler or Felipa Monterro, she attacked Blackness as an alien other tied to racial violence, economic underdevelopment, and brute strength. Whether she followed her father into the ultra-right-wing John Birch society or sent letters to her mother praising the beauty of Aryan men, she sought to defend the authority of strong White rule in a multiracial environment. Whether composing plays, novels, diaries, letters, or a new identity, she was inspired by a love of tough Whites from working-class or southern European backgrounds who could not be caricatured as prudish Nordics or legally classified as Black. As a result, Schuyler generated excessive power to attack forms of Blackness and threatened the authority of Whiteness that she sought to defend. Her story is not just a tale of Black and White; it is also a special blend of tragedy and farce that encourages us to think more deeply about the ironies of a colonial past and the shame of a neocolonial present.

"I Hate My Country"

When she traveled around the world as a concert pianist, Schuyler described her father as a man of color from Madagascar with no ancestral links to Africa. She also demanded the removal of her name from his encyclopedia, *The Negro in America*,[5] and it is difficult to find a starker, more literal depiction of Philippa Schuyler's flight from Blackness than the white piece of paper that George Schuyler pasted over his daughter's entry in his unpublished manuscript of African American life.[6] Yet rather than explore the psychological dimensions of this family romance, historians and biographers have tended to rely on stereotypes about a "tragic mulatto" trapped between Black and White in America, to speculate about the "Mixed Personality Disorder" of "Harlem's biracial prodigy,"[7] and to indulge in armchair psychiatry about Schuyler's "national, racial, and personal identity confusions."[8] Such comments say more about the influence of assertively nationalistic commentators who talk much about the rootlessness of African Americans who try to escape racial shame,[9] and rather less about the routes plotted by Schuyler as a precursor of "that contemporary quest of individuals who resist the one-drop rule and navigate the uncharted waters of multiracial identity."[10] Rather than dismiss Schuyler's self-fashioning as a cautionary tale about "little yellow dream children"[11] or develop a revisionist history that celebrates her struggle to resist the impositions of a one-drop rule, this essay provides some further context for us to analyze Schuyler's pursuit of love and security in the 1950s and 1960s. It is interested in her attempts to unite with something or someone larger than herself in a Cold War context riddled with racism, sexism, and homophobia; her self-conscious adoption of national stereotypes in the hope of becoming a creative artist who would be popular with European audiences; and the voracious and wide-ranging reading that informed her contribution to perennial debates about art and commerce, truth and popularity, revolution and reaction.

Schuyler's attempt to pass as a Mediterranean woman was informed by her reading of iconoclastic writers such as Simone de Beauvoir and Sidonie-Gabrielle Colette. Yet Anaïs Nin, a writer with French, Spanish, and Cuban roots, is perhaps the most intriguing female influence on the motifs of race, sexuality, freedom, and marriage that would play such a major role in Schuyler's self-fashioning. To give one revealing example, Nin's diary described a trip to Harlem in which she sought to repay the wisdom of her psychologist, the Austrian-born Otto Rank, with a night that was filled with the "natural rhythm" and "wild dancing" of Blacks.[12] Such depictions of rational European masculinity were further indulged by Rank's social psychology about birth trauma (the violent separation from the mother) and the so-called masculine ideology of art and myth. In Nin's diaries, Rank tells his most famous American patient, "When the neurotic woman gets cured [from the pain of birth trauma], she becomes woman [or mother]. When the neurotic man gets cured, he becomes an artist."[13] In his own, unfiltered work, he proffers the following maxims: "The woman's strength lies in her sex, the man's in his creative will"; "She needs the man as a rational guide through this man-made world"; "Whereas man develops his psychology to protect himself by control (will), woman takes on his psychology from an opposite motive, that is, to lose herself, to give herself to him."[14]

If Nin found the masculinist views of Rank reinforced by personal contact, Schuyler combined her readings of psychoanalysis, philosophy and literature with trips to the movies. She could lose herself—and fashion a self—while watching epic tales of exotic adventure such as *Lawrence of Arabia* (directed by David Lean, 1962), which won the best picture and best director Oscars at the 35th annual Academy Awards for its exploration of the double consciousness of an Englishman and an Arab; *The Leopard* (directed by Luchino Visconti, 1963), a film based on the novel about Don Fabrizio Corbera, Prince of Salina, and the changes in Sicilian life and society during the *Risorgimento*, which won the 1963 Palm d'Or from the Cannes film festival; and the James Bond series of films, which adapted the novels and short stories created by a White Englishman in the neocolonial settings of Jamaica. In other venues, I have considered Schuyler's relationship to *The Leopard* and *Lawrence of Arabia*.[15] In this essay, I primarily use Schuyler's engagement with Bond to explore what she considered the shame of Black barbarism, her hopes of becoming an exotic femme fatale, and her desire to honor and obey powerful White men.

The Woman of Color and the White Man

Ian Fleming's stories about James Bond were first published at a time of profound anxiety in British life. In 1953 various foreign policy crises displayed the continuing decline of the British military and Winston Churchill, the nation's eloquent and imperialist leader during World War II, suffered a major stroke. The Bond series provided readers with an anti-hero who led the United States and the English-speaking nations of the Commonwealth with his wit, bravery, and bravado. Put more bluntly, Bond was vital to the Anglosphere that Churchill championed in his "Sinews of Peace" address at Westminster College in Fulton, Missouri, on March 5, 1946. Lest we forget, this notion of an Anglosphere often served as a euphemism for White leadership or "White blood" protecting non-Whites from barbarity and irrelevance. One thinks, for example, of Sir Hugh Trevor-Roper, Regis Professor of History at Oxford, who asserted that African history was the study of "unrewarding gyrations of barbarous tribes in picturesque but irrelevant parts of the globe"; of Sir Christopher Masterman, the first British Deputy Commissioner for South India, who promoted the idea that Blacks had "no culture, no architecture, no written language" and were desperately in need of Aristotelian "natural rulers"; and of Austin Ferraz, editor of the *Sunday Mail* of Salisbury, Rhodesia, who thought it was common sense to believe that "out of the 20 million negroes in the US almost none have achieved anything and those who are claimed to have done so—like Ralph Bunche and Thurgood Marshall—are whiter than they are black."[16]

Drawing on his experiences as a student in European universities, an intelligence officer in the British armed forces, and a journalist with Reuters, Fleming's novels also conveyed a concern about the ability of Africans to govern themselves. Black Jamaicans were depicted as kind and lazy "with the virtues and vices of a child" in *Dr No*. In *Quantum of Solace*, Bond describes the "simple, kindly natures" of Black Nigerians who know nothing about birth control. And, when an evil Black genius threatens Bond in *Live and Let Die*, readers are reminded that this clever antagonist has a "healthy dose" of European blood. Yet the racist ideologies that informed Fleming's ideas about race and racial mixing were linked not only to political intelligence; they were also tied to a beauty mystique in which Bond dispatched grotesque villains (such as Le Chiffre, a "Portuguese with a dash of Chinaman") and aligned himself with Solitaire and other racially mixed individuals whom he deemed friendly and beautiful.[17]

Schuyler adapted the racism and beauty mystique of the Bond novels when she hoped to become a Catholic writer and an exotic femme fatale. She chose to pass as a Portuguese woman because she considered Portugal to be "the world's only major nation, having a large non-white populace, to accord half-castes absolute equality with whites," and she reminded the readers of *Jungle Saints* that leading figures in Portugal's parliament were married to women of Chinese descent.[18] Yet while Schuyler praised Portuguese men in Angola who were willing to acknowledge their attraction to non-White women and grant the children of interracial relationships absolute equality with Whites, she also expressed her belief that Blacks were "simple children of nature." Drawing on the pseudo-scientific racism of eugenicists who contrasted the forceful personalities of the Mediterranean "races" with the "sexually conservative" Anglo-Saxons or Nordics,[19] Schuyler praised Portuguese conservatives who were free of that "strained attempt to prove one is a liberal [by asserting the equality of Blacks], so often to be seen in Anglo-Saxon countries."[20] In addition, her missives for the far-right John Birch society condemned the "awful" characters and "primitive savagery" of "pure blacks"[21] and warned readers about the supposed threat of "deviant" homosexuality to Western civilization.[22] She not only argued that "fairies, weaklings, opportunists, climbers, avaricious money-grabbers, socialists and Reds lost the Congo for the West,"[23] but offered the following reflections on her failure to find a real-life Commander Bond while staying near a British military base:

> In Nicosia, [I] went and sat in a bar. Seven Englishmen were seated at the bar stools. I sat next to them for ONE HOUR and not one of them cast ONE GLANCE at me! God, the difference between Englishmen and Italians! . . . No Italian would leave me unlooked-at for one hour! . . . I went to bed, woefully convinced of my decline and failure as a femme fatale.
>
> At dawn, I was awakened by some wild whooping out in the corridor. One of the Englishmen, who had the room on my left, was running around the hall, shouting in purest Anglo-Saxon, to the two Englishmen who had the room on the right. The language (!**%**) he used, and their replies, made it quite clear they were, all seven of them, homosexuals! . . . No wonder the British have lost their empire! . . . They were all RAF officers too.[24]

Bond and BDSM

Fleming created Commander Bond as he contemplated his upcoming marriage on a neocolonial estate in Jamaica that overlooked a private beach. The antics of his hero—perhaps the most famous bachelor in the West—allowed Fleming one way to extend his own bachelorhood and appeal to different classes of readers concerned about Britain's declining role in the world. He wanted the Bond novels to appeal to an "A" readership, but he was also aware that the republication of his books for the mass paperback market, and their serialization in newspapers like the *Daily Express* and magazines such as *Playboy* would attract different types of readers.

Based in Katanga for a musical recital when the region sued for independence and precipitated a civil war in Congo that led to the death of Patrice Lumumba, the country's first democratically elected leader, Schuyler was also enlisted by conservative newspapers who hoped to provide their readers with tales of adventure, intrigue, and sex. In what she considered her best work, Schuyler drew on her experiences in the Congo in the hopes of appealing to readers who were tired of "thought books" without alienating those who could appreciate the sophistication and the background of her stories.[25] As a result, her depiction of a Bondian hero for southern Africa in plays and novels such as *Evil Eville, The Demons of the*

Jungle, and *The White Leopard of Katanga* provide a vivid portrait of an artist anxious about marriage and her position in the wider world.

Schuyler initially assumed that she would need to adapt her plays for an American audience and depicted the Congolese city of Elizabethville as "Evil Eville," a frontier "much like the [American] Wild West." She constructed White male heroes who believed that indigenous Blacks interpreted "the white man's Christian principles, and accordance of excessive liberty to his women" as weakness rather than strength.[26] This meant that she defined Jack, the rugged hero from a working-class background in northern Europe, against middle-class Nordics (who were thought to be excessively prudish and effeminate) and indigenous Blacks (who were depicted as "animals," "primitive savages," and "rapists"). In later drafts of the manuscript, Schuyler described her female characters as "rejoicing" when Jack ordered them out of a car to engage in sadomasochistic sexual encounters that left them bloodied and bruised, much like Commander Bond's sexual conquests were said to enjoy his "sweet brutality" and "semi-rape."[27] If the Blackness of indigenous Africans meant that they were criminalized as rapists, the Whiteness of Jack and Bond granted them a license to inflict bodily harm without punishment. They could even be claimed as potentially progressive figures who offered readers an alternative to mainstream novels and films in which sex outside of marriage was deemed shameful.[28]

With that said, Schuyler could not entirely ignore the shaming practices of male friends such as the sensitive British intellectual who was shocked that she would consider having sex in public and the married Dutchman who disapproved of her interest in sex outside of marriage. Her plays and novels set in Congo often revolve around a female protagonist named Suzanne expressing shame and guilt about extramarital sex, the possibility of having a child outside of wedlock, and her desire to carve out an independent existence as a creative artist.[29] As much as Suzanne might dream of a "glorious and golden" life as a female courtesan in Europe in early drafts of her adventures in Congo,[30] she ends up in later drafts of the manuscript longing to marry a South African mercenary who demands that she seeks happiness "by obedience, by lack of ambition, by abandoning one's plans, by bowing to another's will—the will of 'White Africa.'"[31] Such comments not only provide a contrast to her hopes of achieving success as an independent artist; they also complement Schuyler's own wish to obtain a suitable husband and an "Aryan child."

Looking for Mr. Right

In 1958 Philippa Schuyler penned an article for *Ebony* in which she talked about her life as a young artist who traveled the world but was unable to find her ideal man. Tired of overbearing men who were unwilling to accept her constant traveling as a concert pianist and wanted to keep her in a box as a "slave," Schuyler hoped to meet a man who would support her career. Modeling him on Albert Schweitzer, Schuyler longed for a partner who had a career as a "doctor, writer, poet, scientist, social worker, archaeologist or missionary, someone who brings good to society, not working merely for selfish gain for himself." To go further, her ideal match would be "temperate, charming, intellectual, sweet, affectionate, humanitarian, well-read, never cruel or unjust, never shrewd or conniving, never dissipated or brutal, with high moral standards of honesty, purity and unselfishness, never gambling or improvident, not neurotically insecure or super-critical, but he must be kind and sincerely religious, always looking to God as the true guide and arbiter of human affairs."[32]

Five years later, Schuyler wrote a letter to her mother in which she replaced her desire for a doctor and missionary (like Schweitzer) for a European aristocrat (like Bond):

> What counts is not . . . whether all people are free and prosperous everywhere. What counts is whether I can be successful . . . what do I care whether women are nuclear physicists or ambassadors in a country. I'm an artist! . . . AND I LIKE MEN TO PAY FOR THINGS . . . I don't WANT TO PAY FOR THINGS (I can't anyhow) . . . What I WANT is to spend my life in fine hotels, being courted by noblemen and the rich, being successful in my art, and having everything paid for by people other than myself.[33]

Last but not least, Schuyler drew up a checklist for her prospective husband in her notebook in 1964:

> I. He must be white
> II. He must be European
> III. He must be able to confer on me a nationality I like.[34]

Maurice Raymond, a "cosmopolitan" man from France, fulfilled Schuyler's romantic fantasy because she thought that he combined northern European "cultural superiority" with the "vital force" of "earthy" southern Europeans who were closer to Africa. Even when Schuyler worried about Raymond's intellectual abilities because he came from a working-class background in Lyon, she found solace in his "Aryan looks":

> He is the most Aryan man I have ever known—his mother came from near the German border—so perhaps she had some German ancestry. . . . Imagine—if we had a child it could be perfect—because

it could have . . . His green eyes . . . His Aryan appearance . . . My talent . . . NO NEGRITUDE.[35]

Schuyler's rejection of the "mulatto-minded" culture of her parents in interwar New York is expressed not only in her desire for an "Aryan child" but in her unwillingness to raise a child that might have "Negritude" or be classified as a "Negro child prodigy."[36] Following an affair with George Apedo-Amah—a Ghanaian who upheld the honor of European culture as a member of the French delegation to the United Nations and the European Economic Community—Schuyler could only admit that she loved Apedo-Amah's "personality." She could not tolerate his "nationality" (a euphemism for his "Blackness") and, after their relationship led to an unplanned pregnancy, Schuyler traveled around the world searching for a doctor who would perform a late-term abortion.[37] In a letter to her mother, Schuyler once again turned to a literary form of self-fashioning to explain her decision by evoking Nella Larsen's *Quicksand,* one of the most famous novels of the Harlem Renaissance. In the words of Schuyler:

> Why bring more Negroes into the world? They have their nice side but somehow Negritude just seems to go round and round in circles— and one can't deny that it's better for a child to start life in the white world. I wouldn't even mind having an illegitimate child if I could be sure it would be good looking. All civilizations are brutal—but some are also artistic . . . I will not marry a colored man or an African . . . [I will marry] a white man of European stock, but not a resident European . . . [who has] a virile male force vitale.[38]

In the words of Helga Crane, the mixed-race protagonist of Nella Larsen's 1928 novel, who finds herself always a little different and always a little dissatisfied on her travels around the United States and Denmark:

> Why add more suffering to the world? Why add more unwanted, tortured Negroes to America? Why do Negroes have children? Surely it must be sinful. Think of the awfulness of being responsible for the giving of life to creatures doomed to endure such wounds to the flesh, such wounds to the spirit, as Negroes have to endure?[39]

Schuyler and Fanon: An Unlikely Duet

Good Men Die, an account of Schuyler's time as a war correspondent in Vietnam, was published after her death in a helicopter mission to help Catholic nuns evacuate a number of Vietnamese children from a combat zone. In the book, Schuyler took aim at a specific form of American racism that "place[d] obstacles in place of a soldier marrying a Vietnamese girl," worried about "strong and sensitive . . . half-castes . . . [who] when unattached to or unassimilated by [a Western] society . . . can become violently vocal leaders." Once again, she idealized the French:

> The French tackled this problem with Gallic rationality; they did not avoid it with a narrow refusal to tackle the facts. They granted French citizenship to a half-caste child whose French father admitted paternity, even if the man did not marry the girl. This is more just and certainly more humane. Why should a child's life be ruined? Why should his only heritage be one of misery and shame?[40]

Such investment in the honor of European culture and a "light skin tone" is radically different from the diagnosis of European racism developed by Frantz Fanon, a French war hero, Maritiniquan exile, and Algerian freedom fighter. Whereas Schuyler longed to help the Vietnamese "bar-girls" and the children of their relationships with American men by asserting the honor of a Western identity, Fanon identified with the Indo-Chinese who went into battle against European colonizers whom they blamed for the explosion in "cut-rate boys and women."[41] Whereas Schuyler wrote stories that were based on James Bond novels and films, Fanon expressed his support for the woman in Algeria who could dress up as a Western woman without the "sensation of playing a role she has read about ever so many times in novels, or seen in motion pictures."[42] According to Fanon, it was not enough to assign guilt to manifestations of monstrous racism in Europe and North America; it was also necessary to face the shame of bourgeois barbarism in Africa and Asia that was masked by rhetoric about civilization and empire.

Fanon's insights are rarely cited in seminal texts about shame and guilt in the discipline of psychology. Consequently, many articles have drawn on Helen Block-Lewis's famous definition of shame and guilt (that shame is "directly about the *self,* which is the focus of evaluation" whereas the experience of guilt is "negatively evaluated in connection with something but is not itself the focus of experience"[43]) to assert that shame is a dangerous, painful, and ugly feeling that is "less rational" than guilt. Shame has been equated with blood ties, honor killings, and antiquated notions that threaten social bonds, and guilt has been privileged as a modern, legalistic concept that secures social bonds and solidarity.[44] The focus on turning out healthy modern individuals even means that social psychologists have defined pride as a reasonable emotion while considering shame to be an entirely unreasonable one.[45]

Outside of academia, popular memoirs dealing with shame and pride in America have also shown little engagement with the work of Fanon. Some have dismissed his work as a "dung heap of Freudian analysis" that fails to appreciate

American exceptionalism,[46] and others have followed Barack Obama and portrayed him as an outdated remnant of sixties protests who is of interest only to contemporary radicals on the fringes of college towns.[47] Even when they provide a corrective to studies of Southern honor that ignore the links between Southern pride, Whiteness, and the shaming of Black bodies,[48] sweeping histories of honor and shame in the Western world can omit Fanon's warnings about Western business and its taste for light-skinned "half-breed girls" and "cut-price boys."[49] For example, David Leverenz's recent study of race and shame in American history draws on Samuel P. Huntington's "Clash of Civilizations" and suggests that Barack Obama and other prominent African Americans are evidence of a paradigm shift (from pride in a "light skin color" and "White civilization" to a defense of Western civilization as multicultural and tolerant in contrast to the "rest of the world" and "radical Islam").[50] It does not note the radical spirit of Fanon and other activist intellectuals who have little time for liberal celebrations of nonracialism that guiltily parade the incorporation of some (light-skinned) Blacks into a privileged caste of American politics.

In contrast to the rather functionalist tendencies of psychologists, pundits, and politicians to distance their work from the radical egalitarianism of Fanon, postcolonial theorists have emphasized the continuing importance of Fanon in contemporary battles against imperial nostalgia.[51] Paul Gilroy, perhaps the most influential intellectual in contemporary Britain, has invoked a living Fanon who asks brutally honest questions about the shameful histories that continue to influence social inequalities.[52] In *Postcolonial Melancholia*, for example, Gilroy draws on Fanon to treat shame as a more productive emotion than guilt and critiques forms of corporate multiculturalism that celebrate "less menacing, celebrity half-castes" as part of their commitment to purportedly nonracial, multiracial, or postracial forms of business.[53] He also delivers a pointed critique of Huntington's thesis about the clash of civilizations (which proposes that clashes between "the West" and Islam and China will proliferate after the Cold War and does not know whether to treat Africa as a separate civilization or one that can be subsumed by the West).[54]

If postcolonial theorists consider Fanon a contemporary as part of a broader project to shame the contradictions and confusions of neoliberal universalism and neocolonial governance, we may also want to consider the affinities between Schuyler's rugged individualism in colonial contexts and forms of neoliberalism and neocolonialism in the early twenty-first century. For neither Fanon nor Schuyler seems anachronistic when James Bond enjoys the company of beautiful non-White colleagues in our post–Cold War context and conservatives express anxiety about the possibility of Idris Elba becoming the first "Black Bond." In our digital age, professionals may try to cover up the shame and guilt of race and empire by deleting a file rather than inserting a white piece of paper, but that does not mean that the past is dead. Nor that the shame is past.

Notes

1. Kathryn Talalay, *Composition in Black and White: The Life of Philippa Schuyler* (New York: Oxford University Press, 1995), 36, 208.

2. George Schuyler to Josephine Schuyler, October 20, 1935, Josephine Cogdell Schuyler Papers, Schomburg Center for Research in Black Culture. J. A. Rogers, *Sex and Race: A History of White, Negro, and Indian Miscegenation in the Two Americas* (New York: J. A. Rogers, 1942), 2:408–409.

3. Lincoln Barnett, "Negro Girl, 2 ½, Recites Omar and Spells 5-Syllable Words," *New York Herald Tribune*, February 8, 1934; Joseph Alsop, Jr., "Harlem's Youngest Philosopher Parades Talent on Third Birthday," *New York Herald Tribune*, August 3, 1934.

4. Philippa Schuyler, diary entry, April 15, 1960. Philippa Duke Schuyler Papers, Schomburg Center for Research in Black Culture (hereafter PDSP).

5. Philippa Schuyler, "Une Métisse a la Reserche de son ame," 1950, PDSP; Philippa Schuyler to J. Schuyler, September 22, 1954, and June 9, 1963, PDSP.

6. George Schuyler, *The Negro in America* [c. 1954], George Samuel Schuyler Papers, Schomburg Center for Research in Black Culture.

7. Talalay, *Composition in Black and White*, 294.

8. Jeffrey Ferguson, *The Sage of Sugar Hill* (New Haven: Yale University Press, 2005), 152.

9. Molefi Asante, "Book review: Against Race: Imagining Political Culture beyond the Color Line," *Journal of Black Studies* 31, no. 6 (2001): 847–851.

10. G. Reginald Daniel, *More Than Black: Multiracial Identity and the New Racial Order* Philadelphia: Temple University Press, 2001), 96.

11. Mary Helen Washington, ed., *Invented Lives: Narratives of Black Women, 1860–1960* (New York: Anchor Press, 1987), 160.

12. Anaïs Nin, *The Diary of Anaïs Nin*, vol. 2, *1934–1939* (New York: Harcourt, 1967), 6.e

13. Anaïs Nin, *The Diary of Anaïs Nin*, vol. 1, *1931–1934* (New York: Harcourt, 1966), 291.

14. Otto Rank, *Beyond Psychology* (New York: Dover, 1958), 256–258, 265, 284.

15. Daniel McNeil, *Sex and Race in the Black Atlantic: Mulatto Devils and Multiracial Messiahs* (New York: Routledge, 2009); McNeil, "Black Devils, White Saints and Mixed-Race Femme Fatales: Philippa Schuyler and the Winds of Change," *Critical Arts: A Journal of South-North Cultural Studies* 25, no. 3 (2011): 360–376.

16. Hugh Trevor-Roper, "The Rise of Christian Europe," *The Listener*, November 28, 1963, 871; Christopher Masterman, *Time and Tide*, May 20–26, 1965. Austin Ferraz to P. Wall, September 6, 1966, University of Hull, Brynmor Jones Library Archive, Papers of Sir Patrick Wall, File 48/490.

17. Anthony Synnott, "The Beauty Mystique: Ethics and Aesthetics in the Bond Genre," *International Journal of Politics, Culture, and Society* 3, no. 3 (1990): 407–426.

18. Philippa Schuyler, *Jungle Saints*, 1963, 166–168, PDSP.

19. Gilberto Freyre, *The Masters and the Slaves* (New York: Knopf, 1946).

20. Philippa Schuyler, *The Virgin and the Cross*, 1960, PDSP.

21. Philippa Schuyler, notebooks 1964 and 1965, PDSP; Philippa Schuyler to Josephine Schuyler, [n.d.] 1966, PDSP.

22. Philippa Schuyler, *The White Leopard of Katanga*, 1965, PDSP.

23. Philippa Schuyler, *Who Killed the Congo?* 1962, PDSP.

24. Philippa Schuyler to Josephine Schuyler, April 27, 1960, PDSP.

25. Philippa Schuyler to Josephine Schuyler, July 12, 1963, PDSP.

26. Philippa Schuyler, *Evil Eville*, 1962, ix, PDSP; *Who Killed the Congo*, 1962, i, PDSP.

27. Philippa Schuyler, *The Demons of the Jungle*, 1963, 62–63, PDSP; Paul Johnson, "Sex, Snobbery, and Sadism," *New Statesman*, April 5, 1958; Ian Fleming, *The Spy Who Loved Me* (London: Jonathan Cape, 1962), 15.

28. Philippa Schuyler to Josephine Schuyler, August 15, 1953. PDSP, SCRBC; Tony Bennett and Janet Woollacott, *Bond and Beyond* (New York: Metheun, 1987); Martin Halliwell, *American Culture in the 1950s* (Edinburgh: Edinburgh University Press, 2007).

29. Talalay, *Composition in Black and White*, 156, 247–248. Philippa Schuyler to Josephine Schuyler, April 27, 1960, October 29, 1964, and December 26, 1965, PDSP.

30. Schuyler, *Evil Eville*, 63.

31. Schuyler, *The White Leopard*, 182, 194.

32. Philippa Schuyler, "Why I don't marry: former piano prodigy meets many men on world concert tours, but none her ideal," *Ebony*, July 1958.

33. Philippa Schuyler to Josephine Schuyler, [n.d].1963, PDSP.

34. Philippa Schuyler, notebook 1964, PDSP.

35. Philippa Schuyler to Josephine Schuyler, June 9, 1963, PDSP.

36. Philippa Schuyler to Josephine Schuyler, February 21, 1966, PDSP.

37. Philippa Schuyler to Josephine Schuyler, December 26, 1965, PDSP.

38. Philippa Schuyler to Josephine Schuyler [n.d.] 1966, PDSP.

39. Nella Larsen, *Quicksand and Passing* (New Brunswick, NJ: Rutgers University Press, 1928), 103.

40. Philippa Schuyler, *Good Men Die*, 1967, 196–197, PDSP.

41. Ibid., 196; Frantz Fanon, *Black Skin, White Masks* (New York: Grove Press, 1967), 227.

42. Frantz Fanon, *A Dying Colonialism* (New York: Grove Press), 50.

43. Helen Block Lewis, *Shame and Guilt in Neurosis* (Madison, CT: International Universities Press, 1971), 30; Andrew P. Morrison, ed., *Shame: The Underside of Narcissism* (Hillside, NJ: Analytic Press, 1989), iii; Thomas J. Scheff and Suzanne M. Retzinger, "Helen Block Lewis on Shame: Appreciation and Critique" in *Shame: The Underside of Narcissism*, ed. Andrew P. Morrison (Hillsdale, NJ: Analytic Press, 1989); June Price Tangney and Ronda L. Dearing, *Shame and Guilt* (New York: Guilford Press, 2004).

44. June Price Tangney, "Shame and Guilt in Interpersonal Relationships," in *Self-Conscious Emotions: The Psychology of Shame, Guilt, Embarrassment, and Pride*, ed. June Price Tangney and Kurt W. Fischer (New York: Guilford Press, 1995), 119; Catherine Wheatley, *Michael Haneke's Cinema: The Ethic of the Image* (New York: Berghahn, 2009), 153–187; Jonathan Webber, Forum for European Philosophy panel discussion, London School of Economics, February 21, 2013.

45. Thomas J. Scheff, "Shame in Social Theory" in *The Widening Scope of Shame*, ed. Melvin R. Lansky and Andrew P. Morrison (Mahwah, NJ: Analytic Press, 1997).

46. Gloria Wayde-Gayles, *Rooted against the Wind* (Boston: Beacon Press, 1996), 109.

47. Barack Obama, *Dreams from My Father: A Story of Race and Inheritance* (New York: Random House, 2004), xv, 100.

48. Dov Cohen, Joseph Vandello, and Adrian Rantilla, "The Sacred and the Social: Cultures of Honor and Violence," in *Shame: Interpersonal Behavior, Psychopathology, and Culture*, ed. Paul Gilbert and Bernice Andrews (New York, Oxford University Press, 1998).

49. Fanon, *Black Skin, White Masks*, 169–178.

50. David Leverenz, *Honor Bound: Race and Shame in America* (New Brunswick, NJ: Rutgers University Press, 2012), 6–7.

51. Neil Lazarus, *The Postcolonial Unconscious* (Cambridge, U.K.: Cambridge University Press, 2011), 161.

52. Paul Gilroy, *Against Race: Imagining Political Culture beyond the Color Line* (Cambridge, MA: Harvard University Press, 2000), 78; *Darker than Blue: on the Moral Economies of Black Atlantic Culture* (Cambridge, MA: Harvard University Press, 2010), 155; Nigel Gibson, ed., *Living Fanon: Global Perspectives* (London: Palgrave Macmillan, 2011).

53. Paul Gilroy, *Postcolonial Melancholia* (New York: Columbia University Press, 2005), 99. 128.

54. Ibid., 22.

THREE

Neoliberal Crimmigration: The "Commonsense" Shaming of the Undocumented

Leah Perry

The single "Illegal Alien," from the 1983 eponymously titled album by British rock band Genesis,[1] was ostensibly a light satire about the struggles of undocumented immigrants to the United States, as suggested by its chorus, "It's no fun / Being an illegal alien." The song has, however, been criticized and is rarely played on the radio because it—and the video—explicitly capitalize on nearly every extant racist, sexist stereotype of Mexican criminality.[2] The lyrics, sung by White vocalist Phil Collins in a Mexican accent, describe stereotypically Mexican laziness, drinking (tequila, of course), smoking, relying on illegal economies for documentation, and sordid women. Set in a barrio on the Mexican side of the border, the video visualizes those stereotypes for spectators. Collins and his White bandmates, physically coded as Mexican by their black wigs, large moustaches, and oversized sombreros and serapes, are shown drinking, oversleeping, playing Mariachi music, fighting in line at the passport office, and committing crimes such as passport fraud. The singer is quick to assure listeners that he has "done nothing wrong"—he is no criminal despite mounting contrary evidence and his own assertions that he is willing to commit illegal acts to get over the border.

Like salutary Reagan-era representations of immigration—even one performed by a British band—the song/video nods to the "nation of immigrants" mythos, the notion that the United States is an exceptionally diverse nation that welcomes and provides opportunities for all people from all over the world to make a better life. The Reaganite version of this national narrative responded to (and appropriated) civil rights discourses, multiculturalism, and feminism and was often pointed to by lawmakers and Reagan himself as evidence of America's economic and social ascension under his leadership, as well as its superiority over the Soviet Union and Communism. What the Reagan era "nation of immigrants" trope actually did was reduce civil rights critiques of structural racism and sexism and struggles for material equality to matters of mere representation, individual rights, and individuals' (i.e., tokens') success as evidence of parity. Consequently, "multicultural" people who did not experience America's promises were cast as responsible for their marginalization, and the ways that racism and sexism were endemic to capitalist progression were rendered invisible. As I argue, the negotiation of the "nation of immigrants mythos" with "crimmigration"—the racialized and gendered shaming and stigmatizing of immigrants as criminals that justifies inequality, oppression, and violence in an allegedly ever more inclusive and multicultural nation—is encapsulated in "Illegal Alien." This still prevalent discourse of immigrant criminality that took shape in the 1980s is a key but understudied facet of neoliberalism. Beginning with a closer analysis of the Genesis song and video as emblematic of neoliberal crimmigration, this essay traces the history of that discourse of shame and stigma and what it did and continues to do for neoliberalism.

In "Illegal Alien," the evocation of the "nation of immigrants" trope is flagrantly colored by the racist stigmatization of Mexicans at a moment when Mexicans were the largest group of legal and undocumented immigrants and when Congress was in the midst of a heated five-year debate over immigration that culminated with the passing of the Immigration Reform and Control Act of 1986 (IRCA). The final full stanza of the song appeals directly to the "nation of immigrants" ideology, although this plea for compassion for a striving immigrant is delegitimized because Collins's illegal alien reverts to his criminal tendencies:

> Consideration for your fellow man
> Would not hurt anybody, it sure fits in with my plan
> Over the border, there lies the promised land
> Where everything comes easy, you just hold out your hand
> Keep your suspicions, I've seen that look before
> But I ain't done nothing wrong now, is that such a surprise
> But I've got a sister who'd be willing to oblige
> She will do anything now to help me get to the outside

The alien makes himself undeserving of the human consideration he requests because he is a calculating criminal (he has a plan to get into the country illegally and is willing to prostitute his sister to do it) and he is lazy (things come easy when one holds out one's hand, suggesting that he wants others to support him). The alien has not broken the law yet, but he will and wants to, as suggested in the video from start to finish. There is the promise of crime if this immigrant makes it into the promised land; his assumption that America will take care of him is a proxy for nativist fears that the undocumented come to the country solely to exploit the welfare system, thus becoming burdens on the states and the nation forced to support them. The couplet about exchanging sexual favors from his sister for passage over the border proved so controversial that it was edited out of the song.[3] According to every standard of Reaganite respectability, the Genesis Mexican is deplorable, an embodiment of the problem with Mexican "illegal aliens," big government, taxes, welfare, and anything other than traditional "family values"; he is obviously the wrong kind of immigrant for the "nation of immigrants."

"Illegal Alien" is not an enlightened attempt to expose the struggles of the undocumented to a popular audience; rather, Genesis capitalized (pun intended) on stereotypes of Mexicans and thus perpetuated the problem of racism and exploitation that underscores undocumented immigration. The song baldly dramatizes what Lisa Cacho calls a "de facto status crime," meaning that the status of being of color and connected to a certain space makes one always already a criminal regardless of whether or not a criminal act has been committed. She further notes that under neoliberalism race and racialized spaces make certain actions legible as crimes, and therefore the interpretation and application of criminal law cannot be race-neutral. A person's status is itself the offense and therein is the assumption of future illegal activity.[4] Mexicans occupy a de facto "illegal" status, as "Illegal Alien" indicates—as does the very term "alien," which invokes the nonhuman status of aliens from outer space.[5]

The song and video emblematize the trap that neoliberalism creates with the criminalization of immigrants, a trap that, I argue, was first set in the 1980s and has continued to increase in size, scope, and severity. The stakes were and are far higher than offensive stereotypes. In her important research, Cacho interrogates how human value is contested/condoned via notions of morality that have legal consequences or parallels—that is, given the ubiquitous assumption that the law is ethical, breaking a law casts one as unethical. Law abiding is the prerequisite for rights, recognition, and resources. Consequently, if one is cast as a shameful criminal it becomes impossible for one to be a moral person. This is a racialized, gendered, sexualized, and spacialized process: race, gender, sex, and space become the seemingly inherent explanations for state-sanctioned violence that seems rational.

The criminal, the terrorist, and the illegal alien are treated as the reason for and outcome of lawbreaking, although they are the effect of law. For instance, the "'illegal' or unlawful alien is a status that forms the foundation of immigration law, and, therefore, the unlawful alien cannot be incorporated into immigration or naturalization law."[6] Only exceptions can be made, such as the amnesty that was first offered under IRCA. This overhaul of immigration—designed to appease tensions between free-market economists, such as Reagan himself, who wanted an inexpensive immigrant labor pool, nativists who wanted to restrict immigration, and liberals and immigration and ethnic activists who wanted immigrant rights—provided a path to incorporation for the undocumented who met specific criteria while leaving intact the rightless and criminal status of those who did not. It also restricted welfare for immigrants, amplified border militarization, and established procedures requiring employers to verify the legal status of employees. The rightless statuses created by the law linked race to stigmatized categories such as "criminal" or "alien," and affixed meanings justified why a person or group became the target of state violence, disenfranchisement, and abandonment.

In *The Rule of Racialization: Class, Identity, Governance,* Steve Martinot asserts that, in the post–Civil Rights era "generalization, racialization, and criminalization are interwoven and inseparable in an endless reconstruction of whiteness and white supremacy in which police procedure is today playing a major role." These processes shape class divisions.[7] In the 1980s and 1990s, Latin American immigrants and particularly Mexicans were portrayed and persecuted as the quintessential illegal aliens and immigrant criminals along gendered lines. The three core dimensions of neoliberalism are modes of government rooted in entrepreneurial values; deregulation, liberalization of trade, and privatization of state services; and widespread acceptance of the theory that consumerist free trade will bring unprecedented prosperity to both the "developed" and the "developing" world.[8] Aspects of the neoconservative impetus to police and regiment citizens' personal lives and to use government funds in the name of security coexist and have been incorporated into neoliberal advancement because, as Martinot suggests, in the post–Civil Rights context criminalization creates and rationalizes ongoing racial stratification when overt racism is no longer legally or socially acceptable and stratification is profitable.

This chapter interrogates 1980s discourses of immigrant criminality, arguing that they are key to U.S. neoliberal projects. Neoliberalism is crucial to immigration history because it reshaped the causes and effects of immigration—how and why people migrated and how they were received. Likewise, in keeping with American historical patterns of using immigrants as inexpensive labor (especially after the abolition of slavery and decolonization), immigrant labor is a vital component of neoliberal projects. Gender and racial hierarchies that cohered and were contested through 1980s immigration discourses inaugurated the paradigm for neoliberal immigration. Legal scholar Teresa Miller argues that immigration law in the 1980s became increasingly punitive, functioning as crime control: "immigration control is increasingly adopting the practices and priorities of the criminal justice system,"[9] in a process that scholars refer to as "crimmigration."[10] I show that, as the Mexican border was made more porous for goods and labor, the Reagan administration increased government spending on policing it. This guaranteed the existence of the always already Mexican and, by way of racialization, Latino criminal and the justification of ever more punitive law and procedures. This was echoed in the culture at large with racialized and gendered representations of crime that suggested that certain immigrant bodies were inevitably criminal. This essay focuses on how paradigms of gendered and racialized stigmatization and shaming delineated in the 1980s made the immigrant criminal legible for neoliberalism.

The Invention of the Illegal Alien

Although the term "illegal alien" was not used until the 1970s and has since then been coded as Mexican, the category has historically been affiliated with a variety of racialized groups in accordance with labor needs and domestic and foreign policy.[11] However, casting Mexicans as threats to law and order has been profitable since the nation's formation, as in the aftermath of the U.S.-Mexican War. Under the terms of the Treaty of Guadalupe Hidalgo, the United States annexed Mexican territory in parts of what are now the states of California and Texas and granted Mexicans citizenship (although they did not appear White, when only Whites could be granted citizenship under the 1790 "free white persons" law, which points to the legal creation of racial as well as criminal status). At the same time, the Gold Rush brought waves of White settlers seeking their fortunes into the Southwest. To protect their interests, these settlers uprooted Mexicans[12] and in support the federal government exercised force.[13] For instance, Mexicans were subjected to violence from institutional police forces such as the Texas Rangers, then the Border Patrol, and removal during the Depression-era repatriation of over 400,000 Mexicans irrespective of citizenship status. Authorities claimed that it was cheaper to deport Mexicans than to support them, a common claim and practice: historically, immigrants are targeted in times of economic downturn and often blamed for "stealing" jobs from native citizens.[14] These efforts kept Mexicans marginal until immigration laws restricting their entry were passed.

Yet Mexican labor was desirable to U.S. employers in particular contexts. The Bracero contract labor program for Mexican men, which began in 1942 as a solution to wartime labor shortages, was the prototype for neoliberal Mexican labor importation. It was terminated in 1964 in response to pressure from organized labor and the prevalence of civil rights discourse: contract labor came to be commonly perceived as a form of what Mae Ngai calls "imported colonialism"; that is, laborers of color were brought into the United States, denied the protections and privileges of citizenship, and thus were much like colonial subjects displaced by a colonizing nation's domination of the resources, labor, and market of a colonized territory. The political and cultural economies of the U.S. West and Southwest practiced imported colonialism by creating a migratory agricultural proletariat of Mexicans who were outside of the polity.[15] Ideologically, colonialism was based on ethnocentric patriarchal beliefs that the colonizers were superior to the colonized. This logic characterized the Bracero program, but the stigma of criminality rather than flagrant legal racism resolved the contradictions. Because the Bracero program imposed controls on employers, they often resorted to illegal means to secure the cheapest labor. Thus the program produced the "wetback" or un-documented worker who was not only associated with crime but, by definition, criminal and thus deserving of poor treatment, marginalization, and violence.

It is significant that a hidden gender contract that criminalized women's sexuality sustained the Bracero labor system. Women in Mexico had to uphold domestic responsibilities and do the work that was not done by migrating male family members. Women were also present at recruitment centers and labor camps as vendors, domestic workers, and sex workers. The stereotype of the "wetback" included "destitute females from Mexico [who] cross[ed] the line for purposes of prostitution."[16] The stereotype of the female "wetback" prostitute also erased the wives and female partners of undocumented laborers who often worked as domestics,[17] reifying Mexican women as shamefully and, of course, illegally sexual.

Importing Colonialism/Importing Criminals: The 1980s

In the 1980s, with IRCA amnesty, a new program for temporary labor importation was established and framed as an exceptional measure (and one that, with the new pathway to citizenship for some, was purportedly empowering), and this helped to engender the paradigm of neoliberal crimmigration. The desire for immigrant workers with limited rights was a straightforward demand for an inexpensive transnational labor force as capital was globalizing, although it could be and was dressed up as a democratizing, multicultural endeavor, an example of Reaganite "nation of immigrants" exceptional inclusivity.[18] A more thoroughly institutionalized criminalization of immigrants accompanied this iteration of imported colonialism, making it characteristically neoliberal. According to Paul Smith and Lisa Frank, "by definition and design, crises are opportunities to rework ideological and cultural alignments; crises command public attention (public attention is commanded) precisely because they are the events by and which relevant publics will (or will not) be reconstituted."[19] With an economic depression and widespread unemployment in the 1970s, when the term "illegal alien" became commonplace, Mexicans were blamed for the crisis. The new label made them de facto criminals even though it was policy such as the cessation of the Bracero program, new international trade laws, and new Western Hemisphere immigration quotas passed in 1965 that created increased illegal migration.

The blending of the neoconservative penchant for protecting U.S. political and economic interests with border security and the unilateral use of military power with the neoliberal hallmarks of unfettered international free trade and transnational labor began in the Reagan administration. IRCA worked with the specter of an "immigration emergency" that lingered in the wake of the 1980 Mariel boatlift. When Fidel Castro allowed Cubans to immigrate to the United States, including prisoners and inmates of mental institutions, President Jimmy

Carter unknowingly welcomed them as refugees from Communism, causing a crime panic—a "crisis"—when that fact was discovered and numbers exceeded expectations. The proposed Immigration Emergency Act (versions of which were proposed in 1982 and 1983) was designed to address that crisis and the attribution of Cuban criminality that it engendered, providing an early and strong case for a "commonsense" blending of immigration law and criminal law. IRCA carried on with the failed act's mission, combining the retention and recruitment of inexpensive Mexican labor with increased border security and punitive immigration regulation. The new provisions, which made immigrant laborers more vulnerable to exploitation and abuse, required gendered and racialized ways of knowing that served the new transnational and migratory nature of capital. Pragmatically, punitive measures against immigration-related offenses were included in IRCA because amnesty was largely unpopular with the conservative Reagan administration, despite its approval by many free-market economists. Employer sanctions and beefed-up border security spoke not only to the complaints of organized labor but to nativist fears that undocumented immigrants were stealing jobs from Americans and, significantly, to Reagan's conservative supporters who wanted to "get tough" on crime.

The expansion of the prison system—the logical correlation to "getting tough" on crime—paralleled and overlapped increasingly harsh immigration law. Media panic over another racialized and gendered crisis, gang violence, was also circulating, and the nation undertook the "War on Drugs." Nancy Reagan began the memorable "Just Say No" campaign, which urged Americans to simply abstain from drugs, and the Reagans together declared that the nation was facing a drug epidemic and offered stricter criminal penalties and increased incarceration as the solution. In fact, Reagan historian Michael Shaller postulates that the War on Drugs replaced the Cold War or, more narrowly, that "narcoterrorism" replaced the Red Army as public enemy number one.[20] Reagan approved a 1986 National Security Council directive framing drug trafficking as a threat to the entire Western Hemisphere, and he fingered communist governments in Cuba and Nicaragua as the cause of the U.S. surge in cocaine trafficking and use, providing apprehension and punishment of citizens involved in drug-related crimes as the domestic complement. These factors rationalized increased government spending on policing and military intervention south of the border. Under the direction of William French Smith, the Justice Department brought the FBI into the War on Drugs, and Reagan bolstered the Drug Enforcement Agency (DEA) by adding five hundred agents, setting up thirteen regional antidrug task forces, and increasing the number of drug seizures and convictions.[21]

Domestically, crack cocaine was the centerpiece of the War on Drugs. It was also a clear point at which cohered the Reaganite backlash against and appropriation of feminism and multiculturalism—the former often articulated as efforts to protect allegedly racially neutral traditional "family values" (that is, heteropatriarchal, self-sufficient net contributors). As Black feminist sociologist Patricia Hill Collins observes, crack cocaine was mostly sold and used in Black inner-city neighborhoods and approximately half of the users were women. News stories about crack babies began to proliferate in the 1980s; crack mothers along with single Black mothers and "welfare queens" provided the latest ammunition to shame and stigmatize, and thus pathologize, Black families and especially Black women. In thirty states from 1985 to 1995, about two hundred women, most of whom were Black, were charged with maternal drug use.[22] Development of the prison-industrial complex was also synonymous with the increased incarceration of Black men, and increased gendered and sexualized violence was part and parcel of this process,[23] which manifested in popular culture and the news media with ever increasing representations of Black male violence, as with the prevalence of the stereotypical Black gangster in rap music and hip hop. "Getting tough" on crime therefore became a racialized, gendered endeavor and one with lasting and far-reaching implications. When Reagan left office, annual spending by federal, state, and local authorities to fight the War on Drugs was at $15 billion.[24]

Drugs were a point at which the immigration crisis and the crime/gang violence crisis overlapped, particularly in relation to drug smuggling at the Mexican border and drug sales and use in inner-city communities inhabited by immigrants of color, Latinos, and African Americans; populations of color were blamed for crime and held up as the reason for punitive laws, without discussion of how or why these laws and other policies might have created the crisis in the first place. Additionally, in 1983 Reagan established the President's Commission on Organized Crime, holding hearings in 1984 on Chinese, Japanese, and Vietnamese gangs, which were pegged as emerging organized-crime groups. A 1986 hearing held just months before IRCA was signed focused on Asian gangs, and Congress began to think of immigration law as a complement to criminal law because the former could fight crime by making it more difficult for criminals to become citizens.[25]

But it was Latin American immigrants who were the objects of IRCA's punitive provisions, and as Genesis's "Illegal Alien" shows all too well, Mexicans were the quintessential illegal aliens that lawmakers and most mainstream culture makers had in mind. In 1986, the Immigration and Naturalization Service (INS), the federal agency that managed immigration and naturalization policy until 2003—when, in response to 9/11, its duties were divided among other governmental departments and agencies under the umbrella of the new Department of Homeland Security (DHS)—publicized information about a dramatic increase in Mexican undocumented entries that was associated with Mexico's declining economy and blamed for an amplification of crime, drugs, and terrorism in the United States.[26]

Often spurious evidence of Mexican culpability was not hard to come by: in 1986 the *New York Times* and the *Wall Street Journal* both reported that the Los Angeles County Board of Supervisors had asked Reagan to send more troops to the border because of drug-related crime that was traceable to undocumented immigrants.[27] News magazines, too, were filled with alarmist stories, such as two 1986 *Time* articles, "The Enemy Within" and "Battle Strategies," which blamed crime on undocumented immigrants and framed the problem as a battle between good (American) and evil (Mexican) forces.[28]

While detailed analysis is beyond the scope of this essay, it can be said that in popular films, Latinos have been stereotyped as the help (waiter, maid, bellhop, valet) or as criminals.[29] The border has long been depicted as an abject space,[30] and beginning in the 1980s this characterization has usually been connected to Latino gangs, drugs, and smuggling over the border.[31] Representations of Latina promiscuity, prostitution, gang involvement, welfare abuse, and inadequate and ineffectual parenting have been as prevalent in films and TV shows. Although such representations have sometimes been complex, they have helped to criminalize the undocumented as a racialized and gendered collective, providing more "evidence" of de facto Latino criminality and shamefulness according to Reaganite standards of respectability.

IRCA gave legal form to fears of Latino immigrant criminality with employer sanctions and increased border militarization. Employer sanctions were highly controversial and met opposition from likely contingents such as Latino lobbying groups and liberals, along with big businesses that profited from undocumented labor. Neoliberalism prompted unusual alliances. Sanctions were supported by nativists and less extreme pundits who wanted to combat undocumented immigration, but they were also framed as democratic and equalizing. Generally proponents argued that penalizing employers who hired undocumented immigrants would curtail undocumented immigration because most immigrants came to the country to work. As early as 1981, in the final report of the Select Commission on Immigration and Refugee Policy (SCIRP), which had been formed during the Carter administration to evaluate the immigration crisis and make policy recommendations, Senator Alan Simpson (R-WY), a consistent sponsor of IRCA throughout the five-year debate and its most ardent champion, outlined the need for employer sanctions and other more punitive provisions despite the prevalence of Reagan-era "nation of immigrants" rhetoric. The assertion that America, especially Reagan's America, was an exceptionally inclusive land of opportunity, a sentiment first immortalized with Emma Lazarus's poem on the base of the Statue of Liberty,[32] was bombastically proclaimed in the ostentatious and expensive patriotic spectacle commemorating Lady Liberty's 1986 centennial.[33] Regardless, according to Simpson:

We are just going to be culling [*sic*] the United States of America for suggestions. It is just like the issue of the three-legged stool which is employer sanctions, increased enforcement and some kind of identification system. If we get one without the other two or if we get two without the other one, we have nothing. Yet we will pretend we will and then we will be right back where we were before. It is a tough, tough issue and we realize it, but we are ready to plow ahead and all the political ramifications of it that are so very, very real, and we will be searching throughout this country. . . . I always say to people as they say you can't do that, I say OK, give me what we can do but no fair quoting what it says on the Statue of Liberty. Then they get mad because it is easy to fly into it from that Launchpad [*sic*].[34]

Dismissing concern for the values of inclusive welcome that Lady Liberty symbolized, Simpson and other proponents of IRCA stressed that employer sanctions would end an unfair loophole, the Texas Proviso, which made it legal for an employer to hire an undocumented immigrant even though it was illegal for an undocumented immigrant to take a job. Simpson asserted that the Texas Proviso was a "tacit invitation for unauthorized foreign workers to enter the U.S. in order to find jobs" because it made it legal for employers to hire them.[35] In contrast, free-market supporters and big businesses picked up the "land of opportunity" piece of the "nation of immigrants" trope, forgetting about its immigrant beneficiaries; they countered that the burden of immigration enforcement—the mandate for employers to verify the status of all employees or face sanctions—should not fall on business owners.[36]

But the strongest opposition to sanctions, which surfaced in multiple hearings—and persisted throughout the IRCA debates—came from numerous pundits who argued that employer sanctions would deter employers from hiring persons who looked or sounded foreign, meaning persons of color and persons with accents. The inclusive "nation of immigrants" imperative was not disregarded by everyone, although its Reaganite spin was hard to shake. In a 1982 House hearing before the Subcommittee on Census and Population of the Committee on Post Office and Civil Services, one Democratic lawmaker after another, academics, and Latino activists argued that employer sanctions were racist towards Latinos and people of Caribbean descent, and repeatedly voiced vehement opposition to the proposed identification component of employer sanctions (in this iteration, the bill required that workers—perhaps eventually all Americans—prove legality with documentation). The basic disputation was that Latinos and people of color—both immigrants and citizens—would be excluded from hiring and disproportionately required to prove legality as a result of racist assumptions about their foreignness on the basis of skin color, surname, accent, and so forth.

Senator Alan Cranston (D-CA), the first to testify in the session, conveyed these two points of contention. He favored legalization and strongly opposed the provision requiring individuals working in the United States to have documentation. In his view, this provision was a major step toward a police state, and, hailing from California, where substantial numbers of undocumented immigrants lived and worked, he also argued that rounding up and deporting unauthorized aliens would disrupt communities, families, businesses, the border, and the economies of Mexico and Central America.[37] He noted a continuity between the World War II internment of Japanese Americans and the Nazi's treatment of Jews in Europe; for him, not only were domestic passports a tool of totalitarian regimes but denying legalization and identification requirements were the kind of initial steps that had led to the Holocaust.

Cranston's fellow Californian congressman, Representative Edward Roybal (D-CA) expressed similar concerns, and as co-founder of the National Association of Latino Elected and Appointed Officials (NALEO) and a lifelong advocate for Latino interests, he, too, was vehemently opposed to the law. In fact, in 1986, as chair of the Hispanic Caucus, which he helped found in 1976, he led an unsuccessful opposition to IRCA. While proponents of the punitive provisions in IRCA framed the sanctions as a way to make the law a "jobs bill" by providing more access to work for citizens and authorized workers, Roybal said:

> An employer will not interview anyone under this bill, if he just appears to be a little Hispanic; only blue-eyed blondes will be interviewed. But that individual would have the prerogative of simply not interviewing anyone and, by so doing, discriminating against any individual who may have a Spanish surname or look Hispanic from getting a job in the United States. That is one of the fears we have in the Hispanic communities of this nation.[38]

Along the same lines, Roybal opposed identification cards because he felt that only individuals with Spanish surnames or those who looked Hispanic would be asked for them. Like Cranston, Roybal likened this to the treatment of Jews in Nazi Germany.[39] Simpson also made this connection, although in a different light. In a 1981 interview, just before the IRCA hearings began, he said, "Every time someone talks about the issue [verification beyond signature certification] they flee to the Statue of Liberty. I want to hear alternatives. We'll consider everything but tattoos."[40] This reference to tattoos for identification evoked Nazi concentration camps. Although Simpson later declared that he was misquoted, no retraction or correction was ever made.[41]

Despite the flagrant connections between racialized genocide and employer/employee verification, concern for human rights was not the only impetus behind opposition. American individualism, private property, and free-market values were at play as well, as Cranston argued in his prepared statement that the domestic passport was antithetical to democracy because it "infringes upon our respect for individual liberty in the United States best expressed in the Revolutionary War slogan 'Don't Tread On Me' and New Hampshire's State motto 'Live Free or Die.'"[42] He supported his argument with "nation of immigrants" rhetoric that complemented neoliberalism. The undocumented, he said, contributed to the economy and had thus "earned our acceptance."[43] Hard work—not human rights—made immigrants worthy of American acceptance and individual freedom. Roybal, too, put forth a rather neoliberal argument that immigrants were valuable and had earned rights: framing the United States as the unique nation that offered opportunity to all, he stated that immigrants were the "cream of the crop" because they were hard workers and, "practically starving in their country of origin, they come here to the land of opportunity."[44]

Hard work was the rationale for immigrant rights, and Roybal asserted that the "land of opportunity" was a more desirable, civilized, and humane locale than the sending nations. Both lines of discourse were quintessentially Reaganite and neoliberal in that the justification for immigrants' rights was their contribution to the economy and the notion that America was unique and superior because of the opportunity, equality, and safety it (should) offer to the worthy. Neoliberal rhetoric that frames value exclusively in economic terms makes it so that human beings are only worthwhile and deserving of rights if they work hard and contribute to the economy, don't sap social services or break the law, and—though not mentioned in this congressional session but prevalent elsewhere—adhere to respectable gender and family norms. Thus human rights and/or the inherently transnational lives that so many immigrants led *because of* U.S. foreign and economic policies that impoverished nations on one hand and criminalized immigrants on the other, were concealed by neoliberal discourse and policy even in discussions of antiracism.

IRCA did include an "Unfair Immigration-Related Employment Practices" provision that made it illegal for employers to discriminate against potential employees on the basis of race. In practice, however, sanctions continued to tip the scales of capital in favor of employers and provoked racist criminalization of immigrants and persons who looked or sounded foreign. Penalties for employers were reduced to those associated with civil offenses and a fine of $250 to $2,000 for each undocumented employee; only those who "knowingly" employed unauthorized immigrants were to be penalized.[45] (Criminal law rarely exculpates a perpetrator who "unknowingly" commits an offense, nor does it usually give a criminal the opportunity to prove or stage their unknowingness.) Employers were also decriminalized in implementation of the provision. First, INS aimed to complete 20,000 inspections in 1988, but completed only 12,000 that year and the following year. Second, undocumented immigrants who entered after the 1982 amnesty cut-off date could work under a grandfather clause in IRCA that exempted existing employers from penalization, although it continued to be illegal for all aliens to work.[46] Third, under Section 116 of Title I of the law, "Restricting warrantless entry in the case of outdoor agricultural operations," the INS could not enter an outdoor operation without the consent of the owner and a warrant,[47] giving employers time to conceal undocumented workers. Moreover, the first citation was issued in August 1987 and the first "notice of intent to fine" in October 1987; the first fine was imposed at year's end, at a Wendy's restaurant in Washington D.C. This was odd because the law was created to address undocumented labor in the Southwest, where most illegal employment occurred.[48] In short, employers could continue using undocumented immigrant labor with relative impunity while the undocumented were criminalized, and encouraged by the law to forge documentation for employment.[49]

Finally, statistics reveal that the sanctions intensified racism and made the undocumented especially vulnerable to exploitation by and abuse from employers.[50] Despite the antidiscrimination clause, a 1991 study found that sanctions led to "widespread discrimination against legal but foreign-sounding or foreign-looking workers."[51] Studies by the Mexican American Legal Defense and Education Fund (MALDEF) and the American Civil Liberties Union (ACLU) concurred. Both organizations advocated repeal of the employment verification requirement.[52]

Undocumented status allows businesses to bypass labor and antidiscrimination laws and health and safety regulations. Such violations are sanctioned by immigration law, which makes the undocumented too vulnerable to exercise the worker rights they might have under state labor laws. On the opposite side of the coin, businesses are empowered by immigration law. IRCA employer sanctions privileged employers in the law itself and in its implementation. This created and maintained a population of criminal Latinos, a population of color that was permanently without rights. In contrast, lawbreaking corporate behavior (employing undocumented workers) was a civic infraction unrecognizable as criminal.

IRCA border militarization amplified the gendered and racialized criminalization of immigrants. The Border Patrol and the inspection and enforcement activities of the INS and other federal agencies were enlarged, and to facilitate more efficient adjudication of petitions and applications for entry and legalization, the law expanded examinations and service activities of border agents. These new vaguely defined tasks included a budget of $422 million in 1987 and one of $419 million in 1988. Such large sums were meant to support a 50 percent increase in Border Patrol personnel over two years.[53]

As with the Bracero program, a hidden gender contract underscored these changes: gendering, always key to the criminalization of immigrants, is part and parcel of neoliberal crimmigration[54] and its formation via 1980s immigration discourse. The new criminalizing provisions and their rationales made undocumented female immigrants especially vulnerable to violence, which made them an especially exploitable labor pool. Yet neoliberalism's premium on personal responsibility, competition, and independence ascribe fault to certain groups of people rather than to a fundamentally exploitative capitalist system, and a focus on crime relegates concerns with racism and sexism to the background or trumps them altogether. For example, in the midst of the IRCA debate, *Newsweek* ran a June 25, 1984, cover story, "Closing the Door? The Angry Debate over Illegal Immigration: Crossing the Rio Grande," and *U.S. News and World Report* ran a March 7, 1983, cover story, "Invasion from Mexico: It Just Keeps Growing," each featuring photographs of Latinas being carried over bodies of water into the United States. As the article titles indicate, those crossings were illegal, hostile, and expanding. The magazines explicitly linked Latina fertility to undocumented immigration, providing an example of the gendered intricacies of what Leo Chavez calls the Latino Threat narrative. The *reconquista* narrative, first developed after the U.S.-Mexican War and resurfacing against the backdrop of demands for Latino immigrant labor and the broader incorporation of Third World women into international wage labor, alleges that Latinos are a hostile force intent on invasion of the United States. The focus on women suggests that "the invasion carrie[s] the seeds of future generations," which adds up to economic and social danger. Undocumented Latinas and their American-born children will allegedly beleaguer the welfare state, and women will produce "communities of Latinos who will remain linguistically and socially separate and soon be clamoring for reconquest of the United States."[55]

The reality was far more complicated. Like the Texas Rangers, the newly beefed-up Border Patrol used gendered brutality and rape as a practice of immigration control, supported in modern times by the shaming and stigmatizing of the undocumented through neoliberal crimmigration. The Rangers, established in 1873 to move the Apache and Comanche back into Mexico or onto reservations, targeted Mexicans as threats to the private property of Anglos. Composed of White men who frequently took the law into their own hands, the Rangers enforced the new border by lynching and slaughtering Mexicans and Chicanos.[56] They often used rape and excessive force against women to defend the newly established national border against Mexican "savagery";[57] the Mexican Secretariat of Foreign Relations, the INS, and the U.S. Public Health Service (USPHS) have on record a number of complaints about the mistreatment of women at the hands of the Rangers.[58] A 1998 Amnesty International study found that women detained by the INS were subjected to degrading vaginal searches by male Border Patrol officers and were frequently sexually abused and assaulted. The women were pressured to remain silent, and two women who did complain were accused of lying. In reports filed between 1992 and 1997, Human Rights Watch found sexual abuse to be "rampant" and although INS agents were occasionally prosecuted for rape of undocumented women, the crime was rarely reported.[59] How could or would a population rendered hyper-vulnerable by shaming and stigmatizing law and discourse have a voice?

Antiprostitution provisions in the Immigration Act of 1990 also linked immigrant Latinas' sexuality to deviance and crime, increasing their susceptibility to sexual violence as a mechanism of social and labor control. Along with proimmigration provisions such as an increase in the number of legal immigrants, relaxation of some of the language requirements for naturalization in place since 1906, and revocation of the ban on gay and lesbian immigrants, the law, meant to tie up loose ends left by IRCA, made anyone who had engaged in prostitution or "commercialized vice" excludable for ten years. In this case, antiprostitution provisions might rationalize the systemic disavowal of reports of violence and further discourage survivors from coming forward, allowing employers to use rape and sexual violence to discipline female workers. In short, by rendering Latinas shameful in the law and culture, their punishment seemed logical, and violence against them was unnameable.

Selling Porous Borders and Border Security

Throughout the 1990s, thanks to the neoliberal paradigms inaugurated by IRCA, militarization, criminalization, racialization, gendering, and labor exploitation increasingly complemented each other in international trade and immigration law. The 1994 North American Free Trade Agreement (NAFTA) and the 1996 Illegal Immigration Reform and Immigrant Responsibility Act (IIRIRA), two seemingly contradictory laws, developed IRCA's paradigmatic neoliberal blending of border security and tough immigration law enforcement with the liberalization of international trade and labor. Whereas NAFTA reduced or eliminated tariffs and opened Mexico to imports of U.S. products, including agricultural goods, IIRIRA dramatically increased penalties for immigration-related offenses and boosted militarization at the U.S.-Mexico border. As with IRCA, women were rendered especially susceptible to violence with this amplified blending of policing and free trade.

In his support of NAFTA, President Bill Clinton elaborated on precedents established by Reagan. Along with participating in General Agreement on Tariffs and Trade (GATT) negotiations to liberalize trade in the agricultural and service sectors and playing a key role in setting the agenda for the Uruguay Round (a set of multilateral trade agreements that addressed agriculture, service, and intellectual property rights), the Reagan administration negotiated the Free Trade Agreement (FTA) with Canada. Clinton further developed these policies, and NAFTA incorporated Mexico in the FTA. With the formation of the World Trade Organization (WTO), trade barriers were reduced and some industries were liberalized. Generally neoliberal policies governing an international economic system were solidified. These policies are also known as structural adjustment policies (SAPs) because they literally structurally adjust the laws and economies of nations. That is, to receive economic aid, the World Bank and International Monetary Fund (IMF) required nations, most in the global South, to align their laws and economies with neoliberalism through structural adjustments such as privatization, the removal of import restrictions, and the lowering of local currency values.

Taking a page from the Reagan playbook, the Clinton administration framed neoliberal measures as democratizing and prosperous for an increasingly interconnected and thus interdependent global community.[60] Yet neoliberal policies benefit the U.S. economy by opening the door for cheap immigrant labor for service industries and agriculture and by protecting the comparative advantage of the United States in intellectual property, while causing poverty and consequent legal and undocumented immigration in sending nations. With the requirement that Mexico cease protectionist agricultural policies that allowed subsistence farmers to keep their own land and permitted importation of U.S. goods, wages—and government spending on social services—were simultaneously cut. Within two years of NAFTA's implementation, more than 2 million jobs were lost in Mexico.[61] In turn, widespread poverty led to increased legal and undocumented migration. This was also good for the U.S. economy, creating new consumers and an ample labor pool—the reason for the policy in the first place—and gave rise to more criminalization and securitization of the border to assuage nativist objections to the increasing border flexibility that neoliberal policies had facilitated.

Following IRCA's passage, a steel fence was constructed along the Mexico-U.S. border, large-scale enforcement efforts such as Operation Blockade / Hold the Line (1993) in El Paso, Texas, and Operation Gate Keeper (1994) in San Diego, California, were undertaken, more sophisticated technology was implemented, and INS's budget and personnel were once again expanded, as with the increasing number of border agents, starting at 3,693 in 1986 and reaching 9,212 in 2000.[62] New "control" efforts generated increasing fear of apprehension and persecution on the part of border crossers that was not unfounded given the rise in the number of crossing-related deaths: in 1994, 23 migrants died attempting to cross; in 1995, after Operation Gatekeeper was instituted, there were 61 deaths, increasing to 89 in 1997 and 145 in 1998.[63]

The injustice underscoring such securitizing measures was not lost on inhabitants on both sides of the border in El Paso and Ciudad Juarez, who had planned a "We are all Fronterizos" celebration to climax with a "Day of Unity" celebrating neoliberalism's promise of unity and shared prosperity. This was destroyed by the erection of the "Berlin Wall" of the border.[64] But another injustice occurring was neither criticized nor acknowledged, although it strikingly exposed the gendered violence underscoring neoliberal crimmigration. Ciudad Juarez, the largest exporting zone on the border with approximately 350 manufacturing plants in the 1990s and about 180,000 workers, most of whom were paid the equivalent of $23 per week,[65] was the location of the murders of several hundred Mexican women that had begun in 1994. By 2008, 400 women had been murdered and an estimated 1,000 had disappeared.[66] Most were poor and dark-skinned, and had migrated to the borderlands from southern Mexico and Central America to work in *maquiladoras* (the assembly-line factories owned by U.S. companies located in Mexico that use cheap Mexican labor to produce duty-free and tax-free products). Impunity has surrounded the murder because the Mexican government has refused to acknowledge their systematic nature and has criminalized and blamed the victims. One criminologist asserted that the influence of the United States caused these women to join the workforce earlier than they otherwise might have, leading to promiscuity and other transgressive sexual behavior such as lesbianism and prostitution that made them more likely to be victimized.[67]

Neoliberal shifts called for the incorporation of Third World women into wage labor, and the neoliberal assertion that international wage labor leads to empowerment for women in "developing" nations rendered capital exploitation an impossibility. The United Nation's Woman's Decade (1976–1985) was framed as a feminist and multicultural initiative. At the very moment that immigrant women were being made increasingly vulnerable by criminalizing immigration laws in nations of the global North and SAPs in the global South, international campaigns were circulating the idea that international wage labor would empower women. Furthermore, the "sexism that devalued the domestic work of women" carried over into women's employment in manufacturing industries to make women especially desirable as employees. Sweatshop garment piecework is often seen as an extension of traditional "women's work" in the home, and women are wanted for assembly lines because they are perceived as easy to control, as in Mexico, where young women are recruited for factory work because of a popular perception that they are naïve and obedient and unlikely to join or form unions.[68]

The securitization of the U.S. side of the border in the midst of increasing border fluidity for capital and goods provided quite a contrast to the impunity surrounding the Ciudad Juarez crimes. The United States had secured the border while exploiting the labor of Mexican nationals in *maquiladoras* and the labor of Mexican migrants and immigrants at home. The Ciudad Juarez feminicide showed with frightening clarity that women workers were truly disposable. It also legitimated the ongoing hegemony of patriarchal culture because, despite grass-roots and nongovernmental organization (NGO) efforts to stop the violence, the shaming and stigmatizing of the victims allowed the government to avoid responsibility for the security of its female citizens or, in the case of the United States, the security of its female laborers.

While the Ciudad Juarez feminicide and the increase in border-crossing deaths that corresponded with increased militarization indicate that women workers and the undocumented had much to fear, and expose a slippage between neoliberal rhetoric and neoliberal material reality (i.e., that it is fundamentally exploitative, harmful, and potentially deadly to populations that are already vulnerable to violence and exploitation—women, people of color, the poor, the undocumented), U.S. law turned Mexicans and other "illegal aliens" into increasingly dangerous criminals who thereby had no recourse for protections and rights. Anthropologist Roger Lancaster suggests that the production of fear in relation to undocumented immigration rationalizes a spike in punitive laws because "where fear is the order of the day, protection is the name of the game."[69] This was certainly the case in 1996, when a new Republican Congress (following the "Gingrich Revolution" of 1994), passed three laws that directly affected immigrants: The Illegal Immigration Reform and Immigrant Responsibility Act (IIRIRA), the Personal Responsibility and Work Opportunity Reconciliation Act (PRWORA), and the Anti-Terrorist and Effective Death Penalty Act (AEDPA). Legal and undocumented immigrants were stripped of fundamental individual rights and benefits, such as Supplemental Security Income (SSI), food stamps, and due process, and many were subject to long-term detention and deportation as a result of past offenses.[70] In essence, IIRIRA made immigration law function more like criminal law and, like Operation Hold the Line, it balanced NAFTA border permeability with punitive action, cementing the gendered criminalization of Latin American immigrants.[71]

More specifically, IIRIRA flagrantly criminalized Latin American immigrants even though undocumented entry, a federal misdemeanor crime since 1924, was usually treated as a civil rather than a criminal offense.[72] IIRIRA increased militarization of the Mexican border again, featured new deportation measures for undocumented immigrants, placed income-based restrictions on family reunification, and mandated permanent and obligatory deportation for "aggravated felonies." In 1988, AEDPA, the Reagan-era prelude to this increased criminalization, created the category of "aggravated felony" for deportable crimes (i.e., those punishable with a sentence of five or more years, including murder and drug and firearm trafficking). IIRIRA expanded this list so that there was no meaningful distinction between murder, shoplifting, assault, and tax evasion. AEDPA added seventeen newly deportable crimes, with loosely defined "crimes of moral turpitude" becoming grounds for removal. IIRIRA was also retroactive, applying to convictions on or prior to its enactment, and it contained several seemingly contradictory provisions in terms of state power. On the one hand, 287(g) expanded the role of local law enforcement in immigration control and PRWORA's delegation of the authority of states to deny welfare benefits to legal immigrants. Other provisions rendered immigration lawyers impotent by making all immigration cases subject to this federal law and the new category of deportable offenses.[73] Yet all roads led to the same destination: the draconian restriction of immigrant rights and little to no recourse for challenge, given that immigrant crime was the rationale for such harsh changes. Revised in both 1998 and 2001 under allegations of unconstitutionality and cruelty, many provisions were repealed, undocumented entry was still treated as a civil rather than criminal offense in many cases, and the law did little to decrease immigration and illegal labor migration.[74] But IIRIRA along with these other laws nonetheless secured the systemic reproduction of a criminalized immigrant underclass.

Moreover, in the 1990s there was an increasing use of private actors and individuals to police immigrants (beginning with California's Proposition 187 and its imperative to report suspected undocumented immigrants, and continuing with laws and initiatives into the 2000s).[75] This complemented neoliberal downsizing of the state and was a rather literal example of the neoliberal ideology of personal responsibility. In fact, between 2004 and 2008 about 300 laws were passed in 43 states that required government workers and private citizens to verify the legal status of persons and report those without the proper documentation.[76]

According to Philip Kretsedemas, "The mission of immigration enforcement is defined as much by the imperative of labor market regulation as by the imperative of border control."[77] In the context of neoliberal governance, punitive immigration policies are not conventionally restrictionist because they do not cut back on immigration. Nor does immigration increase the crime rate, as shown by a 1997 National Research Council (NRC) review[78] and research that indicates that undocumented immigrants are actually more inclined to play by the rules to avoid detection.[79] This, then, is not the point, either. Rather, policies create a climate in which legal status widens the gaps between segments of the U.S. population and the unauthorized immigrant becomes "an affront to conventional notions of citizenship, which equate political, social, and civic rights with the criterion of legal residence."[80] Some are protected and nurtured while others are "subjected to disciplinary techniques designed to stimulate maximum productivity, but with much less concern for the individual."[81] This is the fundamentally gendered and racialized process of neoliberal crimmigration.

For instance, immigrant women of color were harmed in specific ways under IIRIRA. In 1998 Ana Flores, a permanent resident from Guatemala with two citizen children ages nine and eight, faced deportation because she defended herself against an abusive husband. Under the expanded definition of "aggravated felony," her act of self-defense was grounds for deportation.[82] Almost 75 percent of all H-1B visas are issued to men, and 75% of H-4 dependent visas are issued to women. H-4s are ineligible for social security numbers, cannot work legally, and cannot do much of anything—such as open a bank account or rent an apartment—without spousal consent/assistance. Therefore, female victims of abuse are essentially legally bound to abusers. Along with the IIRIRA crimmigration provisions, the neoliberal focus on ostensibly gender-neutral economic criteria not only "reinforced heteronormative gender identities and a gendered model of economic activity that portrayed men as economic agents and providers and women as caregivers,"[83] but also directly reinforced immigrant women's vulnerability to violence. And yet the Immigrant Marriage Fraud Amendment of 1986 (IMFA) indicated that the abuse of immigrant women was an issue that U.S. lawmakers were already well aware of.

IMFA, passed days after IRCA, authorized the INS to scrutinize immigrant marriages to citizens or legal permanent residents in order to identify and remove immigrants who attempted to obtain legal status through a bogus marriage. Under IMFA, a citizen or legal-permanent resident spouse must file on behalf of his or her immigrant spouse for conditional residence, and the marriage must remain intact for two years for the spouse to achieve independent legal status. If this sounds like a trap, it is because "the immigrant wife may be economically and psychologically dependent upon her spouse, limiting her alternatives to the relationship and placing her at increased risk for domestic violence." In fact, Congress amended IMFA in 1988 so that battered wives could petition on their own behalf.[84]

Although initiatives such as the United Nation's Women's Decade promised women empowerment through wage work and neoliberalism was touted as a universally beneficial system, increasing efforts to secure the border in the midst of border flexibility for goods and labor rendered immigrant women and especially Latin American immigrant women—both documented and undocumented—an extremely vulnerable and hence extremely cost-effective labor force. This was accomplished by linking Latin American immigrant women with sexual deviance and prostitution and by the erasure of women in securitizing and militarizing initiatives. In short, IRCA and subsequent legislation, along with media discourses, repackaged paradigms of Mexican and Latin American criminality to support rising neoliberalism and delineated a prototype for later laws, particularly in the aftermath of 9/11, that linked immigration and terror to justify increasingly draconian and extreme measures.[85]

The "War on Terror" initiated by the George W. Bush administration made immigration restriction and internal security seem more urgent than ever before. To protect the United States from terrorists, who were racialized as Muslim and

Arab, with the so-called PATRIOT Act of 2001, law enforcement agencies received more authority to search the records of citizens and immigrants and to detain and deport immigrants suspected of terrorism-related acts.[86] As always, implementation was racialized.[87] Terrorism rationalized a second war in Iraq and occupations in the Middle East, all of which drew on neoliberal utopianism to portray economic rights as human rights. Bush, eager to capture a pool of inexpensive Latin American immigrant laborers, also supported 2006 reform proposals, including amnesty, described as "strikingly similar" to IRCA.[88]

The Democrat Barack Obama has also advanced a neoliberal agenda. By-passing opposition in a Republican-dominated Congress and accusations that the Development, Relief, and Education for Alien Minors (DREAM) Act rewards illegality and crime,[89] in 2011 he used an executive order to enact some aspects of the DREAM Act to offer conditional permanent residency without a path to citizenship to qualified (i.e., valuable neoliberal subject) aliens (such as students and soldiers, all sans felony convictions). In 2012, the administration stopped deporting those who met DREAM's criteria. In a word, the qualified must be good neoliberal citizens—that is, working or attending school; although many have benefited from the act, under it adherence to neoliberal ideals is the measure of human value. Meanwhile the 2009 American Recovery and Reinvestment Act has provided over $400 million to bolster security at the U.S.-Mexican border and the 2013 DREAM has been criticized as an "enforcement-first" policy.[90] Obama's neoliberal agenda also includes support of the NAFTA model, Bush-era trade initiatives,[91] and Middle East interventions.

In April 2013, the Senate bipartisan "Gang of Eight" once more combined border security and economic opportunity in a neoliberal crimmigration proposal. Along with a path to citizenship and the privileging of high-skilled immigrants (scientists, engineers) and immigrants in "low-skilled areas" (laborers), the proposal bolsters security with a "biometric work authorization card" and a "biometric green card."[92] Like Simpson's 1980s desire to consider "everything but tattoos" to verify legal status, this biological tracking evokes Nazis and eugenics. Like IRCA and later laws, it does not directly name race; however, when most undocumented immigrants continue to be of Latin American origins and when any real or imagined connection to Islam or the Middle East can cast one as a terrorist, punitive measures simply seem necessary to protect citizens' safety.

Alicia Schmidt Camacho argues that "the criminalization of the migrant has occurred since the nineteenth century alongside the development of a capitalist economy that actively recruited laborers from Mexico and Latin America. State officials and labor contractors have long colluded to produce the ideal migrant, the temporary worker stripped of labor rights and the entitlements of citizenship."[93] Reagan-era discourses of immigrant criminality that shamed and stigmatized immigrants along racial and gendered lines seemed to explain why certain immigrants "deserved" punishment, exclusion, and violence, and thus helped to secure an inexpensive, pliable labor pool for the ostensibly exceptionally democratic, inclusive "nation of immigrants." With public ascriptions of gendered and racialized shamefulness, the paradigm for neoliberal crimmigration that was inaugurated in the 1980s seemed like "common sense." It continues to seem like "common sense" with fresh layers of fear and threat added after 9/11. This persists alongside ongoing demand for cheap immigrant labor and new generations of immigrant consumers. But what might be more accurately and justly considered shameful is that, in the "nation of immigrants," neoliberal crimmigration has proven profitable far beyond its "playful" incarnation in Genesis' "Illegal Alien."

Notes

1. The song peaked at no. 46 on the U.K. charts but did not chart in the United States, even though Genesis is to date one of the best-selling groups of all time. The band formed in 1967, and in 1970 Phil Collins replaced original vocalist Peter Gabriel. The band was at the height of its popularity in the 1980s and 1990s. The album that included "Illegal Alien" was in fact their third no. 1 album in the United Kingdom and reached no. 9 on the U.S. Billboard charts; several tracks continue in rotation on soft-rock and light radio stations. *Invisible Touch,* the 1986 follow-up to *Genesis,* resulted in five top five singles and one no. 1 single in the United States. Collins left the band in 1996 for a relatively successful solo career, and the band officially reunited in 2006. Genesis is among the top thirty highest-selling recording artists of all time, and was inducted into the Rock and Roll Hall of Fame in 2010. "Illegal Alien" itself was not wildly popular, but Genesis was and is (at time of writing if one searches "Genesis," the band, and not the opening book of the Christian Bible, is the first hit). Even "Illegal Alien" is well known enough to turn up on blogs, music magazine websites, and You Tube, and it was rated no. 13 in *Blender* magazine's list of worst songs of all time. See "Genesis," *Official Charts,* http://www .officialcharts.com/artist/_/genesis/; Marc Lee, "Final chapter in the book of Genesis?" *Telegraph,* June 2, 2008, http://www.telegraph.co.uk/culture/music/3673737/Final -chapter-in-the-book-of-Genesis.html.

2. Scott Thill, "Genesis' 'Illegal Alien': Worst Song Ever? Or Worst Video Ever?" *Wired. com,* May 30, 2008, http://www.wired.com/listening_post/2008/05/genesis-illegal/.

3. Steven Hyden, "It's No Fun Bein' A Really Good, Really Offensive Genesis Song," *A.V. Club Blog,* February 15, 2008, http://www.avclub.com/articles/its-no-fun-bein-a-really -good-really-offensive-gen,9841/.

4. Lisa Cacho, *Social Death: Racialized Rightlessness and the Criminalization of the Unprotected* (New York: New York University Press, 2012), 34–38.

5. Kevin Johnson, "'Aliens' and U.S. Immigration Laws: The Social and Legal Construction of Non-Persons," *Inter-American Law Review.* 28, no. 2 (1996): 1509–1579.

6. Cacho, *Social Death,* 5–6.

7. Steve Martinot, *The Rule of Racialization: Class, Identity, Governance* (Philadelphia: Temple University Press, 2003), 175.

8. See Manfred B. Steger and Ravi K. Roy, *Neoliberalism: A Very Short Introduction* (New York: Oxford University Press, 2010); David Harvey, *A Brief History of Neoliberalism* (New York: Oxford University Press, 2005); Aihawa Ong, *Neoliberalism as Exception: Mutations in Citizenship and Sovereignty* (Durham, NC: Duke University Press, 2006); Jafaar Aksikas and Sean Johnson Andrews, "Neoliberalism, Law and Culture: A Cultural Studies Intervention after 'The Juridical Turn,'" in "Cultural Studies and/of the Law," ed. Jaafar Aksikas and Sean Johnson Andrews, special issue, *Cultural Studies*. 28, no. 5–6 (2014): 742–780.

9. Teresa Miller, "Citizenship & Severity: Recent Immigration Reforms and the New Penology," *Georgetown Immigration Law Journal* 17 (2003): 611–666, 612.

10. Juliet Stumpf, "The Crimmigration Crisis: Immigrants, Crime, and Sovereign Power," *American University Law Review*. 56, no. 2 (2006): 367–419, 376; Allison S. Hartry, "Commentary Gendering Crimmigration: The Intersection of Gender, Immigration, and the Criminal Justice System," *Berkeley Journal of Gender, Law, and Justice* 27, no.1 (2012): 7–14.

11. Claudia Sadowski-Smith, "Unskilled Labor Migration and the Illegality Spiral: Chinese, European, and Mexican Indocumentados in the United States, 1882–2007," in "Nation Past and Future," ed. David G. Gutierrez and Pierrette Hondagneu-Sotelo, special issue, *American Quarterly* 60, no. 3 (Sept. 2008): 779–804; Mae M. Ngai, *Impossible Subjects: Illegal Aliens and the Making of Modern America* (Princeton: Princeton University Press, 2004), 202.

12. Marci R. McMahon, "Manifest Domesticity in the Era of Globalized Nation: Alma Lopez's *California Fashion Slaves*," paper presented at the Migration, Border, and Nation-State Conference, Texas Tech University, Lubbock, April 8–11, 2009.

13. Joseph A. Stout, *Border Conflict: Villistas, Carrancistas, and the Punitive Expedition, 1915–1920* (Fort Worth, TX: Texas Christian University Press, 1999).

14. Abraham Hoffman, *Unwanted Mexican Americans in the Great Depression: Repatriation Pressures, 1929–1939* (Tucson: University of Arizona Press, 1974), 86–87.

15. Ngai, *Impossible Subjects*, 13.

16. Ibid., 149.

17. Alicia Schmidt Camacho, *Migrant Imaginaries: Latino Cultural Politics in the U.S.-Mexico Borderlands* (New York: New York University Press, 2008), 82.

18. See Leah Perry, "Overlooking/Looking Over Neoliberal Immigration: Amnesty Policy in the 'Nation of Immigrants,'" in "Cultural Studies and/of the Law," ed. Jaafar Aksikas and Sean Johnson Andrews, special issue, *Cultural Studies*. 28, no. 5–6 (2014): 844–868.

19. Paul Smith and Lisa Frank, "Introduction: How to Use Your New Madonna," in *Madonnarama: Essays on Sex and Popular Culture*, ed. Paul Smith and Lisa Frank (Pittsburgh, PA: Cleis, 1993), 12.

20. Michael Shaller, *Reckoning with Reagan: America and Its President in the 1980s* (New York: Oxford University Press, 1992), 85.

21. Lou Cannon, *President Reagan: The Role of a Lifetime* (New York: Public Affairs, 1991), 730.

22. Patricia Hill Collins, *Black Sexual Politics: African Americans, Gender, and the New Racism* (New York: Routledge, 2005), 131.

23. Jerome G. Miller, *Search and Destroy: African-American Males in the Criminal Justice System* (New York: Cambridge University Press, 1996), 88; Elizabeth Shulte, "The Sick

Face of Racism in the U.S.: More Black Men in Jail than College," *Socialistworker.org*, September 6, 2002, http://socialistworker.org/2002-2/420/420_12_JailsVCollege.shtml. See also Michelle Alexander, *The New Jim Crow: Mass Incarceration in the Age of Colorblindness* (New York: The New Press, 2010).

24. Shaller, *Reckoning with Reagan*, 85.

25. Cacho, *Social Death*, 65, referencing Senator William V. Roth (DE-R) before the U.S. Senate Permanent Subcommittee on Investigations of the Committee on Governmental Affairs, *Emerging Criminal Groups, Hearings before the Permanent Subcommittee on Investigations of the Committee on Governmental Affairs*, U.S. Senate, 99th Cong., 2nd sess., September 24, 1986, 50.

26. Aristide R. Zolberg, "Reforming the Backdoor: The Immigration Reform and Control Act of 1986 in Historical Perspective," in *Immigration Reconsidered: History, Sociology, and Politics*, ed. Virginia Yans-McLaughlin (New York: Oxford University Press, 1990), 315–339, 329.

27. *New York Times*, February 15, 1986, and April 29, 1986; *Wall Street Journal*, May 14, 1986. For an example of a government text, see Congressional Research Service. "Immigration Enforcement within the United States" (Washington, D.C.: Government Printing Office, 2006).

28. Roger Rosenblatt, "The Enemy Within," *Time*, September 15, 1986, and "Battle Strategies," *Time*, September 15, 1986.

29. Clara E. Rodriguez, "The Silver Screen: Stories and Stereotypes," in *Latin Looks: Images of Latinas and Latinos in the U.S. Media*, ed. Clara E. Rodriguez (Boulder, CO: Westview, 1998), 78.

30. See David R. Maciel and Maria Rose Garcia-Acevedo, "The Celluloid Immigrant: The Narrative Films of Mexican Immigration," in *Culture across Borders: Mexican Immigration and Popular Culture*, ed. David R. Maciel and Maria Herrera-Sobek (Tucson: University of Arizona Press, 1998), 149–202.

31. Frank Javier Garcia Berumen, *The Chicano/Hispanic Image in American Film* (New York: Vantage, 1995); Clara E. Rodriguez, "Keeping it Reel? Films of the 1980s and 1990s," in *Latin Looks: Images of Latinas and Latinos in the U.S. Media,* ed. Clara E. Rodriguez (Boulder, CO: Westview, 1998), 180.

32. Lazarus' 1883 poem "The New Colossus" christened Lady Liberty the "mother of exiles" who would provide "world-wide welcome" to "huddled masses yearning to breathe free." See *Liberty State Park, Liberty Science Center*, http://www.libertystatepark.com/emma.htm. According to Lazarus biographer Esther Schor, "The sonnet identified the statue's mission—and by extension that of America—as the provision of refuge for the oppressed." Schor, *Emma Lazarus* (New York: Random House, 2006), 191.

33. Simone Davis, "Checking in the Mirror: Liberty Weekend's Patriotic Spectacle," *Journal of American Culture* 19, no. 2 (1996): 61–70.

34. Select Committee on Immigration and Refugee Policy (SCIRP), *Hearing, Final Report of SCIRP before the Subcommittee on Immigration and Refugee Policy of the Senate Committee on the Judiciary and Subcommittee on Immigration, Refugees and International Law of the House*

Committee on the Judiciary, 97th Cong., 1st sess. (Washington, D.C.: Government Printing Office, 1982), 88.

35. U.S. Senate, *Immigration Reform and Control Act,* 99th Cong., 2nd sess., 132 Cong Rec S 16879, October 14, 1986, http://web.lexis-nexis.com/congcomp/printdoc.

36. Ibid.

37. House Subcommittee on Census and Population, Immigration Reform and Control Act of 1982. *Hearings,* 97th Cong., 2nd sess. (Washington, D.C.: Government Printing Office, 1983), 2.

38. Ibid., 13.

39. Ibid.

40. Charles R. Babcock, "Migrant Policy Said to Benefit Western Bosses," *Washington Post,* July 19, 1981, A1.

41. Alan Simpson, *Right in the Old Gazoo: A Lifetime of Scrapping with the Press* (New York: William Morrow, 1997), 89–90.

42. House Subcommittee on Census and Population, *Hearing,* 6.

43. Ibid., 2.

44. Ibid., 13.

45. IRCA, Pub.L, 99-603, 100 Stat. 3359, Nov. 6, 1986.

46. Aristide R. Zolberg, *A Nation by Design: Immigration Policy in the Fashioning of America* (Cambridge, MA: Harvard University Press, 2006), 173.

47. IRCA.

48. Zolberg, *A Nation by Design,* 373.

49. Eithne Luibheid, *Entry Denied: Controlling Sexuality at the Border* (Minneapolis: University of Minnesota Press, 2002), 233, n. 20.

50. Ibid.

51. Michael Fix, ed., *The Paper Curtain: Employer Sanctions' Implementation, Impact, and Reform* (Washington, D.C.: Urban Institute Press, 1991), 91.

52. Zolberg, *A Nation by Design,* 373–374.

53. IRCA Title I, Section B, Sect. 111.

54. Hartry, "Commentary Gendering Crimmigration," 20.

55. Leo Chavez, *The Latino Threat: Constructing Immigrants, Citizens, and the Nation* (Stanford, CA: Stanford University Press, 2008), 83–84.

56. Grace Kyungwon Hong, *The Ruptures of American Capital: Woman of Color, Feminism and the Culture of Immigrant Labor* (Minneapolis: University of Minnesota Press, 2006), 136.

57. David Montejano, *Anglos and Mexicans in the Making of Texas, 1836–1986* (Austin: University of Texas Press, 1987), 117–120.

58. Alexandra Minna Stern, *Eugenic Nation: Faults and Frontiers of Better Breeding in Modern America* (Berkeley: University of California Press, 2005), 73–74.

59. Human Rights Watch, *Brutality Unchecked: Human Rights Abuses along the U.S. Border with Mexico* (New York: Human Rights Watch, 1992), 35, cited in Luibheid, *Entry Denied,* 121.

60. Steger and Roy, *Neoliberalism,* 55–56.

61. Carlos A. Heredia, "Downward Mobility: Mexican Workers after NAFTA," *NACLA* 30, no. 3 (1996): 34–40.

62. Joseph Nevins, *Operation Gatekeeper: The Rise of the "Illegal Alien" and the Making of the U.S.-Mexico Boundary* (New York: Routledge, 2002), 196–197.

63. Ibid., 145.

64. Zolberg, *A Nation by Design*, 401.

65. Rosa Linda Fregoso, *MeXicana Encounters: The Making of Social Identities on the Borderlands* (Berkeley: University of California Press, 2003), 7.

66. Melissa W. Wright, "Field Note: Ciudad Juarez, Mexico," in *Women's Studies Quarterly* 34, no. 1/2 (2006): 94–97; Camacho, *Migrant Imaginaries*, 264.

67. Fregoso, *MeXicana Encounters*, 5.

68. Camacho, *Migrant Imaginaries*, 243.

69. Roger Lancaster, "Panic Attack: Sex and Terror in the Homeland," *NACLA Report on the Americas* 41, no. 6 (2008): 31–36.

70. Jean Hardisty, "Rights for Some: The Erosion of Democracy," *Public Eye* 15, no. 2 (2001): 1.

71. An analysis of Bill Clinton's immigration politics is beyond the scope of this essay; however, it can be said that he was not anti-immigration or anti immigrant despite the draconian laws that were passed during his presidency. He repealed some welfare cuts after 1996 given the economic stability of the nation, and the Citizenship U.S.A. program, run by Al Gore, increased naturalization by loosening some requirements such as English and civics tests for persons over sixty-five with twenty years of residence. From October 1995 to September 1996, 1.2 million immigrants were naturalized, eliminating a backlog of 500,000. See Zolberg, *A Nation by Design*, 420. At the same time, Clinton has been frequently characterized as the first properly neoliberal president: NAFTA, along with many other globalization efforts, passed with his enthusiastic support, and he espoused the universal benefits of globalization, which, I argue, is largely dependent on the exploitation and criminalization of undocumented immigrants.

72. "Unlawful Entry a Crime since '29," *Rocky Mountain News*, June 11, 2009, http://www.rockymountainnews.com/news/2006/jun/11/unlawful-entry-a-crime-since-29.

73. Illegal Immigration Reform and Immigrant Responsibility Act of 1996, Pub.L, 104–208, Div. C, 110 Stat. 3009-546.

74. Roger Daniels, *Prisoners without Trial: Japanese Americans in World War II* (New York: Hill and Wang, 1993), 246.

75. Christina Gerken, *Model Immigrants and Undesirable Aliens: The Cost of Immigration Reform in the 1990s* (Minneapolis: University of Minnesota Press, 2013), 240; see also Pia Moller, "Restoring Law and (Racial) Order to the Old Dominion," in "Cultural Studies and/of the Law," ed. Jaafar Aksikas and Sean Johnson Andrews, special issue, *Cultural Studies*. 28, no. 5–6 (2014): 869–910.

76. Gerken, *Model Immigrants and Undesirable Aliens*, 240.

77. Philip Kretsedemas, "Immigration Enforcement and the Complication of National Sovereignty: Understanding Local Enforcement as an Exercise in Neoliberal

Governance," in "Nation and Migration: Past and Future," ed. David G. Guitierrez and Pierette Hondagneau-Sotelo, special issue, *American Quarterly* 60, no. 3 (2008): 553–573, 555.

78. Zolberg, *A Nation by Design,* 427.

79. See Leo Chavez, *Shadowed Lives: Undocumented Immigrants in American Society,* 2nd ed. (New York: Wadsworth, 1998).

80. Kretsedemas, "Immigration Enforcement," 553.

81. Ibid., 561.

82. Grace Chang, *Disposable Domestics: Immigrant Women Workers in the Global Economy* (Cambridge, MA: South End Press, 2000), 9.

83. Gerken, *Model Immigrants and Undesirable Aliens,* 23.

84. Michelle J. Anderson, "A License to Abuse: The Impact of Conditional Status on Female Immigrants," *Yale Law Journal* 102, no. 6 (1993): 1401–1430.

85. Teresa Miller, "Blurring the Boundaries between Immigration and Crime Control after September 11th," *Boston College Third World Law Journal.* 25, no. 1 (2005): 80–123.

86. Uniting and Strengthening America by Providing Appropriate Tools Required to Intercept and Obstruct Terrorism Act of 2001 (USA PATRIOT Act), Pub L.107-56. 115 Stat. 272.

87. Rachel Ida Buff, "Deportation Terror," in "Nation and Migration: Past and Future, ed. David G. Guitierrez and Pierette Hondagneau-Sotelo, special issue, *American Quarterly.* 60, no. 3 (2008): 328–352.

88. Rachel L. Swarns, "Failed Amnesty Legalization of 1986 Haunts the Current Immigration Bills in Congress," *Washington Post.* May 23, 2006, http://www.nytimes.com /2006/05/23/washington/23amnesty.html.

89. Hans Von Spakovsky, "Could a Texas Judge Derail Obama's DREAM Act Amnesty Plans?" *Fox News,* May 6, 2013, http://www.foxnews.com/opinion/2013/05/06 /could-texas-judge-derail-obama-dream-act-amnesty-plans/.

90. Jim Bach, "Federal Dream Act Looks Unlikely, As Obama Focusing on Security, Experts Say," *Diamond Back,* March 5, 2013, http://www.diamondbackonline.com/news /national/article_1953b892-8552-11e2-92dc-0019bb30f31a.html.

91. Bryan Buchanan, press officer (trade/globalization), Public Citizen's Global Trade Watch. telephone interview, July 6, 2011.

92. Alan Gomez, "Senate Gang of Eight releases immigration bill," *USA Today,* April 17, 2013, http://www.usatoday.com/story/news/politics/2013/04/17/senate-files -immigration-bill/2089879/.

93. Camacho, *Migrant Imaginaries,* 2.

FOUR

The Look of Sovereignty:
Style and Politics in the Young Lords

Frances Negrón-Muntaner

The day was October 18, 1970, and a young man by the name of Pablo "Yoruba" Guzmán was doing all the talking. Armed with an Afro, U.S. military fatigues, and Cuban shades, Guzmán—the Minister of Information for a radical group called the Young Lords—was demanding that any police officer who came into the East Harlem Methodist Church step aside. The Young Lords had occupied the church after a funeral march to protest the suspected murder of one of their members, Julio Roldán. To make sure that firearms would not be planted on the premises, Guzmán styled his actions with great care: dressed as a commander himself, he body-searched the captain in charge of the operation, forcing him "to assume the position spread."[1] The order produced the desired results. Not only did the police fail to find any weapons, the very next morning one New York newspaper headline read: "Policemen Frisked by the Young Lords."[2]

The Lords' road to citywide recognition had been both long and short. Launched on July 26, 1969, the New York Lords were initially a branch of the Young Lords Organization of Chicago, a street gang turned political group led by José "Cha Cha" Jiménez. In existence since 1959, the group's primary goals were to defend Puerto Rican neighborhoods and demand respect from rival Italian, Appalachian, and Latino gangs.[3] The radicalization of the Chicago Lords unfolded after Jiménez received a sixty-day sentence on a drug possession charge over the summer of 1968. While in prison, Jiménez read works by Thomas Merton, Martin Luther King, and Malcolm X; he also became familiar with the thought of Puerto Rican nationalist leader Pedro Albizu Campos and the Black Panthers' concept of self-defense.[4]

Perhaps as a sort of poetic justice, the founding Lords, who had initially carved a name for themselves as a turf gang, invested much of their political capital in fighting gentrification in Chicago's Puerto Rican communities. From the outset, however, the New York Lords were different.[5] For one, many had little association with street gangs. In fact, a number of the Lords' core leadership had some college education and had belonged to traditional left groups before joining the organization. Furthermore, if the Chicago Lords had tense relations with the media and in the eyes of the public never quite shed their gang origins, the New York Lords were another story. In the words of former Lord Miguel "Mickey" Meléndez: "We had different working methods [from Chicago] and the New York media at our disposal."[6] The groups' divergence eventually became official when, in May 1970, the New York group broke off from the Young Lords Organization of Chicago to become the Young Lords Party.

To this day, scholars debate how and to what extent the New York Lords changed public institutions in the city or achieved revolutionary goals. Yet often overlooked are the ways in which the Young Lords significantly disrupted a symbolic economy founded on the stigmatization of Puerto Ricans as criminally prone if politically docile and, in the process, transformed not only how the world saw Puerto Ricans but also how they saw themselves. Equally critical, they equipped an already upwardly mobile sector of the community to fully participate in New York's political and cultural life. In more ways than one, the Lords' afterlife has shown—and this is an important choice of words—that some Puerto Ricans could "make it" at the same level of New York's other historic ethnic minorities, particularly European Jews and Italians. In Guzmán's terms, "The concept of winning, right, that is the number one contribution of the Young Lords Party—that is what we are, man, the concept of winning."[7]

But how did the Young Lords' leadership turn what one former Chicago Lord called a "ragtag army" into a winning (political) party? After all, they identified and were identified with one of the most politically disempowered communities in New York. In addition, their core leadership comprised five to ten people who could typically mobilize only a few hundred members to demonstrations, even if they claimed a membership of a thousand.[8] Just as significant, the organization's median age was close to eighteen, with some prominent members like Deputy Minister of Finance Juan "Fi" Ortiz being as young as fifteen.

Historian Mervin Mendez attributes to the Young Lords' youth one of the reasons for their success. "The eyes of children are not hypocritical," Mendez remarked in an interview. "They're very honest, deadly honest."[9] While many, including the Young Lords, saw their youth as more of a political liability, I concur with Mendez on one thing: looking and being looked at are at the center of the New York Lords' story. For a major part of the Young Lords' achievements relied on what could be called the "look of sovereignty"—that is, a way to style, display, and move the body to denote that a political actor is willing and able to exercise self-governance and full citizen rights at any time he or she determines. This look was likewise a part of an evolving visual vocabulary that could be recognized by the state, the mainstream media, and radical groups in and outside the city.

At another level, the Lords' successful deployment of style underscores that, although the concept of sovereignty is commonly understood in relation to the prerogative of states to control national territory, it is not solely a matter of law; sovereignty is also a performative and aesthetic act. In the words of philosopher Michel Foucault, one of the few theorists to take note of the relationship between style and sovereignty: "If I want people to accept me as king, I must have the kind of glory which will survive me, and this glory cannot be disassociated from aesthetic value."[10] The Lords' stylized performance further implies that, given how the identity of racialized and colonized groups is routinely shamed by dominant cultural discourses, their political mobilization often requires the act of refashioning or restyling the public self. For style, as scholar Jesús D. Rodríguez Velasco has argued, is intimately linked to how citizens "express their will to form an active part of . . . sovereign power."[11]

That the Young Lords fully understood the importance of style to politics makes their trajectory a rich archive to inquire into the effects and limits of both practices. An engagement with Lords style also partly explains why they remain the most widely recognized of New York Latino radical organizations of the late 1960s and early 1970s. Whereas other contemporary groups such as the Real Great Society (RGS) were similarly pivotal and generative—it was RGS, after all, that incubated the Young Lords in their East Harlem offices—the Lords and their iconography have come to signify radical politics itself for subsequent generations of activists.[12] Additionally, the Young Lords' sartorial history accentuated that style is not an afterthought to political action but rather a practice that materializes at the exact moment when dissent is articulated and a new political body brought forth. Or as Guadeloupian writer Maryse Condé once put it, "The revolution starts with new clothes."[13]

Change of Clothes

The struggle to refashion Puerto Ricans in New York did not, of course, begin with the Young Lords. New York Puerto Ricans have historically been aware of their low status in the city's symbolic and political economies and have pursued ways to redress it. During the post–World War II period, for instance, many young men tried to valorize themselves by belonging to gangs and styling themselves accordingly. In the words of former Young Lord Chairman Felipe Luciano, "My first models of resistance were Puerto Rican men. I saw Puerto Rican men stand up to the Italian gangs, oblivious to the fact that these guys might put a hit on them. I saw them stand up . . . in T-shirts, with pegged pants and curly hair coming down their foreheads."[14] Those who played the politics of respectability also sought redress by means of style, wearing the standard suit and tie in the hope of gaining access to the U.S. party machineries, the island's Commonwealth's Office in New York, or the War on Poverty programs of the post–World War II period.[15]

But coming onto the scene at a time of global political radicalization and the expansion of visual media technologies, the Young Lords opted for a different strategy to transform the perception of Puerto Ricans and their conditions. They seized the very site of shame and subordination—the body—and restyled it to maximize its potential as a mobile political sign that staged and anticipated their liberation from colonial, racist, and patriarchal structures of power. In this way, "costume," as Daphne A. Brooks has suggested in another context, was a path for self-transformation and freedom.[16] That the Young Lords specifically focused on the body was not a coincidence. Similar to other groups in the United States and Puerto Rico, the Lords understood that the violence visited on Puerto Rican bodies through inferior health services, mass sterilization, poor nutrition, substandard housing, and inadequate education was political. Moreover, an emphasis on the body spoke to the colonial stereotype of Puerto Ricans as incapable of sovereign action because of their individual and collective body politic's presumable weakness. Since the start of U.S. rule on the island in 1898, officials dismissed Puerto Ricans' self-governance claims and demands for political participation by alluding to the community's sickness, ignorance, poverty, and lack of hygiene.

To counter a politico-symbolic economy that barred Puerto Ricans from resources and visualized them as disposable, the Young Lords worked hard to produce a different body for *boricuas*: well-fed, well-dressed, and well-educated; drug and lead-free. This was a body guided by a new consciousness that could "stand up" to the system[17] and take control of the Puerto Rican nation's destiny by discipline, organization, and coordinated action. By restyling and beefing up the body, the Lords aimed to shed what former Young Lord Mickey Meléndez called the "colonial pathology of docility" and replace it with "an image of Puerto Ricans as tough and inventive defenders of their rights as citizens."[18] In this and other ways, the Young Lords fashioned a public body that moved U.S. Puerto Ricans into political modernity, which in the words of Wendy Parkins, "depends on the concept of an individual who is not subject to the authority of any other except by consent and who is also free to withdraw this consent."[19]

In a broader sense, the Young Lords' desire to improve their political performance is linked to how shame is constitutive of Puerto Rican ethno-national identity in a colonial context. As I have argued elsewhere, U.S. colonial discourses have historically imagined Puerto Ricans as Black, poor, and lacking as national subjects. Not surprisingly, many of their forms of survival, including escape, avoidance, or unarmed resistance, have been similarly considered "queer" in the sense of both odd (non-normative) and effeminate (weak, cowardly).[20] Given this context, Puerto Ricans' performances as national subjects are often aimed at the American gaze. A "dirty look" that not only deems Puerto Ricans low, criminal, and "other" in relation to first-class, upstanding, normative American subjects but demeans them in the eyes of other groups as well. Insisting on being seen otherwise, the Lords asserted that Puerto Ricans had nothing to be ashamed of; on the contrary, what was shameful was the racist, colonial, and patriarchal gaze.

Equally significant, in contrast to the island Puerto Rican elites who emphasized their racial, class, and gender normative identities, the Young Lords engaged with, rather than denied, the racialized and queer cast of Puerto Rican identity. On the one hand, they embraced feminist politics and at times overtly identified with the stigmatized political location of LGTB people, particularly gay men. On the other hand, in a manner different from how mainstream political leaders frequently deployed a national discourse of ambiguity toward U.S. sovereignty, the Young Lords' sovereign acts offered an oppositional (if problematically) masculinist alternative: one that challenged American imperial "muscular" style with the muscle of national liberation aesthetics deployed by African American, Cuban, and Vietnamese revolutionaries.

In sum, to contest multiple sites of symbolic and political dispossession, the Young Lords developed a range of "self-actualizing performance[s]" that were striking in their economy.[21] A group without significant financial or institutional support, the Young Lords promoted low-cost imaginative practices such as symbolic disruption, sartorial reinvention, and dramatic storytelling to stage a radical alternative to the status quo. In this way, the Young Lords built on Felix Padilla's observation that "the only significant resource Puerto Ricans possessed was the capacity to make trouble . . . and force authorities to respond."[22] With style and stunts, the Lords set out to conquer New York.

Lords of Style

As the Young Lords themselves have noted, the Black Panthers largely inspired their style. From the party's founding in 1966, Black Panther imagery and gestures like the raised fist became a widely cited shorthand to signify empowerment and revolution for radicalized minorities. The Black Panthers' strategic use of style, and the media's tendency to primarily cover the organization's most spectacular actions, often made Panther fashion better known than their platform or programs. Media consumers, for instance, may not have been aware that the Black Panthers wanted a United Nations–sponsored referendum on Black self-determination or a general amnesty for all imprisoned Black men. But the majority of TV viewers knew what the Panthers looked like: "They were splendidly outfitted . . . black leather jacket, slacks, shoes, and beret . . . turtleneck shirts; dark glasses optional," in the words of historian William Van Deburg.[23]

A cross between urban street style, outlaw fashion, and Third World revolutionary aesthetics, the male Panther's look accentuated the wearer's power. This is evident in, for instance, the use of the black leather jacket, a garment that since its origins in early twentieth-century Germany enclosed a complex history that signified military power, rebellious masculinity, outsider status, and social disaffection.[24] Long firearms, military formation choreography, and the display of "scowling facial expressions" similarly defined the Panther look.[25] Whereas Black Panther women could also be seen carrying guns and wearing black leather jackets, their style was less regulated and often perceived by critics as a statement of high fashion instead of political practice. In the notorious terms of "Radical Chic" chronicler Tom Wolfe, Panther women were more inclined to wear "tight pants and Yoruba-style headdresses, almost like turbans, as if they'd stepped out of the pages of Vogue, although no doubt Vogue got it from them."[26]

For the Young Lords, drawing from the Black Panthers was an effective way to make Puerto Ricans visible. Different from African Americans, Puerto Ricans at the time were mostly concentrated in a few neighborhoods in the Northeast, Illinois, and Ohio, and seemed racially ambiguous according to American standards. Fashioning themselves as "a kind of Puerto Rican equivalent to the Black Panthers"[27] allowed the Lords to be readily identified as a desirable ally for other radical groups and as a revolutionary organization that would take the rights of Puerto Ricans by any means necessary. In citing the Black Panthers through the use of berets, leather jackets, and/or Afros, the Lords were engaging in what style theorist Nathan Jones has called "sartorial metaphor": "borrowing . . . the social characteristics of another—status, relationships, and attribute—by adopting his dress."[28]

Identifying with the Black Panthers was also about challenging racism among Puerto Ricans. If race is nearly always downplayed in Puerto Rican national politics, many Young Lords wore their Blackness literally on their sleeve by dressing in African and African American–inspired fashions. This trend was embodied in the style of Young Lords like Guzmán, who sported a Malcolm X look, an Afro, and occasionally a dashiki. In addition, while the Young Lords remained a Puerto Rican majority organization, Black style signaled its openness to accepting all groups in their organization and communicated its desire to work on behalf of the "people" rather than narrowly defined communities. Fittingly, a significant number of Young Lords—from 25 to 30 percent—were not Puerto Ricans and many were African Americans.[29] Importantly, this practice of inclusion went beyond the rank and file. Some of the top Lords like Guzmán were "halfies" (in his case, of Cuban and Puerto Rican parents), and Denise Oliver, who went on to serve as Minister of Economic Development, was African American.

Simultaneously, the Young Lords knew that, to be taken seriously as Latino revolutionaries, they could not be perceived as just an imitation of Black groups.

At the level of style, the Young Lords addressed this by infusing their Panther-inspired attire with accessories that accentuated Puerto Rican identity. For instance, whereas the Panther beret was black, the Lords' own was purple, a detail that is easy to miss if looking at black-and-white footage or photographs. Purple explicitly referenced the Young Lords' Chicago gang origins since this was their distinct color as a street gang. Moreover, the Lords adopted Chicago's "YLO button," which showed a "fist holding a rifle and a Spanish phrase, 'Tengo Puerto Rico en mi corazón'—'I have Puerto Rico in my heart' against a silhouette of the island."[30] The beret was arguably the item that most identified the New York Lords: "People knew us by the beret and the buttons that we wore on them," recalls former Lords leader Iris Morales. "If we did not want to be seen or engage as a Young Lord, we would take off our beret."[31]

An equally significant addition was the Puerto Rican flag. This was a key accessory. During the first half of the twentieth century, the flag emerged as a symbol of defiance to U.S. colonial authority in large part because of its suppression by the local government. Pro-independence groups like the Nationalist Party led by Pedro Albizu Campos often displayed the flag at public events despite its being outlawed (or precisely because it was). Although the Estado Libre Asociado officially adopted the banner in 1952, the fact that it could still not be legally flown "alone"—without the American flag—carried its oppositional meanings well into the 1970s.[32] After Puerto Ricans migrated to the United States and expanded their participation in American institutions, the flag came to signify ethno-national identity in multiple locations, from New York's Puerto Rican Parade to war zones in Korea. Whether they intended to call attention to the "national question" and/or underscore their ethnic difference,[33] many Young Lords wore the Puerto Rican flag on their heads, chest, and hands—anywhere that they could hang it.

A good number of Young Lords similarly wore "U.S. Army-issued field jackets, combat fatigues,"[34] and black boots. While wearing U.S. military garments may appear incongruous given the Young Lords' opposition to American colonial policies and foreign interventions, these sartorial choices communicated a range of ideas regarding their aspirations, experience, and form of organization. Army attire, for example, connoted the Young Lords' paramilitary structure, which included a central committee consisting of five people: a chairman and the ministers of information, education, defense, and finance. Fatigues also referenced the contradictory experience of Puerto Rican service in the U.S. military and opposition to the Vietnam War. "We had a lot of Vietnam vets and they wore their uniform," adds Morales. "They were proud that they had fought in Vietnam but ambivalent about the fact that they had killed Vietnamese."[35] In wearing the uniform, the Lords aimed to remove the stigma of passivity and weakness, and be seen as warriors: an image associated with heroism, strength, and honor in the American popular imagination.

The common use of olive green clothing further emphasized the Young Lords' identification with Third World revolutionary movements and projected their actions as those of revolutionary soldiers against the state and its representatives. This affinity was present from the very beginning, starting with the date chosen by the Young Lords to stage their first public event: July 26, 1969. The day overtly referenced the Cuban July 26 Movement, which became the military arm of the anti-Batista forces that eventually propelled Fidel Castro to power in 1959. Honoring their key political genealogies—nationalist, Black, and Third World—the Young Lords introduced themselves to New York "clad in fatigues resembling the BPP [Black Panther Party] and holding aloft a banner of a rifle over the Puerto Rican flag as their insignia."[36]

The Young Lords' constant citation of the basic Third World guerrilla uniform also explicitly signified their aspiration of combating U.S. colonialism in Puerto Rico. According to Meléndez, "We began to believe in the possibility that we could become an independent and self-governing nation, controlling our own economy and our own destiny. We redefined ourselves in this tradition of struggle and resistance against powerful foreign intervention."[37] Yet the rare display or use of the ultimate sovereignty accessory—guns—suggested that even if they identified with liberation movements in the United States and abroad, defended their own right to armed struggle, and in print constantly included drawings and photos of guns, theirs was a conflict fought primarily in the symbolic rather than the military arena.

This reality is evident in the sole New York action in which guns were widely wielded in public: the aforementioned funeral of Young Lord Julio Roldán. Arrested on October 15, 1970, for allegedly trying to set an East Harlem apartment on fire, Roldán was taken to the Manhattan House of Detention for men, otherwise known as the Tombs.[38] A few days after his arrest, Roldán was found dead in his jail cell, hanging by a belt. Although the police labeled the death a suicide, the Young Lords believed that Roldán was murdered. In response, the Lords occupied what they had renamed the "People's Church" for a second time. On this occasion, they entered the building carrying arms, in a show of force designed to signal that their organization would not tolerate the killing of its members.[39] But because the Lords were not interested in confronting the police or being arrested, they devised a magnificent exit strategy: before leaving, they broke down the guns and hid them in the clothes and purses of seemingly harmless neighborhood *doñas* leaving the church.

The Young Lords' downplaying of guns is in contrast to the Black Panthers and speaks to different histories and contexts despite significant affinities. The

Panthers initially became visible as the Black Panther Party for Self Defense to confront police brutality and "a law-and-order culture" in California.[40] Arms also stood for the Black Panther rejection of nonviolence as a resistance strategy and frustration with the limitations of the Civil Rights Movement. Fittingly, the Black Panthers' first statewide action, on May 2, 1967, was an armed entrance into the California state capitol at the same time that the legislature was considering the Mulford Act, a gun control bill that would have barred residents from carrying concealed weapons. At the end, even after dropping "self-defense" from their name to avoid being considered "a paramilitary organization"[41] and emphasizing service programs, guns remained a loaded symbol of empowerment for the Black Panthers.[42]

In this sense, while both groups displayed guns for symbolic reasons, and the Young Lords similarly recognized police brutality and prison conditions as a threat to Puerto Rican well-being, much of the Lords' core politics emerged from being marginalized and unrecognized rather than targeted and attacked. In addition, through their close study of past Puerto Rican nationalist armed revolts, the Young Lords were arguably aware of the risks of these actions, the potential for state violence against community members, and the high price paid by pro-independence militants who often enjoyed little support. Not surprisingly, even on the occasions when he advocated armed struggle, the Young Lords' Minister of Defense Juan González underscored the importance of coalescing with other allies, particularly Blacks and radicalized workers, and the tactical need to "divide up the work necessary to destroy amerikkan power."[43]

When going it alone, the Young Lords then tended to carry weapons under circumstances perceived as extreme and only to stress that Puerto Rican political will and/or citizenship had to be respected. In this sense, the Young Lords were generally unwilling to engage in the definitive sovereign action: determining who lives and who dies. Even Mickey Meléndez, one of the Lords' highest-ranking military members, who at one time was also given the task of building up an "underground armed branch,"[44] described the scene at the Methodist Church in exclusively performative terms: "For the first time, we would brandish weapons. They were meant to be symbolic; we wanted to force the city to negotiate with us for prison reforms. We were angry and wanted to show how serious we were, publicly and on TV."[45] This is consistent with Nathan Joseph's observation that, in certain contexts, "the importance of weapons may derive less from their actual efficacy than their associated cultural values. The right to weapons has long symbolized the wellborn or even the ordinary adult male in a warlike society."[46]

Inherent in Joseph's gendered comment is that looking like the Young Lords had different implications for men and women. As a visual sign, the male Young Lords' armed image signaled that Puerto Rican men were capable of violence. In the words of José Yglesias, the Lords' look was about "being a macho, a real male, means standing up to the Man."[47] Or, in the more explicit terms of former Young Lord Richie Perez, "When we integrated campuses . . . we got to [kick ass] too . . . throw racists down the stairs. We did non-violent actions—but it was a TACTICAL question, not a matter of PRINCIPLE. It was important that our antagonists knew this."[48] The idea was to make it clear that Lords men could—and would—defend themselves and their rights by force if they so decided.

Though the male Lords' look projected a sovereign masculinity, dressing as a "Lady Lord" had as much, if not more, to do with power differentials between genders. By wearing clothing associated with men and war such as combat boots in private and public spaces, women signified a rejection of the traditionally defined gender roles of housewives and mistresses so closely associated with the "macho" culture some men were attempting to uphold. In the words of Iris Morales, who was married to Chairman Felipe Luciano at the time, "War begins at home."[49] Women's adoption of the Young Lords uniform was ultimately a sign of discontent in relation to gender expectations and a demand that women be treated as equals in and out of the organization.

But although women may have valued military dress, their style, like that of female members of the Black Panthers, was generally less regimented than the men's. In addition to the fact that many women embraced fashion choices that affirmed their sexual autonomy, such as the miniskirt, there was another important reason: it did not take long for Lords women to figure out that dressing the part was not enough to be recognized as sovereign or equal. As the Young Lords increasingly thought of themselves as a paramilitary organization, sexist ideologies arguably became more dominant in day-to-day operations and women's discomfort with their low status grew apace.[50] Consequently, eight months into the life of the Young Lords, the women members staged the first transformative insurrection experienced by the organization. And, not coincidentally, in one of the most colorful accounts of the Lords' feminist revolt, Denise Oliver narrates the inciting incident via dress metaphors.

The triggering event took place at the home of poet and activist Amiri Baraka (LeRoi Jones). Chairman Felipe Luciano, who was intrigued by Baraka's strand of nationalism, went to meet him accompanied by several Lords men and Denise Oliver. According to Oliver, when she arrived at Baraka's home, she noticed that women "crawled into the room on their hands and knees wearing elaborate headdresses decorated with fruit"[51] while "Baraka's coterie of male guards and supporters . . . wore dashikis and gave power handshakes to the male Lords." Uncomfortable with the scene, Oliver reportedly asked Baraka about the role of women in his organization but was ignored throughout the gathering. After Oliver left, she called a meeting with other Lords women and urged them to pressure the male leadership for greater inclusion in the top command. Oliver succinctly summed up the reason that this course of action was urgent: "[because] if we didn't do something we would end up on our hands and knees with fruit on our heads."[52]

To bring the point home, the Lords women proceeded to create their own caucus, formally pressured for change, and threatened to stop working for the organization.[53] Some women also reportedly refused to have sex with the men until the Central Committee met their demands. (Lord internal regulations prohibited sex outside of the group for fear of government infiltration.) By June of 1970, the Lords women had won a series of victories that substantially altered their status.[54] Among these were the elevation of two women to the central committee and other positions of power and the complete overhaul of point 5 in the party program, the only item that the Young Lords amended while an active organization. Whereas before the Young Lords argued in their platform that "machismo must be revolutionary and not oppressive," the new point 5 read: "We want equality for women. Down with machismo and male chauvinism."[55] For the Lords women, the rationale for the amendment was simple. In the words of Oliver, "machismo was never gonna be revolutionary. Saying 'revolutionary machismo' is like saying . . . 'revolutionary racism.'"[56]

Ready for Their Close-Up

Arriving at the right look and mending the gendered splits, however, was only the first step. Once refashioned, the Young Lords had to move their bodies and their audience by telling compelling stories in which they were the protagonists of a political drama about the city's failure to serve and protect its people. Importantly, these performances were directed not only at the state or other radical groups but also at Puerto Ricans and other community members. According to the *New York Times* journalist Joseph Fried, one of the first reporters to cover the Young Lords, their main goal was "to show the people of El Barrio, East Harlem's Puerto Rican slum, that such activity was necessary to get city action to meet community needs."[57] Aiming to inspire respect among some, and fear in others, the group captured the imaginations of thousands of people who had never met a Young Lord in person or directly benefited from Lord actions.

Since a wide base of support was necessary to challenge institutions, offer services, and "awaken" Puerto Ricans to their own political potential, the Young Lords heavily promoted their corporeal movements to the mass media, effectively recruiting them to act as their co-producers. "Look, you know," wrote Guzmán, "the media is gonna have to be used. Until we can put out the *Daily News* regularly, until we have a TV station and a radio station, chalk it up. Everybody on welfare got a TV set, everybody got a radio, everybody buys the *Daily News* and *El Diario*, so as long as the people got access to these things, we might as well use them to the best of our advantage."[58] Moreover, as New Journalist Tom Wolfe once observed, "Without publicity it has never been easy to rank as a fashionable person in New York City."[59] In other words, politics required publicity and publicity required that you make news. And to make news you had to not only "look good" but also tell a moving story.

The Young Lords' discovery of the importance of effective (and entertaining) media representation to contemporary politics was not met with universal approval. The traditional left deeply disliked the Lords' style and tactics. The leaders of the Movement for Puerto Rican Independence (MPI), for instance, were particularly clear when they called the Young Lords "a group of immature young people looking for publicity" and a "bunch of crazy exhibitionists."[60]

Despite the Left's bad reviews, the Young Lords' emphasis on the media was not arbitrary. The group came into being at a time when media outlets were significantly expanding and there was an unprecedented hunger for television news. News programs were similarly changing into more stylish and dramatic presentations that sought to build audiences rather than promote traditional journalistic values such as "content and social responsibility."[61] In addition, city residents increasingly constituted their social and political identities via their interaction with mass media products. Knowing how to attract and grasp media attention was at this time paramount to any disruption of hegemonic discourses around race, colonialism, and citizenship.

Furthermore, although the Young Lords were not the first Puerto Rican group to recognize the importance of performance to politics—anarchists like Luisa Capetillo and the Nationalists under Albizu Campos understood it, too—they were the first U.S.-based organization to do so in a context where the mass media had become a major political power, as great as, and at times greater than, the state in allocating the cultural capital of groups seeking support for their claims. In this sense, improving Puerto Rican looks through style, performance, and choreography was both a mode of "self-defense" as the Black Panthers would have it and a means to quicken the pace of political empowerment and accumulation of cultural capital.

In attempting to capture media attention, however, the Young Lords faced structural challenges. Unlike affluent Whites who could easily access news and media infrastructure, Puerto Ricans had few resources to call attention to their concerns. In contrast to African Americans, who despite marginalization had a more sustained presence in U.S. media and greater prominence in American national discourse, Puerto Ricans were rarely recognized as a U.S. ethnic minority or a separate national group, so their claims were often dismissed as irrelevant and/or anti-American. Moreover, they were often confused with immigrants and

Blacks and required additional effort to gain separate notice. It was thus not a co-incidence that Puerto Rican activists and organizations were known for extreme stunts, such as the Nationalist Party's 1954 shooting on Congress to bring attention to Puerto Rico's colonial situation or twice climbing the Statue of Liberty and unfurling Puerto Rican flags in support of various causes, including evicting the U.S. Navy from Vieques.

To counter their limitations, the Young Lords developed two key performances with a "sense of drama . . . and a flair."[62] The first was the well-coordinated stunt, exemplified by their first mass action in July of 1969, known as the "Garbage Offensive." According to Mickey Meléndez, the Lords picked garbage, no pun intended, because that is what *barrio* residents identified as their number one neighborhood problem. This was an astute choice because, as historian Johanna Fernández has observed, not only were *barrio* residents concerned with the issue; it had also become a sensitive matter for the city at large. The fact that New York's sanitation infrastructure was outdated, city workers underpaid, and the growing volume of waste increasingly difficult to manage was on the minds of many New Yorkers.[63] But a third account that is particularly fitting for my argument is that the Young Lords decided to concentrate on the overwhelming problem of trash in East Harlem because, as Yoruba Guzmán put it, "garbage is visible and everybody sees it."[64]

In addition, "garbage" was what many New Yorkers considered Puerto Ricans to be. A 1948 travel book, *New York Confidential* by Jack Lait and Lee Mortimer, minced no words in describing the new immigrants: "They are mostly crude farmers, subject to congenital tropical diseases, physically unfitted for the northern climate, unskilled, uneducated, non-English-speaking, and almost impossible to assimilate and condition for healthful and useful existence in an active city of stone and steel."[65] Even after decades of living in New York, Puerto Ricans continued to be largely seen as unassimilable to the city's values and norms. Former congressman Herman Badillo, for instance, once commented that when he began registering Puerto Ricans to vote in the late 1950s, he heard a man say, "We have to do something about that guy Badillo. He's been bringing all this garbage to register and to vote."[66] Ten years later, Guzmán would similarly conclude that "[the] D.O.G [Department of Sanitation] looks upon Puerto Ricans and Blacks as though they are something lower than garbage."[67] So, making the garbage visible—and purposefully representing it as a sign of how "dirty" the system was rather than as a measure of Puerto Rican worth—was a highly effective way of prompting New Yorkers to look at Puerto Ricans in an entirely different light.

Influenced by prior Real Great Society actions and named after the 1968 Vietnamese Tet Offensive, the Young Lords and other community members decided to meet every Sunday to clean up the garbage. To this end, the Lords requested supplies from the city and were summarily ignored. After experiencing similar treatment more than once and seeing that the trash was not collected or, if it was, was left "strewn in the street," the Lords changed their tactics.[68] For over a month, the Lords and other residents pushed the garbage further and further onto 110th Street and Third Avenue and made piles that partly obstructed traffic. On August 17, something unexpected happened: the protesters decided to set the garbage on fire.

Setting garbage on fire was, according to political scientist José Ramón Sánchez, a turning point in relations between Puerto Ricans, the state, and New York City at large.[69] Whereas residents had piled up garbage and swept the streets before the Young Lords came onto the scene, the style deployed by the Lords suggested that this was not business as usual. The idea was no longer to ask the authorities for help but to make their failure to visible, thus deflecting shame onto a system that did not live up to its self-proclaimed standards of cleanliness, efficiency, and order. And, from the Lords' point of view, what the garbage made evident was at least twofold: that "the system does not serve them [Puerto Ricans]" and that Puerto Ricans, while they were surrounded by garbage, were not responsible for the conditions in which they lived.[70]

Yet to establish themselves as prime-time players and to be widely recognized as sovereign political actors—that is, subjects who did not require state or church approval to act on their desires—the Young Lords needed to dramatize their movements and capture New York's attention on a grander scale. To achieve this, they began making use of a second tactic—the "kidnapping" building crisis—an open-ended dramatic performance that invited spectators to join and assist in changing prevalent conditions.[71] The first action to embody the new tactic was the takeover of the First Spanish Methodist Church on the corner of 111th Street and Lexington. The impasse began when the pastor, Reverend Humberto Carranza—a Cuban exile to whom the Young Lords must have seemed like miniature Che Gueveras—repeatedly refused the Lords' request for space to house several programs, including a day care center and a popular free breakfast program over a four-month period. Frustrated with the lack of progress, the Young Lords decided to take the church. On December 29, 1969, they began an eleven-day occupation during which hundreds of people participated in their programs.

The Young Lords' biggest victories may have been at other levels. The Garbage Offensive and the takeover of First Spanish Methodist had instituted the Lords as representatives of Puerto Ricans in what they perceived as a global revolution and had decisively transformed Puerto Rican expectations of themselves. In Guzmán's words, "Before the Young Lords Party began—people used to walk with their heads down like this, and the pigs would walk through the colonies, man, like they owned the block. They'd come in here with no kind of respect in their eyes. But after the Garbage Offensive and the People's Church it was a whole

The Look of Sovereignty   97

new game."[72] In the end, the longer-term impact of these actions had less to do with whether the city picked up the garbage in East Harlem somewhat more frequently than before or offered church space. Rather, it had to do with how they transformed Puerto Ricans from spectators into political actors, unhinging enduring stereotypes of Puerto Rican passivity and ineffectiveness.[73]

Emboldened by their accomplishments, the Young Lords went on to organize other, similar high-profile actions such as the "liberation" of an X-ray truck to conduct community tuberculosis tests on June 17, 1970, and the occupation of Lincoln Hospital, nearly a month later, on July 14.[74] Prompted by the outrage of proposed budget cuts and inhumane treatment of patients, the Lincoln takeover was a classic Young Lords action: it included the occupation of an unpopular hospital that most agreed was a "butcher shop." In addition, the siege lasted only twelve hours, attracted news cameras, and made no use of physical force. Notably, the hospital's chief administrator, Dr. Antero Lacot, described the action as "helpful" in "trying to dramatize a situation which is critical."[75]

Ultimately, the Young Lords offered a familiar and popular story line to the media featuring disempowered youth with a just cause that was likely to end well for all involved. In Guzmán's terms, "The people dig an underdog, that was the great appeal of the Mets at one time, and you have to understand that that's exactly what we are, underdogs."[76] Despite the Lords' revolutionary rhetoric, they chose relatively easy targets that could lead to tangible improvements. According to Sánchez, "They appeared dangerous yet used church space for a free breakfast program and free medical care."[77] This is one of the main reasons that the Young Lords generally obtained sympathy from journalists, broad sectors of the public, and even some individuals and organizations that they targeted. Likewise, their New York actions did not seek military control or revolutionary overthrow of the state but access to resources, self-transformation, and expansion of the political imagination.

Heart of Lords

For over a year, the Young Lords won nearly every publicity battle if not every political fight. Some may have disagreed with their look or tactics, but few disagreed with their reasoning. This is evident in that the Lords were often arrested for trespassing and other offenses but the charges would eventually be dropped. Still, the Young Lords began losing momentum after 1972, when they engaged in a series of public actions and internal debates that began to alter their image and strategy. Their first political turn arguably had taken place earlier, on June 8, 1970, when they marched in the annual Puerto Rican Parade alongside members of the Movement for Puerto Rican Independence and the Puerto Rican Students Union. During the parade, the group embarrassed some participants and organizers when they pelted officials and Puerto Rico's pro-statehood governor Luis A. Ferré with tomatoes, oranges, and eggs.[78]

Moreover, while bringing guns to Julio Roldán's funeral in 1970 was a symbolic gesture that did not end in armed confrontation, it anticipated a turn toward more traditional nationalist military politics, one that boomeranged. As journalist Ansel Herz has argued, "Unlike previous building occupations, the second takeover of the 'People's Church' did not achieve any tangible victory for the community of El Barrio. No one was ever held responsible for Roldán's death. The open display of weapons did, however, agitate the FBI and lead to increased surveillance and repression."[79] In other words, as the Lords moved from dramatic actions focused on community needs toward a pro-independence agenda, the political ground began to shift. Not only did this new orientation deeply polarize the Young Lords and community members, it also made the media lose interest. All that the Lords had achieved seem to fade away.

Yet from the start the Young Lords had a constitutive duality that came to undo them as a political force: they may have been bent on being recognized as an integral, if distinct, part of New York and in solidarity with other anti-imperialist movements at home and beyond. But, as the Young Lords' button proclaimed, they had "Puerto Rico en el corazón" and it started weighing heavily. The Lords came to believe that acts of political imagination and community service in East Harlem did not go to the heart of Puerto Rican subordination and therefore could not free Puerto Ricans, decolonize the island, or confer the dignity of nation-state status."[80] After all, point 1 in the Young Lords' platform was "We want self-determination for Puerto Ricans, liberation on the island and inside the United States" and point 6 stated, "We want community control of our institutions and land."[81]

In contemplating growth for the organization within a context of declining mass activity, the Young Lords made a fateful decision: In March 1971, they launched Ofensiva Rompecadenas and started to develop a presence in Puerto Rico. This decision was not unanimous. It was, however, largely founded on a shared analysis that rested on two assumptions: one, that Puerto Ricans made up a single nation and therefore the occupied island was every *boricuas'* national land base; and, two, that the origin of Puerto Rican disempowerment and stigmatization in the United States was the colonial status of Puerto Rico. In the succinct words of Felipe Luciano, "Puerto Rico is oppressed as a nation, it is a colony of the united states [*sic*] and the colonial status of Puerto Ricans follows them from the countryside to New York City."[82]

Based on this assessment, the Young Lords decided that they should reallocate energies and resources to winning independence and liberate the "two-thirds of our people [who] are in chains in Puerto Rico."[83] If Puerto Ricans were an "internal" colony of the United States, the only path to liberation was to externalize it through formal decolonization. "And this is why we must rise up together," wrote Lord leader Gloria Gonzalez. "Boricuas in the u.s. [sic] and Boricuas on the island, to put an end to yankee abuse . . . we must re-unite our Nation."[84] Only then would the new body and the old heart produce a truly free and sovereign Puerto Rican.

The Young Lords proceeded to open branches in Ponce, Aguadilla, and San Juan. Dressed in their full Young Lords uniforms, their first major appearance was on March 21, 1971, as part of a commemorative march for the Ponce Massacre of 1937. But their presence was generally not welcome. Although the Lords' commitment to national sovereignty did not go unnoticed by sectors of the independence movement and later prompted outreach campaigns on the mainland,[85] most island nationalists felt little need for the "Nuyorican" warriors on their own turf. Counting on nationalist and leftist traditions over a century old and apparently feeling that the Young Lords had come to "show the other *independentistas* how to make revolution," many dismissed the new arrivals.[86] While there is limited research on this part of the Young Lords history, anecdotes from political activists of this period suggest that the New York Lords were seen as similar to other U.S.-born Puerto Ricans: low class, non-Spanish-speaking, *atrevido* Americans.[87]

In listening to their hearts, the Young Lords had come face to face with a nearly unbearable truth: if a great part of their transformation into revolutionaries had to do with realizing that they were Puerto Ricans and not Americans, the "real" Puerto Ricans did not think that they were Puerto Ricans at all, much less that they were needed to win any political battle. In Juan González's words, "One of the biggest mistakes . . . the Young Lords ever made was . . . [to think] that we could figure out how to organize an independence movement on the island. Because the reality is that we're US-raised Puerto Ricans and the experience that we knew was the urban ghettoes of the United States."[88] This realization had great implications.

During more than a year of strenuous work, the Young Lords had fashioned themselves into a disciplined body ready for political power. Style was a form of discipline, and discipline was a way to produce a sovereign self: "We stressed self-discipline . . . we attempted to remake ourselves—change our thinking and behavior—while we fought to change the world."[89] But, one could say, Puerto Rico broke the Lords' heart, in some ways severing the heart from the body. And this severance revealed the tensions between two different conceptions of sovereignty. The first was a lowercase form that emphasized symbolic disruption, recognition as citizens, and the politicization of class, ethnicity, gender, race, sexuality, and colonial subordination.[90] The second, an uppercase version, understood self-determination in nation-state terms and ultimately could only be fought in—and over—Puerto Rico. The gap exposed a fissure between the potentially sovereign body of the

"Nuyorican" and her nonsovereign heart, Puerto Rico, one that would eventually make the Young Lords Party implode.

At the exact moment that the Young Lords aimed to overtly challenge U.S. sovereignty in Puerto Rico by migrating part of their operation to the island, the state moved to disassemble the organization's potential success by stepping up surveillance, increasing the number of infiltrators, and intensifying police harassment of individuals and property.[91] Equally important, the move south literally dislocated rather than stretched the Lords' body politic. In Iris Morales' words, "We started to lose the relationship with the community which was what had kept us and made us strong . . . people then didn't have a place where they would come and talk to us about the police brutality issues, they didn't have a place where there could be a free breakfast program or a free clothing drive."[92] In addition, the embrace of more conventional goals such as national sovereignty displaced other fundamental political objectives that had so defined the politics of the Young Lords, including dismantling racism and sexism.[93]

Lastly, this dislocation became a deep fracture when Marxist-Maoist members led by Gloria Fontanez transformed the party into the Puerto Rican Revolutionary Workers Organization (PRRWO) in July 1972. The PRRWO's leadership, which included former core Lords, derided the Lords' prior nationalist analysis in favor of revolutionary proletarianism, arguing that only a working-class revolution in the United States would eliminate the threat of American imperialism. Some of the Lords were now even accused of being "rightist" and "reactionary." As the PRRWO's new leaders saw it, "Puerto Rico is not a divided nation. Puerto Rico is a nation in Puerto Rico, and the Puerto Ricans inside the U.S. are an oppressed national minority part of the North American working class."[94] Significantly, a measure of the proof that the PRRWO offered for the Lords' political errors was sartorial: "Left extremism was being developed and this was seen in the way we dressed, as if we were an army, our way of talking, of living, so different from the rest of the working people."[95] In time, the PRRWO's dogmatism led to violent internal struggle, authoritarianism, and ineffectiveness.

Still, whereas the PRRWO is almost universally regarded as the Young Lords' "darkest hour," and their stance that the working class was the only possible revolutionary class as misguided, its leaders were not altogether wrong in assessing the Lords' project as that of an already upwardly mobile group ("lower petty bourgeoisie" in their terms). This is evident in their reasons for cutting off their ties to Chicago to become the Young Lords Party—the original Lords were considered too "street" and not sophisticated enough—and in their urgent quest for a base once social movements began to change in the early 1970s.[96] Called the "intellectuals" by the Chicago group, the New York Lords' leadership composition also implied a distrust of, or at least a distance from, the masses: although the leadership stressed service to "the people," all decisions were made by a central committee, mostly composed of college-educated young men, who shared Che Guevara's assumption that a small group of militants could bring about significant change and foster revolutionary conditions.

Not surprisingly, one of the most tangible long-term effects of the Young Lords' political practice was the ways in which it enabled Puerto Rican upward mobility and greater participation in New York's mainstream institutions and mass media structures. As Guzmán summed up, "Ask any Latino professional in Nueva York who advanced in government or the corporate world between, say, 1969 and 1984, and you'll be told they owe part of their opportunity to the sea change of perception that Young Lords inspired."[97] Similarly, not a few Young Lords went on to careers inside the legal system and mass media as producers, radio personalities, judges, organizers, nonprofit directors and/or lawyers. For instance, Felipe Luciano was a radio personality on Fox 5 and WLIB radio. At present, Yoruba Guzmán is a newscaster for WCBS/Channel 2, Juan González is a *Daily News* columnist and co-host of the show *Democracy Now!* and Iris Morales is a lawyer and filmmaker.

In the end, the Lords did not bring liberation to Puerto Rico or Puerto Ricans in the United States in the conventionally sovereign terms they envisioned. Their "look of sovereignty" paradoxically exposed the limits of style, of nationalist Puerto Rican politics, and of sovereign discourse itself in a context of global economic restructuring and enduring colonial power relations. Yet regardless of the Young Lords' internal struggles, by becoming lords of style, they upended the premise of Puerto Rican identity as inherently low, passive, and disposable and displaced the stigmatizing shame of racialization and colonialism from their bodies to state and media structures. Furthermore, the Young Lords' trajectory, including its failures, freed U.S. Puerto Ricans to inhabit different and multiple political locations as New Yorkers, Blacks, Latinas, queer Latinos, and/or global citizens, among others. In the process, the Lords left behind a rich record of imaginative acts in challenging times. They also showed—and this is an important word— the possibility of thinking about politics as a daily practice of self-fashioning and transformative action rather than a utopian state somewhere beyond our reach.

Notes

1. Pablo Guzmán, "La Vida Pura: A Lord of the Barrio," in *The Puerto Rican Movement: Voices from the Diaspora*, ed. Andrés Torres and José E. Velázquez (Philadelphia: Temple University Press, 1998), 155–172, 165.

2. Quoted in Mickey Meléndez, *We Took the Streets* (New Brunswick, NJ: Rutgers University Press, 2005), 186.

3. For additional context for the Young Lords of Chicago, see Lilia Fernandez, *Brown in the Windy City: Mexicans and Puerto Ricans in Postwar Chicago* (Chicago: University of Chicago Press, 2012); Jakobi Williams, *From the Bullet to the Ballot: The Illinois Chapter of the Black Panther Party and Radical Coalition Politics in Chicago* (Chapel Hill: University of North Carolina Press, 2013); and Jeffrey O. G. Ogbar, "Puerto Rico en mi Corazón: The Young Lords, Black Power and Puerto Rican Nationalism in the U.S., 1966–1972," *Centro Journal* 18, no. 1 (2006): 148–169, 154.

4. Johanna Fernández, "The Young Lords and the Postwar City: Notes on the geographical and Structural Reconfigurations of Contemporary Urban Life," in *African American Urban History since World War II*, ed. Kenneth L. Kusmer and Joe W. Trotter (Chicago: University of Chicago Press, 2009): 60–82, 66.

5. Although beyond the scope of this essay, the differences between the trajectory of the Chicago, New York, and other branches of the Young Lords were at times substantial. These involved differences not only in membership composition and goals but also in relationships to city structures, level of support from the media, impact of counter-intelligence programs such as COINTELPRO, the presence of other radical organizations, and public discourse around key issues.

6. Meléndez, *We Took the Streets*, 136.

7. Pablo "Yoruba" Guzmán, "Before People Called Me a Spic, They Called Me a Nigger," in Young Lords Party and Michael Abramson, *Palante: Voices and Photographs of the Young Lords Party* (New York: McGraw-Hill, 2011), 73–83, 82–83.

8. Johanna Fernández, "Between Social Service Reform and Revolutionary Politics: The Young Lords, Late Sixties Radicalism, and Community Organizing in New York City," in *Freedom North: Black Freedom Struggles outside the South, 1940–1980*, ed. Jeanne Theoharris and Komozi Woodard (New York: Palgrave Macmillan 2003), 255–285, 261.

9. "Interview with Puerto Rican Historian Mervin Mendez: The Young Lords and Early Chicago Puerto Rican Gangs," January 27, 2002, http://www.uic.edu/orgs/kbc/latinkings/lkhistory.html.

10. Michel Foucault, interviewed by Paul Rabinow and Hubert Dreyfuss, "On the Genealogy of Ethics: An Overview of Work in Progress," in *The Foucault Reader*, ed. Paul Rabinow (New York: Pantheon Books, 1984), 334.

11. Jesus D. Rodríguez-Velasco, *Citizenship, Monarchical Sovereignty, and Chivalry in the Iberian Late Middle Ages* (Philadelphia: University of Pennsylvania Press, 2010).

12. For further discussion of the Real Great Society, including its relationship with the Young Lords, see Luis Aponte Parés, "Lessons from El Barrio—The East Harlem Real Great Society/Urban Planning Studio: A Puerto Rican Chapter in the Fight for Urban Self-Determination," *New Political Science* 20, no. 4 (1998): 399–420.

13. Maryse Conde, *Heremakhonon* (Boulder, CO: Three Continents, 1985).

14. Quoted in Ed Morales, *Living in Spanglish: The Search for Identity in Latino America* (New York: St. Martin's Press, 2002), 83.

15. Amílcar Antonio Barrero, *Vieques, the Navy, and Puerto Rican Politics* (Gainesville, FL: University Press of Florida, 2002).

16. Daphne A. Brooks, *Bodies in Dissent: Spectacular Performances of Race and Freedom, 1850–1910* (Durham, NC: Duke University Press, 2006), 5.

17. Che Ja, "Free the Hungry System," *Palante*, October 16, 1970, 10.

18. José Ramón Sánchez, *Boricua Power: A Political History of Puerto Ricans in the United States* (New York: New York University Press, 2007), 196.

19. Wendy Parkins, "Introduction: (Ad)dressing Citizens," in *Fashioning the Body Politic: Dress, Gender, Citizenship* (Oxford, U.K.: Berg, 2002), 1–17, 1.

20. Frances Negrón-Muntaner, *Boricua Pop: Puerto Ricans and the Latinization of American Culture* (New York: New York University Press, 2004).

21. Brooks, *Bodies in Dissent*, 3.

22. Quoted in Lilia Fernandez, *Brown in the Windy City: Mexicans and Puerto Ricans in Postwar Chicago* (Chicago University of Chicago Press, 2012), 173.

23. William Van Deburg, *New Day in Babylon* (Chicago: University of Chicago Press, 1992), 156.

24. Mick Farren, *The Black Leather Jacket* (Medford, NJ: Plexus Publishing, 2007).

25. Jane Rhodes, *Framing the Black Panthers: The Spectacular Rise of a Black Power Icon* (New York: New Press, 2007), 107.

26. Tom Wolfe, *Radical Chic and Mau Mauing the Flak Catchers* (New York: Picador 2009), 5.

27. "Militants Vow to Continue Protest at Harlem Church," *New York Times*, January 4, 1970, 61.

28. Nathan Joseph, *Uniforms and Nonuniforms: Communication through Clothing* (New York: Greenwood Press, 1986), 13.

29. Johanna Fernández, "Denise Oliver and the Young Lords Party: Stretching the Boundaries of Struggle," in *Want to Start a Revolution: Radical Black Women in the Black Freedom Struggle,* ed. Dayo F. Gore, Jeanne Theoharis, and Komozi Woodard (New York: New York University Press, 2009): 271–293, 271.

30. Joseph P. Fried, "East Harlem Youths Explain Garbage-Dumping Demonstration," *New York Times*, August 19, 1969, 86.

31. Phone interview, Iris Morales, April 28, 2015.

32. Nancy Morris, *Puerto Rico: Culture, Politics, and Identity* (Westport, CT: Praeger, 1995), 50–52.

33. Guzmán, "Before People Called Me a Spic, 75.

34. Meléndez, *We Took the Streets,* 94.

35. Phone Interview, Morales.

36. Fernández, "Between Social Service Reform and Revolutionary Politics," 264.

37. Meléndez, *We Took the Streets*, 81.

38. "Young Lords Take Over Church; Protest Death," *Jet*, November 26, 1970, 52.

39. Richie Perez, "Julio Roldán Center Opens," *Palante* 2, no. 14 (1970): 4.

40. Amy Abugo Ongiri, *Spectacular Blackness: The Cultural Politics of the Black Power Movement and the Search for a Black Aesthetics* (Charlottsville: University of Virginia Press, 2009), 42.

41. Alondra Nelson, *Body and Soul: The Black Panther Party and the Fight against Medical Discrimination* (Minneapolis: University of Minnesota Press, 2011), 62.

42. Rhodes, *Framing the Black Panthers,* 106.

43. Juan González, "Armed Struggle," *Palante* 3, no. 13 (1971): 8.

44. Ansel Herz, "The Young Lords: Examining Its Deficit of Democracy and Decline," https://libcom.org/library/young-lords-party-examining-its-deficit-democracy-decline. This article was originally located at: http:athomehesaturista.worpress.com.2009/09/01-the-young-lords-party-examining-its-deficit-of-democracy-and-decline/.

45. Meléndez, *We Took the Streets,* 182.

46. Joseph, *Uniforms and Nonuniforms,* 22.

47. José Yglesias, "Right On with the Young Lords," *New York Times,* June 7, 1970, 32.

48. Richie Perez, "A Young Lord Remembers," May 2000, http://libcom.org/library/young-lord-remembers.

49. Judy Klemesrud, "Young Women Find a Place in High Command of Young Lords," *New York Times,* November 11, 1970, 78.

50. Denise Oliver, *in Palante, Siempre Palante* (documentary), directed by Iris Morales, 1996.

51. Jennifer A. Nelson, "'Abortions under Community Control': Feminism, Nationalism, and the Politics of Representation among new York City's Young Lords," *Journal of Women's History* 13, no. 1 (2000): 158–180, 162.

52. Nelson, *Body and Soul,* 162.

53. Phone interview, Morales.

54. Ibid, 159.

55. Young Lords Party, "Palante," in *The Puerto Rican Experience: A Sociological Sourcebook,* ed. Francesco Cordasco and Eugene Bucchioni (Totowa, NJ: Rowman and Littlefield, 1973), 246–275, 272.

56. Young Lords Party and Abramson, *Palante: Voices and Photographs of the Young Lords Party* (New York: McGraw-Hill, 2011), 52.

57. Joseph P. Fried, "East Harlem Youths Explain Garbage-Dumping Demonstration," *New York Times,* August 19, 1969, 86.

58. Young Lords Party and Abramson, *Palante,* 261.

59. Wolfe, *Radical Chic,* 30.

60. "¿Young Lords o 'landlords'?: Ex miembros hablan de lo que hacen hoy," *El Diario-La Prensa,* March 4, 1989, 46.

61. Rhodes, *Framing the Black Panthers,* 63.

62. Guzmán, "Before People Called Me a Spic," 75.

63. Fernández, "Between Social Service Reform and Revolutionary Politics," 269.

64. Young Lords Party and Abramson, *Palante,* 246–275, 258.

65. Jack Lait and Lee Mortimer, *New York Confidential* (New York: Crown, 1948), 126.

66. Adriana Bosch, executive producer, *Latino Americans,* Public Broadcast System and WETA, 2013.

67. "Young Lords Block Street with Garbage," in *The Young Lords: A Reader,* ed. Darrel Enck-Wanzer (New York: New York University Press, 2010), 185.

68. Fernández, "Between Social Service Reform and Revolutionary Politics," 265.

69. Sánchez, *Boricua Power,* 2007.

70. Fried, "East Harlem Youths Explain Garbage-Dumping Demonstration," 86.

71. In the video *Palante, Siempre Palante* (1996), Felipe Luciano's describes taking the first building in this way: "We literally kidnapped the church."

72. Guzmán, "Before People Called Me a Spic," 82.

73. Richie Perez, "A Young Lord Remembers."

74. Fernández, "The Young Lords and the Postwar City."

75. For more details, see Alfonso A. Narvaez, "Young Lords Seize Lincoln Building: Offices Are Held for 12 Hours—Official Calls Points Valid," *New York Times*, July 15, 1970, 34, and Fernández, "The Young Lords and the Postwar City," 76.

76. Guzmán, "Before People Called Me a Spic," 78.

77. Sánchez, *Boricua Power: A Political History of Puerto Ricans in the United States*, 203.

78. Yglesias, "Right On . . ."

79. Herz, "The Young Lords Party."

80. For further discussion of the relationship between sovereignty and political modernity, see Yarimar Bonilla, *Non-Sovereign Futures: French Caribbean Politics in the Wake of Disenchantment* (Chicago: University of Chicago Press, 2015).

81. Young Lords Party, "13 Point Program and Platform," in *The Puerto Rican Experience: A Sociological Sourcebook*, ed. Francesco Cordasco and Eugene Bucchioni (Totowa, NJ: Littlefield, Adams, 1973), 272–275, 272.

82. Felipe Luciano, "On Revolutionary Nationalism," *Palante* 2, no. 2 (1970): 10.

83. "Beat is Gettin' Stronger," *Palante* 3, no. 4 (1971): 2.

84. Juan Gonzalez, "Armed Struggle," *Palante* 3, no. 13 (1971): 18.

85. Andrés Torres, "Introduction: Political Radicalism in the Diaspora—The Puerto Rican Experience," in *The Puerto Rican Movement: Voices from the Diaspora,* ed. Andrés Torres and José E. Velázquez (Philadelphia: Temple University Press, 1998), 1–22, 7.

86. "Resolutions of the Puerto Rican Revolutionary Workers Organization," in *The Young Lords: A Reader,* ed. Darrel Enck-Wanzer (New York: New York University Press, 2010), 235–244, 240.

87. Carmen Teresa Whalen, "The Young Lords in Philadelphia," in *The Puerto Rican Movement: Voices from the Diaspora,* ed. Andrés Torres and José E. Velázquez (Philadelphia: Temple University Press, 1998), 107–123.

88. *Palante, Siempre, Palante.*

89. Richie Perez, "A Young Lord Remembers."

90. For a fuller genealogy of sovereignty in U.S. Native American, Pacific Island, and territorial contexts, see Frances Negrón-Muntaner, ed., *Sovereign Acts* (University of Arizona Press, 2016), forthcoming.

91. *Palante, Siempre Palante.*

92. Ibid.

93. Phone interview, Morales.

94. "Editorial," in *The Young Lords: A Reader,* ed. Darrel Enck-Wanzer (New York: New York University Press, 2010), 234.

95. "Ibid., 234.

96. Fernandez, *Brown in the Windy City,* 202–203.

97. Guzmán, "La Vida Pura," 165.

PART 2

Disciplining the Body Politic: Domestic and Foreign Policy

Suicide as an Invocation of Shame in Mohsin Hamid's *The Reluctant Fundamentalist*

Renee Lee Gardner

> If today I heard that some American had committed suicide rather than live
> in disgrace, I would fully understand.
> —J. M. Coetzee, *Diary of a Bad Year*[1]

Mohsin Hamid's *The Reluctant Fundamentalist* is set in a café in Lahore, where
a Pakistani man named Changez tells an unidentified—and, in Anna Hartnell's
terms, "wholly silent"—American the story of his love affair with both the United
States and an American woman. Changez studied at Princeton, started work in
New York City shortly before September 2001, and returned to Pakistan shortly
after 9/11. He may or may not have become a terrorist in the years following the
attacks. The American with whom Changez speaks may or may not be a CIA as-
sassin. The novel may end in one or both of their deaths or neither may be in real
danger. The entire narrative is delivered in the second person, via Changez's side
of the conversation; thus everything we learn about the American, the United
States, and Changez's likely dead lover Erica is offered not merely via Changez's
consciousness but via his deliberate word choice. This structure subverts the empowered West–versus–subaltern East binary by lending voice to the othered (Pakistani) character while silencing the traditionally empowered (American) ones. For
this reason, *The Reluctant Fundamentalist* is an especially enlightening lens through
which to consider the American government's aggressive response to 9/11 as well
as its consequences. Of particular interest to this essay are the actions of wealthy
Manhattanite Erica, who makes literal the silencing of privilege by willingly embodying—and thus modeling—a shame that was missing from American consciousness during the reactive post-9/11 years and by responding to that shame
with politically purposeful self-abnegation.

By name and action, Erica is a clear representative of both pre- and post-9/11
America. The monikers Hamid uses in this novel make evident the high degree

to which his characters and structures are meant to be allegorical. For example, the valuation firm Changez works for, Underwood Samson, clearly represents the corporate nature of the United States ("Underwood Samson" and "United States" share initials). Erica is a personified version of *America*, and her deceased, "old world" boyfriend Chris brings to mind, in Anna Hartnell's terms, "not only Europe's Christian roots but also Christopher Columbus's encounter with the Americas."[2] Margaret Scanlan labels Erica "the best of America" and notes that she "shares with [Changez] her 'insider's world.'"[3] Thus we begin to see the non-militaristic side of America's reaction to 9/11. The nation portrayed via Erica is not the violent, retaliatory America we might expect but a shame-filled and apologetic America, longing for the past and punishing itself (herself) with and for that longing. By presenting this version of America as his primary national allegory, Changez offers a model for a way of being that is not predicated on dominance.

This is significant because in all national ideologies—and in most counter-ideologies—dominance is privileged over vulnerability. Despite our devotion to dominance, however, I argue that the cost of ignoring vulnerability is immense and the danger profound. Resistance to precarity has led to no end of historical disasters, not least the war-filled years since the attacks of September 11, 2001. Although the events of that day could have led to an admission of American complicity—an acknowledgment of political missteps and global overreaches—it was widely met instead with patriotic pride, righteous devotion to American exceptionalism, and a cultivated hunger for vengeance at any (outside) cost. In these terms, Erica's shame-induced self-harm becomes especially interesting because it reveals an alternative to America's widespread refusal to bear responsibility. My goal in delving into Erica's suicide is to unravel the prevailing logic that privileges dominance over submission by considering anew the long-held tradition of female self-abnegation. In *Precarious Life*, Judith Butler asks that we find an escape from the mandates of sovereignty dictated to us by virtue of our position as citizens. She suggests that when "national sovereignty is challenged," we should struggle not to sustain it but to "dislocat[e] from First World privilege": to "imagine a world in which [our] interdependency becomes acknowledged as the basis for global political community."[4] I contend that Erica performs such a "dislocation," willingly enacting the consequences of cultural and historical disgrace on her own body. She becomes the one aspect of America to which Changez remains loyal, even after his apparent fundamentalist shift. Thus in *The Reluctant Fundamentalist*, despite the tragedy of her death, Erica serves as the best possible hope for a peaceful "global political community."

In my exploration of Erica's suicide, I likewise make use of J. Halberstam's term "shadow feminism," which she argues exposes "the limits of a feminist theory that already presumes the form that agency must take."[5] Because of liberal feminism's influence over academic notions of power, critics tend to perceive women only as agents when they resist, challenge, or subvert authority, thereby pursuing actions translatable as "liberating" in nature. Halberstam calls for an approach to feminism by which we might come to see within such unliberated acts as "masochism, sacrifice, [and] self-subjugation," not "failed masculinity" but success in new terms.[6] Though her suicide is made almost invisible by the prescriptive nature of the rhetorics of liberation, Erica's subversion of those rhetorics is apparent when considered through the lens of shadow feminism, which exposes the potential of self-abnegation as it manifests in Erica's shame and in her refusal to adhere to the righteous doctrine of self-protection promoted by sovereignty. *The Reluctant Fundamentalist* functions as a commentary on American resistance to shame. In ending her existence as a wealthy, White, heterosexual woman who benefits from America's refusal to accept responsibility for its consequences, Erica models an unwillingness to live as such for others and for her government as well.

In *Diary of a Bad Year*, J. M. Coetzee's protagonist, J. C., claims provocatively that—in light of the wars in Afghanistan and Iraq—"if [he] heard that some American had committed suicide rather than live in disgrace, [he] would fully understand."[7] This suggests not only that we are all complicit in the political activities of our nation-state but that the shame of that complicity might well overpower our will—or even our right—to live. Erica is not murdered; she takes her own life, thereby demonstrating agency within a complex political system. I therefore read Erica's self-abnegation as demonstrative of both a profound level of agency and a profound potential for undermining the state even after her death. I want to be careful, however, not to suggest that Erica deserves to die for her existence as a privileged American citizen. Indeed, such a reading is in direct opposition to what I propose because it relegates Erica to the prolonged status of victim: if she *must* pay for the sins of neo-imperialism, then her self-sacrifice is not a choice; her shame is set on her and not willingly adopted. Yet shame is not set on her, is not, indeed, reflected in post-9/11 U.S. actions. Rather than reading Erica as an example that others might follow, then, I perceive her suicide as a radical and symbolic way out of the mandates of nationalistic aggression, an opening to other possibilities. Butler claims that our vulnerability to "death at the whim of another" is "reason for both fear and grief." But she goes on to ask if "the experiences of vulnerability and loss have to lead straightaway to military violence and retribution," insisting, "There are other passages. If we are interested in arresting cycles of violence to produce less violent outcomes, it is no doubt important to ask what, politically, might be made of grief besides a cry for war."[8] In Erica's death, we have found one such alternative path. The political ends Erica seeks are divested of notions of invincibility, are instead deeply rooted in the inherency of bodily susceptibility. Thus her reaction to shame works to subvert long-held narratives that insist on the necessity of war at any cost. In her suicide, Erica proves that other passages exist: that shame and complicity can be avoided and precarity embraced. And if other passages exist, we might abandon the dangerous default passages of unabashed warfare and aggression.

Scanlan contends that *The Reluctant Fundamentalist* "is a Rorschach inkblot test exposing our own interpretive strategies, histories, and desires."[9] And Hamid himself states in an interview with Deborah Solomon that the ambiguity of the novel's ending forces readers to face their own assumptions: that we experience the closing scene between Changez and the American via whatever prejudices we bring to our encounter with the characters.[10] Scanlan argues that—while most 9/11 novels merely reaffirm the East/West binary—*The Reluctant Fundamentalist* "internalize[s] a conflict in ordinary people." Such internalization can be seen via the private reactions its characters have to public events. Scanlan claims that the novel's "hesitations, qualifications, and complexities of lived experience become alternatives to the lethal polarities of public rhetoric," which it "challenge[s]" by "revis[ing] the West's vision of itself as a haven for the oppressed."[11] Although the focus of Scanlan's analysis is the complexity with which Hamid portrays Changez, her contentions apply to Erica, as well. Considered in such terms, Erica's death can be seen as politically generative precisely because—by shamefully self-abnegating in the face of America's retaliation—she rejects American self-aggrandizing and offers a way around the "lethal polarities" that dominate 9/11 discourse. Readers may not identify with Erica or even sympathize with her, but I argue that her suicide functions as an indictment, demanding recognition of what Paul Gilroy terms "postcolonial melancholia": that until the nations responsible for colonization face and grieve their own capacity for destruction, guilt and fear of reciprocity will linger on for those whose governments have taken the liberty of establishing a hierarchy of human worth on behalf of the world.[12] Readers don't have to condone Erica's means to grasp the dis-ease that fuels them.

Erica's acceptance of vulnerability manifests in traditionally feminine ways, making the distance between her approach and the masculine, militaristic approach of the United States government all the more clear. In the wake of 9/11, Erica is inconsolably struck by the grief of an old loss. As Changez attempts to win Erica's affection, she withdraws further into herself, succumbing to self-pity, nostalgia, and a destructive (literally self-wasting) eating disorder: all markers of shame. Kristiaan Versluys contends that the events of 9/11 exposed an emptiness that had been present in the lives of Americans for some time, and that it thus merely provided an outlet for—and was not the origin of—the cultural grief felt in the wake of those events.[13] Because of her allegorical status, Erica's unraveling serves as an exaggerated example of the weight of such grief: it offers insight into America's self-absorbed response to the terrorist attacks. As Scanlan notes, the United States breaks down in ways similar to the way Erica breaks down in the post-9/11 period: "The nation committed to progress is determined to 'look back.'"[14] This is the America not of outwardly focused vengeance but of navel-gazing self-doubt. In her self-abnegation, Erica absorbs fear and grief instead of propelling those emotions onto the Muslim (or merely dark-skinned) other, as do the bulk of Americans Changez encounters. Butler notes that "certain forms of grief [are] nationally recognized and amplified" while "other losses become un-thinkable and ungrievable." Butler clarifies this distinction, observing that "the names, images, and narratives of those the US has killed" are largely unknown to us, while America's "own losses are consecrated in public obituaries that consti-tute so many acts of nation-building."[15] Before her suicide, Erica is a wealthy, at-tractive, White American; thus her death is visible. Yet ironically, because of those same characteristics, we are conditioned to read her as a victim, especially in the context of 9/11. Perceiving her death instead as a clear and deliberate choice sub-verts the network of assumptions that sprung up in post-9/11 rhetoric, problema-tizing the clarity with which we see American deaths and making visible the deaths of non-Americans.

Ironically, Erica's shame-filled suicide manifests the same troubling violence that marks America's shame-resistant vengeance. Butler calls violence "a touch of the worst order, a way a primary human vulnerability to other humans is ex-posed in its most terrifying way, a way in which we are given over, without con-trol, to the will of another."[16] So what does it mean when violence is imposed on the self, when it is the will of the self that brings about such "primary human vul-nerability"? I argue that this manifestation of violence functions in simultaneous reaction to and against the state, which Butler claims, "shores itself up, seeks to reconstitute its imagined wholeness, but only at the price of denying its own vul-nerability, its dependency, its exposure."[17] Violence, therefore, is central to the dis-grace of sovereignty against which Erica works. Yet she performs it in ways that subvert the standard (sovereignty-mandated) outward trajectory of aggression. This violence is directed inward.

Because of the direction of self-abnegation's violence, we don't typically as-cribe power to its perpetrators. In The History of Sexuality, Michel Foucault uses the term bio-power to outline what he sees as "an explosion of numerous and di-verse techniques for achieving the subjugation of bodies and the control of popu-lations" marking the modern period.[18] He contends that "genocide is . . . the dream of modern powers . . . not because of a recent return of the ancient right to kill" but "because power is situated and exercised at the level of life."[19] Indeed, when individuals kill other individuals, we attribute to them a great deal of power. We make clear that they are responsible for death, and we rely on our judicial system to take their power away, which it often does by demonstrating its own power to take life. Yet because sovereignty does not extend to the citizen, we don't ascribe this level of power to individuals taking their own lives or, especially, to women doing so. Foucaultian logic reveals a potential nationalistic reason for such a dismissal: that suicide is threatening to an institution (a nation) that claims as its sovereign space the right to kill. Foucault writes that suicide was (and is) against the law because it was (and is) seen as "a way to usurp the power of death which the sovereign alone . . . had the right to exercise," contending that a "determination to die . . . was one of the first astonishments of a society in which political power had assigned itself the task of administering life."[20] We still see this "astonishment" at work in the reactions Erica garners from other characters, readers, and critics. But by perceiving suicide as connected to the state, we are able to see the danger such an action poses to the illusion of sovereignty and the reasons behind its dismissal as the desperate ends of an agentless being. In taking her own privileged life, and in garnering pity for her supposed powerlessness, Erica casts the countless lives taken by American military might into stark contrast. Through Erica, we see America's victims.

Thus we begin to see the motives underlying our dismissal of self-abnegation as weak and powerless: that if it is politically motivated, female suicide is so flagrantly rebellious as to constitute a "real and credible threat" (to borrow the language of the post-9/11 U.S. government) to national sovereignty. Such behavior effectively amounts to rejection of the cultural construction of bio-power, which works, according to Nealon and Giroux, to regulate behavior precisely because it "invent[s] a species or life-form lurking behind the acts of criminality: the delinquent, the monster, the sociopath, the pervert." Such citizens "may or may not have *done* anything illegal or transgressive, but their lives are nonetheless outside the slippery slope of biopolitical normativity," and thus they must be villainized.[21] I argue that Erica's actions position her outside of "normativity." Indeed, she conforms so exaggeratedly to demands for female submission that she fails to conform at all, thereby threatening the norms by pointing out their otherwise obscured fault lines. Nealon and Giroux claim that "because power (like life) is so ubiquitous that it's nearly impossible to localize, it's easiest to locate social power . . . where power clamps down on various forms of resistance."[22] Power is most apparent, they suggest, when it is "brought to light against 'resistant' acts or practices that power wants to eradicate."[23] In the illogic of Erica's suicide, we are positioned to see the danger of sovereignty as well as a potential way to overcome it.

The potential power of the submissive side of America represented by Erica becomes especially apparent when considered alongside Hamid's second U.S. allegory: Underwood Samson (U.S.), the valuation firm for which Changez works, whose subscription to national notions of capitalistic dominance is far more destructive than Erica's naval-gazing nostalgia. Scanlan argues that "at first Changez is too pleased to have made it through the firm's rigorous selection and training process to criticize its aims," but that as time goes on he begins to notice that "the firm is a powerful force, embodying a fundamentalist conviction in American domination of world markets."[24] Considering the aggression inherent to western military might, it makes sense that, as Scanlan points out, "Underwood Samson is 'not nostalgic whatsoever'"; that, unlike Erica, it "remains focused on productivity, fundamentals, 'the task of shaping the future with little regard for the past.'"[25] Changez's career with Underwood Samson—especially in the context of the retaliatory war in Afghanistan that develops during his short tenure at the firm—exposes the unapologetically dangerous side of American culture, which makes visible the symbolic potential of Erica's suicide.

Indeed, especially with a corporate (masculine) foil like Underwood Samson, it is easy for readers to see the nostalgic and vulnerable side of America's national consciousness manifest in a female character. Erica punishes herself in the decisive act of suicide in response to a perceived wrongdoing (a terrorist attack), but she does so by wracking herself with grief for events beyond her control (the death of her lover as well as those killed in the towers), by denying herself sustenance (she starves herself in keeping with cultural norms that govern women and weight), and by refusing to let go of the single-minded suffering through which she ultimately destroys herself. Because she self-abnegates in such feminized terms, it is easy to read Erica as a victim. Ironically, however, her allegorical status problematizes our ability to do so. Erica represents a nation that is deeply averse to weakness even as she herself embraces it. Her self-abnegation can thus be read as national abnegation as well. Although her suicide has no literal impact on the imperialistic decisions her government makes on her behalf, her death resists complicity in those decisions and may thus be read as in keeping with the kind of deliberate nobility about which Coetzee's *Diary of a Bad Year* protagonist theorizes. Changez says, "The United States was supposed to be the place that could not be attacked, where life was safe from violence."[26] Erica's power as an allegorical figure is in her ability to demonstrate—and even to perform—a manner of vulnerability that America at large fervently resists.

John Milbank explores that vulnerability—and America's resistance to it—asking why we grieve certain deaths (the people who died in the towers) and not others (the deaths our retaliation brought about). First, Milbank argues that we are all invested in the idea that sovereign nations have the right to take life judiciously but individuals don't. He writes: "Killing on this scale is something only the state is supposed to be capable of"; thus for Erica to kill herself is to attack the sovereign structure of the state itself.[27] Second, like Versluys, Milbank argues that our grief-stricken response served as a justification to act on certain already present desires.[28] He discusses use of the term "liberty"—which, although it is meant to convey agency, amounts to national and not personal power—claiming that globalization puts national ideas of liberty in danger and that, as a consequence, nations require an enemy if citizens are to stay locally (nationally) loyal. Tracing America's quest for such an enemy, Milbank asserts that the new American empire is even more dangerous than past empires in that we have found in the "war against terror" a long-term adversary.[29] This is the dangerous America to which Erica offers contrast and against which her suicide arguably leads Changez to retaliate.

Milbank goes on to expose a political similarity between terrorism and our reaction to it, saying that the war against terror functions as "an effort to resolve the crisis of state sovereignty in the face of globalization." Yet he likewise suggests that, because "both the Western and the different Islamic state forms face the same crisis," the war on terror shares similar means and ends to terror itself, as both "terrorism and counterterrorism . . . are attempts to resolve this crisis."[30] Erica's obsession with the self and her paradoxical self-destruction undermine both the shared and the contradictory elements of terrorism and counterterrorism. She refuses to perpetuate the illusion of an enemy—rejecting a foundational tenet of both terrorism and counterterrorism—but in her willing self-abnegation, she forces America into the position of vulnerability exhibited by suicide bombers. She makes no bid for power—nationalistic or otherwise—and thus she refuses to perpetuate the demands for sovereignty exhibited by both the perpetrators of 9/11 and the retaliatory U.S. government.

In the pre-9/11 period, however, Hamid's allegorical references to the United States remain fairly undifferentiated; far from being subversive, Erica's state of *being* is submissive in state-sanctioned ways. Changez first meets Erica on holiday in Greece, where he learns that "she hated to be alone . . . .She attracted people to her; she had presence, an uncommon *magnetism* . . . . a naturalist would likely have compared her to a lioness: strong, sleek, and invariably surrounded by her pride."[31] The sexuality of this metaphor is important, as Erica tempts Changez in ways not dissimilar to those exhibited by Underwood Samson. Before their relationship turns romantic, Changez sees Erica almost naked.[32] The significance of this moment is given context when Changez notes that "being in Pakistan heightens one's sensitivity to the sight of a woman's body."[33] It is precisely the American quality of immodesty that Changez picks up on in this encounter with Erica: her willingness to submit to his gaze and the gaze of others on the beach that day. Before 9/11, then, her submission is in keeping with cultural expectations regarding women. In her pre-9/11 submissiveness, Erica manifests no cultural shame.

Indeed, in her pre-attacks state of being—which is a product of class- and nation-based privilege as it interacts with a feminine willingness to submit—Erica seduces Changez easily. Her "magnetism" proves captivating in Greece, but it is not until they return to the United States that Changez begins to understand how different Erica's reality is from his, and how secure she can be from certain vulnerabilities if she wants to be. Far from finding it offputting, however, he is transfixed by Erica's family's stature. Of a dinner they share with Erica's parents at their Upper-East-Side apartment, Changez says, "Erica received me with a smile; her tanned skin seemed to glow with health. I had forgotten how stunning she was," observing too that in her "short Mighty Mouse T-shirt" she "did not appear to have been quite as preoccupied with issues of dress selection as I had been."[34] While Changez has agonized over what to wear, Erica's privileged position carries with it a degree of assuredness. In observing this, Changez's attraction deepens—letting us know that before 9/11 he is drawn to privilege—but his awareness of the significance of Erica's wealth creates tension. As Erica leads Changez about the city in the month before the attacks, he notes: "I realized I was being ushered into an insider's world . . . to which I would otherwise have had no access."[35] In her sovereignty-claiming state of being, Erica's openness to Changez functions as an invitation to the touted pinnacle of the American dream, which Changez gladly accepts.

Even before the fall of the towers, however, Erica is unwell. In this way, her post-9/11 abnegation is in keeping with Versluys's observation that the grief most Americans felt over the events of that day was a product of already present sorrow. For Erica, however, even that sorrow is linked to the nation-state. Changez recalls a moment from their early interactions when he saw in Erica's eyes "something *broken* . . . like a tiny crack in a diamond that becomes visible only when viewed through a magnifying lens." So, too, Changez repeatedly notices that Erica is "introspective," prone to "withdraw, to recede a half-step inside herself."[36] This "broken[ness]" comes from grief. Erica's boyfriend Chris—whose death from cancer resulted in Erica's hospitalization for, among other things, an eating disorder a year before she met Changez—is central to her "rece[ssion]" and thus to this symbol of America's nostalgic longing for the past. Describing Chris, Erica fondly recalls, "His nurses had been charmed by him: he was a good-looking boy with . . . an *Old World* appeal."[37] As critics note, Chris embodies a Christopher Columbus–styled America. This makes Erica's comparison of Changez's homesickness to her longing for Chris all the more interesting; she says, "I kind of miss home, too . . . except my home was a guy with long, skinny fingers."[38] In implicitly likening Pakistan to America, Erica indicates that there's a degree to which she is already positioned to mourn her own nation.

Erica gives us details of this grief, noting on a picnic that when Chris died she "stopped talking to people. I stopped eating . . . . They told me not to think about it so much and put me on medication."[39] For Changez, this "evoked . . . an almost familial tenderness . . . . I offered her my arm and she smiled as she accepted it . . . . We had never before remained in contact for such a prolonged period . . . her body was so strong and yet belonged to someone so wounded."[40] In this passage, we see not only the degree to which Erica has already begun the process of self-destruction but the fact that the physical intimacy Changez shares with her is tied up in that destruction via her past with Chris. It thus becomes evident that—though Changez struggles to identify with what we might call a "new world" America—the nation's present cannot be separated from its "old world" history. Even in the days before 9/11, Erica (America) is influenced as much by her (its) past as by the present. Thus, instead of claiming her position of privilege in the aftermath of America's history, she self-abnegates in response to it, yielding to the historical pain of her nation by shifting her shameful gaze inward.

Erica's self-abnegation manifests only its internal potential—she is positioned to undermine narratives of sovereignty only by refusing to participate in them—until Changez begins to read her as an American allegory and until he begins to see her as worthy of grief. Once he attaches both personal and political meaning to her, however, Erica's process of self-abnegation stands to undermine his devotion to the United States. In what is arguably the novel's most controversial passage, Changez recounts for the American his initial experience of the 9/11 attacks, which he learned about via a television in a hotel room in Manila. He recalls: "I turned on the television and . . . watch[ed as] . . . the twin towers of New York's World Trade Center collapsed. And then I *smiled*. Yes, despicable as it may sound, my initial reaction was to be remarkably pleased."[41] The coldness of his response causes Changez anxiety, as does his inability to feel sadness until—observing his colleagues' concern for their family members—he remembers that Erica is in New York. He notes: "I was almost relieved to be worried for her and unable to sleep; this allowed me to share in the anxiety of my colleagues and ignore for a time my initial sense of pleasure."[42] Here we see that Erica is Changez's path to grief. Via his position as a Pakistani, he cannot perceive America as a victim. Yet because of Erica's simultaneously privileged and feminized state of being, it is easy to perceive her as such.

Because she is not a victim of the attacks, Changez's sympathy is warranted only when Erica becomes a victim of her own willingness to self-destruct. Nevertheless, in terms of Butler's (and Milbank's) contrast between grievable and ungrievable beings, Erica fits profoundly in the former category, even though she has not been directly injured by the attacks. Moreover, she is perceived as grievable not just to her insider group of Americans but to her Pakistani suitor as well. In this way—though entirely unharmed—Erica is positioned as the novel's primary victim of terrorism. This is in keeping with Susan Faludi's finding: that instead of working to understand the complexities of 9/11, Americans responded with fear, reverting to 1950s gender dynamics wherein men are seen as heroes and women as victims in need of rescuing.[43] This is ironic in that the majority of that day's casualties were men and the attacks were perpetrated in our commercial and governmental centers. At first glance, this indicates that in *The Reluctant Fundamentalist* Hamid perpetuates perceptions of female victimization. I argue, however, that the readiness of this reading is a result of liberal feminism's assumptions about women and power. When considered instead in terms of shadow feminism, we begin to see the way in which Erica's shame breaks down this construct. Although he is ostracized as he travels back to America after 9/11, Changez's connection to Erica intensifies his sense of connection to the country: her grievability functions at first to unite Changez with America. Only when she meets it with shame does Erica's privilege undermine Changez's devotion to the United States, disrupting assumptions about both privilege and female victimhood.

In the weeks following 9/11, Erica shifts from demonstrative pseudo-victim to self-destructive agent.[44] Observing this process, Changez notes that Erica is becoming "utterly detached . . . Her eyes [are] turned inward."[45] What her abnegation models, then, is that the biggest danger to America is not terrorists, or even loss, but its devotion to sovereignty. Significantly, this is Erica's state when Changez first touches her intimately. Erica gets a bruise while practicing tae kwon do, and, looking at the tender spot of the bruise itself, Changez recalls: "Without thinking, I extended my hand. Then I hesitated. She returned my gaze watchfully, but her expression did not change, so I touched her, placing my fingers on her bruise. She rested her hand on the back of her head as I traced the line of her ribs."[46] Here we see Erica begin to submit to vulnerability, to open up to being touched where she has already been hurt. That night, Changez tries to parlay the intimacy of the bruise-touch into a sexual encounter: Erica "did not respond; she did not resist; she merely acceded as I undressed her . . . she was silent and unmoving . . . I found it difficult to enter her."[47] Hartnell says that this scene exposes the "impenetrable" aspect of the Erica/America allegory, but I find that the passivity with which Erica yields to Changez complicates the rigidity of a word like "impenetrable." She is not "aroused," but neither does she "resist." Instead, she is "silent and unmoving," neither shameful nor pursuant. I read this scene as an early manifestation of Erica's post-9/11 subjugation. In allowing Changez access to her body, the symbolic victim of terror attacks—the wealthy, White symbol of female vulnerability—begins a process of self-exposure that will end in her death. She does so voluntarily, and she does so literally at the hands of a brown-skinned man. And doing so is political. Shortly after this encounter, Changez watches the start of America's bombing of Afghanistan.[48] In this context, Erica's submission to Changez stands in stark opposition to the aggression of American military might.

Erica refuses the assumption that *life itself* is irrefutably and invariably precious, that it must be valued above all else. Giorgio Agamben offers a frame for such a refusal by critically deconstructing the elements of what we broadly refer to as *life*, using the Aristotelian binary of *zoē* and *bios*. Agamben describes *zoē* as "the simple fact of living common to all living beings" and *bios* as "the form or way of living proper to an individual or a group."[49] In Aristotelian terms, the life that we commonly consider an integrated reality is actually an amalgam of our biological or cellular existences (our *zoē*) and our political or cultural existences (our *bios*). Ironically, because of narratives of sovereignty, we are led to believe that our real lives are our bodily presences (our *zoē*) and that nothing should impinge on our pursuit of physical continuation. Though *bios* includes citizenship and sovereignty, *zoē* is still privileged, which is evident by the fact that sacrifice of it is seen as abhorrent. If instead we define life in terms of the complex relationship between *bios* and *zoē*—and we allow that we are constituted by both constructs—those same sacrifices become rich with generative meaning. When we assume that self-abnegating women are powerless, we read their self-destruction as evidence that they have failed to appropriately live. Agamben's distinction allows us to complicate this view of suicide as the ultimate surrender of power and agency. Nealon and Giroux further this discourse, discussing German philosopher Theodor Adorno, who contends that life "has to be animated, configured, or deployed within a context, given a particular sense, for it to live."[50] By considering *bios* as interactive with—but separate from—*zoē*, we see that the choice to sacrifice the latter for the former might be read as the process of performing just such an "animation": of "configur[ing]" the life of a woman-citizen within a context whose meaning we might be able to perceive. Suicide can thus be seen as a way of reconfiguring the political implications of *bios* and not simply as eliminating *zoē*. Without such a lens, however, *lifelessness* is dismissed as *powerlessness*.

Erica deliberately destroys *zoē* by sacrificing *bios*. Her unbeing is clearly historically grounded: it is tied intimately to her privilege and to the grief of 9/11. What Erica resists when she rejects life, then, is arguably sovereignty itself. Erica is a sovereign subject, but she refuses that reality by willingly modeling the forced denial of sovereignty experienced by the victims of America's post-9/11 retaliation. In *Frames of War*, Butler argues that "a sovereign position not only denies its own constitutive injurability but tries to relocate injurability in the other."[51] While the United States government "relocate[d] injurability" onto Afghani (and later Iraqi) citizens, Erica makes no attempt to "deny [her] own . . . injurability" or to refuse responsibility for the travesty of America's retaliation. Butler goes on to insist that violence is usually "a way of relocating the capacity to be violated (always) elsewhere" because "it produces the appearance that the subject who enacts violence is impermeable to violence."[52] In refusing to "relocate" the violence she perpetrates, Erica demonstrably rejects the illusion of personal sovereignty, and in that rejection she destroys a *bios* she cannot abide. In killing herself, Erica ceases to be an American. She stops being privileged by happenstance of birth. In her self-abnegation, she refuses the shame of complicity.

Even before her death, Erica's self-abnegation drastically undermines Changez's devotion to America. When Changez invites her to his apartment again—and Erica "acquiesce[s]"—Changez observes that she is "vanishing before [his] eyes."[53] And of their second sexual encounter, Changez notes that Erica doesn't "move her lips or shut her eyes." As with their first time together, she submits but her compliance is not fed by desire. She receives and accepts his passion, but she does not participate in it. Because she does not "shut her eyes," Changez "shut[s] them for her," after which he asks, "Are you missing Chris?" When she admits that she is, Changez tells her, "Then pretend . . . pretend I am him," and he later recalls: "In darkness and in silence, we did."[54] His use of the word "we" makes clear that Erica is not the only one pretending. In terms of *The Reluctant Fundamentalist*'s system of allegories, this is the most concrete example of Changez's attempts to assimilate into American culture.

In his role as Chris, Changez understands Erica's vulnerability anew. He recalls that "the entrance between her legs was wet and dilated, but was at the same time oddly rigid," such that it lent the encounter "a violent undertone." Changez thinks Erica is bleeding, but he recalls: "When I reached down to ascertain with my fingers whether it was her time of the month, I found them unstained." Finally, Erica "shuddered . . . grievously, almost mortally; her shuddering called forth [Changez's] own."[55] Although she experiences pleasure in this scene, Changez is aware of the depth of her surrender. He carries this awareness with him in the months to follow, and it impacts his relationship with the United States. Changez realizes that Erica is "disappearing into a powerful *nostalgia*, one from which only she could choose whether or not to return."[56] His allowance that Erica is empowered to "choose" even in this compromised state is evidence of his newfound understanding of the agency driving her vulnerability. In one of the novel's most overtly didactic passages—occurring in the aftermath of Erica's deterioration—Changez "wonder[s] how it was that America was able to wreak such havoc in the world—orchestrating an entire war in Afghanistan, say, and legitimizing through its actions the invasion of weaker states by more powerful ones . . . with so few apparent consequences at home."[57] And he later tells the American in Lahore, "As a society, you were unwilling to reflect upon the shared pain that united you with those who attacked you."[58] Erica functions as an embodiment of America that is willing to suffer such "consequences"—willing to share in the shame of the attacks of September 11—and her willingness makes the resistant side of America all the more visible to an increasingly dismayed Changez.

Suicide as an Invocation of Shame in Hamid   *121*

Weeks after Changez visits Erica in a mental institution—which is the last time he sees her—he learns that she has disappeared. A nurse tells him that they never found her body but "her clothes had been found on a rocky bluff overlooking the Hudson, neatly folded in a pile."[59] She is presumed to be dead and to have taken her own life in the heightened vulnerability of nudity. Changez leaves America for good shortly after Erica's disappearance. In his outsider status, Changez seems to understand the complexity of Erica's surrender. He attempts to honor it as he departs the United States by leaving his "jacket on the curb as a sort of offering, [a] last gesture before returning to Pakistan, a wish of warmth for Erica—not in the way one leaves flowers for the dead, but rather as one twirls rupees above the living." Although Changez has been affected by Erica's shame, however, America at large is still deeply invested in dominance and sovereignty, which is disturbingly visible in this scene. Changez recalls that, after leaving the jacket as a gesture, he "saw that [he] had caused a security alert, and [he] shook [his] head in exasperation."[60] Like Erica's self-sacrifice, Changez's gesture is misread. Both of these misreadings have potentially dangerous consequences for America. Reading the actions of Changez as potentially terroristic leads to the possibility that Changez becomes—by the novel's end—a "reluctant fundamentalist." And if we dismiss Erica's suicide as a product of mental illness, the generative possibilities of her sacrifice are rendered invisible. Erica's death functions as an overt rejection of U.S. demands for self-protection at any external cost: a shame-based unwillingness to share complicity in the actions of her nation-state. And her suicide has the potential for significant external ramifications: she undermines Changez's loyalty to America such that her death triggers his abandonment of it and possibly his active resistance to it. Thus, Erica provides a model for the acceptance of shame that destabilizes post-9/11 wartime America. The degree to which America mimics that acceptance is likely to determine whether such destabilization allows the nation to flourish or condemns it to eventual destruction.

Notes

1. J. M. Coetzee, *Diary of a Bad Year* (New York: Penguin Group, 2007), 43.

2. Anna Hartnell, "Moving through America: Race, Place and Resistance in Mohsin Hamid's *The Reluctant Fundamentalist*," *Journal of Postcolonial Writing* 46, no.3–4 (2010): 343.

3. Margaret Scanlan, "Migrating from Terror: The Postcolonial Novel after September 11," *Journal of Postcolonial Writing* 46, no. 3–4 (2010): 274.

4. Judith Butler, *Precarious Life: The Powers of Mourning and Violence* (Brooklyn, NY: Verso, 2004).

5. J. Halberstam, *The Queer Art of Failure* (Durham, NC: Duke University Press, 2011), 6.

6. Ibid., 4.

7. Coetzee, *Diary of a Bad Year*, 43.

8. Ibid., xii.

9. Ibid., 277.

10. Deborah Solomon, "The Stranger: Interview with Mohsin Hamid," *New York Times Magazine*, April 15, 2007, 16.

11. Ibid., 266–267.

12. Paul Gilroy, *Postcolonial Melancholia* (New York: Columbia University Press, 2006).

13. Kristiaan Versluys, *Out of the Blue: Fiction and September 11th* (New York: Columbia University Press, 2009).

14. Ibid., 117.

15. Ibid., xiv.

16. Ibid., 28–29.

17. Ibid., 41.

18. Michel Foucault, *The History of Sexuality: Volume 1: An Introduction* (New York: Vintage Books, 1990), 140.

19. Ibid., 137.

20. Ibid., 138–139.

21. Jeffrey Nealon and Susan Searls Giroux, "Life," in *The Theory Toolbox: Critical Concepts for the Humanities, Arts, and Social Sciences*, 2nd ed. (Lanham, MD: Rowman and Littlefield, 2012), 216.

22. Ibid.

23. Ibid., 218.

24. Ibid., 275.

25. Ibid., 276.

26. Mohsin Hamid, *The Reluctant Fundamentalist* (Orlando, FL: Harcourt, 2007), 39.

27. John Milbank, "Sovereignty, Empire, Capital, and Terror," in "Dissent from the Homeland: Essays after September 11," special issue, *South Atlantic Quarterly* 101, no. 2 (2002): 306.

28. These include "a continuous war against 'terrorists' everywhere; a policing of world markets to ensure that free-market exchange processes are not exploited by the enemies of capitalism [and] an opportunity to reinscribe state sovereignty" (Ibid.).

29. Milbank's work traces America's pursuit of an enemy via such historical occasions as Western expansion, World War II, and the second Red Scare (Ibid., 309–310).

30. Ibid., 314–315.

31. Ibid., 21–22.

32. Ibid., 24.

33. Changez goes on to recount how "one's rules of propriety make one *thirst* for the improper . . . once sensitized in this manner, one numbs only slowly, if at all; I had by the summer of my trip to Greece spent four years in America already . . . but still I remained acutely aware of visible female skin" (p. 26).

34. Similarly, in a scene at his boss's house in the Hamptons, Changez notes that "Jim's house was so splendid, I thought even [Erica] might be impressed. And that, as you will come to understand, is saying a great deal" (pp. 44, 50).

35. Ibid., 56.

36. Ibid., 52.

37. Ibid., 27.

38. Ibid., 28.

39. Ibid., 59.

40. Ibid., 60.

41. Ibid., 72.

42. Ibid., 74.

43. Susan Faludi, *The Terror Dream: Myth and Misogyny in an Insecure America* (New York: Picador, 2008), 5.

44. In their first post-9/11 encounter, Changez notes that Erica's "lips were pale, as though she had not slept—or perhaps had been crying," and she admits: "I keep thinking about Chris . . . I don't know why. Most nights I have to take something to help me rest. It's kind of like I've been thrown back a year . . . . I feel haunted" (p. 80).

45. Ibid., 86.

46. Ibid., 89.

47. Ibid., 90.

48. Ibid., 99.

49. Giorgio Agamben, *Homo Sacer: Sovereign Power and Bare Life*, trans. Daniel Heller-Roazen (Stanford: Stanford University Press, 1998), 1.

50. Ibid., 213.

51. Judith Butler, *Frames of War: When Is Life Grievable?* (Brooklyn, NY: Verso, 2009), 178.

52. Ibid.

53. Ibid., 104.

54. Ibid., 105.

55. Ibid., 105–106.

56. Ibid., 113.

57. Ibid., 131.

58. Ibid., 168.

59. Ibid., 163.

60. Ibid., 168.

SIX

Fat, Shame, and the Disciplining Practices of Health Expertise

Meghan Griffin

Medicalization and Public Health

To describe the social situation surrounding food, weight, and health in the United States today is to describe, at least in part, the relation of medical science to the individual and the body. The acts associated with selecting, preparing, and consuming food are no longer primarily centered on energy replenishment, but have become problematized spaces for the exercise of social and political control through shame-centered surveillance and practices of public policing. In the 1960s, Michel Foucault analyzed the discourse shaping doctor-patient relationships and the social structures supporting and informing medical practice. Focusing on shifts in patient care during the late eighteenth century, he defined the workings of the physician's gaze and the move of the "clinic" into the population through medical education and home-based care. This essay builds on Foucault's work to consider another turn—the *dispersion* of medicine itself into cultural interactions between citizens through shame-producing surveillance of one's own body and criticism of the bodies of others. It draws attention to some of the forces shaping Americans' relation to food, eating, and health and the ways that health expertise circulates as a disciplining practice implemented through shame.

In *The Birth of the Clinic*, Foucault outlines the emergence of clinical practice and its shift in the medicalization and treatment of populations in a series of moves progressing from the presentation of disease as a temporary interruption in an otherwise healthy and whole person toward a notion of disease as ever present, ever looming, and in need of constant monitoring. Doctor and patient engaged in "ever-greater proximity, bound together, the doctor by an ever-more attentive, more insistent, more penetrating gaze, the patient by all the silent, irreplaceable qualities that, in him, betray—that is, reveal and conceal—the clearly ordered forms of the disease."[1] Because the gaze focused on disorder of the physical systems requiring a doctor's specialized knowledge, "the capacity to talk sensibly about disease shifted from the patient to the doctor."[2] Diseases, not wholly embodied patients, became the object of study and treatment. One result of this shifting gaze is the broadening of what "disease" means. The American preventive medical system now focuses on long-term care, lifestyle medicine, and staving off illness. Historically, medicine acted when disease was acute, when life was threatened, and when care was a necessary condition of survival. Foucault names this a luxury of modern civilization: "Before the advent of civilization, people had only the simplest, most necessary diseases."[3] In contrast, medicalization allows for "the unwarranted transformation of a broad range of bodily, psychic, and social experiences into problems of medicine or of medical definition."[4] This aspect of the medical gaze problematizes previously benign spaces of health, and "health seems to diminish by degrees" as spaces for health intervention flourish.[5]

As the focus of medicine grows to include previously benign aspects of the body and its functions, doctors become increasingly vigilant regarding the body's signs and symptoms. Social and political structures organize to support this work. During the period that the clinic flourished, Foucault also traced the beginnings of epidemiology and the reporting techniques for characterizing and naming instances and outbreaks as epidemics. Provincial doctors operating in clinics began to catalogue and report symptoms and diagnoses to a central authority for tracking. This had very clear benefits for managing epidemics: the ability to mobilize support to a specific area, the ability to name the malady and share information across locations, the ability to ascertain specific conditions that may support or discourage outbreaks. What resulted, though, was the looming prospect of the epidemic and the structures that watch carefully to monitor contagion. Any individual illness now holds the potential of the epidemic and is always already conceived as a potential threat to the population at large. Mobilizing the science of epidemiology means that medicine travels outside the confines of the doctor-patient relationship and is now a policing social force to describe "how one should feed and dress oneself, how to avoid illness, and how to prevent or cure prevailing diseases."[6] The medical gaze thus has moved toward an open space, a totality, in the monitoring and reporting of signs and symptoms.

Through the lens of epidemiology, a doctor sees not "the patient in his singularity, but a collective consciousness, with all the information that intersects in it, growing in a complex, ever-proliferating way until it finally achieves the dimensions of a history, a geography, a state."[7] This collective consciousness allows medical space to pervade social space and daily lived experience. The result is "a generalized presence of doctors whose intersecting gazes form a network and exercise at every point in space, and at every moment in time, a constant, mobile, differentiated supervision."[8] We see this medicalization enacted by Dr. Thomas Farley, Commissioner of the New York City Department of Health and Mental Hygiene, describing his interest in obesity and his undifferentiated, amorphous patient population. In the summer 2012 HBO documentary *The Weight of the Nation*, Farley says, "I've been interested in obesity for a long time. But now I'm responsible for a city of 8.3 million people. Every one of those people I consider to be my patient as a doctor."[9] Whether any individual wants to be perceived as Farley's patient, whether one wants to come to him for care, Farley conceives of himself as everyone's doctor, responsible for every person's health. Epidemiology has changed the practitioner's role, the treatment of individual illness as contagion potential, and the apparatus of the state for monitoring and correcting related living practices. We see this turn in the treatment of fat as disease (one of the modern conveniences of a generally healthy population), in the concurrent treatment of obesity as an epidemic couched in the language of contagion, and in the public health focus on eating and activity.

Foucault's history of the clinic and his attention to the medical gaze, the medicalization of the population, and the turn to health as a civic duty deeply inform the modern concern with fat, health, and the population. Foucault describes a time in which "each individual must be alerted; every citizen must be informed of what medical knowledge is necessary and possible."[10] With a population educated in nutrition, disease prevention, and care the "privileged relation between medicine and health involved the possibility of being one's own physician."[11] Foucault notes this turn in vaccinations, where the family becomes responsible for both individual care and the social body, engendering a "'private' ethic of good health as the reciprocal duty of parents and children to the social, state, medical, policing bodies."[12] The "medicalized and medicalizing family" maintains a central role in Foucault's analysis as a unit capable of operating as a temporary clinic, resulting in what he calls a "medical staffing of the population" based on a civic duty for the larger public's health.[13] We see this now in the duty of each person to work toward a "normal" body weight. The BBC, for example, launched a website in July 2012 that asks the question, "Where are you on the global fat scale?" and calls on the individual to place her weight as an individual person, a member of her nation, and an inhabitant of earth under consideration. When I entered my body weight, I learned that "If everyone in the world had the same BMI as you, it would add 149,147,207 tonnes to the total weight of the world's population."[14] I was also informed that while I have a BMI higher than 85% of the women in my country, I also have a BMI higher than 99% of the women aged 30 to 44 in the world.[15] None of this information was immediately relevant to my own health, but it served as a warning of what the global consequences would be if everyone were like me. A fat me makes for a fatter America and a fatter world. These statistics demonstrate the undesirability and shame I ought to feel about my body and my weight.

Whereas Foucault considered the training and educating of families and staffing of clinicians within communities, I posit that we now face a different type of staffing of the population. Rather than individually trained citizens mobilized for self-care and care of the family for the good of the larger population, we face now individually trained citizens, supported by the rhetoric of medical understandings of health, driven to action by social programs and public policy and energized by fear of epidemics of contagion to shame one another (not just oneself or one's family) as a way to increase compliance with medical health norms. In this economy of surveillance, anyone with the appearance of fitness, leanness, and health is turned into a guru, essentially endowed with medical knowledge concerning health and healthy behaviors, and socially licensed to correct others through the pervasive medical message that conflates body size with health and conflates healthy body size with healthy behaviors. The thin person who enters her data on the "Where are you on the global fat scale?" website will see that her body weight amplified to global proportions would reduce the collective weight of the world.

What initially mobilized the population for self-care has developed into a social hierarchy based on adherence to medical priorities and interpretations of signs. Thin people, with the social capital endowed by medical constructions of health in relation to fatness, have become American cultural symbols of health, endowed with an ethos regarding health and nutrition unrelated to any sort of deep or serious knowledge of public health:

> Fatness leaves the domain of morality for the halls of the surgeon (liposuction or highly risky gastric bypass) to then be set free by fat liberationists, only to be returned to medicine by endocrinologists who cede some of the bodies (those whose disorder is will) to the morality plays of reality television.[16]

Add to this the public school, the church, and the news media, and we have a description of how concepts of fatness circulate within a medicalized American society. In the eighteenth century, the physician became "the great adviser and expert, if not in the art of governing, at least in that of observing, correcting, and improving the social 'body' and maintaining it in a permanent state of health." Today that power is transferred to factions of the population based on body size.[17] And while we endow thin Americans with cultural capital, assuming that they have knowledge regarding health, we concurrently shame and disempower any fat person by assuming that his fat is evidence of nutritional illiteracy or noncompliance. The moves Foucault defined in eighteenth-century medicine equip the current social atmosphere where healthy weight and eating behavior are socially mobilized. It is within this framework that I review some of the contemporary themes surrounding health and body size. To begin, let us consider one of the most fundamental and essential elements of life and health: food.

What Is Food?

Given the primacy of food as a sustaining force, it may seem unnecessary to define it. However, ways of thinking about food have changed dramatically in modern history, particularly when traced alongside the history of nutrition science and the discourse of quantification. Within this framework, "calories, proportions, minutes, servings, and groups" are used to describe what had previously been known simply as food.[18] This move allowed scientists to order, classify, and control food by breaking it down into constituent parts. Individual eaters also began to understand food in terms of nutritional components rather than holistic experiences of taste. In many ways, this schema feeds rationality, reduction, and objectivity rather than integration, sensation, or pleasure.

The calorie, for example, measures a food product's ability to provide energy to the body. However, it is used across a variety of media to measure the amount of heat required to raise a gram of water by one degree Celsius. Adopting this measurement allowed scientists to "contrast amounts of heat given off by engines, supernovas, and people," effectively reducing—or at least correlating—the human frame to a machine and couching its functions in terms of industry.[19] Not only do the calorie and other measures of quantification frame food and eating *within* a mechanistic way of viewing the body and its processes; this discourse also serves to silence certain other factors regarding food and eating. The qualitative experience of wellness and satiety, for example, has little merit in the discourse of quantification. This way of viewing food sets up a system of values that allows some ways of eating to be healthy and good and others to be insufficient or bad. This is the environment eaters navigate today, and one in which medical and nutritional information is collected, communicated, and disseminated to the public. The discourse of quantification, then, is not simply one possible way of treating food but the dominant discourse so pervasive that alternate ways of thinking about food are no longer possible outside of this framework.

This is not to suggest that the calorie or other measures of quantification are invented or fictional properties of food. Indeed, we know that food does contain caloric energy and nutrients in certain measure. However, the prescriptive ways in which this discourse has been implemented by the U.S. Department of Agriculture (USDA) through recommended daily allowances (RDAs) and food guides privileges these quantifiable facts over qualitative aspects such as a food's visual appeal, smell, seasonality, locality, or taste. In the use of the food guide pyramid and other tools, the USDA's audience is the "cultural subject," not samples of a real population but an audience invoked. Real eaters and their specificities and preferences related to eating are considered less important than that which science and quantification can catalogue about food. For eaters, compliance with recommendations regarding numerical calculations of enough, too much, and appropriate intake, is more important than pleasure or taste.

As cultural subjects, citizens hailed by the USDA are compared to externally generated numbers by technologies of governance, which include everything from food scales to photo representations of a healthy meal. The good meal, far from what an embodied eater might expect, has nothing to do with taste or pleasure but is described in terms of meeting a threshold for grams of fiber or limiting other elements like grams of sugar. These are not properties of food our bodies can readily identify, yet they are the very properties the discourse of quantification makes known and privileges. In this schema, direct experience is secondary to quantifiable fact.[20] When a user attempts to abide by these measures, the food journal becomes a technology of governance that allows us to translate food products into the discourse of quantification in ways that can be categorized, tallied, counted, and assessed according to the recommendations of the USDA.

As citizens, we follow these prescriptive eating practices because we adhere to the assumption that "the hidden chemical elements, and the quantities of those elements, of a food are its most important features" and that abiding by the recommendations will, in fact, lead to improved health.[21] Conversely, when ill health is reported, we now look to food as its source.[22] Reducing food to its nutritional portfolio is the very *reason* for eating as described in popular media. In recent scientific accounts of the physiology of eating, the process is described thus: food is an energy source for macro- and micronutrients and the oxidation of energy. A food's energy value is measured as its caloric content minus the use of energy in the digestion and normal bodily function, or the basal metabolic rate (BMR). In this configuration, eating is an equation—calories in versus calories out—a matter of scientific rationality rather than experiential pleasure.

When pleasure is no longer a consideration, the only task of the eater is to find the perfectly balanced human-food equation where intake is precisely matched to caloric energy output, resulting in perfect energy and weight balance. When it comes to theorizing appetite (or the internally regulated *appestat*), our metaphors come from engineering and the imagery of perfectly regulated systems wherein behavior (hunger, eating, and satiety) are controlled by cycles of depletion and repletion. This attitude toward food remains the foundation for nutrition practice and medical dietary advice today. Quality (how good a food is) becomes subject to quantification (how much of a nutrient it has); the *experience* of food doesn't matter in this configuration of food and of bodies.

The unstable realm of seasonality and quality and the individual realm of preference for taste, texture, and food combinations are difficult to track and scale on a public policy level. Instead, nutrition science focuses on the intrinsic nutritional characteristics of foods. The problem, however, is that science repeatedly proves that our understanding of calories and nutrients is limited. Almonds, for example, appear on many "good snack" lists as high in nutrients and capable of staving off hunger. Nuts are notoriously high in fat (good, healthy, unsaturated fat) and calories, though, and have to be consumed in controlled portions. An August 2012 study shows, however, that the traditional Atwater values assigning a USDA serving (one ounce or about twenty-three almonds) a value of 165 calories are inaccurate. Researchers have discovered that something in the fiber structure of almonds means that not all of those calories are absorbed and that the net caloric value of a serving of almonds comes in at around 130 calories.[23] This has implications not only for almonds themselves but for other food products containing almonds and for the general reliability of Atwater calorie estimates. And because this caloric difference is based on the absorption of fat in the gut, it stands to reason that there may be differences between individuals—or even *within* one individual—based on food combinations or individual bacterial profiles or between almonds grown in different regions or at different times of year, or almonds at differing levels of freshness. The calorie as a stable, consistent, reliable measure of food energy simply cannot account for the many factors that inform food energy uptake.

Despite studies revealing the variability of caloric content in food and the continued findings that there is no significant difference between the amounts of food consumed by large versus lean people, the discourse of quantification perpetuates the notion that larger body size is a result of overconsumption of food or of inactivity. During a time when types of malnutrition and general food scarcity defined the populace, scientists understood caloric information as a matter of home economics and encouraged families to spend limited money on higher-calorie foods. Thus, using nutritional formulas could save both the health and the wealth of Americans during a time when scarcity defined both. This discourse of quantification, rationality, and morality remains, although we are no longer in a period of scarcity. Our way of thinking about food and health is based on a model of food availability that no longer defines the current situation.

Through the publication of food guides, the public became accustomed to eating in a prescribed way that addressed some particular social issue (fiscal scarcity, times of plenty, and later weight management). Across the various guides, "Learning to eat according to scientific principles, and understanding food through a series of numbers, would facilitate the eater's achieving whatever social goal the food guide purported to have."[24] These guides moved from selecting foods based on what the body needs to selecting foods based on budgetary constraints and later to avoidance of vitamin and mineral deficiencies based on age and sex. For Mudry, "The RDAs represent the moment in which the person, in the process of eating, falls away, and the judgment of the goodness of a meal and the goodness of an American becomes a measurement." Users of the guides were asked to adhere to "the letter and spirit of enumerated food by counting food groups, vitamins, nutrients, or pennies committed the household to solving a pressing problem of the era."[25]

By 1956, the move toward adequacy took a turn toward avoiding *over-indulgence*. By 1977, Americans were eating more calories than they needed (according to scientists) and the language of the food guides changed. The 1977 *Dietary Goals* report included seven dietary goals. Of those, four "began with the word 'reduce,' one began with 'avoid,' and one with the words 'limit the intake.'"[26] For professionals (scientists and nutritionists), preferences and cultural norms mattered only when they presented barriers to optimal prescribed eating. By this point, even the nutritional portfolio of food lost value to the regime of limiting caloric intake. During this era, foods relatively low in calories were recommended over those higher in caloric and nutritional density.

In alignment with the shift toward limiting food intake, the Nutrition Labeling and Education Act (NLEA) required food packaging after May 8, 1994, to include nutrition facts. The nutritional portfolio of food became omnipresent, even though scientists know that "30 to 40 percent of your total physical response to a meal occurs during the 'cephalic phase of digestion,' which is . . . the time you spend seeing, smelling, and tasting your meal."[27] That cephalic phase is rendered subject to another kind of cephalic phase, which relies on rational thinking and interpellation within the discourse of quantification. Particularly when weight management enters the equation, cues of hunger and satiety are ignored in favor of eating by caloric value and numerical configuration.

Because of the conflicting messages surrounding food (all of which are positioned within or in response to the discourse of quantification), there is a cultural desire for food and appetites that are self-governing and self-regulating, and that fulfill the requirements of the discourse of quantification. Deborah Lupton outlines this desire by describing how "vitamin gels and 'smart pills' have become the alternative to organic food, taking the non-natural to its apotheosis. The fantasy of cyberspace and virtual reality is to leave behind the organic body . . . nourishing only the mind/computer with space-food-like capsules."[28] The fleshy body itself—both of the eater and of the food's own embodiment—is repudiated in favor of a disembodied capsule-like food product that answers the call of the discourse of quantification.

Mudry points out that this system of numbers that point to other numbers—nutrition pointing to finance and back again—creates a self-referential system that continues to drive attention away from taste and experience and toward quantification. This self-referential system is a nutritional simulacrum in the Baudrillardian sense, creating a reality that comes to replace the real. Lupton's nonfood is presented not only in science fiction accounts of food and eating but also in daily

Disciplining the Body Politic

experience as food substitutes (such as protein supplements or meal replacement drinks). These products are culturally positioned as "virtuous and ascetic . . . not only because of [their] lack of palatability but also because [they are] viewed as being good for brain functioning (the 'software' of the body that is closest conceptually to a computer). In its elevation of function over pleasure, 'non-food' therefore suggests the ability to transcend the body's needs for sensual gratification, privileging mind over matter."[29] The Cartesian dualist approach to the body—and to food—produces the discourse of quantification as superior to the embodied reality of eater and food.

One outstanding difficulty with the discourse of quantification and the zero-sum model of caloric balance is the reality that we do not yet fully understand how the body functions in digesting, processing, and utilizing food or in desiring and achieving satiety through the eating process. The simple fact of the BMI, for example, is complicated by the fact that a calorie deficit (required for weight loss) leads directly to a dip in the BMI "shortly after the onset of a significant negative energy balance, disproportionately to and preceding any meaningful weight loss, which may be blunted by this physiological response."[30] A person would have to eat successively less food in order to maintain a negative energy balance as a way to achieve weight loss over extended periods of time. As an obese person works to lose weight through food restriction, he may drive "[her] weight to below set-point . . . in turn causing an elevation of hunger."[31] The physiological *drive* to eat and the affectivity of the hunger and satiety spectrum are not figured into the discourse of quantification and are not fully understood.

Fat and Health

We are, on average, larger than our ancestors. This increase in size has resulted in what public health officials—in the legacy of Foucault's work on the clinic—have labeled an epidemic. That choice of language, of course, "maintains a powerful metaphoric connection to contagion," and we begin to conceive of fat as a spreading virus, ready to infect any population, household, or person.[32] The idea of "infectobesity" is reinforced by graphics on television news programs that show obesity "spreading" across the country from the coasts toward the midsection. When we think of obesity (or increased body fat) as an epidemic, it becomes, as Foucault traced, a national rather than an individual problem. What we know, however, is that fat is historically "in the eye of the beholder. Each age, culture, and tradition has defined acceptable weight for itself, and yet all have a point beyond which excess weight is unacceptable, unhealthy, ugly, or corrupting."[33] This point is clearly labeled for modern Americans as the point of medical obesity. Rather than pointing to a failed organ, system, or process in the body, obesity functions as "a phenomenological category, which reflects the visible manifestation of bodily size."[34] As a result of obesity epidemic discourse, people enter into some relation with fatness, even when they are *not* fat or overweight. The fat body shames not only the individual who has "failed" to control it but the nation itself.

Etiology

While the impact of fat on the well-being of any individual remains uncertain even during the height of this obesity epidemic, researchers have worked to identify the causes of increased body fat. Of course, engaging in "cause-seeking rhetoric, we presume that some intervention into the 'problem' is necessary."[35] If the cause of obesity can be identified, the thinking goes, so too can a cure.

In nearly every account of the etiology of obesity, fatness is considered the result of some broken, damaged, or otherwise disturbed physical or psychological system. In these cases, whether causes are traced along a biological path "or along a social path to traumatic childhood experience, proponents of essentialist positions argue that fat identity is the unfortunately inevitable outcome of a causal relationship with some original variable gone awry."[36] That variable might have to do with "genes, hormones, fear of being sexually attractive, and dozens of other causes for fatness . . . each one advanced with the understanding that finding a remedy would be a financially rewarding proposition."[37] In any case, fatness supposedly evidences deviation from health, stability, and normality.

This understanding of obesity resulting from some foundational disruption of physical, psychological, or social eating practices is evidenced in practitioners' assumptions about the causes of their client's body size. Nutritionist Karin Kratina, in her dissertation project from the University of Florida, begins to notice a "parallel process" in her overweight clients: some problem in their personal life coincides with a problem in their eating habits.[38] For trained nutritionists, "the commonly accepted reasons for obesity are: (a) emotional, when compulsive eating becomes a compensation for emotional and psychological problems; (b) regulatory, when the brain's appetite control center is not functioning properly; and (c) cultural, when parents, family and friends overeat and inappropriate feeding habits are learned."[39] In each of these cases, increased body weight equates with some broken or maladaptive physiological system.

Because weight is attributed to one or all of these factors, succeeding in weight loss and weight control means somehow correcting all of the problems and behaviors that allowed for weight gain.[40] Culturally speaking, this requires a systems approach where "forces governing appetite control . . . are in a constantly dynamic state and encompass biological, psychological and environmental events."[41] Part of this dynamic state includes fat cells themselves, which of course are active living organisms that are involved in chemical processes regulating a variety of bodily functions.[42] For practitioners, this interplay between body and environment means looking inward, understanding the physical pull of hunger on the drive to eat (and "over" eat). Here, the distinction between hunger and appetite is important for professionals: it has been suggested that the obese are less able to perceive internal feeding cues (hunger) and rather respond more readily to external cues (appetite).[43] Hormones that signal hunger (ghrelin) and fullness (leptin) have a noticeable impact on the drive to eat; the balance of these hormones varies across individuals and within individual bodies over time. In some literature, the hunger/appetite distinction marks the difference between restrained (dieting) and unrestrained eaters. If you restrain eating to the point of ignoring hunger, you will binge. Practitioners of the Health at Every Size Approach advocate the view that if you eat unrestrained, you will eat what you want and need and lose interest when you are done. "Done," however, varies naturally across the population.

For some practitioners, the emphasis falls less on an integrationist approach and more on singling out a root cause for increased hunger/appetite. One theory is that "subjects who are predisposed to obesity all show heightened hedonic responses to fat-containing stimuli," including children of fatter parents, people who want to restrict fat intake for weight control, nonobese subjects at higher ends of normal body weight, and those already or previously obese.[44] The idea that food high in fat is overwhelmingly pleasurable is also linked to high-sugar foods: "The more sugar and fat you consume, the more opioids released. Because the reaction is so pleasurable, you consume more of these foods to continue to receive the pleasurable reaction, creating a powerful, neurochemical drive to overeat those foods."[45] Thus the lesson is that pleasurable foods cause overconsumption. Eaters have the option of carefully limiting these pleasurable foods or eliminating them altogether (also known as abstinence from certain foods in the language of Overeaters Anonymous).

In addition to certain food types, eating *patterns* are said to contribute to obesity. Popular dietary knowledge teaches that breakfast is the most important meal of the day and that nighttime snacking should be avoided. Eating misaligned with circadian rhythms is reported to increase body weight, as people with higher body weights are said to eat less in the morning and more in the late evening. It is recommended instead that we eat a hearty breakfast and then smaller meals throughout the day. Smaller, regular meals are associated with better "glucose tolerance test responses, lower insulin concentrations, and improved lipid profiles, compared with less frequent eating."[46]

Eating patterns are, it turns out, strongly genetic, and associations between eating patterns and body size are largely dependent on genetic factors.[47] The fat mass and obesity (FTO) gene on chromosome 16 has been associated with fatness, but was recently linked to "impaired satiety responsiveness, suggesting that FTO's correlation with increased body mass index partially involves effects on appetite."[48] That the satiety response is "impaired," of course, refers only to the difference in satiety between non-FTO and FTO-carrying children in the study. And even after controlling for body weight, genetic obesity risk alleles are associated with the number of eating episodes per day as well as consumption of dairy and protein.[49] The risk alleles studied in this research include FTO and MC4R, SH2B1, BDNF, INSIG2, TNNI3K, NISCH-STAB1, MTIF3, MAP2K5, QPCTL/GIPR, and PPARG.[50] Genetic research on a population of 249,796 confirmed "14 known obesity suscep-tibility loci and identified 18 new loci associated with body mass index."[51] More-over, the genes associated with obesity function differently: some impact waist circumference while others impact BMI, and only 60% overlap and affect both.[52] The list of known alleles associated with obesity demonstrates the complexity of an individual's own drive to eat and experience of satiety and the biological con-straints for regulating those intensities.

Outside of behaviors linked strongly with genetics, other physiological fac-tors are at work in body weight. Lily O'Hara, a public health policy researcher, outlines additional factors contributing to obesity:

> Physiological factors related to the gut, such as deficiency in Toll-like receptor 5, an immune system protein present in the gut, metabolic endotoxemia caused by bacterial lipopolysaccharide from Gram-negative intestinal microbiota, which leads to low grade chronic in-flammation, the composition of microbiota in the gut, and infection with helicobacter pylori. Other types of infection have also been iden-tified as contributing to increased body weight, including chlamydia pneumonia and human adenovirus 36.[53]

These factors are not under any individual's conscious control. Combined with genetic risk factors for obesity, exposure to these pathogens, bacteria, and viral in-fections might "activate" obesity genes. As with alleles, the way these organisms affect body weight is not well understood and is in constant interplay with other factors. Lifestyle, for example, such as sleep patterns and stress, also impact body weight. Even in short-term trials, loss of regular sleep "leads to impaired glucose metabolism, dysregulation of appetite, and increased blood pressure."[54] Likewise, excessive sleep can be associated with some forms of metabolic disease. Stress hor-mones such as cortisol have a direct link to fat storage, and chronic stress can lead to long-term weight gain. In a nineteen-year study of more than ten thousand in-dividuals, researchers concluded, "Chronic work stress predicts general and cen-tral obesity."[55]

There are many theories as to the cause of increased body fat among today's population, yet not one has adequately provided a solution for reducing body fat or even determined whether it is truly desirable or necessary to reduce body fat to levels considered historically normal. We do know that the energy balance equation alone is insufficient to account for the drive to eat or the ways in which food interacts with hormonal systems in an individual's body. Perhaps what the statistics on obesity demonstrate most convincingly is the "erosion of qualitative conceptions of health."[56] Given these factors, "one must accept etiological ambiguity and resist the temptation to affix a cause, even an apparently forgiving one, to the health condition of fatness—in other words, stop asking 'why?' about fat identity, and start acting out about it."[57]

Lipoliteracy

With health defined largely by the BMI, individuals and populations are diagnosed as underweight, normal, overweight, or obese (and some BMI charts further differentiate types of obesity, such as "morbid" and "super morbid"). The BMI is used by doctors and insurance companies and is taught in elementary schools so that children learn their categorical placement. It "hails" the population by drawing even the nonfat into a relation with fatness. Once created, BMI tables classify and discursively construct body sizes into labeled groups. Because it is interpellated through the BMI, the entire population is required to become "lipoliterate" in that we are all in some relation to fat and are adept at reading the body (our own and others) for fatness and meanings associated with it. As a numerical categorization, obesity "not only evokes a mode of scientific empiricism that offers measurements, weights and sizes"; it has "embedded 'fat' flesh in popular understandings as always already a virtual confession of pathology."[58] The interpellated fat person, at any age, is literate about her own status as fat and is constructed as pathologically diseased by obesity's association with illness and bad health when the classifications actually produce the concept of obesity rather than describe it.

What the body mass index effectively accomplishes is a model of normality rather than a response to some pathological abnormality. Thus, the normal BMI becomes a model for health and a standard way to assess health, even when the BMI has only *general* correlations to health and cannot account for individual differences in lifestyle or physiology. Because of the BMI, "a fatty who exercises, eats her veggies, meditates, and never diets might not be in a high-risk category at all, but we'll never freakin' know, because everything is skewed so far in favor of blaming adiposity itself."[59] For example:

> [When researchers] looked at a nationally representative group of more than 170,000 U.S. adults, they found the difference between

actual weight and perceived ideal weight was a better indicator of mental and physical health than BMI. In other words, *feeling* fat has stronger health effects than *being* fat.[60]

So while a person might be healthy by all other measures, a BMI in a high-risk category stands as a cause for any future health problems that develop, even when there is no certainty than BMI-associated health problems will develop. What *is* certain, however, is the negative health effect of labeling people as potentially unhealthy without any indication of physiological illness.

And because of the medical model, we *all* feel fat. If we are not now fat, we fear becoming fat. Our lipoliteracy informs us as to our relation to fat, and we are in continual state of fat surveillance that requires monitoring of ourselves and compliance with advice from nutritional experts. This professional gaze is ever present (even when physically absent), so "women must continually produce bodies that are acceptable to that gaze. Thus a woman's own gaze becomes a substitute for a man's gaze, and she evaluates her own body as ruthlessly as she expects it to be evaluated by him."[61] Part of our lipoliteracy includes the ruthless self-monitoring of fatness. The BMI thus creates "temporal and spatial decomposition" of bodies into a sphere of numerical data in need of regulatory practices and controlled surveillance.[62]

Self-surveillance also bleeds into surveillance of others. When I can control my body fat, I may begin to feel superior to those who cannot (or do not). When I can control my body fat, I may assume that if all people performed my same actions, they might all achieve the same results. The process of quantification through the BMI "describes microhierarchization":

> . . . superiority or self-loathing based on each calorie or gram of food consumed or not consumed, in each belt notch, pound, or inch gained or lost, in each clothing size smaller or larger. Each micro-rung on the weight-based hierarchy exerts pressure to covet the next increment thinner and regret the next increment fatter, leaving little room for people to recognize and revolt against the overall system that alienates us from our own bodies.[63]

Microhierachization exists among fat individuals, and at the other end of the weight spectrum includes those with disordered eating patterns such as anorexia nervosa, bulimia nervosa, or—the newest DSM IV diagnosis—eating disorders not otherwise specified (EDNOS).

Pro-ana groups, engaging in some of the same logic used by size acceptance groups, argue that some people are simply naturally thin and ought to be left to their thinness without harassment from the medical community. Sites such as pro-ana-nation.com and prettythin.com provide "thinspiration" and support for those pursuing bodies thinner than the medical model of health allows. Although fatness and thinness are culturally entirely different experiences, the existence of pro-ana communities reflects the complicated relationships we have as a society with our bodies, our eating practices, and medically defined health. Through the BMI—on both ends of the spectrum—we are interpellated into a relationship with ourselves and with each other that circulates around the discourse of fatness. The cultural pushback, then, may be to push back with a holistic, experiential description of health and wellness rather than one is driven by numeric data. Such an allowance would free women of all sizes to practice health rather than rigid body surveillance.

Permanent Body Size Modification

As we have seen, medicalization of fatness essentializes fat as the result of some original (yet unidentified) variable gone awry, yet "not all essentialist positions are anti-fat; some prefer to focus on the present fact of fatness and the impossibility of changing it, using this resignation as a platform for civil rights size acceptance movements."[64] For such groups, weight is seen as a human characteristic that varies across the population on a bell curve similarly to height. Thus the BMI's "underweight," "overweight," and "obese" categories would be variants of normality rather than abnormalities. Despite lipoliteracy and self-surveillance, permanent body weight modification is rare, and body size seems to be determined more by genetics than any other factor. According to the 2008 *American Journal of Clinical Nutrition*, 77 percent of body size is genetic, leaving only 23 percent under the control of conscious will, the foodscape, and other environmental factors.[65] Fat activists have come to agree that, while "a balanced, nutritious diet and exercising are good for you," it is "stone cold bullshit that those things will make you permanently thin if your body is not so inclined."[66]

The National Association to Advance Fat Acceptance (NAAFA) includes among its membership many women who "have experienced short periods of being at average weight. Most achieved their weight loss through drastic measures like liquid diets, fasting, diet pills, or gastric bypass surgery, and all gained at least as much weight back as they had lost."[67] According to the National Institutes of Health, "Success rates for long-term weight loss are not good: of those who intentionally lose weight, most will regain about one-third of their weight within the first year, and virtually all will return to their baseline weight within five years."[68] It is well-established that any previously "obese individuals who have lost weight are . . . at high risk of subsequent weight regain and re-establishment of obesity."[69]

With those odds, it is difficult to reconcile the injunction to lose weight and achieve a normal BMI with the reality that such permanent body size modification is statistically impossible.

Yet the population continues to diet, knowing that "short-term weight loss is associated with reductions in risk factors for cardiovascular disease, including improvements in blood pressure, glycemic control, and lipid and lipoprotein profiles" during the period of reduced weight.[70] With each diet, however, the likelihood of regaining weight increases. The process of weight cycling has been shown "to decrease metabolic rates at rest and during exercise, increase lipoprotein lipase activity (making the body more efficient at storing fat), and increase the proportion of fat to lean tissue in the body. With each weight loss/regain cycle, weight is increasingly redistributed from lower body subcutaneous fat, shown to have a protective effect against heart disease, diabetes, cancer, and high cholesterol, to abdominal visceral fat, which does not confer these positive effects."[71] With each cycle of weight loss and regain, the body becomes markedly less healthy. In addition, we know that the dieting process "results in personality changes that include increases in apathy and depression, and decreases in mental alertness, comprehension, and concentration."[72] These feelings often continue once the diet has ended for a period at least as long as the diet itself lasted.

And diets, despite claims, are not always effective in reducing weight. In 2004, the creator of the South Beach Diet, Arthur Agatson, organized the Osceola County HOPS (Healthier Options for Public School Children) program, which implemented school-based gardens and integrated nutrition science in math and life science courses. Despite Agatson's expertise and the county's compliance with the program, there was no change in the prevalence of obesity at the end of the program.[73] In larger-scale studies, it was found that "when energy intake is held constant, short- and long-term trials confirm that diet composition has (perhaps surprisingly) very little effect on energy balance or body weight."[74] The National Weight Loss Registry attempted to define what makes 5 percent of dieters successful at maintaining weight loss for a period of five years: "Food frequency questionnaires indicated that [these dieters] consumed a diet adequate in minerals and vitamins, but low in calories (1,306 kcal/day for women; 1,685 kcal/day for men), averaging about 23 to 25 percent fat, 55 to 56 percent carbohydrate, and 18 to 19 percent protein. Participants were also very physically active, expending an average of about 2,800 kcal/week or approximately 400 kcal/day."[75] The registry participants had lost an average of 66 pounds each for a period of 5.1 years, but their net calorie intake was very restrictive at just 906 calories per day for women. In general, diets are ineffective and the ones indicated by the National Weight Loss Registry are largely unsustainable and do not meet the guidelines established by the USDA.

The pervasive cultural messages—from our national discussion of childhood obesity to daily news reports on fat and diet cures—shape the landscape of Americans' daily practices and habits. With all of the attention directed at fat, a person is interpellated into a dialogue with it. A person must be lipoliterate, must in some measure comply—or desire to comply—with standards of health and beauty. The common result of this situation is a population that persistently diets ineffectively.

Alongside the discourse that shapes fat in terms of "excess body weight," the BMI, and obesity lie the lived, embodied experiences of fat people. The subject of the discourse of quantification is always compared to a normative standard, and there are inevitably those marked as *too* fat or *too* big and in need of body size intervention. The spoiled identity of fatness is so culturally pervasive and powerful that fat people may hate even their own bodies.[76] Culturally, the woman labeled fat "represents the worst of the woman—unmanaged, out of control, her desires overtaking her reason."[77] The fat body is read as a failure to comply with common-sense principles of eating and nutrition. The pervasive notion that fat equals poor body management and ill health results in mistreatment of fat people.

Because of the anti-fat trends of the medical, nutrition, and diet industries, fatness has turned into a subject-marking experience. In many ways, "the lived experience of fatness inhabits the same space as . . . the embodiment of race and sexuality."[78] While body size, race, and sexuality have clearly different social histories and result in varying levels of discrimination, fat people are marked as socially *othered* and somehow *less-than*. There are differences in the ways fat men and fat women are treated culturally, but "fat, unlike gender, *is* written on the body for *all* to see" and results in a subjectivity that marks personhood.[79] In the same way that thin Americans are assumed to have medical and nutritional expertise based upon their body size, so fat Americans are shamed by the obvious fact of a larger body. And this isn't a pressure that we can point to one institutional force to correct: this shame does not stem only from the medical establishment or from celebrity culture or from issues related to gender and beauty. No, this fat shame is enacted through a *dispersion* of these forces, acting with and through and among citizens and in multiple layers of American social relationships. It is in this dense, complex, and shame-filled network that the power of medicalized health circulates.

In this final dispersion of Foucault's epidemiology, the only avenue to reclaim the power of the individual is to draw awareness to the ways in which the network of shame is activated and enacted. Fat activists are engaged in a project to "revamp their subjectivities, accord new usefulness to the signifier of fat, and to explore new linkages of affinity and action."[80] These activists work against the health/beauty/ medicine triplex to recognize fat as neither simply an aesthetic state nor a medical condition but a *political* situation. In the project of fat activism, the very act of *being fat* is a subversive cultural practice that challenges received notions of health, beauty, and what is natural. Fat activism rejects the shame of fatness, trading in the idea that the body must be perfected to thinness for a focus on the body as a location to revolt against American fat shame and the misguided notion that body size demonstrates health expertise.

Notes

1. Michael Foucault, *The Birth of the Clinic* (New York: Routledge, 2007), 518–520, Kindle ed.

2. Cindy Patton, ed., *Rebirth of the Clinic: Places and Agents in Contemporary Health Care* (Minneapolis: University of Minnesota Press, 2010), 1513–1514, Kindle ed.

3. Foucault, *Birth of the Clinic,* 535–536.

4. Patton, *Rebirth of the Clinic,* 99–101.

5. Foucault, *Birth of the Clinic,* 538–539.

6. Ibid., 723–727.

7. Ibid., 797–801.

8. Ibid., 829–831.

9. HBO Documentary Films et al., "Part 1: Consequences," in *The Weight of the Nation,* 2012, http://theweightofthenation.hbo.com/films/main-films/Consequences.

10. Foucault, *Birth of the Clinic,* 837–839.

11. Ibid., 912–914.

12. Michel Foucault and Paul Rabinow, *The Foucault Reader* (New York: Pantheon Books, 1984), 281.

13. Ibid., 285.

14. BBC, "Where are you on the global fat scale?" *BBC News Health,* http://www.bbc .com/news/health-18770328, last modified July 12, 2012.

15. Ibid.

16. Patton, *Rebirth of the Clinic,* 104–105.

17. Foucault and Rabinow, *Foucault Reader,* 284.

18. Jessica Mudry, *Measured Meals: Nutrition in America* (Albany: State University of New York Press, 2009), 2.

19. Ibid., 5.

20. David Abram, *The Spell of the Sensuous: Perception and Language in a More-Than-Human World* (New York: Vintage Books, 1997).

21. Mudry, *Measured Meals,* 16–17.

22. Deborah Lupton, *Food, the Body, and the Self* (London: Sage Publications, 1996), 77.

23. Janet Novotny, Sarah K. Gebauer, and David J. Baer, "Discrepancy between the Atwater Factor Predicted and Empirically Measured Energy Values of Almonds in Human Diets," *American Journal of Clinical Nutrition,* 96, no. 2 (2012), 296–301, doi: 10.3945/ajcn.112.035782.

24. Mudry, *Measured Meals,* 50.

25. Ibid., 75.

26. Ibid., 82.

27. Linda Bacon, *Health at Every Size: The Surprising Truth about Your Weight* (Dallas: BenBella Books, 2010), 189–190.

28. Lupton, *Food, the Body, and the Self,* 92.

29. Ibid., 92.

30. David Mela and Peter J. Rogers, *Food, Eating, and Obesity: The Psychobiological Basis of Appetite and Weight Control* (London: Chapman & Hall, 1998) 44.

31. Ibid., 5.

32. Sander Gilman, *Fat: A Cultural History of Obesity* (Cambridge, U.K.: Polity, 2008), 19.

33. Ibid., 3.

34. Gilman, *Fat,* 18.

35. Kathleen LeBesco, *Revolting Bodies? The Struggle to Redefine Fat Identity* (Amherst: University of Massachusetts Press, 2004), 14.

36. Ibid., 14.

37. Ibid., 85.

38. Karin Marguerite Kratina, *Fat Talk and Related Conversation: What Women Have in Mind When they Engage in Food and Body Discourse* (Ph.D. diss., Gainesville: University of Florida, 2003), 15.

39. Ileana M. Mancusi, *A Comparative Study on Presently and Previously Obese Individuals in Food Diary Records And Lifestyle Data by Subjects Attending a Weight Control Program* (M.A. thesis, University of Central Florida, 1985), 7–8.

40. Ibid., 20.

41. Mela and Rogers, *Food, Eating, and Obesity,* 2.

42. Bacon, *Health at Every Size,* 26.

43. Mancusi, *A Comparative Study,* 120.

44. Mela and Rogers, *Food, Eating, and Obesity,* 104.

45. Bacon, *Health at Every Size,* 104.

46. Mela and Rogers, *Food, Eating, and Obesity,* 126.

47. Lily O'Hara, "The HAES Files: Uncommon Knowledge about Changes in Body Weight–Part 1," *Health at Every Size Blog,* May 1, 2012, http://healthateverysizeblog.org/2012/05/page/6/.

48. Jane Wardle, Susan Carnell, Claire M. A. Haworth, I. Sadaf Farooqui, Stephen O'Rahilly, and Robert Plomin, "Obesity Associated Genetic Variation in *FTO* Is Associated with Diminished Satiety" *Journal of Clinical Endocrinology & Metabolism* 93, no. 9 (2008): 3641, doi: 10.1210/jc.2008-0472.

49. Jeanne M. McCaffery, George D. Papandonatos, Inga Peter, et al., "Obesity Susceptibility Loci and Dietary Intake in the Look AHEAD Trial," *American Journal of Clinical Nutrition* 95, no. 6 (2012), doi: 10.3945/ajcn.111.026955.

50. Ibid.

51. Elizabeth K. Speliotes, Cristen J. Willer, Sonja I. Berndt, et al., "Association Analyses of 249,796 Individuals Reveal 18 New Loci Associated with Body Mass Index," *Nature Genetics* 42, no. 11 (2010): 937–948, doi:10.1038/ng.686.

52. O'Hara, "The HAES Files."

53. Ibid.

54. Ibid.

55. Eric J. Brunner, Tarani Chandola, and Michael G. Marmot, "Prospective Effect of Job Strain on General and Central Obesity in the Whitehall II Study," *American Journal of Epidemiology* 165, no.7 (2007): 828, doi:10.1093/aje/kwk058.

56. Mudry, *Measured Meals*, 176.

57. LeBesco, *Revolting Bodies*, 120.

58. Samantha Murray, *The "Fat" Female Body* (London: Palgrave Macmillan, 2008), 3.

59. Kate Harding and Marianne Kirby, *Lessons from the Fat-o-Sphere: Quit Dieting and Declare a Truce with Your Body* (New York: Perigee Book, 2009), 175.

60. Bacon, *Health at Every Size*, 126.

61. Jana Evans Braziel and Kathleen LeBesco, *Bodies Out of Bounds: Fatness and Transgression* (Berkeley: University of California Press, 2001), 62.

62. Lisa Cartwright, *Screening the Body: Tracing Medicine's Visual Culture* (Minneapolis: University of Minnesota Press, 1995), xvi.

63. Sondra Solovay, Esther D. Rothblum, and Marily Wann, *The Fat Studies Reader* (New York: New York University Press, 2009), xv.

64. Braziel and Lebesco, *Bodies Out of Bounds*, 84.

65. Gilman, *Fat*, 18.

66. Harding and Kirby, *Lessons from the Fat-o-Sphere*, 10.

67. Debra L. Gimlin, *Body Work: Beauty and Self-Image in American Culture* (Berkeley: University of California Press, 2001), 137.

68. Solovay et al., *The Fat Studies Reader*, 38.

69. Mela and Rogers, *Food, Eating, and Obesity*, 48.

70. Kratina, *Fat Talk and Related Conversation*, 50.

71. Ibid., 54.

72. Ibid., 220.

73. Gilman, *Fat*.

74. Mela and Rogers, *Food, Eating, and Obesity*, 100.

75. Solovay et al., *The Fat Studies Reader*, 39.

76. Lebesco, *Revolting Bodies*, 110.

77. Murray, *The "Fat" Female Body*, 55.

78. Lebesco, *Revolting Bodies*, 11.

79. Braziel and Lebesco, *Bodies Out of Bounds*, 79.

80. Lebesco, *Revolting Bodies*, 110.

SEVEN

Citizenship at Odds: Disability, Liberalism, and the Shame of Interdependence

Noel Glover

Given the reality that some persons with disabilities will necessarily be in situations of intense dependency and reliance, can liberty and autonomy—with their emphasis on freedom from—really be the lodestars liberalism has assumed? Despite liberalism's assumption that dependency is the opposite of autonomy, disability may force a reconciliation between autonomy and dependence.
—Dianne Pothier and Richard Devlin, *Critical Disability Theory: Essays in Philosophy, Politics, and Law*[1]

Shameful Sharing: Education, Liberalism, and the Interpersonal Self

In school people are meant to come together. Throughout each day, we meet with familiars and encounter strangers. Sometimes we are trespassers, infringing on the being of others; other times we are welcomed participants, assisted and encouraged by a community of others. In our daily lives, we intermittently approach and reproach others, flee from them, and return to them in due course. As Sartre might say, we are *pursued-pursuers*, transcendences transcended. Our experiences in education alert us to the notion that existence is in many ways something we share with others. For students, questions concerning "who I am" implicitly invoke the being of others; who we are for others and who others are for us are modalities reflected in our intimations of self. These individual and inner experiences are not our own; they depend radically on the other's response. We depend on others to house our existence, and we are also then subject to them and their conditions of being and living.

My essay examines the condition of shame as a widely felt but minimally understood element of experience for both students and teachers in school. Shame is a pervasive affect, "and this ubiquity itself lends to [it] a kind of invisibility."[2] As a result, many everyday experiences of shame go undetected or, worse, misattributed. In American culture—a culture of spectacle—instances of exposure and shame pertain to a kind of appearing that is ardently regulated and overcoded by social mores. Students, for instance, become standardized by these sociopolitical and moral conventions, concretizing a notion of political actor—exerciser of rights—as precisely he or she who has been deemed "fit to be seen"[3] by a history of normalizing practices and by the interpersonal grounds on which the student as citizen is *revealed*. The bodies of students in school in North America are governed by certain practices that foment membership in school and the nation that depend on compliance and, of course, on punishment for failure to comply. In this way, shame is frequently obscured by the very meaning-making rituals employed to bring it into view.

As a point of departure, this essay presents the following hypothesis: shame can be at once both intensively constructive and extensively destructive, having profound personal and sociocultural implications for the interiority as well as the intersubjectivity of the shame subject. The subject I have in mind is the student, although, as I will try to make clear, the trafficking of shame in the classroom permeates the specificities of its subjects, impacting teachers no less than students and, more than that, investing itself in pedagogical relations quite broadly. Accordingly, I will configure shame as a complex constellation of emotions. Furthermore, I will present the shamed individual as someone objectified, dependent, alienated, and yet, concomitantly, someone who is *inter*dependent, vulnerable, and responsible. Often shame is raised as a generative limit obtaining between delusions of omnipotence and realizations of weakness and need. What is paramount, therefore, when analyzing the role of shame amidst the delirium of meeting and greeting of education and its pedagogical relations is keeping with the variability and multiply intelligible realities of the affect. I will treat shame not just as a singular moment that punishes a singular act (which may more accurately characterize affectations of guilt) but as an affect that is lived *through,* carried, transferred, and periodically reanimated. This essay harkens to the multiple narratives that concertedly sing the tune of shame, resounding temporally, outward like ripples in the interpersonal social body, enduring in each of us, and echoing in our education.

Liberalism in America offers a telling and productive vision against which this essay will cast the image of the shamed (inter) subject. The liberal paragon of the self-sufficient, productive, and invulnerable citizen is fertile ground for the sting of shame. As Martha Nussbaum remarks: "Because we all have weakness that, if known, would mark us off as in some way 'abnormal,' shame is a permanent possibility in our lives, our daily companion."[4] To need assistance or to call for newly organized forms of social or legal recognition is to expose the injured reality at the heart of the human condition, a reality plagued by limitation, at times even unproductively so. This is a reality that when brought to the fore is often considered shameful. Liberalism thus poses a worthwhile paradox: While feeling shame is a strident reminder of the primordial sensitivity of the self to the regard of others, a sensitivity inherent to what it means to be human, our current liberal society employs the stigma of shame to disavow precisely this kind of display of vulnerability and dependence. Shame, then, depending on how it is wielded, received, and understood, either can remind us of a fundamental mutuality enacted between individuals (which may promote, for example, an atmosphere of inclusivity and assistance in educational practices) or can cause us to renounce this very reciprocation (which can discourage, for example, support and accommodation for students making "special" requests or having "special" needs). I will argue that this divergence marks a difference in kind between two climates of shame conferral. Leaning on Nussbaum,[5] I will refer to experiences of shame that reintroduce mutuality as "self-regarding." This is shame conferred primarily according to a recognition beginning with the self. I will also refer to experiences of shame that punish and alienate as "other-regarding." This is shame conferred primarily according to the actions and intentions of the other and without the consent of the shamed self.

The reified fiction of the unremitting and self-sufficient student-citizen will represent one half of the lens for our vision of shame in American culture. Against this fiction, I will cast an actuality: the lived and contradistinctive reality of the student in a situation of disability. Allison Carey observes: "While the storybook ideal citizen exudes intelligence, independence, and the ability to contribute to the national well-being through hard work, political participation, and bravery, people with . . . disabilities tend to be characterized by their deficiencies"; as such, I would add, they tend also to be marginalized by other-regarding shame.[6] Because disability necessarily troubles attempts at generalization, I will endeavor to refer explicitly in my discussion only to a particular situation of disability—that of an individual with a hearing impairment.[7] But, of course, I acknowledge that this kind of analysis will unavoidably treat both more and less than the singular reality of this specific situation. I will try to show that, through a deconstruction and re-animation of the phenomenological contours of the shame experience, we can reopen the underlying vulnerability of the self and restore the foundational interdependence between self and other at the center of the social contract, a contract so vital to educational experience. In this way, differences in ability can be reasons for coming together, for assisting each other, for learning together, rather than being simply reasons for coming apart.

While many of my claims concerning shame deal with what I suspect is a fundamental aspect of the human condition, the setting I have in mind—indeed, the very condition I will recommend as a crucible for the emotional realities of shame—is education or, less specifically, pedagogical relations. Thus, I am interested in what we might ask of education in the interest of retelling, which is to say reconceptualizing, shame experience and shame conferral within liberal ideology. Deborah Britzman suggests: "We can begin from the subjective fact that education is a place where strangers meet and where individuals can experience not only the nature of knowledge but also a transformation of human nature through a capacity for feeling and being affected."[8] Following this suggestion, I will claim that it is not one's capacity for independent contribution to a given or imagined community that should distinguish the projects of the ideal student; rather, one's capacity to perceive need in others and thereby contribute *with* one's given or imagined community, affectively, should typify the citizenship of pedagogy in a liberal society. It is toward this *"being-with"* that this essay leans, toward the amplification of a fundamental emotional sharing, beginning perhaps within the realm of education and resounding outward into the sociocultural networks of our everyday coming together.

As Carl Schneider remarks, "Because our culture has tended to obscure the way in which our communication is simultaneously a disclosing and a concealing, we are often unaware of the covering that accompanies our meeting, and frequently are conscious of it only insofar as we are uneasy when it is missing."[9] Perhaps we would do well, then, to *uncover* ourselves when we meet, and join together in our uncovering. The exposure of shame may be the very thing we need to reconnect, to re-entwine, to reimagine the many routes toward self-improvement, indeed toward education, routes made all the more numerable with the help of others.

Two Kinds of Shame

I will devote the first section of this essay to elucidating, in phenomenological terms, the conditions under which shame is conferred, and the profound affinity between shame and shamelessness, with an eye to eventually turning these remarks over to pedagogy and asking how teaching and learning are inhabited by certain kinds of shame conferral and how education might translate some of its more pernicious affective scenes into more constructive alternatives. French phenomenologist Maurice Merleau-Ponty posits that "in so far as I have a body, I may be reduced to the status of an object beneath the gaze of another person, and no longer count as a person for him," and he concludes: "Shame and shamelessness express the dialectic of the plurality of consciousnesses."[10] Embodiment invariably commits us to the dialectic of self and other—the wax and wane of objectification at the shores of subjectivity. As a result, any encounter with the other can result in a reconfiguration of the perceptual plane, a reanimation of the phenomenal world.

"There is no shame except in having none," declares French philosopher Blaise Pascal.[11] This is, of course, the negative formulation of the claim that there is always shame, that shame is omnipresent. And while it would be unconvincing to argue that we are perpetually suppressing or overcoming a constant torrent of shame, we should find compelling the notion that we are always in a relational affective stance that invariably includes shame, or that includes at least some referential intimation of the enduring impacts of shame on our existence. Each encounter with the other is propelled, in a way, by a history of interaction with shame, an odyssey of felt revelations and associative acts—objectifications that are lived through, which is to say absorbed and carried along with us.

Shame is caused by a painful feeling of exposure and causes in turn an intense desire to cover oneself from view. To feel ashamed is simultaneously to feel seen, disclosed in a limited or reduced way by the gaze of another. We more than behave differently when under the gaze of another; we *are* different. Experiencing shame before another is an instance of ontological transformation—a radical metamorphosis. Commonly, shame conferral is understood as interpolating and debilitating, as stigmatizing and reductive, as the cause of a destructive and disorienting reflexivity in the shame subject. A popular and intuitive account portrays shame as a form of affective punishment for moral deviance.[12] But what of shame's less recognizable and thus perhaps more influential psychological and phenomenological realities? Is there a sense in which feeling shame also marks a change in the shame subject, not on moral or sociological grounds but on premoral and ontological grounds? Perhaps feelings of shame also communicate a movement of the self *toward* the other, a relinquishing of narcissistic projects in favor of mutual recognition, in favor of the profound complicity and vulnerability that obtains between all human beings.

Eve Sedgwick observes that "shame floods into being as a . . . disruptive moment . . . in a circuit of identity-constituting identificatory communication."[13] The significance of these momentary floods pervades the living narrative into which they crash—a kind of deconstructive symbiosis. "Indeed, like a stigma," Sedgwick says, "shame is itself a form of communication."[14] Shame more than interrupts; it joins the circuitry of identity-constitution. "In interrupting identification, shame, too, makes identity."[15] Habits of expression and emotional response linked to shame are part and parcel of a larger identificatory communication that comprises an entire self-system: self-appearing-before-other. Shame is a basic ingredient in the perceptual plenum of each lived-through instance of exposure before others. Having a "sense of shame," as the verbalism goes, pertains here to the affective residue posed by an ongoing communication that includes interior histories as well as exterior forecasts of shame. "Shame . . . is not a discrete intrapsychic structure," suggests Sedgwick, "but a kind of free radical that (in different people and also different cultures) attaches to and permanently intensifies or alters the meaning of—of almost anything."[16] The permanence of this free radical's capacity to intensify or alter meaning cannot be overstated. There is something strikingly persistent, underlying, and wide-ranging about shame. It is every bit, as Nussbaum puts it, our daily companion.

In school our perfunctory coming together and coming apart with others is a perpetual oscillation between modes of becoming: becoming shameful and becoming shameless, becoming a speaking subject and becoming a spoken-to object, seen by proximal others and seer of others. As Andrew Morrison suggests, "Shame and narcissism inform *each other* [my italics], as the self is experienced, first alone, separate, and small, and, again grandiosely, striving to be perfect and reunited with its ideal."[17] The student strives for perfection, but depends on many others for its conferral. And, when caught in this endeavor, seen promulgating the narcissism of singular completeness, it is in and through feelings of shame that the student is often reminded of his or her basic interdependence and incompleteness. We should think of shame and narcissism, shame and pride, then, together as the same subject. Informing each other as they do, there is no experience of shame that has not simply turned the corner on narcissism, and there is no narcissistic display that does not first arise out of a sense of shame.

According to Sedgwick, "Shame is the affect that mantles the threshold between introversion and extroversion."[18] The interruption of shame is an emphatic line of flight that runs along an equally grounded line of desire extended between self and other. Reasons for feeling shame in school, therefore, can tell us as much about a student's desire to be seen as about a socially projected desire for her to hide. These unfolding displays of shame and shamelessness, *both* incited by daily appearances before others, point to the same underlying human quiddity: to exist and to take part in the tributary performances of identity therein, pedagogical and otherwise, is to be placed within an ontology of fundamental connectivity to a plurality of others. Where education is responsible for symbolizing, or representing, these conflicts, it is responsible, too, for thinking them together—the desire to see and the hatred of being seen.

Merleau-Ponty says that, just as "the parts of my body together comprise a system, so my body and the other's are one whole, two sides of one and the same phenomenon."[19] In practice, however, and because shame can be such an uncomfortable and stultifying impediment to the contributions of the "ideal student," we construe the phenomenal coin of self and other as rendering a choice: "I must choose between others and myself, I must choose between being a subject or being an object." But as Merleau-Ponty intriguingly conditions: "We choose one against the other, and thus assert both. The other transforms me into an object and denies me, I transform him into an object and deny him, it is asserted."[20] One never reaches the status of absolute subject, of unseen seer, or of absolute object; *both are asserted*. The shame we confer on others is part of a dialectic that also invariably includes our own shame. And occasionally, therefore, the becoming object of one student may actually condition a remedial effort on behalf of another. Sometimes when we feel ashamed for having misrecognized the requests or needs of others, it is precisely through our shame that we can begin a process of clarification and recognition.

The very situation in which we come to feel shame[21] in the first place can initiate a perceptual shift toward the clear realization of the subjectivity of another. For example, if we have brusquely dismissed a student for not listening "properly" before discovering (and having our discovery exposed before others!) that the student has a hearing impairment and requires only that we speak with more attention, the shame we feel may incite a leaning not away but toward the other. Feeling shame here may cause us, among other things, to discontinue stigmatizing behavior toward others in situations of hearing impairment. It is an invitation, if you will, to feel shame. So while shame often deals in alienation, the stark invocation of the initial turn toward otherness inherent to the exposure of shame may also establish a posture in which both self and other are opened, made aware of their mutuality. Shame reminds us that being is fundamentally shared. In shame, self and other find themselves in a formative altercation, naked, face to face, and struggling for recognition, positioning themselves within the primitive ontological hierarchy of object seen and subject seeing.

"Shame is by nature recognition," says Jean-Paul Sartre. "I recognize that I am as the other sees me."[22] The recognition is of an outside beyond the self. "The perception of the other-as-object refers to a coherent system of representations that is not mine," culminating in, as Sartre notes, "the radical negation of my experience."[23] The danger of this recognition—a danger at the heart of all shame experience—is that the *kind of sensitivity that shame renders depends acutely on the origin of its conferral*. What we face here, a problem faced perpetually in education, is a problem of reference: shame can be at once a favorable and an invidious affect depending on the circumstances under which it is motivated.

We can therefore distinguish meaningfully between two kinds of shame conferral. First, shame conferred in reference to the self's *recognition* of his or her object-relation to the other—a regard for otherness that begins in the self and invokes an other whose investment in this conferral is secondary—is an example of shame that is self-regarding. For instance, I may feel ashamed of the way I have treated a student because of what the exposure of this treatment says about my regard for his otherness. This is the case, for example, as mentioned earlier, when one has failed to recognize a difference in another's hearing capacity and has, in effect, mistreated him. When this misrecognition is disclosed before the gaze of another, it can potentially, turn the objectifying gaze inward toward the self, invoking the realization: "Before this other, whom I have failed to recognize, I, too, am irredeemably other!" For shame that is self-regarding, *recognition precedes conferral*. The self comes to recognize her status as object within a coherent system of representations located outside all possible experience for her, and feels shame in the acknowledgment of this limited and dependent position. Inherent to this kind of shame conferral is not just the recognition of one's object status but, more meaningfully, the recognition also that this object status is a fundamental aspect of one's being-in-the-world. My suggestion is that self-regarding shame is favorable.

Second, and alternatively, when shame is conferred in reference to the other's *treatment* of the self, through stigmatizing and objectifying behavior, and this treatment in effect induces a regard for otherness along with feelings of reduced status, and when the stigmatizing other has a primary investment in the conferral of shame, namely the regulation of the shamed self, this is an example of other-regarding shame. Other-regarding shame generally occurs when we refuse to accommodate a student's "unusual" request—for instance, a student with a hearing impairment asks for clarification, repetition, or more permanent forms of assistance in the classroom but is met with exasperation or an expectation that he or she must learn how to participate in a more "usual" way. In shame that is other-regarding, *conferral precedes recognition;* the self is treated as an object and *thereby* recognizes his or her object state. Therefore, even as this student may recognize his or her object status before the other, he or she *does not* at the same time recognize the fundamental and shared nature of this status. Instead, in this situation the shamed student often has a strong sense that her feelings of shame are unnatural and unwarranted, resulting in an exigent desire to remove shame by shaming others. My suggestion is that other-regarding shame is invidious.

Moreover, I think that other-regarding shame is frequently employed as an effective and operative standardizing process within pedagogical relations. Self-regarding shame, in contrast, is a process by which the self becomes acquainted with an all too human vulnerability to otherness and, by extension, also to the limitations and dependencies that characterize much of human existence; however, it is a process that has yet to find much currency within educational practices. Perhaps what I am suggesting, then, is the need for a change in the climate in which shame is both dealt and felt in and within the encounters through which teaching and learning take place, to change, finally, *how* we commonly perceive otherness.

Shame, in aligning self and other against the limits of a freedom contracted in their meeting, seemingly summons an ambivalent directionality: the freedom to be seen by the other and the freedom to remain concealed, the freedom to be shameless and the freedom to be shamed: *the freedom to be both subject and object.* The question, then, is how these equal freedoms—freedoms that inevitably enjoy *unequal* interpersonal expression between varyingly able and disabled students—can be made in some way commensurate or proportionate at the level of social interaction and in the interest of equal human dignity. Perhaps if we better understand the duplicity of shame in our everyday encounters with others, and if we can become better equipped to distinguish between self-regarding and other-regarding experiences of shame, we may learn to resist the commonplace desire to stigmatize the "abnormal," instead perceiving otherness and need as natural and interconnecting, as simple requests for new kinds of recognition. Perhaps, finally, it is a matter of the emotional context of education, of how we learn, together, with others, how we learn, finally, to live with others, together.

In the next section, I will project a more concrete application of shame experience. I am interested in descrying how self-regarding and other-regarding shame each gain expression in liberal society and, in particular, how shame straddles the limit between the simulated image of the productive, self-sufficient, and independent student on one hand and the unsparing reality of the assisted, supported, and interdependent human being on the other. For Sally Munt, "shame is a force that acts upon the self, constituting social subjects who are marked and shaped by its interpellating propensities of recognition, misrecognition and refusal of recognition."[24] The task now is to face these refusals. Indeed, at times shame is a facile instrument for social sculpture, but at bottom it may be a reminder that we are always incomplete, that while identity extends only up to the borders of the other, subjectivity extends well beyond those borders. And perhaps educators, after all, are best equipped to be both containers and disseminators of this reminder. I turn now to liberal America to see if such a reminder can feasibly reach us.

Recognizing Difference: Dis/Abled Citizenship and the American Body Politic

Yet, as a general proposition, disability demands a coming to terms with difference.
—Dianne Pothier and Richard Devlin, *Critical Disability Theory: Essays in Philosophy, Politics, and Law*[25]

While perhaps leading the way globally in terms of legally defined rights for people with disabilities (the Rehabilitation Act, the Individuals with Disabilities Education Act, and the Americans with Disabilities Act), the United States still relies heavily on a concept of citizenship founded on unrealistic expectations of independence and productivity. In effect, the American legal model has historically "equated disability with incompetence."[26] Moreover, as Paul T. Jaeger and Cynthia Ann Bowman state, "Disability rights laws in the United States are more concerned with classifying disability than classifying discrimination . . . many other nations have disability rights laws that prioritize defining discrimination in terms of the barriers to inclusion that are socially created."[27] The rigorous and categorical classification of disability in America allows rights laws to control the terms and realities of disability, which in turn promotes state control over difference and foments reintegration rather than recognition—the remodeling of the citizen with a disability rather than the remodeling of the social scenery in which a disability first becomes perceived as a "problem." I will argue that the real problem here is one of ideology, an effect of perception. In other words, the problem is with a model of perceiving born out of liberal ideology. According to Dianne Pothier and Richard Devlin, "Liberalism, as a dominant ideology and principle of social organization, has a particularly hard time dealing with disability."[28]

Breckenridge and Vogler further suggest that "concepts of citizenship, the economy, and the body are embedded in understandings of what constitutes well-being, understandings that generally exclude or marginalize the forms or realities of disability."[29] Understandings of well-being and citizenship exclude the forms or realities of disability. It is in and through certain patterns of perception—habitual seeing and modes of encounter—that we repeatedly exclude the realities of those with visible "abnormalities," reacting to unconventionally unconcealed others with fear and an objectifying gaze. Merleau-Ponty holds that perception is "the background from which all acts stand out, and is presupposed by them"; he further claims that "the gaze gets more or less from things according to the way in which it questions them, ranges over or dwells on them."[30] An industrious and pernicious refusal of recognition is played out in the way our acts sometimes presuppose *only certain kinds of perception.* In this regard, liberalism, for instance, carries "deep structural assumptions such as its narrative of progress, which many persons with disabilities find hard to imagine given the current context of state downsizing, budget cutting, and retrenchment."[31] The self-sufficient perceiver in a liberal society can be a frequent supplier of other-regarding shame simply by being unable to incorporate within his or her worldview a vision of disability that exceeds the narrative of misfortune, failed autonomy, or arrested development. To be a "productive" citizen is in many ways to range over and dwell on others with the reductive gaze of absolute subject—that seer who refuses the reciprocity of the gaze of the other and the interdependence such reciprocity demands.

Unsurprisingly, living within the boundaries of a sociocultural identity for which legally defined rights are still inconsistently and ambiguously upheld[32] causes many individuals to feel shame. The misrecognition of rigid classification can be a violent objectification. To exercise rights in the United States, one is expected, first, to make peremptory socioeconomic contributions. Difficulties in contributive power are quickly translated into difficulties in legal security. The right to have rights rests on one's capacity to exercise those rights. As Maryam El-Shall notes, "Such terms as will, consent and freedom mask the reality of difference and inequality created by the history of having denied the willpower, consent and freedom of particular groups."[33]

My claim, then, is that the practice of perceiving an individual with a hearing impairment according only to the generalized existential contours of his impairment is a learned proclivity. Hence, it seems appropriate that one might turn to education for a response, or rather, for the potential to unlearn and relearn these perceptual proclivities. The particular request made by an individual with a hearing impairment is a singular and uncomplicated one that calls merely for a difference in the kind of response we are used to providing. As Sartre demarcated, the other's projects draw a limit against our own. If the limit drawn by the other fails to meet the imagined limit against which he becomes culturally "fit to be seen," then the other's request goes decidedly unrecognized. Again, as El-Shall observes: "When the narrative is cast as one of a collective of discrete individuals acting in their own self-interest, those who fail to meet the standards of 'our' narrative have only themselves to blame."[34] This cultural narrative is ripe with the potential for other-regarding shame, but as a narrative it is also vulnerable to practices of retelling, practices that find their most formative impetus within the trajectories of education.

But when proposing the retelling of a story, it is important to consider what was so seductive about the story in its original form. Why does the narrative of self-interest and self-sufficiency appeal so uncritically to so many? Perhaps the human dependence and difference displayed by disability unveils the veritable image of the human condition, an image that our cultural mythology does not easily support. And so, willingly and preferably, we objectify requests for assistance so as to conceal our own sense of shame and vulnerability. Perhaps we are ashamed that we may not measure up to the mythical standards set by our fantasy of independence and autonomy, and as a result we find most distressing the sight of our own limited and interdependent existence reflected in the being of an exposed and differently abled other.

There is a mirror effect to this kind of ashamed shaming—this is why the narrative is so pervasive: it is both a story we are told by others and a story we tell ourselves. Reflected, reactionary shame, rife in American culture, has a psychical instantiation: the deeply seeded desire for invulnerability and therefore for only certain kinds of narcissistic patterns of perception. Nussbaum says that, because "shame has its origin in a primitive desire to be complete and completely in control, it is potentially linked to the denigration of others and to a type of aggression that lashes out at any obstacle to the self's narcissistic projects."[35] What is peculiar, then, is how the self comes to interpret the limitations and dependencies of the other as an obstacle to *his or her own narcissistic projects,* unless it is the case, as

Sartre professed, that the other holds a secret within his or her being—the very secret of what we are—and therefore that the "profound meaning of [our] being is outside of [us], imprisoned in an absence."[36] Human existence is a fragile happenstance. The irrecoverable singularity of the self is an imperfection and precariousness that begs for the primordial response of the other—a response that is at once remedial and constitutive. But when a culture (and a cultural narrative) asks that we be perfectly and productively subsistent on our own—perpetually diverting us from thoughts and stories about our true and rudimentary incompleteness—we render the needs of others as obstacles, obstacles posed by objects, and therefore accordingly deserving of shame.

Gershen Kauffman states that "attitudes of the wider culture become internalized through the various scenes of shame that are initially encountered in interpersonal settings."[37] Interpersonal settings reflect and are reflected in the attitudes of the wider culture. When liberalism stigmatizes displays of difference, it conditions a climate of other-regarding shame. This climate is reproduced in classrooms in behaviors and in the very narratives that attribute meaning to them. The various scenes of shame conferral that accompany teaching and learning become internalized projections that fund a perceptual currency. We meet and learn together according to a perceptual background partly established by the liberal narrative, and our affective propensities serve to strengthen its resolution. When our fabricated sense of completeness is damaged by encounters with differently abled others (as when we are asked to accommodate the audial capacity of an individual with a hearing impairment), it is because these limitations are, at bottom, mirrored versions, reproductions, of our own true yet disavowed nature that we so easily become invested in their swift denial. It is reactionary, therefore, the shame we confer against those who fail to perform a pantomime of normalcy. Discomfort with a primitive narcissistic shame procures a discomfort with others who challenge the sacrosanct morphology of the independently contributive student-citizen. And, finally, the kind of social differences through which education enacts its influences come to reflect this very discomfort, together with its limited range of meaning.

Thus, disability in American culture, and particularly in pedagogical relations, all too frequently occasions instances of other-regarding shame, instances in which our *treatment* of others inculcates feelings of shame in *them*, feelings that are promulgated by the perceptual background of a wider cultural narrative and attitude that has, historically, revered misrecognition in the name of efficiency. As Julia Kristeva aptly describes, "The disabled person opens a narcissistic identity wound in the person who is not disabled; he inflicts a threat of physical or psychical death, a fear of collapse, and, beyond that, the anxiety of seeing the very borders of the human species explode."[38] The threat of physical or psychical death and the anxiety of just glimpsing the borders of the human species, let alone seeing those borders explode, put at risk the image of invulnerability that liberalism so meticulously and so delicately assembles. In response to this threat, as Jaeger and Bowman suggest, "the most basic social relation to disability may be to pretend that it is not there."[39] To objectify and alienate the other, debilitate him socially, mark him off physically, and force him to feel out of place, is to deny his request for recognition, a request made in the form of a distinctive pronouncement of interdependence, a request that is fundamental to human subjectivity.

Perhaps what I am suggesting is that the tensions and duplicities inherent to the everyday shame experience of students, and teachers, offer us an opportunity: that by crafting a lucid vision of shame we may also be initiating a process of cultural and ideological transformation. In the co-construction of a vocabulary of shame, we might also increase our comfort with the reality of our interdependence and, in effect, increase our comfort in returning the supplicating gaze of the other with an appropriate regard for his or her otherness, for vulnerability that is shared yet unequal, with a sense of shame that is at bottom *self*-regarding. This kind of transformation is a task, first and foremost, I think, for encounters with others—indeed, encounters with the difference of other understandings— in education. Difference might more easily be faced, not ignored, in education. I believe this facing is born of self-regarding shame and obscured through other-regarding shame.

The perceptual shift intrinsic to the reversal of other-regarding for self-regarding shame begins with a capitulation: the self must relinquish its designs on completeness and abnegate its claim to absolute subjectivity. As Donna Haraway urges, "Only partial perspective promises objective vision."[40] The image of the autonomous student is only ever a partial perspective, relational and assembled by an entire community of perceiving others. Allison Carey notes that the "receipt of physical assistance should not preclude one from being seen as autonomous. . . . Dependence is part of the human condition; we are not autonomous but, rather, inter-connected, relational beings. . . . Exposing the interconnectedness of all people reveals the myth of independence and positions dependence as the 'normal' state of being in which all people require support and assistance."[41]

It is toward this kind of exposure and the retelling of a cultural myth that this essay makes its claims to influence the directionality of a collective consciousness. Our interconnectedness is never more exposed than when we feel self-regarding shame. Feeling shame before an other without dismissing her otherness or without being regulated by the conferral is an opportunity to deconstruct the fiction of independence that so diligently motivates the shaming and stigmatizing of dependent others. The decisive point is how shame is used, and described; therefore, perhaps what is decisive for education is precisely the manner in which teaching and learning are also emotional relations. How we perceive and understand the role of shame in positioning self and other between the poles of objectivity and subjectivity and how we come to recognize each other in and through our dealings with shame are part and parcel of the very education of education, of how, as Britzman suggests, "it is the responsibility of education to symbolize these conflicts rather than repeat them."[42]

What I am arguing is something similar to Dianne Pothier and Richard Devlin's critical disability theory, which "emphasizes the inevitability of difference, [and] demands the material reorganization of our basic social institutions, and . . . challenges the assumptions of sameness and assimilation in a profound way."[43] In practice what this might look like is a new foundational myth: the myth of interdependent citizenship and education. In this myth, our sense of shame at our varyingly dependent human existence inspires the acknowledgment rather than the refusal of our profound sensitivity to otherness, our vulnerability and connectivity to others. A more diverse awareness of shame, then, can actually help us retool the customs with which we manner our capacity to perceive need in others.

Nussbaum explains that there may be experiences of shame that are "not only non-narcissistic but actually antinarcissistic, reinforcing a sense of common human vulnerability, a sense of the inclusion of all human beings in the community, and related ideas of interdependence and mutual responsibility."[44] This is precisely how I have envisioned the role of self-regarding shame. It is my belief that a better understanding of our own sense of shame can produce a greater facility in perceiving the primordial otherness of surrounding others and therefore induce a heightened sensitivity to those others who may most clearly challenge our practiced completeness and narcissistic projects.

Nussbaum argues that "education needs to focus constantly on the needs and anxieties of the inner self, at the same time developing the capacity to perceive need in others."[45] According to the Individuals with Disabilities Education Act, a student with disabilities must have access to the most typical educational situation possible, be integrated or "mainstreamed" into general classrooms as often as is feasible, and in general be placed in the "least restrictive environment possible" for his or her education.[46] But, as Jaeger and Bowman contend, students with disabilities are still being undereducated, socially stigmatized, and emotionally traumatized.[47] This is due in part, I believe, to an unyielding cultural insistence upon reintegration, to the potential double stigma of not only failing to integrate but also failing to reintegrate. The liberal education model still employs an unfounded faith in the causal relation between self-sufficiency and productivity, convinced concurrently that this causality is an inherent social, political, and moral good. The expressed goal is one of reintegration and typicality rather than the more tolerant and inclusive aim of gaining appropriate awareness for the singular needs and capabilities of each student. What is needed are new strategies for recognizing the emotional life of *both* students and teachers, models of inclusion, not clinical classification and the abstract rights they (ambiguously) evoke. In effect, educational assistive services have in some ways become merely the regulative measures by which individuals in situations of disability are impelled toward a mainstream of categorization and standardization.

As argued earlier, these attitudes and the kind of perceiving they presuppose promote a mendacious vision of absolute independence, and they nurture desires for completeness that can in turn catalyze rampant and incapacitating exchanges of other-regarding shame. As long as the "abnormal" request continues to counter the current of the mainstream and thereby expose the very borders of the stream itself, the projects of the "abnormal" other will continue to be received and recognized as an obstacle to the narcissism of the self, a revelation that lays the ground for covetous personal demands for complete subjectivity. We might find a way, keeping with our nebulous affect, to supplant the other-regarding shame in pedagogical relations with a methodology for thinking about what it means to be seen seeing in the classroom.

Julia Kristeva says, "I am weary of the term *integration* of the disabled: it has a whiff of charity about it toward those without the same rights as others. I prefer *interaction*, which expresses a politics that has become an ethics, broadening the political pact to the frontiers of life."[48] Perhaps *interaction* is indeed the ethos at the heart of all that I have said so far. In fact, *integration*, on its side, seems to be precisely the end toward which other-regarding shame reaches, conferring object-status so as to incite a desire to hide difference, weakness, or dependence and regain typical self-sufficiency en route to achieving narcissistic subjectivity. Interaction, on the other hand, is born out of self-regarding shame. Dependence and sensitivity to the regard of others define self-regarding shame, an interaction for which vulnerability and mutuality are basic ingredients. According to Kristeva, "Inscribing vulnerability at the center of the political pact (understood as taking care of others) seems to me to be the best antidote to barbarity."[49]

With interaction as the bottom line for the education of students in situations of disability, we begin an attempt to change the particular relational patterns that characterize this telling meeting point in our society. Replacing the myth of independence for the more complicated and multifarious myth of interdependence in the classroom is a matter of changing attitudes, changing the practices of perceiving, and, in effect, changing the way in which we tell the stories of nurturance, sponsorship, and interaction in education. Accepting our own interdependence is a first step on the way to recognizing the interdependence of others, and it hinges on the capacity to perceive need in others, a capacity, as I have argued, that can be recovered and elaborated in and through experiences of self-regarding shame. It is a question of how teaching and learning might incite a new kind of thinking about inclusion and interaction, as well as about the shame each of us carries with us along with our various and often atavistic weaknesses. This anti-narcissistic project, gathering-in moments of self-regarding shame, keeping with instances of heightened sensitivity to otherness, and living through our mutuality with others, also "requires revising the idea of the citizen as independent bargainer and replacing it with a more complex image of a being both capable and needy, who moves from helplessness to 'mutual interdependence,' and, unfortunately, often back to helplessness again."[50]

A Politics of Transformation

As Nussbaum argues, there is a "minimum needed to appear in public *without shame* [my italics], as a citizen whose worth is equal to that of others."[51] Our sense of shame may be ever enduring, redolent with the secrecy of our objectivity, but our fundamental susceptibility to the other's gaze does not commit us to a lifetime of other-regarding shame. To be human, limited and in need, capable and constantly developing, is to merit both assistance and dignity. Each individual has the right to appear *without* shame—that is, without being seen and treated as an object. At the same time, however, it is meaningful to add that each individual has an obligation to appear *with* a sense of shame, a regard for the other, attending to her otherness with her very being. Merleau-Ponty advises:

> Once the other is posited, once the other's gaze fixed upon me has, by inserting me into his field, stripped me of part of my being, it will readily be understood that I can recover it only by establishing relations with him, by bringing about his clear recognition of me, and that my freedom requires the same freedom for others.[52]

Once the other is posited, the self becomes fixed and on guard. But it is not by reversing this conferral with the other or by transferring our perceived abatement and denudation onto the other that we win recognition. "[T]his mastery is self-defeating, since, precisely when my value is recognized through the other's desire, he is no longer the person by whom I wished to be recognized, but a being . . . who no longer counts in my eyes."[53] A culture that champions self-sufficiency also champions self-defeat. It is in establishing relations with the other or, in other words, by *interacting* rather than *integrating*, by drawing on our object-state so as to appreciate our mutuality, that we can bring about the collaborative recognition that we seek, an image that necessarily includes *both* self and other. As Schneider puts it, "The point is not to throw out shame and enthrone autonomy; but to recover an appropriate sense of shame and of the mutuality that is its foundation."[54]

While the distinction between self-regarding and other-regarding shame may only amount, in the last analysis, to a conceptual essentialism, the larger aim of this project is simply the bifurcation itself. If shame is indeed our everyday companion, we would do well to begin thinking of the affect as multiply articulate, expressive of two or more realities, generating two or more zones of becoming, intensifying—from multiple perspectives at once—what it means to be seen and discovered, stripped and incomplete, both subject and object. Shame is not always disconsolate; it is sometimes a reminder that we have misrecognized, or refused recognition to, others. It is sometimes an encounter with difference. It is sometimes a reminder that our freedom requires the same freedom for others. As independent citizens, we will always be disturbed by the true proximity of the other, leaning in ever so close, filling in the edges of our being, drawing the very limits of our very limited existence. The existential intermingling of experiences of shame may perhaps form one of the rare paths by which we can regain clear recognition between self and other, one of the rare paths by which we can overthrow the widespread liberal fixation on self-sufficient citizenship and transform the myth of independence into one of interdependence. There is a violence in our practices of perceiving that demands that we reflect on the kinds of shame our cultural narratives are wielding, particularly within educational practices. And there is a politics of perspective in our classrooms that insists we pay more attention to how difference is being confronted. The vision of citizenship offered by liberalism is, quite frankly, insufficient, unable to appropriately encounter disability. But self-regarding shame offers a unique vision and a unique kind of viewing, a lucidity perhaps, for perceiving interdependence. I urge that we gather-in (and gather in) our experiences of shame, come together in and through our shame, in the classroom and on the street. What we need, desperately, and what I have only really hinted at here, is a shift of mythological proportions, larval still in its current capacity for transformation but carrying a secret weight and truth, the portents of which are held within a look, glimpsed, grounded, and growing each and every time we come together.

Notes

1. Dianne Pothier and Richard Devlin, *Critical Disability Theory: Essays in Philosophy, Politics, and Law* (Vancouver: University of British Columbia Press, 2006), 16–17.

2. Robert Metcalf, "The Truth of Shame: Consciousness in Freud and Phenomenology," *Journal of Phenomenological Psychology*, 31, no. 1 (2000): 2.

3. This turn is in reference to Hannah Arendt's discussion of Emmanuel Kant's political philosophy. Kant claimed that "morality means being fit to be seen." Arendt, *Lectures on Kant's Political Philosophy* (Chicago: The University of Chicago Press, 1992), 49–50.

4. Martha Nussbaum, *Hiding from Humanity: Disgust, Shame, and the Law* (Princeton, NJ: Princeton University Press, 2004), 173.

5. In reference to J. S. Mill, Nussbaum distinguishes between actions implicating only the agent and consenting others (self-regarding) and actions implicating the interests of nonconsenting others (other-regarding). Nussbaum, *Hiding From Humanity*, 269.

6. Allison C. Carey, *On the Margins of Citizenship: Intellectual Disability and Civil Rights in Twentieth-Century America* (Philadelphia: Temple University Press, 2010), 1.

7. This choice, of course, does not come at random, but rather results from a personal context. My twin brother lost his hearing at the age of eight while battling meningitis. He wears a cochlear implant and hearing aid with considerable "success." He proudly identifies as hard of hearing.

8. Deborah P. Britzman, "Thoughts on the Fragility of Peace," *Life Long Learning in Europe*, no. 2 (2014).

9. Carl D. Schneider, *Shame, Exposure and Privacy* (Boston: Beacon Press, 1977), 38–39.

10. Maurice Merleau-Ponty, *Phenomenology of Perception* (New York: Routledge, 2007), 193.

11. Blaise Pascal, *Human Happiness* (London: Penguin Books, 2008), 78.

12. See, for instance, James B. Twitchell, *For Shame: The Loss of Common Decency in American Culture* (Collingdale, PA: Diane Publishing, 1997).

13. Eve Sedgwick, "Shame, Theatricality, and Queer Performativity: Henry James's *The Art of the Novel*," in *Gay Shame*, ed. David M. Halperin and Valerie Traub (Chicago: University of Chicago Press, 2009), 50.

14. Ibid.

15. Ibid., 51.

16. Ibid., 59.

17. Andrew P. Morrison, *The Underside of Shame* (New York: Analytic Press 1989), 66.

18. Sedgwick, "Shame, Theatricality, and Queer Performativity," 52.

19. Merleau-Ponty, *Phenomenology of Perception*, 412.

20. Ibid., 420.

21. If the shame is self-regarding, as I will distinguish.

22. Jean-Paul Sartre, *Being and Nothingness* (New York: Washington Square Press, 1992), 302.

23. Ibid., 309, 310.

24. Sally R. Munt, *Queer Attachments: The Cultural Politics of Shame* (Burlington, VT: Ashgate Publishing, 2008), 203.

25. Pothier and Devlin, *Critical Disability Theory*, 12.

26. Carey, *On the Margins of Citizenship*, 2.

27. Paul T. Jaeger and Cynthia Ann Bowman, *Understanding Disability: Inclusion, Access, Diversity, and Civil Rights* (London: Praeger, 2005), 76.

28. Pothier and Devlin, *Critical Disability Theory*, 2.

29. Carol A. Breckenridge and Candance Vogler, "The Critical Limits of Embodiment: Disability's Criticism," *Public Culture* 13, no. 35 (2001), 351.

30. Merleau-Ponty, *Phenomenology of Perception*, xi, 177.

31. Pothier and Devlin, *Critical Disability Theory*, 9.

32. See especially Carey's extended discussion of the ambivalence surrounding intellectual disability and the exercise of rights in the United States, *On the Margins of Citizenship*, chap. 1.

33. Maryam El-Shall, "Yes, Who Can? Who 'We' Are in American Liberal Discourse," *Thirdspace: A Journal of Feminist Theory and Culture* 10, no. 1 (2011), 15.

34. Ibid., 12.

35. Nussbaum, *Hiding from Humanity*, 207.

36. Sartre, *Being and Nothingness*, 475, 472.

37. Gershen Kaufman, *The Psychology of Shame* (New York: Springer, 1996), 275.

38. Julia Kristeva, *Hatred and Forgiveness* (New York: Columbia University Press, 2010), 29.

39. Jaeger and Bowman, *Understanding Disability*, 18.

40. Donna J. Haraway, *Simians, Cyborgs, and Women: The Reinvention of Nature* (New York: Routlege, 1991), 190.

41. Carey, *On the Margins of Citizenship*, 17, 18.

42. Deborah P Britzman, *The Very Thought of Education: Psychoanalysis and the Impossible Professions* (New York: State University of New York Press, 2009), 12.

43. Pothier and Devlin, *Critical Disability Theory*, 21.

44. Nussbaum, *Hiding from Humanity*, 213.

45. Ibid., 203.

46. Jaeger and Bowman, *Understanding Disability*, 81.

47. Ibid., 96.

48. Kristeva, *Hatred and Forgiveness*, 34.

49. Ibid., 34.

50. Nussbaum, *Hiding from Humanity*, 312–313.

51. Ibid., 284.

52. Merleau-Ponty, *Phenomenology of Perception*, 416.

53. Ibid., 193.

54. Schneider, *Shame, Exposure and Privacy*, 1977.

PART 3

Bodies on Display: Performing Shame in Visual Arts

EIGHT

Shame and Shitting: Postfeminist Episodes in Contemporary Hollywood Films

Madeline Walker

> We know of course that women are habitually constipated, but to represent them in fiction as being altogether devoid of a back passage seems to me really an excess of chivalry.
> —Somerset Maugham, *Cakes & Ale*[1]

Maugham's observation in 1930 was apt—descriptions of women defecating were rare in nineteenth- and early twentieth-century literature because of historical propriety and a cultural anxiety about defecation, the final taboo. In James Joyce's bawdy *Ulysses*, it is not Molly Bloom but Leopold Bloom who famously sits on the toilet and defecates in episode 4, Calypso. Depictions of women shitting in literature have continued to be uncommon. Two rare European examples are Leni's extraordinary "paperless" status (able to execute a bowel movement so cleanly that paper is not needed) in Heinrich Boll's 1971 *Group Portrait with Lady* and Sabina voiding her bowels as erotic spectacle in Milan Kundera's 1984 *The Unbearable Lightness of Being*. The near invisibility of the female bowel movement in literature can be contrasted with a recent exposure of women's defecation in Hollywood film. Most spectacularly, we see Lillian in the 2011 box office hit *Bridesmaids* collapsed in the middle of a Chicago street "crapping her wedding dress": female bowel movement turned into visual spectacle. Filmmakers make less direct but still notable references to the female bowel movement in *North Country, Without a Paddle,* and *The Help*. What happened? Silence about women's bowel movements in social discourse, film, art, and literature has shifted not simply to a more open depiction of the topic but to the reveling—as in two recent Hollywood films—in the "shamelessness" of exploding the taboo through open portrayal of women shitting in public. If, as Hilary Radner writes, films contain a "highly schematic representation of contemporary discourses in which the tensions and controversies of an era are writ large," then Hollywood films chart the discursive constructions operating in American society.[2] The spotlight on women's bowel movements,

I suggest, may be the signal of societal discomfort with women going too far—a clarion call to twentieth-century female propriety through shaming.

In this essay, I draw on Freud and postfeminism to structure my analysis of scenes in *The Back-up Plan* (2010), written by Kate Angelo, and *Bridesmaids*, written by Annie Mumolo and Kristen Wiig. My own strong visceral reaction to shitting episodes in these movies inspired me to contemplate why I felt shamed by those scenes. Although my response derived partly from a lifetime of coprophobia, it was also the result—I recognized—of popular American culture's gendered scripts around women and defecation. I argue that the "shameless" depiction of women defecating in public may be viewed as a shaming device that reinscribes Freud's injunction that women's unruly bodies must be disciplined to maintain civilized life. At the same time, this device of public defecation demonstrates one of postfeminism's central dictums: the feminine subject must, at all times, maintain self-regulation or risk the shame of being seen as out of control. In *The Back-up Plan*, the state of being out of control is associated with second-wave feminism, an embarrassing movement that may have benefited women but is depicted as irrelevant for contemporary postfeminist subjects.

Historically, the message that women's bodies must be controlled was conveyed through reining in women's sexuality; more recently it has been portrayed through anal shaming. If feminists worked to dismantle shame and repression as forms of social control over women, postfeminism operates in *The Back-up Plan* to reshame them as bodies out of control, contrasting unruly figures with their self-regulating foil, the protagonist Zoe (Jennifer Lopez). As in *Bridget Jones's Diary*, in *Bridesmaids* we see postfeminist "heroines" who have benefited from all of the gains of feminism and are now free to enjoy their autonomy as conscious consumers of white weddings and bleached anuses. The metanarrative hovering over the crucial "I crapped my wedding dress" scene is that feminism has done its equalizing work: we can enjoy raunchy bathroom humor about women now, too. But a postfeminist sensibility inscribes another message on that scene: don't let your body out of your control, especially in public.

Shattering the taboo of showing or discussing female defecation in public, these films do not—as might be expected—liberate a repressive notion of female propriety by leveling men and women as both possessing anuses and both needing to move their bowels. On the contrary, by shaming women who expose too much, the movies operate—to varying degrees—as disciplinary devices to put women back in their place. Postfeminism serves as a corrective sensibility in these movies, though in different ways. (Here, I borrow the word "sensibility" from Rosalind Gill and will discuss her term "postfeminist sensibility" in detail a bit further on.)[3] In these and many recent "chick flicks" women's own surveillance both within the films and in the assumed audience shames and shapes filmic images of women losing control of their bowels. If one of the central imperatives to postfeminism is self-discipline, as Marjorie Jolles argues, then these two movies remind women of the shame in failing to control themselves and their bodies.

In the *Back-up Plan*, the beautiful and independent Zoe gives up on finding love and decides to become a single mother through artificial insemination. On the same day she is inseminated, she meets Stan (Alex O'Loughlin), and they eventually fall in love. After the usual conflicts and reverses of the "rom-com," Stan and Zoe end up happily together. Zoe, having profited from its gains, rejects feminism as no longer necessary. Feminist women in the film are depicted as anachronistic, ugly, and unfeminine man haters whose bodies are out of control, as demonstrated by a woman birthing like an animal, public defecation, and a mother breastfeeding her three-year-old child. In *Bridesmaids*, a film about the ups and downs of the relationship between Annie (Kristen Wiig) and her best friend Lillian (Maya Rudolph), who chooses Annie to be her maid of honor, there is a knowing postfeminism at work that might be considered almost a post-postfeminism. Scenes of out-of-control defecation poke fun at the ways that typical chick flicks and Disney movies display the gutsy, entitled heroine as tough and authentic yet impossibly beautiful and perfect. In *Bridesmaids*, the heroines shit, too. But the metaphor that life is diarrhea if you don't get hold of it—the protagonist Annie's lack of impulse control leads to an out-of-control life—plays out alongside the literal diarrhea of the dress scene, always illustrating that not to self-regulate, as a good postfeminist should, results in shame.

Some readers may wonder whether it is significant that the screenwriters for both of these films are women—is this a case of postfeminist screenwriters shaming other women? The answers are neither clear nor obvious. *Bridesmaid's* co-producer Judd Apatow was apparently responsible for inserting the diarrhea and vomit scenes to appeal to male viewers.[4] However, the way the scenes are handled and the undercurrent of shaming might well be the design of the female writers. More important, though, the shaming effect is a product of our culture as much as it is the result of how the scenes are treated. Women are socially torqued to feel shame about their bowel movements—go no further than your local pharmacy to see "Just a Drop" bathroom odor eliminator on the shelf, a product marketed mostly to women.

Theoretical Background: Freud and Postfeminism

Although Freud and postfeminism may seem like peculiar mates, they resonate curiously with one another. The theoretical basis for my argument, in brief, turns on an old idea found in the Bible, Shakespeare's *Taming of the Shrew* and Freud's *Civilization and Its Discontents*: Unruly women need to be tamed by men for the good of civilization. In postfeminism, however, the role of the male disciplinarian who keeps the woman in line is turned back on women themselves. Woman has internalized the surveillance role and must ensure that she is always in control (or *appears* to be in control): beautiful, sexy, and feminine. Her self-control is ostensibly exerted for her own pleasure—not for men's. The movies I examine are illustrations of rare breaches of that control—when women defecate in public, a final taboo is ruptured and a cultural anxiety about a complete loss of control, signaling the end of Western civilization as we know it, is set in motion. That loss of control, I suggest, is linked to feminism's old but still lurking unruliness. My illustrations of this phenomenon in two chick flicks may seem banal in relation to such a sweeping idea as the downfall of civilization; however, seen in the context of postfeminism's objective to reference feminism only to then disavow it—the trend seems ominous. McRobbie argues that popular culture has been "perniciously effective" in this undoing, casting feminism into the "shadows," where young women will continue to keep their distance.[5]

Freud

Although many of Freud's theories seem ridiculous and outmoded, his ideas about anal eroticism, the anal stage, and anal character have nonetheless permeated North American culture to the degree that we talk casually about being "anal." His *Three Essays on Sexuality* published in 1905, in which he posited the three stages of human development—oral, anal, and genital—contains some of the most culturally familiar material in his oeuvre. At the same time, messages about unruly women as enemies of order and civilization inform many images in popular culture. Freud posited in *Civilization and Its Discontents* (1929) that woman's libidinous and unruly nature must be repressed for men to do the work of building civilization: "Women soon come into opposition to civilization and display their retarding and restraining influence."[6] This belief, that women are sexually unbridled and uncontrolled and thus a threat to the order of civilization, lies just under representations of women as the more restrained or reticent sex. Although it is now commonplace in Hollywood film to see women depicted as having intemperate sexual appetites, it is still rare to see public or private representations of women defecating. And these representations are few compared with the slew of men and boys depicted for decades in movies and television shows as the butts and enjoyers of toilet humor, for example, in *American Pie, Superbad, Scary Movie,* and *Animal House.*

Potty humor might be associated with regression—being thrown back to the anal stage where children enjoy their "creations" and play with their feces. Mastering control of the bowels and sublimating anal eroticism is a necessary path to becoming adult and civilized, just as it is a requisite learning site of where self ends and the external world begins. According to Freud, "Sublimation of instinct is an especially conspicuous feature of cultural development; it is what makes it possible for higher psychical activities, scientific, artistic or ideological, to play such an important part in civilized life."[7] Thus, Freud suggested that both oral and anal eroticism needed to be rerouted into genital satisfaction for the individual and in turn the culture to become civilized. However, according to Freud there are some people who develop "anal characters" as a result of being too attached to the pleasurable experience of the bowel movement in early life. These people, having eventually to sublimate and compensate for those early pleasures, end up being "orderly, parsimonious and obstinate."[8]

Regardless of the "truth" of anal character, the concept of being "anal" has flourished in popular culture. Although Freud seemed to have rather jaded view of those character traits in his early writing, by the time he wrote *Civilization and Its Discontents*, he calls them "valuable and welcome."[9] Similarly, in pop culture the *Urban Dictionary* denotes being "anal" as being "uptight"; nevertheless, the positive associations of being orderly, clean, and controlled are viewed as desirable in contrast to disorder and being out of control. For example, the public diarrhea scene in *Bridesmaids* is contrasted with the male lead's "anal" character. In one scene, as Nathan and Annie get to know each other, they sit on his police car at dawn, chatting and flirting after meeting by accident in an all-night grocery store. They share his bag of baby carrots. Annie finds an "ugly" carrot that she rejects, but Nathan says he'll eat it because it brings good luck. Annie snatches it from him, exclaiming "Ew!" and flinging it to the ground. Nathan then picks it up: "Don't litter; I'll fine you. . . . It's just that I am anal about that kind of thing."[10] Although we may joke self-deprecatingly about being "anal," we also value "anality" as a positive trait, just as we do perfectionism. To be anal is to be organized, tidy, clean, and mature in opposition to the unruliness of letting it all out, as Annie demonstrates with her verbal diarrhea and Lillian shows with her literal diarrhea in the movie. Nathan, the figurehead of law and order in the movie, has positive character traits of loyalty, constraint, good values, and orderliness that are contrasted with Annie's lack of judgment, morals, and control.

The anal stage, according to Freud and his followers, is also coterminous with the formation of identity. A child begins to recognize where she ends and the external world begins during the period of toilet training. As Hocquenghem, following Freud, writes, "The functions of this organ [the anus] are truly private; they are the site of the formation of the person."[11] Hocquenghem discusses the anus in the context of homosexual desire; however, his use of Freud is relevant to the discussion of public defecation and women:

> Freud sees the anal stage as the stage of formation of the person. The anus has no social desiring function left, because all its functions have

become excremental . . . . The anus does not exist in a social relation, since it forms precisely the individual and therefore enables the division between society and the individual to be made . . . one does not shit in company.[12]

Thus, the breaching of the private woman through public defecation in the two films I examine is akin to a breach of identity and autonomy. The symbolic breakdown of social order effected by women shitting out of place is also the breakdown of women's self-surveillance, a salient ingredient of postfeminism.

Postfeminism can be viewed as a "sensibility" that includes women's stringent monitoring of their selves and their bodies, with an apparent disconnection from the forces exerted by culture and society. In other words, women—as ideal neoliberal subjects—are entirely responsible for their own bodies and actions and, as Gill explains, have successfully and frighteningly internalized male judgment by being harsh judges of their own appearance and actions. I will explain this and other aspects of postfeminism next, but let me just point out now that the Freudian injunction that the child learn control of the anus in order to achieve entry into society and the further staining of women as the agents of social breakdown put an extreme pressure on females to hold back, to be in control, to be "anal." When this injunction is broken through spectacles of public defecation, the women in the films and the viewers are meant to feel the multivalent breach of barriers—of female identity, autonomy, self-control, and privacy; and to feel the threat to the postfeminist view of women as self-made, powerful, beautiful, and sexy. Indignant at this breach, the viewer is compelled to side with postfeminists. This is how these films shame women and discipline them.

Finally, images of women out of control are loosely connected with feminists in both of the films as examples of whom not to be like. Similar to the "old maid" in the card game, second-wave feminism in these films is the placeholder for all that is to be avoided or shunned. I will flesh out this idea later in this essay.

Postfeminism

Like postmodernism, postfeminism is a multivalent term without a stable definition. However, Rosalind Gill's description of it as a contradictory "sensibility" wherein the discourses of feminism and antifeminism are intertwined and conflicting is one useful way of conceptualizing this ill-defined and fluid collection of theories.[13] Gill acknowledges that postfeminism has been used to "signal an epistemological break with (second-wave) feminism, an historical shift (to a third wave), or a regressive political stance (backlash)."[14] These conceptualizations are not only contradictory, writes Gill, they do not tell us what actually constitutes postfeminism. Her pragmatic solution is to describe a "postfeminist sensibility" comprising six stable characteristics (described later) that illustrate the contradictoriness of postfeminism, its commensurability with neoliberalism, and its salience in current popular media.

I purposely do not take up Hilary Radner's concept of neofeminism (in *Neo-Feminist Cinema*) here because she conceptualizes neofeminism not as a turn away from feminism but as coterminous with second-wave feminism, offering women a new model for femininity inspired largely by Helen Gurley Brown. Although Radner shares with other theorists the idea that post/neofeminism is tightly intertwined with neoliberalism and consumer culture, she has a much more sanguine view of the emancipatory nature of neofeminism than the more ominous views of Gill and especially McRobbie, who see postfeminism as a sort of fake feminism. My own argument relies on illustrating postfeminist shunning of feminism and feminists in film, which is an integral part of Gill's and McRobbie's theorizing but not aligned with Radner's views. I believe the postfeminist sensibility to be so salient in contemporary media culture—in which feminism is feared and attacked yet taken for granted while neoliberal values are trumpeted—is a pretense of women's "empowerment," with anal shaming its latest manifestation. Thus, in this essay I use *postfeminism* and *postfeminist sensibility* to refer to a set of ideas, promulgated by Gill (and McRobbie to some extent), that permeate the movies I examine.

Postfeminism is displayed regularly in popular culture, "a primary realm where gender ideology is actively produced, consumed, negotiated, and transformed."[15] In fact, many feminist theorists see popular culture in the form of media (advertisements, television, magazines, film) as the primary site for the undoing of feminism (see Brunsdon, Gill, Jolles, and McRobbie). In the case of contemporary chick flicks or rom coms, there is always already an implicit divide between what McRobbie calls the "spectre of what feminism once was"[16] and the postfeminist woman, who is hostile to her mother's brand of feminism. This provides a canvas for the conflicts and tensions arising from those relationships—between young "postfeminists" and those stained with old-school (second-wave) feminism. This tension is ratcheted up with what I call the breaching of the final (anal) taboo—feminists don't care really because they are viewed as "monstrous"[17] and therefore shameless about bodily functions, but postfeminists feel appropriate shame for being out of control and defecating in public. These displays may even be read as a kind of generalized warning: this is what will happen if feminism is reconstituted.

Gill's six stable characteristics of postfeminist media culture are useful signposts for reading the contemporary rom-com. First, femininity is seen as a bodily property belonging exclusively to postfeminists (thus Zoe in *The Back-up Plan* is always feminine, even when giving birth or urinating, whereas the feminists in her Single Mothers and Proud support group are all unfeminine). Second, there is a shift from objectification by men to subjectification by women themselves, which might be read as a form of internalizing the oppressor. Third, the injunction to be self-surveillant, although long a requirement for "successful femininity,"[18] has now saturated all pockets of life: women must monitor and continually transform their entire selves, including their appearance and attitudes, with real vigilance. At the same time, they must always appear carefree and confident about their presentation. Fourth, there is an emphasis on choice and autonomy and the elision of cultural and political influences. Gill uses the example of women getting Brazilian waxes and breast implants presumably to please themselves or to make themselves look beautiful for their own pleasure. The makeover paradigm is the fifth characteristic of postfeminist media culture. Finally, sexual differences between men and women, which some feminists worked to de-emphasize, is again highlighted as "natural."

Although not all of Gill's ideas have relevance to my discussion, the overall sensibility of postfeminism—that is, a contradictory discourse that takes for granted many of the accomplishments of feminism and at the same time trashes feminists as ugly man haters and celebrates a sexy, powerful, autonomous "new" woman—is evident in two of the films I explore. And the requirement that women be self-surveillant and constrained is also very much at play in these films. In *Bridesmaids*, for example, the woman who does not self-police—who has diarrhea of the mouth and actions and instigates the public humiliation of her best friend's shitting on the street—is, by the end of the movie, reined in by her policeman boyfriend. In *The Back-up Plan*, the leading lady Zoe has reaped the gains of feminism (autonomy, choice, sexual and reproductive freedom), yet rejects the apparent demands of being a feminist as illustrated by the members of the Single Mothers and Proud group (ugly, unfeminine, humorless, and bent on kooky, seemingly outdated rites and rituals such as home birth and child-led weaning).

The Freudian notion of women's unbridled energies needing to be reined in by men for the good of civilization is here transformed into women reining themselves in through careful self-surveillance, self-regulation, and pretend autonomy (e.g., I love being beautiful and free). In the movies I explore, the contradictory character of postfeminism is clear—undisciplined women who shit out of place (even if the elimination—diarrhea—is out of their control) are disciplined through cultural shaming or tainted by their representation as second-wave feminists. Sometimes shaming is effected with a knowing wink typical of rom coms and chick flicks, but shame is nonetheless the result. Although of course I cannot "prove" that female viewers feel shame during these films, there are some media reports and comments that bear out my assessment, which I will discuss.

Shame

Shame has been defined as the emotion that makes one feel "I am no good" and includes the experience of "wishing to hide, disappear, or die."[19] The self feels in some way "not human, not a full person."[20] To paint the literature in very broad strokes, writers on shame can be roughly divided into those who defend it as useful in regulating self and others and those who read it as a toxic and something to be liberated from. The first camp tends to view shame as a cleansing emotion and a mark of humanity (e.g., Deonna, Rodogno, and Teroni; Schneider).[21] The other camp comprises those who consider shame debilitating, amoral, and primitive (e.g., Brene Brown, Nussbaum, Sanders et al.).[22]

Although Lewis claims that the shrinking feeling produced by shame is not related to "the public or private nature of the situation"—he argues that we can feel shame privately or among people—there is a strong connection between shame and the exposure of something private in the public sphere.[23] Carl Schneider suggests that when the barriers concealing activities considered private, such as bodily functions, are breached, the result is shame, disgust, obscenity or pornography.[24] Drawing on the work of Max Scheler, Schneider says that when shame is exploited to elicit displeasure or shock the effect is obscenity. Thus, the obscene is "a deliberate violation of the sense of shame."[25]

The obscene, then, is a way of treating human physicality, making a public spectacle out of what should remain private. Obscenity involves making private events public in a way that denigrates our humanity.[26] In this light, public defecation—particularly by women because of persistent ideas about propriety and femininity—makes a spectacle out of what should remain private, thus shaming the shitter and branding the event as obscene. By extension, the female viewer of the obscene event is shamed.

I offer a caveat here: rather than feel shame, male viewers seem to relish these spectacles. In fact, *Bridesmaids* was praised by male reviewers precisely because of the "shamelessness" of the vomit and diarrhea scenes reportedly inserted by co-producer Judd Apatow to increase male attendance.[27] According to the *Hollywood Reporter*, the anticipated opening weekend box-office take for *Bridesmaids* was $15–17 million; however, the actual take was $24.6 million, attributed to more males in the audience (33%) than expected.[28] And Ricky Gervais, celebrating the defecation scene, said, "Defecating in a sink was less demeaning then what most of you have done to make it in show business" when presenting the Critics Choice Award to *Bridesmaids*.[29] Many female critics, on the other hand, were put off by the same scenes that brought in male viewers. NPR's Ella Taylor wrote, "We want to see girls behaving badly—though preferably without the vomit and poop scenes that Apatow reportedly shoehorned in for fear of losing the guy demographic. That stuff played just fine in *Knocked Up*, but it's not needed here." And Carol Mallory wrote, "To mock women defecating is crude, demeaning and not achieving equality . . . only ridicule."

I view shame as a cultural tool to shame "shameless" women and to deliberately violate the sense of shame for obscene purposes. The overarching cultural view is that if the female characters in the films I examine do not feel uncomfortable or uncomfortable enough in their own shame over public defecation, female viewers should feel it for them, along with the shock of obscenity arising from the exploitation of their shame. Freud wrote that people who "look on at excretory functions" are at risk of suffering from "perversion" if their disgust is "overrid[den]"; thus, feeling shame is a necessary adjunct of watching what ought to remain private.[30] The alternative is to be as debased as the shitters. Arousing sympathetic shame in the viewer serves to put women back in their place—the fact that they have anuses should not be drawn to public attention, they should have more control, they should be more discreet. And when women watch women defecating publicly—even if it is beyond their control (i.e., diarrhea), their own sense of shame comes into play.

Although it is too simplistic to claim that American cinema is a mirror of American society, we can nonetheless see in the movies our cultural anxieties "writ large" and read a trajectory about anality and women in recent film.[31] The breakdown of civilization includes breaking the last taboo of the private anus, defecation, and women. These films not only show this final breakdown but, through a postfeminist lens, they reshame these out-of-control women in various ways to keep them in line. What is interesting to me is that women are shown only in situations where defecation is not in their control (i.e., diarrhea and passing stool during birth). We cannot imagine a Hollywood movie showing a woman on the toilet, reading, like Leopold Bloom perusing "Matcham's Masterstroke,"[32] and taking quotidian pleasure in a normal bowel movement. The absence of that image, I hypothesize, is the result of postfeminism's contradictory force: Contemporary women have reaped the rewards of feminism, including the freedom of sexuality and full ownership of the body, and yet are held captive by the regressive ideas that femininity is a bodily property, sexual differences between men and women are paramount, and women must be self-monitored. Thus, although the anus is the great anatomical equalizer between men and women, bodily femininity precludes the publicity of the bowel movement as something we all do—after all, women choose to be attractive and sexy at all times, and although sitting on the toilet to urinate has been represented as sexually titillating (see *Not another Teen Movie* and

The Sessions), sitting on the toilet to defecate has not. We have passed the barrier of sexual shaming (*pudendum*, the word for female external genitals, derives from the Latin *pudere*, to be ashamed) and moved to the final frontier of shaming around the bowel movement—and in particular women's bowel movements because men having bowel movements has already been comedy fodder for years.

Bridesmaids: "I Crapped My Wedding Dress"

Bridesmaids is about Annie, a charming but loser-ish forty-something single woman and her relationship with her best friend Lillian, who chooses Annie to be maid of honor in her upcoming wedding. The plot follows Annie's uneasiness in the role of maid of honor as she competes against the perfect, beautiful Helen (Rose Byrne). Helen finally usurps Annie's role after a number of hilarious battles that show Annie as imperfect, out of control, and outlandish and Helen as controlled, groomed, and "anal." A narrative accompanying the main story is Annie's love interest, an attractive cop with a British accent, Nathan Rhodes (Chris O'Dowd), who stops her for broken tail lights and ends up in bed with her. Annie temporarily wrecks both this relationship and her friendship with Lillian as a result of being out of control, but will is pulled back under control in the final scene—disciplined by her anal competitor, Helen, and her anal boyfriend, Nathan, who jokingly puts her in the back of his police car after the white wedding that ends the comedy.

The scenes that interest me in this movie concern a public outbreak of diarrhea among the bridesmaids. Annie, characterized as someone who consistently makes bad decisions in her life, chooses a questionable Brazilian restaurant in a seedy neighborhood. The waiters serve up big hunks of meat to the bridesmaids. All but proper (anal) Helen partake in the feast. After lunch, they go to an upscale bridal salon that Annie has chosen to purchase their bridesmaid dresses. When they are all in their full regalia, each bridesmaid in a different expensive dress, the food poisoning begins to take effect. Megan (Melissa McCarthy), an overweight, dykey woman (the groom's sister), makes a beeline for the bathroom, competing with Rita (Wendi McLendon-Covey), who has been depicted throughout the movie as out of control in her graphic language and desire to have extramarital sex. As Rita gets to the toilet first, kneeling down and vomiting into the bowl, Megan hoists her squat body, wrapped tightly in a wine-colored dress, onto the sink, where sound effects illustrate her noisy diarrhea while she yells "Look away, look away!" A high-angle shot closes the scene, showing Megan and Rita respectively shitting and puking. The effect of a mannish, comedic character shitting in a sink is less shocking and shaming than the later scene, where we see the attractive bride having diarrhea in the street. However, Megan's shitting in a sink is a warm-up of sorts—she is associated with feminism more than any other character in the movie because she doesn't care about femininity or her weight and she is bellicose, inappropriate, and outspoken. Thus, her public diarrhea is not too disturbing because of her mannish appearance and might be taken as equivalent to iconic scenes of men having diarrhea—for example, Paul Finch (Eddie Kaye Thomas) in *American Pie* and Harry Dunne (Jeff Daniels) in *Dumb and Dumber*. Moreover, Melissa McCarthy, who plays Megan, also plays the feminist ringleader of the single mothers group in *The Back-up Plan*, cementing that typecasting in American comedy.

Meanwhile, Helen and Annie wage their war of bridesmaid competition in the main boudoir, with Annie (sweating and ill-looking) insisting she's fine and Helen egging her on by offering candied almonds. Next, we see Lillian in a white wedding dress running out of the store to get to a bathroom across the street. She dodges traffic, moaning "It's happening," like an incantation, four times. She then collapses in the street, the white fabric ballooning up around her. "It happened, it happened," she says, motioning a car to go around her. Shame often results in an inability to speak—here rendered as repetition of the same words.[33] Women in the audience are invited to feel Lillian's shame with her as we witness her face and her paralysis while performing a most private act in public. Although passersby may be male, the audience is primarily made up of women—Annie, Helen, and Whitney as well as female viewers. Similarly in *The Back-up Plan* it is only women who witness the stool-in-the-water scene; Stan, the male protagonist, is in the other room and only enters later. Annie, now on the sidewalk watching says, "Wow you're really doing it aren't you—you're shitting in the street." Helen and Whitney stand together, also watching but talking about dresses. As if nothing has happened, Helen says, "We'll just take five of the Fritz Bernaise [the fictional dress designer]. They really do look better." During the scene where Annie drives Lillian home, Annie asks, "Are you alright?" "I crapped my wedding dress," Lillian answers, as if replaying the traumatic scene in her mind. "I crapped my wedding dress." Annie pulls over, gets out, and retches (off camera) at the side of the car. Although at this point it does not seem that Annie will get diarrhea, much later in the film, she says to Helen, "I shit my pants on the way home." Thus this reported event, too, takes place off camera.

These rich scenes in the elegant wedding boutique and its bathroom, on the street fronting the store, and in the car home, show women shitting uncontrollably (i.e., having diarrhea). The portrayal of such shitting—by Megan and Lillian in particular—may first appear to be emancipatory. Finally, we can show and witness women in the same bawdy, animal positions as we have shown and witnessed men in for decades. The juxtaposition of the white wedding dress and public diarrhea serves to highlight the contrast between the usual romantic comedy (ending in a white wedding) and this hybrid content, mixing the raunchy guy comedy (*American*

Pie-style) in a chick flick. The shameless portrayals (shameless in the sense that the movie creators have no shame) are in fact shaming portrayals, because the women whose bodies are out of control are unable to accomplish the self-surveillance and "keeping it together" so important to a postfeminist sensibility.

Carl Schneider argues that shame is understood visually—we try to hide when feeling shame, to disappear from view. Thus, Megan's insistent "Look away, look away" (and the camera's bird's-eye view, obeying her command by looking, though not away, from a distance) illustrates how shame operates. Lillian's shame results from her exposure and inability to hide as she defecates (even though covered by her gown) in the middle of the street. The visual sense here is of loss of face translated into loss of self and power: the crumpled dress around her is like the Wicked Witch of the West (in *The Wizard of Oz*) dissolving in water—her magic all gone. Her power as a postfeminist heroine, an attractive, independent woman who has chosen a white wedding despite (or because of) radical feminism's rejection of this patriarchal ritual, is lost in a moment when she shits her panties.

Another aspect of postfeminist sensibility is the salience of the makeover, illustrated later in the film. When Annie attends the bridal shower at Helen's mansion, she become furious with Lillian, whom she thinks has been taken in by Helen's inauthentic friendship: "Get your head out of your ass," she says to her old friend, and then "I bet it's bleached." Lillian retorts, "We went to the salon and I got my asshole bleached and I love my new asshole." Lillian is of mixed race, the product (in the film) of a Black father and a White mother. She is also the character who soiled a white wedding dress in public with diarrhea. So here we have her bleaching her anus, a postfeminist move showing her supposedly autonomous choice to have an invasive and possibly harmful procedure to bleach away the brown—not just the perceived "stain" of feces/diarrhea but the stain of being Black in a White group. Here Lillian goes public with a private, personal body transformation—thus turning the potentially cleansing act of bleaching skin into another shameful scene ("shameless" paradoxically equals "shameful"—the connotations of shame cannot be bleached from the word even with the suffix "less"). If, as Nathan has joked about her, Annie is the "maid of dishonor," Lillian is the bride of shame.

The "makeover paradigm" is another illustration of the postfeminist as perfect neoliberal subject: women have the will, the personal power and choice, the financial means, and the interest in changing their bodies—even if it means to temporary lighten a dark anus. The implicit comparison is with the stereotypical bra-burning second-wave feminist who is purposefully unkempt and rejects any "unnatural" procedures. As McRobbie has pointed out, postfeminism is a "double entanglement"[34] because its celebratory claims of being "beyond feminism" are predicated on the very achievements of the feminists they claim to be beyond.

Having control over her body as a result of the work of second-wave feminists is ironically taken by Lillian to the self-harming extreme: anal bleaching.

The Back-up Plan: Out-of-Control Pretty and Out-of-Control Ugly

In *The Back-up Plan*, Zoe—embodying postfeminism—is the beautiful, freedom-loving, independent, entrepreneurial protagonist whose feminine charms are continually set against the ugliness of feminism. A scene that illustrates this more than any other is the water birth. Zoe and Stan are invited to attend a home water birth of one of the members of the Single Mothers and Proud group that Zoe previously belonged to. The members are shown as unattractive feminists: the leader Carol (played by Melissa McCarthy, the mannish Megan from *Bridesmaids*) is an overweight, chanting, drum-banging woman. The birthing woman, Lori (Maribeth Monroe), is depicted as masculine looking with tattoos and greasy hair. She is making frightening animal sounds as she sprawls in a child's swimming pool set up in the living room, a starkly different image from the one Frederick Leboyer had in mind in his 1975 *Birth without Violence*, in which he popularized the gentle water birth. Zoe is Lori's "focal point," so she is prevented from leaving the room and has to witness not only the birth but also Lori evacuating her bowels in the water. Zoe says, "Jesus what is that?" while stools float into her view and another tough-looking woman, Ridley, is asked by the leader to dispatch the shit, which she does using a toy fish net. The movie viewers are spared the shame, seeing only something dark in the net, whisked away quickly. "Perfectly natural, sometimes the bowels just release,"[35] remarks the unflappable leader of the group, who continues to bang her drum while others chant and the birthing mother continues to groan and growl. This scene contrasts with Zoe's own birthing scene at the end of the movie, which is sweaty but serene, draped, and feces-free. The implication is that birth out of control is horrible and even traumatic, and that during a primitive birthing like Lori's, one's primal nature is unleashed, revealing not only literal shit but the figurative shit of the subconscious. On the other hand, Zoe's birthing, properly controlled in a hospital setting by a kindly, avuncular obstetrician and by Zoe's own impeccable self-surveillance, is appealing and unthreatening. Jennifer Lopez's status as domesticated Latina subject here signals a third way (neither Black nor White) that serves to resolve anxieties between second-wave and postfeminist polarities. The usual identification of the Latina in Hollywood films as fertile, childbearing, and a sexual threat is here traded for a tamed version of the raced female, to be contrasted with the second-wave feminist dyke in the water birth scene.[36] As a result, ethnically marked Zoe seems more "American" than White Lori.

The water birth scene highlights the *sine qua non* of postfeminism—that feminism is sealed (safely) in the past—feminists are dusty, ugly, and irrelevant man haters, and all they might stand for, including home births and unregulated stools, is also ugly and irrelevant. The name of the group "Single Mothers and Proud" implies a contrast to Zoe, who is rejected by the group because she is no longer single once she falls in love with Stan. Their "pride" is an object of expected viewers' scorn—what have they to be proud of? They really ought to be ashamed of themselves—none of them is attractive enough to keep the men who impregnated them, whereas Zoe attracts and keeps a man who is not even the father of her twins.

Postfeminism, while portraying feminism as all used up, also shows women as having benefited from the movement and its accomplishments. For example, Zoe has used the choice and freedom available to her to be a single mother and have a child by artificial insemination (reproductive freedom is one of the alleged gains of feminism, although this partial gain is again under threat, considering the ongoing attacks in the United States on that freedom in relation to abortion). She is portrayed as exercising her freedom as a liberated woman, and yet she is always beautiful, never "gross," and would never make choices that might jeopardize either her femininity or her bodily difference from men (two ingredients of postfeminist sensibility). In other words, during a "natural" home birth, a woman might let loose and act like an animal (scream, pass stools) and thus seem more like a human or a man. When Zoe gives birth near the end of the movie, she is properly in stirrups, covered, and with no accidental bowel movement, not even a real groan. She has every right to be proud and not ashamed, unlike the "proud" single mothers of the support group who feel pride when they should feel shame.

As in *Bridesmaids*, in *The Back-up Plan* the shame we feel as viewers and that Zoe feels is highly visual—we want to shrink into ourselves or flee when we feel this emotion. Zoe feels ashamed *for* Lori—who appears to be shameless. Zoe wants to flee the scene, but is held back by Carol. The single mothers group members are shameless about the natural release of feces into the water—Zoe feels the shame they ought to feel with her own discomfort, and we, the viewers, are invited to feel ashamed of the spectacle of a public, unladylike bowel movement. The movie becomes a vehicle of shaming shameless feminists/women, but always in the name of comedy—wink, wink; nudge, nudge. Gill has pointed out that irony and knowingness are potent ingredients in postfeminism. Cultural irony, she claims, is about having it both ways: "expressing sexist or homophobic or otherwise unpalatable sentiments ironically while claiming this was not actually 'meant.'"[37]

Early in the movie, Zoe visits Stan's farm and finds a pot of simmering stew on the stove. Ravenous, she starts to eat the stew sloppily and is surprised with feces-looking brown slop all over her face when Stan enters the kitchen. The post-feminist heroine feels properly repulsed and shamed by excrement, but can show gusto for fecal-looking stew, therefore accomplishing the displacement of the less acceptable anal stage for the oral stage (in Freud's hierarchy). We can enjoy these fruits of an already accomplished feminism—freedom to eat like a man—but the movie's creators must continue to show us just the frontispiece; we cannot imagine Zoe having a bowel movement. She is beautifully out of control again in the barn, when she enters into abandoned lovemaking with Stan and has multiple orgasms and then retches in the sink—all of these representations of being beau-tifully out of control can be contrasted with Lori's grunting, straining, animalis-tic body giving birth and expelling turds in the water, shown as repulsive, horrific, not-woman, feminist—all of the things postfeminists love to hate.

Finally, after giving birth to twins perfectly and invisibly, Zoe is in bed with Stan after he has put the babies to sleep. Again, the gains of feminism (equal par-enting) are taken for granted. Stan starts to report on his daughter Penny's defeca-tion, and Zoe says, "Don't talk about Penny's poop when I'm about to kiss you." The subject of bowel movements is taboo because even though feminism has lib-erated aspects of women's lives—they are sexually free, can choose artificial in-semination, share parenting equally with their mates, can choose to be sexy and beautiful because it pleases them—the good postfeminist knows that feminism can also unleash the uncivilized parts of females that need to be tamped down. These uncivilized parts are exemplified by women breastfeeding babies way beyond what is appropriate (thus making them more like cows than women), women shitting when birthing, and women talking about the decay and reality of their bodies like Zoe's best friend Mona (Michaela Watkins), who is way too bawdy and graphic about the trials of being female. Although we see Zoe peeing (although she has the propriety to feel uncomfortable under the dog's surveillance—peeing needs pri-vacy), having multiple orgasms, puking, and eating like an animal (Stan: "Would you like a trough?")—these appealing scenes provide contrast to Lori's animalis-tic and exhibitionistic shitting and groaning while birthing that is marked as dis-gusting. Zoe's version is losing herself momentarily in eating like an animal: she retains a charming propriety and is never like the feminists.

Shame and the Breakdown of Civilization

To conclude this essay, I would like to turn to a scene in a third movie that illustrates and prefigures the approach of Hollywood postfeminism toward anal shaming. A 2001 comedy directed by Joel Gallen, *Not Another Teen Movie (NATM)*,[38] parodies the popular teen movies of the 1980s and 1990s (many produced by John Hughes), such as *She's All That, Pretty in Pink,* and *10 Things I Hate about You.* Fol-lowing the plot in *She's All That, NATM* is about a high school soccer hero trying to turn an "ugly" unpopular girl into a prom queen in six weeks as part of a bet. *Not Another Teen Movie* closely follows that plot, ramping up the sex jokes and—of interest to me—adding excremental material that is particularly to do with female characters (an element not present in *She's All That*). The teen movies of the 1980s and 1990s, and their brethren, movies for young men like *Dumb and Dumber*, *American Pie*, and *Animal House*, often depicted men and boys enjoying stereotypical toilet humor. However, girls and women were not generally shown as part of this humor.

In *NATM*, a scene extraneous from the plotline showing women as the defecating agents of the breakdown of civilization stands out because of its emblematic character. From above we see a sweet, ladylike girl in a school toilet stall. The camera shows us three boys who have crawled through the HVAC system to peep at her from above (we, the viewers, share their voyeurism). The film cross cuts to the scene below in the English classroom, where a poetry lesson is occurring. A boy in a back row shouts, "You know what I think about poetry?" and then lets out a loud, long fart. Back to the boys in the HVAC system: They describe being semi-turned on ("snake happy in pants") while the girl below is just urinating but grossed out and expressing nausea when she starts to defecate. The girl seems shocked at her own body's noises (she farts; then we hear intestinal gurgling when she seems to have diarrhea). More cross cutting occurs in the next minute or so with a continual back and forth between classroom and bathroom. The English teacher, indignant, says, "Is that what your generation considers humor? Shakespeare, Moliere, Oscar Wilde: these were humorous . . . the sublime poetic genius of a clever turn of phrase." Suddenly, back in the WC, the ceiling gives way and the boys fall on top of the defecating girl. They all crash through the floor into the English classroom below, the toilet spraying the English teacher with a stew of feces and urine. In the final image, the three teenage boys, the girl, and the teacher are all splayed on the floor of the classroom, a tangle of limbs coated in excrement in a scene of chaos reminiscent of carnage scenes in war movies, with human waste replacing blood. The scene suggests that by making public the extremely private act of female defecation (a final taboo) we incite a global return to the anal phase, to undifferentiation, leading to a breakdown of civilization to a state of chaos. The English teacher's final words are evidence: "Your modern day, moronic, feeble minded, sophomoric excuse for wit is merely a parade of nasty, filthy, vulgar, human excrement!"

As Mark Olsen points out, the screenwriters, in the schoolteacher's words, "anticipate—and mock—the criticisms they will receive."[39] Reviewers will see the same old moronic bathroom humor as a sign of the immaturity of the generation. But what reviewers did not notice perhaps, and what I see as an important shift with this movie after the 1980s cycle of teen films and the 1990s take on those films, is the full inclusion of women in the outing of the anus, defecation, and bathroom humor.

The anus has been, in literature and art, the last bastion of the private, and women have been the last bastions of the private anus. In *NATM*, the writers seem to enjoy the "shamelessness" of depictions of taboo anal topics—there is everything here from analingus (a male character appears with a banana sticking out of his anus for his girlfriend to eat), to both men and women talking about defecating on a lover's chest as sex play, to watching women defecate, to wallowing in human waste—all presented as homogeneous fodder for laughs. This 2001 movie, intended for mostly male audiences, provides a foreshadowing of the appearance of the public female anus and defecation in the rom-coms of the 2010s. *The Back-up Plan* and *Bridesmaids,* as I have demonstrated, however, are limned with the postfeminist sensibility that shames both characters and viewers in scenes of female defecation. The audience laughs but is warned: self-surveillant females, don't let down your guard or your anus and its activities may become public knowledge and you, too, will be shamed.

Carl Schneider argues that elimination is "respected by a sense of shame" partly because we feel so ambivalent about the act and products of defecation. As children, we viewed our anal products as "valuable parts of ourselves that we were giving away,"[40] and Freud argued for an elaborate parallel between feces and money or gold. On the other hand, Schneider asserts that feces are "devalued by our culture" and associated with filth and decay. The result of this contradiction is a thread of societal ambivalence: "Elimination, in short, is an ambivalently valued human experience: on the one hand, the symbol of creativity; on the other hand, the symbol of mortality."[41] The scene in *NATM*, then, brings this ambivalence out of the (water) closet, so to speak, by bringing together in an undifferentiated stew both human waste, which is valued as the body's creative product during the anal stage, and the human products of art and intellect—great works of literature. The fact that woman incited the shameful stew is significant and marks the beginning of a new cultural trend toward the anal shaming of shameless women in American film.

Notes

1. Somerset W. Maugham, *Cakes and Ale* (Harmondsworth, Middlesex, UK: Penguin Books Ltd., 1958 [1930]), 103.

2. Hilary Radner, *Neo-Feminist Cinema: Girly Films, Chick Flicks and Consumer Culture* (New York: Routledge, 2011), 2.

3. Rosalind Gill, "Postfeminist Media Culture: Elements of a Sensibility," *European Journal of Cultural Studies* 10, no. 2 (2007): 148.

4. Ella Taylor, "In 'Bridesmaids,' a Divorce from Chick-Flick Norms," *NPR*, May 12, 2011.

5. Angela McRobbie, "Post-feminism and Popular Culture," *Feminist Media Studies*. 4, no. 3 (2007): 255.

6. Sigmund Freud, "Civilization and Its Discontents" (1929), *The Freud Reader*, ed. Peter Gay (New York: W. W. Norton, 1989), 745.

7. Ibid., 742.

8. Freud, "Character and Anal Eroticism" (1908), *The Freud Reader*, 294.

9. Freud, "Civilization and its Discontents," 742.

10. Annie Mumolo and Kristen Wiig, *Bridesmaids*, directed by Paul Feig (Universal City, CA: Universal Pictures, 2011), DVD.

11. Guy Hocquenghem, *Homosexual Desire* (1978), trans. Daniella Dangoor; preface to 1978 ed. by Jeffrey Weeks, new introduction by Michael Moon (Durham NC: Duke University Press, 1993), 96.

12. Ibid.

13. Gill, "Postfeminist Media Culture," 148.

14. Ibid., 147.

15. Marjorie Jolles, "Going Rogue: Postfeminism and the Privilege of Breaking Rules," *Feminist Formations* 24, no 3 (2012): 44.

16. Angela McRobbie, *The Aftermath of Feminism: Gender, Culture, and Social Change* (London: Sage Publications, 2009), 1.

17. Ibid.

18. Rosalind Gill, *Gender and the Media* (Cambridge, U.K.: Polity Press, 2007), 261.

19. M. Lewis, "Embarrassment: The Emotion of Self-Exposure," in *Self-Conscious Emotions: The Psychology of Shame, Guilt, Embarrassment, and Pride*, ed. J. P. Tangney and K. W. Fischer (New York: Guilford Press, 1995), 210.

20. K. Sanders, S. Pattison, and B. Hurwitz, "Tracking Shame and Humiliation in Accident and Emergency," *Nursing Philosophy* 12, no. 2 (2011): 85.

21. See Julien A. Deonna, Raffaele Rodogno, and Fabrice Teroni, *In Defense of Shame: The Faces of an Emotion* (Oxford, U.K.: Oxford University Press, 2011); and Carl Schneider, *Shame, Exposure and Privacy* (Boston: Beacon Press, 1977).

22. See Brené Brown, *I Thought It Was Just Me (but It Isn't): Telling the Truth About Perfectionism, Inadequacy, and Power* (New York: Penguin / Gotham, 2007); Martha C. Nussbaum, *Hiding from Humanity: Shame, Disgust and the Law* (Princeton, NJ: Princeton University Press, 2006); and K. Sanders, S. Pattison, and B. Hurwitz, "Tracking Shame and Humiliation in Accident and Emergency," *Nursing Philosophy* 12, no. 2 (2011): 83–93.

23. Lewis, "Embarrassment," 210.

24. Schneider, *Shame, Exposure and Privacy*, 50.

25. Ibid.

26. Ibid., 51.

27. Taylor, "In 'Bridesmaids.'"

28. Pamela McClintock, "'Bridesmaids' Rocks Weekend Box Office with $24.6 Million Opening," *Hollywood Reporter*, May 15, 2011, 1.

29. Carol Mallory, "Misogynistic 'Bridesmaids' Wins Praise from Gervais at the Golden Globes," *The Wrap*, January 16, 2012, 1.

30. Freud, "Three Essays on the Theory of Sexuality," in *The Freud Reader,* ed. Peter Gay (New York: W. W. Norton, 1989 [1925]), 251.

31. Radner, *Neo-Feminist Cinema,* 2.

32. James Joyce, *Ulysses* (New York: Random House, 1986 [1922]), 56.

33. Lewis, "Embarrassment," 210.

34. McRobbie, *The Aftermath of Feminism,* 6.

35. Kate Angelo, *Back-up Plan,* directed by Alan Poul (Los Angeles: CBS Films, 2010), DVD.

36. Myra Mendible, "Introduction: Embodying Latinidad, an Overview," in *From Bananas to Buttocks: The Latina Body in Popular Film and Culture* (Austin: University of Texas Press, 2007), 9.

37. Gill, *Gender and the Media,* 266–267.

38. Mike Bender and Adam Jay Epstein, *Not Another Teen Movie,* directed by Joel Gallen (Culver City, CA: Columbia Pictures, 2001), DVD.

39. Mark Olsen, Review of *Not another Teen Movie,"* *Sight and Sound,* 12, no. 8 (2002): 47.

40. Schneider, *Shame, Exposure and Privacy,* 70.

41. Ibid.

NINE

Distancing Maneuvers: Collective Shame in Iraq War Films

Michael Rancourt

In her book *Memorial Mania,* Erika Doss observes that America is obsessed with its military history and the persistent need to express gratitude to the soldiers who fight and die in its wars, ostensibly to "keep us free." This is apparent, according to Doss, in the glut of stone memorials, monuments, plazas, bridges, sports stadiums, and highways dedicated to wars, veterans, war heroes, and common soldiers. She argues that "the touristic experience of visiting [national memorials] . . . is a primary means of learning about and becoming an emotionally engaged member of the nation."[1] Thus, many Americans develop a sense of national identity that is partially built on gratitude toward soldiers and reverence for the nation's militaristic past. Doss is not alone in examining the link between American public memory and national identity or in such expressions in physical memorials and other public discourse on America's wars. Scholars have looked at how speeches, public performances, and popular media help shape public memory and national identity, with many noting that popular film now influences the way Americans remember the past even more than do history books or museums.[2] War films have great potential to influence public memory not only because of America's obsession with its militaristic past but also because they combine, perhaps more clearly and completely than other texts, many of the discursive elements scholars have seen as the building blocks of public memory, among them images,[3] narratives and myths,[4] and emotions.[5]

Evocations of emotion in popular war films can serve powerful purposes beyond mere entertainment or the cathartic experience of the cinema because, as psychologist Jesse Prinz argues, emotions constitute moral judgments, and such judgments promote behavior monitoring and modification.[6] In other words, as popular war films evoke emotions in their viewers, they also position viewers as citizens judging the nation's history and its military endeavors. It is valuable, then, to study the range of emotions audiences are invited to feel by texts that help shape public memory, especially those texts that deal with the nation's military past.

Although Doss focuses on discourses of gratitude in war memorials, it is more frequently pride and shame that serve as the dominant emotions in war films, emotions that often correspond to judgments about the honor or dishonor of American history. For instance, in the 1980s and 1990s, films critical of the Vietnam War dominated the genre, typically evoking strong emotions about the nation's military actions, its political failings, and the suffering of veterans.[7] In a chapter dedicated to shame in her book *Imagining America at War*, Cynthia Weber examines who the American people "wish they had never been," finding that films about Vietnam reveal a sense of shame at the heart of the national imaginary over its imperialist past. In short, these films struggle to respond to what John Hellmann describes as the Vietnam War's shattering of the myth of American exceptionalism.[8] Weber's findings also resemble those of other scholars who have contemplated the effect of the humiliation of the Vietnam War on veterans, political elites, and other citizens.[9]

Celebrations of the fifty-year anniversary of the triumph of World War II and so-called "good war" films like Steven Spielberg's much heralded *Saving Private Ryan* (1998) helped rehabilitate the national myth and elevate gratitude and pride over shame.[10] However, following the 2003 invasion of Iraq, a new cycle of war films would begin to rehash some of the same themes and narratives, playing on many of the same emotions, as their Vietnam predecessors. After a wave of critical documentaries beginning in the election season of 2004, the first notable narrative films dealing directly with the Iraq War appeared in 2007; these were low-budget offerings from established Hollywood directors, namely Paul Haggis with *In the Valley of Elah* and Brian De Palma with *Redacted*. The same year, British documentarian Nick Broomfield directed his narrative debut with the low-budget and commercially unsuccessful but now often-cited *Battle for Haditha*. These films constituted the first set of narrative Iraq War films that stirred controversy and contributed significantly to the debate about the war. They also mobilized a sense of shame about America's involvement in war that harkened back to the anti-war films of the 1980s and seemed to leave behind the pride of *Saving Private Ryan*. In addition to these early examples, two later films, Kathryn Bigelow's *The Hurt Locker* (2009) and Paul Greengrass's *Green Zone* (2010), deserve attention because they were the most critically and/or financially successful Iraq War films while continuing many of the critiques of other films of the period.

To understand the way these films mobilize shame in the service of a critique of American politics and culture, it is important to pay close attention to the "smaller" emotional moments throughout a film and how they tangle with larger themes and narratives. Communication scholar Greg M. Smith provides a method by which to embark on such analysis, arguing from the cognitivist perspective that film theorists have paid too much attention to the psychoanalytic perspective and have consequently neglected the ways films evoke a wide range of emotions beyond desire. His "mood-cue approach" encourages critics to pay close attention to the "emotional markers" through which films "elicit brief moments of emotion"[11] that contribute to the overall mood of a given film and thus influence the way audiences perceive and enjoy it. By attending to the emotional moments, it becomes possible to see how critical Iraq War films create emotional contrasts, such as pride versus pity, to evoke the larger emotion of shame in service of a moral judgment against the authorities responsible for the war.

This essay contributes to the study of shame and American culture by considering the way Iraq War films evoke feelings of shame in order to position spectators as critical of shameful aspects of American culture. To examine these phenomena, I begin by reviewing concepts of shame established by psychologists and other researchers interested in the way such feelings manifest themselves and provoke responses at the individual and group levels. Here, I explore one kind of "distancing maneuver" by which individuals defend themselves against shame by dissociating from the shameful aspects of their individual or collective identities. This, combined with the mood-cue approach and theories of spectatorship from film theory, offers the insight necessary to analyze the mobilization of public shame in war films. I apply this perspective first to an analysis of the vulnerable veteran in Vietnam War films, especially those dealing with issues of the wounded male body narratively and cinematically coded as passive and "feminized." By examining the effects of war on the veteran's body and the effects of these bodies on public discourse, I am able to identify a second type of "distancing maneuver" by which publics reframe combat as nonthreatening to the body of the American soldier by relying on "clean war" technologies to create distance between soldiers and war's dangers. This perspective then guides my analysis of the way Iraq War films refute this Gulf War–era technological promise while shaming the American people for forgetting the lessons of Vietnam. I argue, then, that as these films evoke discordant emotions and an overarching sense of shame, they also expose the false promise of the "clean war," thus shaming the country that subjects young soldiers and civilians to suffering and death for dubious political purposes. Unlike films from the post-Vietnam era, however, the shame is not visited on the individual wounded soldiers. Instead, it is a collective shame that critical publics can deal with by distancing themselves from the Bush Administration and those who supported the war. The result is a fractured collective identity and a struggle over the dominant meaning of the war in public memory.

"Distancing Maneuvers" in Individual and Collective Shame

When pundits and critics invoke the concept of collective shame, they intuitively transfer the individual psychological concept to the larger community to suggest an analogy between the kind of situation that may cause an individual to feel ashamed and the kind that challenges the collective's narratives of pride. For instance, in December 2012 many editorials in national newspapers referred to the recurring deaths of children from gun violence as a "national shame," suggesting a perpetual flaw in the nation's collective ability to address an important issue and complicating myths of America as a nation that values and protects children's lives. By analogy, parents who failed to take the necessary actions to protect their children might feel judged and have to face emotions such as guilt, shame, and humiliation if something tragic were to happen to their children. These feelings are often grouped together and confused with one another, but a closer look at the distinction between them reveals the ways in which identity and behavior are important considerations on both the collective and the individual level.

Psychologist Evelin Gerda Lindner distinguishes between shame and humiliation, writing, "Shame can be defined as a humbling experience a person agrees to; humiliation describes those experiences a person does not agree to."[12] To agree is to accept the viewpoint of others and to feel the shame and see oneself as the object of the others' shaming gaze. This is similar to guilt, although the distinction is that psychologists usually see guilt as referring to ill feelings about one's behavior (*what I do*) whereas shame refers to negative feelings about one's identity (*who I am*). When extended to the level of the collective, both guilt and shame become issues of in-group identification, prompting individuals not only to see themselves through others' eyes but to see themselves as complicit in the actions of others. Lickel et al.[13] find that, whereas those experiencing collective guilt for in-group members' actions are motivated to make reparations, those feeling collective shame are motivated to distance themselves from the in-group or the offending members. This is a defensive position that seeks to "save face" rather than acknowledge complicity or fault.

Studies of responses to shame on the individual level are also revealing when it comes to conceptualizing collective shame. In her seminal work on shame and guilt, Helen B. Lewis notes that among the psychological responses to shame experienced by individuals are hiding, running away, and bypassing. In bypassing the shame, the individual minimizes the affective response to the shaming situation through a "distancing maneuver" by which the person sees him-or-herself from the outside, through the eyes of "the other," but without acknowledging the negative feelings of being seen.[14] According to Lewis, typical feelings of shame feature a dividing of the self "experiencing condemnation from the other . . . [and] simultaneously acutely aware of itself,"[15] but the distancing maneuver allows the individual to dissociate from this self-awareness in order to degrade the source of the shame. In collective shame, this process is actually simpler to conceive because it is merely a process of dissociating from in-group identification.

The influence of shamed dissociation is especially evocative in considering how rhetorical scholars view public memory and national identity. As Michael C. McGee argues, national identity is "more process than phenomenon" in that it is "conjured into objective reality, [remains] so long as the rhetoric which defined [it] has force, and in the end [wilts] away."[16] These myths are far from stable in the always partial, partisan, and contested terrain of public memory.[17] This means that as narratives of shame, in contrast to widely held beliefs about national identity, become prominent in public discourse, they threaten to lead many to dissociate from the dominant national identity. It is in this way that American national identity can be seen to fracture along moral lines, especially when opposing groups construct their collective memories of events in order to preserve their own identities. Perhaps the clearest example of this fracture is the tension between the myths of American moral superiority exemplified in the mythos of World War II and the failings of the Vietnam War.[18] As Hellmann argues, Vietnam was a "disruption of the American story"[19] that demanded revision of either the meaning of Vietnam or the meaning of America in order to have a coherent national mythos. The way Americans tell the story of Vietnam, then, is revealing of the way they deal with collective shame and the competing narratives and myths in the construction of public memory and collective identity.

Vietnam, Shame, and the Body

The Vietnam War remains a highly contentious event in American public memory, remembered by some as a betrayal of the American people by the government and by others as a betrayal of the soldiers by the anti-war movement.[20] It has been a source of individual shame for the veterans, who may feel judged for being the first generation in American history to lose a war, as well as collective shame for the American people for subjecting the veterans and the Vietnamese people to such violence for little or no tangible purpose. Together, the shame, guilt, and humiliation over the war have been described as the Vietnam syndrome. The term initially referred to the now familiar condition of post-traumatic stress disorder and is believed to have been coined by Henry Kissinger in describing the ailment of veterans returning to the United States physically and emotionally scarred.[21] However, it soon came to refer to the humiliation America as a nation suffered from the failures of Vietnam, a distinct meaning some attribute to Ronald Reagan, who in a 1980 campaign speech at the Veterans of Foreign Wars convention referred to the Vietnam syndrome as a loss in the propaganda war to the North Vietnamese. Reagan argued that the North Vietnamese had succeeded in crippling American foreign policy by making the American people timid and guilty as if they had done something shameful.[22] In this light, the use of the term *syndrome* suggests a national psychological ailment, which, as Marita Sturken observes, "was an image of emasculation, a disease that prevented the government from displaying strength."[23] The disease, then, was an affliction of the public memory mapped onto the body of the suffering veteran and visible in both policy and public commemorations such as the much debated and celebrated Vietnam Veterans Memorial and the films that help Americans remember the war.

Scholars have found that post-Vietnam-era films provide critiques of the war ranging from the deeply personal effects on veterans to broad cultural implications. Susan Jeffords, for instance, sees popular films as sites for reclaiming the masculine ideal whereas Sturken identifies a number of historical narratives filmmakers construct along these lines, including the brutality suffered by the soldiers, especially the victimized infantry "grunt."[24] Among the most prominent films to address these themes and evoke a sense of shame are the two Hollywood productions based on the life of veteran-turned prominent anti-war activist Ron Kovic. Hal Ashby's *Coming Home* (which was "inspired" by Kovic's story) and Oliver Stone's *Born on the Fourth of July* (based on Kovic's autobiography of the same name) together provide a way to examine how Vietnam War films position spectators to identify with, and share the shame of, the wounded veteran and to free themselves from blame by distancing themselves from the presumed collective identity of the nation that supported or acquiesced to the war.

A reading of *Born on the Fourth of July* according to the mood-cue approach outlined by Greg M. Smith offers a way to examine how the film's images, sound, and narrative provide what he calls a "periodic diet"[25] of small emotional moments that contribute to the larger mood—in this case an overarching sense of shame over the Vietnam War. For Smith, the opening of a film is important for setting mood, and this is particularly true in *Born on the Fourth of July*, where the first twenty-five minutes appeal to emotions such as pride, patriotism, and nostalgia for a simpler time both in the American mythos and in the life of the individual. It opens first with a narrated scene of children playing "war" in the Long Island woods in 1958, then moves to a small-town Fourth of July parade. In the midst of the parade, the protagonist, a young Ron Kovic (Bryan Larkin, later Tom Cruise), spots wounded veterans marching toward his family and excitedly tells his father, "Daddy, soldiers." The boy's wonder and pride in them, however, conflicts with the portrayal of the veterans, most of whom are visibly disabled and who wince at the sound of firecrackers. The scene shifts to slow motion and the music swells, highlighting this incongruence and foreshadowing what will become a major source of emotional and narrative tension in the film. In the following scenes, Ron has his first kiss, hits a home run in a Little League game, and gathers with his family around the television to watch Kennedy's inaugural address, concluding with the famous line, "Ask not what your country can do for you; ask what you can do for your country." Such moments are almost cliché appeals to the nostalgic emotions of the audience, establishing a proud, patriotic mood similar to that of a previous generation of war films. However, through the course of the film the narrative serves to challenge those feelings, upsetting such emotions as the boy becomes a man victimized by a political regime that indoctrinates the young through patriotic appeals, only to use them up and mistreat them for dubious political ends.

After scenes showing Ron as a high school wrestling star and patriotic Marine enlistee, the film moves to Vietnam, where the mood shifts quickly through emotions of confusion, disgust, and pity. As Sturken observes, the "murky red haze" of the lighting in the combat scenes evokes confusion[26] as Ron and his squad engage in a brief firefight and then enter a village to find that they have wounded and killed innocent civilians. In the hut where Ron attempts to treat the dying victims, dark lighting, abrupt camera movements and oblique angles, and swirling music evoke feelings of stress and continued confusion. The audience is also disgusted by the sight of graphic wounds on the dying civilians. The rural domestication of the mise-en-scène inside the hut and the dialogue's repeated assertion of the innocence of the dying civilians also help to evoke a strong sense of pity for them. Moments later, among the sorrow, pity, and confusion, Ron ends up firing on and killing his fellow Marine as he flees the village. Here, the mood has shifted drastically, and in comparison to the pride and nostalgia of the opening of the film, the audience is now prompted not only to feel more negative emotions but to reconcile the gap between the positive emotions earlier in the film and the negative ones now dominating. This contrast only increases when Ron is shot through the leg and chest, leaving him paralyzed.

In both *Coming Home* and *Born on the Fourth of July*, the audience is prompted toward pity rather than admiration for the male protagonist, whose position as the masculine ideal of the soldier is reduced to a "feminized"[27] and emasculated object: wounded, disabled, and incapacitated. This is not to suggest that veterans with disabilities are always represented as feminized in American cinema. In fact, as Russell Meeuf argues, John Wayne's character in John Ford's 1953 film *The Wings of Eagles* overcomes his paralysis to "single-handedly [win] World War II" (as Meeuf puts it tongue in cheek) and actually enhances his masculinity.[28] Meeuf calls on Lara Mulvey's theory of the dominant male gaze and the passive female objectification in cinema, writing, "The immobile spectacle of Wayne's body . . . [transforms] the once-mobile male body into a passive and therefore feminized object to be gazed at by other characters and the spectator, a static object to be fetishized or interrogated and punished for its masculine failures."[29] The World War II hero can overcome this would-be *feminization* in a way that veterans with disabilities in post-Vietnam films cannot. In contrast, the male protagonists in *Born on the Fourth of July* and *Coming Home* are "lowered" to a position of limited mobility and helplessness. It is their shame that they cannot overcome their paralysis, and it is the shame of the nation that they were sent to an unjust war. As a consequence, male spectators accustomed to identifying with the male movie star whose "glamorous characteristics are . . . not those of the erotic object of the gaze, but those of the more perfect, more complete, more powerful ideal ego,"[30] instead find themselves uncharacteristically confronted with a passive and therefore more *feminized* male protagonist whom they pity. For Sturken, the casting of Cruise, who was familiar to audiences for his portrayal of the masculine ace fighter pilot in *Top Gun* three years before the release of *Born on the Fourth of July*, made the contrast all the more poignant.[31] Although they dominate the narrative in some ways, Ron and Luke, the protagonist in *Coming Home*, are presented as helpless and weak within the story world, both literally and figuratively emasculated by the horrors of war and incapable of reintegrating into society. The narratives depict this emasculation and evoke this pity in scenes where characters discuss their inability to get erections and scenes in which veterans are shamed and humiliated by this particular aspect of their paralysis, in some cases displaying the rage against the "rejecting other" that psychologists identify as a typical response to shame and humiliation.[32] However, the films also feature a *lowering* of the veteran through film techniques such as high camera angles that frame them as diminutive characters and code them as passive objects rather than the powerful men who typically dominate the screen in war films.

Through narrative and cinematic processes of rendering the once dominant male passive, the characters become the objects of the spectator's gaze that implicates the audience in their shame. First, viewing the emasculated male can be a source of shame for the spectator positioned as the active male, who instead of finding a strong figure in control of his actions and surroundings is confronted with a male in a pitiful, passive, objectified position. The ableist shame here can also be a homophobic one that comes from dominating the male who had previously "stood" as a soldier, the pinnacle of manliness. This is the case, at least, until the veteran "rises," not necessarily from his wheelchair but from his position of passiveness. In both *Coming Home* and *Born on the Fourth of July*, a significant turnaround for the male protagonist comes when he joins the protest movement and becomes a vocal critic of the war. Cinematically, this is complemented by a reframing of the characters with camera angles and movements that suggest rising and empowerment. In *Born on the Fourth of July*, for example, in the scene in which Ron leads a group of veterans protesting at the Republican National Convention, he is confronted by security guards (shot from low angles, making them fill the screen and appear more powerful). Ron tells a reporter during this face-off, "My name is Ron Kovic, and I am here tonight to say that this war is wrong." As he says this, he props himself up out of his chair and the camera drops down, raising him in the shot as the emotion in his voice rises. As Ron becomes an active, empowered protagonist through his opposition to the war, the anti-war spectator identifying with him no longer feels pity and is vindicated and freed from blame and the shame of his emasculation. In this way, both *Born on the Fourth of July* and *Coming Home* position the viewer as first shamed by the war and then freed from that shame by criticism of it. The emotion of this scene is admiration, perhaps even pride, in Ron's rising. Consequently, the ultimate shame of Vietnam belongs to the government (as Ron suggests in his impassioned speech) and those who support the war for sending the young, able-bodied American male to risk his life and body for questionable reasons. Spectators are then freed from shame because they are on Ron's side, set in opposition to the war and the contingent of the American people who would subject him to its horrors. It is in this way that the emotional appeals of such films both evoke shame and prompt viewers to distance themselves from the shameful collective identity in order to preserve both their positive conceptions of self and the masculinity of the American male body.

Technological Distancing and the "Clean War"

Although Iraq War films resemble their Vietnam predecessors in some ways, they differ significantly in their treatment of the veteran. So far, there are no prominent narrative Iraq War films that bring the audience to pity the veteran or feel shame for the emasculation of the male soldier. Indeed, disability rarely receives attention. This is not true of documentaries or coverage in the news media, where stories about veterans with disabilities and the mismanagement of their medical claims and neglect of their health have fueled much discourse on shame. For instance, the documentary *Body of War* features Thomas Young, whose spinal cord was severed by a bullet in 2004, talking freely about his inability to get an erection or use the bathroom without assistance. However, the film quite deliberately juxtaposes Young's positive attitude toward his injuries with the seventy-seven U.S. senators who voted to authorize George W. Bush to invade Iraq in October 2002, suggesting that the shame of the war belongs not to the veteran but to the politicians responsible for putting Young and thousands of others in harm's way. The viewer does not feel shame by identifying with him, but is rather positioned by his side like the viewer of *Born on the Fourth of July* who is positioned on Ron's side to cast a moral judgment against the government. Perhaps as a result of the "Support the troops, not the war" approach that dominates the anti-war movement and seeks to avoid the further victimization of veterans in the popular media that supposedly occurred during Vietnam,[33] narrative Iraq War films have avoided such representations of veterans with disabilities. The result has been a tendency to represent the vulnerability of the human body against the technologies of war without dwelling at length on those who survive their injuries and must face the challenge of reintegration into society and living with disabilities.

Technology, in fact, has been a focal point of recent representations of war, especially since the 1991 Persian Gulf War's images promoting a "clean war" narrative[34] that stood as a counter to the "war as hell" narratives proliferating in Vietnam War films and the larger public discourse. It is in the context of the so-called "clean war" as a response to the Vietnam syndrome that Iraq War films have pointed the shame away from the victims and toward (some of) the American people. Rhetorical scholar Roger Stahl identifies the "clean war" and techno-fetishism as two of the major tropes in the discourse on the Persian Gulf War:

> The clean war prosecutes with smooth, sterile, and smart weapons, while the weapons of the enemy are "dirty bombs" designed to spread poison or germs. Rather than destroy, the clean war seeks to "disarm," blessed with the moral authority of hygienic high technology.[35]

Technology, then, promises to create distance between the spectator and the horrors of war, a distance doubly symbolized by the technological simulation of danger for the film spectator. In the mythos of American war culture, the promise of technology is a kind of "distancing maneuver" to relieve shame, to ensure not only that America dominates on the battlefield but that American soldiers will be kept safely away from danger and, if they should be wounded, will be given the benefit of world-class medical technology to help them return to their normal lives. Paul Achter notes that this narrative has led to either an erasure of the wounded veteran body in the news media or a framing of representations that highlights recovery through medical technologies and the moral character of those who are strong enough to endure and even thrive after their injuries. This reliance on technology, however, to sanitize war is far from new. Christina S. Jarvis recounts the promise of medical technologies to restore physical health and masculinity to World War II veterans, noting particularly a 1945 article in *Time* that reported on the successful transplant of testicles to an officer who had been struck by a German "castrator mine."[36] Even in World War I, with the advent of the first armored vehicles, technology had promised to ensure the safety of soldiers, and in fact the firearm itself, dating back hundreds of years, was conceived as an extension of the soldier's body designed to establish a safe distance from the enemy while allowing the armed soldier to disarm the enemy.[37] This has been a logic underlying war technology for centuries, but nowhere is the promise of technology more prominent than in the Persian Gulf War. The distancing technology of firearms, monitoring systems, and smart bombs of that war helped American officials rebrand war as a "war without war"[38] and consequently enabled George H. W. Bush to claim that America had finally been cured of the Vietnam syndrome. It was the promise of the distancing and sanitizing power of technology that supposedly allowed America to overcome the shame of what it had done to soldiers in Vietnam.

In many ways, the notion of "clean war" was dominant in American mainstream media right up through 9/11, the beginning of the Afghanistan War, and the invasion of Iraq, when the Bush Administration, especially Vice President Cheney, promoted the coming war as one in which the United States would be "greeted as liberators." Although military commanders who spoke to the press in the lead-up to the war were not claiming that it would be a repeat of the 1991 Gulf War, they emphasized air power and the importance of quick strikes while at the same time acknowledging that a ground war was a possibility.[39] The press promulgated this "clean war" mentality by emphasizing the power of technology to reduce casualties.[40] Thanks to the rhetoric of "shock and awe" and the promise of a technologically enhanced "clean war," many regular people did seem to imagine the war to come as more like Kuwait than Vietnam. In what serves, in retrospect, as an illustration of the idealization of the "war without war," in one late February 2003 *Washington Post/ABC News* poll 72 percent of respondents said they supported the coming invasion but only 37 percent said they believed that it would incur "a significant number of U.S. military casualties."[41] Once the war began, part of the psychological warfare/public relations operation of the military and the Bush Administration was to ensure that the images coming out of Iraq supported the administration's framing and did not challenge the "clean war" narrative. Journalists were given greater access to the troops than their Gulf War counterparts, but what they were allowed to see and what they reported were not necessarily revealing images of the truth of the war.[42] Instead, they produced images that focused on the technology and later the human interest[43] but never the human cost to civilians or soldiers. This was the context in which filmmakers began creating vivid images and narratives that would correct this sanitized vision and show the human cost exacted on coalition soldiers and the Iraqi people in spite of the technology, a motivation explicitly stated by several Iraq War narrative filmmakers.[44] These films, released between 2007 and 2010, expose the horrors of war and in so doing shame the nation that fails to live up to its professed democratic ideals.

Emotion and Closeness in Iraq War Films

Although Iraq War films avoid displaying the disfigured and disabled bodies of soldiers and veterans in order to shame the American people, they do find other ways to expose the human cost of war and the falsity of the promise of a clean war by evoking a range of emotions in the viewer. These emotions are not the pity of *Born on the Fourth of July*, for in Iraq War films the characters are not made passive or emasculated. They are victimized and thus evoke sympathies along the same lines as pity, but their dignity remains intact. In *The Hurt Locker*, for instance, the war leaves the American soldier psychologically unable to return to civilian life or to connect with his family. In *In the Valley of Elah*, the torment of what the soldier witnesses turns brothers in arms against each other. In *Redacted* and *Battle for Haditha*, the stress of combat leads young soldiers to crack under pressure and commit horrible, inhuman acts against Iraqi civilians. *Battle for Haditha*, in fact, presents this violence against civilians in a way that prompts viewers to feel sympathy for and identify with *the other*. It poignantly reminds audiences that the technology of war, designed to keep its dangers at a distance from American soldiers, only heightens the danger for the innocent bystander—whom it is difficult to accurately label guilty or innocent from such distance. In the film, many scenes are dedicated to a young Iraqi couple, Hiba (Yasmine Hanani) and Rashied (Duraid A. Ghaieb), and their family as they plan a party and go on about their daily lives. In the end, Rashied is among those innocent civilians killed by U.S. Marines in a raid searching for persons who detonated a roadside bomb, and Hiba is later devastated to find him dead. The spectator here is prompted to feel sympathy for the Iraqi victims but also to feel sadness and sorrow for their pain. The viewer does not side with the American sniper who kills Rashied and then celebrates with laughter and high fives. In contrast to this humanization through intimacy, even Vietnam films such as *Born on the Fourth of July* and *Platoon*, which both portray the massacre of innocent Vietnamese people, fail to give voice or depth of character to the victims. In Iraq War films, despite the "cleanliness" promised by politicians and the media, the closeness of the actual war brings the audience face to face with victims of violence. In fact, in *Battle for Haditha*, the spectator is "closer" to the Iraqi civilian than to the American sniper who kills him.

The U.S. troops in these films have the benefit of technologically mediated images with which to survey the scene, whether drones in *Battle for Haditha*, Apache helicopters in *Green Zone*, or remote-control bomb-disarming robots in *The Hurt Locker*. The audience is shown these views from a distance, but is then given a glimpse of the problems with these technologies when the scenes on the ground reveal a much more complicated truth. The contrast between the view from the sky and the view on the ground can be read as commentary on the questionable use of surveillance intelligence to justify the invasion of Iraq, including the satellite imagery shared by Secretary of State Collin Powell as proof of Iraq's weapons program in his highly publicized presentation to the United Nations in February 2003. From the sky in these films, people are either "friendlies" or "hostiles," but on the ground this binary proves far too simplistic. The shame here is the war itself, which places the young U.S. soldier and the young Iraqi on opposite ends of a rifle scope and leaves neither untouched by the questionable motives of the Bush Administration.

The contribution to the discourse of shame is perhaps most significant in *Green Zone* because its star power and large budget allowed it to reach a wider audience and have a greater impact on the public debate about the war. The film does not directly re-create the emotional appeal of films like *Born on the Fourth of July*, but it can similarly benefit from a mood-cue analysis that reveals it to be an extension of the emotional and critical work of films of the post-Vietnam era. In this film, Matt Damon plays Army Chief Warrant Officer Miller, who leads a team of soldiers searching Baghdad for weapons of mass destruction (WMD) in the first days of the war. As site after site turns out to have no evidence of weapons, Miller becomes frustrated and eventually suspicious of the intelligence that led the United States to war.

The film opens with "shock and awe," first with overt cues to the viewer through audio of news reports on a dark screen in which reporters describe Baghdad under attack the first night of the war, concluding with one reporter's statement, "There is no doubt tonight that war has begun and the Iraqi capital is experiencing 'shock and awe.'" Following this is a visual of the first moments of the war. It would be an overstatement to suggest that the audience is moved to actually feel shock or awe, because the perspective in the opening is that of the Iraqi people, especially a high-ranking Baathist general (under Saddam Hussein), but the image and sound of the opening certainly invoke a sense of chaos and a feeling of confusion. Unlike the audience viewing the confusion of *Born on the Fourth of July*, however, the audience here does not yet have a protagonist with whom to identify or a previously established mood that this confusion challenges. A shaky camera follows a frantic group of Iraqis fleeing an apartment amid a driving, drum-heavy musical score, flashing lights, and off-screen shouting and screaming. As this brief scene ends, the music comes to an abrupt stop and the camera pans from the fleeing general's caravan heading down the street to a fiery explosion in the distance, followed by a shot of the river and buildings of Baghdad silhouetted against a bright fire in the dark night. Here the spectacle of war and the spectacle of the cinema unite finally to approximate the "awe" of "shock and awe" in the viewer. A viewer may even feel a sense of pride in the effectiveness of this spectacle and the Iraqis scrambling to get out alive. In this way, *Green Zone* can be said somewhat to resemble the opening of *Born on the Fourth of July* in that both appeal to positive emotions associated with America and its military.

After a fade to the title screen, the viewer is treated to a scene in which a serious Damon takes charge of a chaotic situation. Quick cuts and more unsteady handheld camera work contribute to the already established confusion, though this time the audience has a specific protagonist with whom to identify. As they confront a narrative not yet clear to them, they do so alongside Damon's character, who is equally ill-informed of the narrative into which he has been cast. Miller gives orders and leads a small team of soldiers to take out a sniper and enter what is reportedly a military storage site that is believed to hold nerve agents. Amid the confusion, Miller's strength and competency invite admiration and identification, as well as some level of pride in the strong masculine leadership of young U.S. soldiers. However, the larger mood at this point is building toward the suspense of an action movie, especially for viewers who see *Green Zone* through expectations they bring from Damon and Greengrass's previous collaborations in the Jason Bourne series. This suspense is later heightened when Miller and his soldiers are bottled up in traffic, which makes them vulnerable to attacks. The confusion and chaos turn into a mild fear, again with swelling music and chaotic movements of people and the camera. The audience is firmly on Miller's side by now, and he has already started questioning the intelligence that led to the belief that Hussein had WMDs. The audience is beginning to see that the noble Miller is vulnerable to the violence of war and the confusing situation all for nothing. The source of chaos in this scene in fact turns out to be not the threat of insurgents but civilians who are in upheaval because they have no water, a signal of the incompetence of the Bush Administration's planning.

Like *Battle for Haditha*, however, the viewers' sympathies are not just for the American protagonists. They are invited to identify with an Iraqi named Freddy (Khalid Abdalla), who is introduced when he witnesses a group of apparently important Iraqis going into an apartment building; some of them, including the general, viewers may recognize from the "shock and awe" scene at the opening. Somewhat surprisingly, and uniquely for a U.S. war film, viewers are given a point-of-view shot from Freddy's perspective, giving him a privileged position as a source of knowledge and even identification for viewers. Although the film has been dominated by the American perspective up to this point, Freddy is immediately made a sympathetic character. As viewers get closer to him, they get closer to the Iraqi people and get distance from the blame of the arrogant American politics the film criticizes. The next time they see Freddy after his act of witnessing, he is literally being held on the ground by a U.S. soldier—a visual representation of humiliation[45]—and Miller comes to his rescue to listen to his report of what he has seen. Viewers then feel sorry for the humiliation of a character to whom they have given sympathy, and they feel relieved that Miller, representing the good, critical American, respects his dignity. This is not to say that Miller fully understands what it means to be respectful of the Iraqi people, but he is at least willing to get closer and willing to listen.

Freddy's emotion is most apparent later when he delivers an impassioned speech after Miller offers him a reward for helping capture an Iraqi who had been part of the meeting Freddy witnessed. After Freddy flees with an important notebook, he is chased down an alley and caught trying to climb a fence. When the U.S. soldier who catches him accidentally pulls off his prosthetic leg (he says he lost his leg in the Iran-Iraq War), Freddy must give up running. Miller then assures Freddy he will be safe and offers a reward for his assistance to which Freddy responds passionately. As he is shown in close-ups with rising music, all the while balancing on one leg, he tells Miller:

> You think I do this for money? You think I don't care about my country? I see what's happening. You don't think I see what's happening in it? And all the people, they have no water; they have no electricity; you think I do this for reward? You don't think I do this for me? For my future? For my country? For all these things? Whatever you want here, I want more than you want. I want to help my country.

Freddy is not what he appears to be to the American who is suspicious of Iraqis as insurgents or as mere opportunists. The mood is no longer just suspense, and pride in the "shock and awe" campaign has long faded away. The film has moved from confusion, fear, and awe to admiration for both the noble American and the noble Iraqi and suspicion of the corrupt forces trying to silence them. As in *Born on the Fourth of July*, the emotional cues of the film accumulate to form a larger mood and an associated moral judgment that tangles with the film's narrative and U.S. myths of pride, technology, and war. This is a rising shame in response to the emotional contrasts of Freddy. The very presence of his wounded body is inscribed with both the horrors of war and the false promise of technology even if the healthy body of the Hollywood star, Damon, serves as a denial of those horrors on the American body. Freddy is an emotional focal point and an embodied criticism of both America's obsession with technology and its own goals in Iraq, goals that are central to the critique in *Green Zone* and to the critical memory of those opposed to the Bush Administration.

Although *Green Zone* satisfies the expectations of the dominant male spectator, Damon as the movie star who fills the screen (and one recognized as the title character from *Saving Private Ryan*) only controls the narrative until the point at which Freddy takes charge of the story. As the film moves toward its conclusion, Miller chases and tries to save the general, who is also hunted by corrupt Americans with whom he fabricated the fictional threat of WMD to justify the war. The chase is monitored by a commander who makes decisions watching a video feed from an Apache helicopter above the city. As the chase ends, it is Freddy who kills the general (with a technology suited for short-range combat, a pistol), telling Miller, "It is not for you to decide what happens here." Any inkling of pride or awe in the American war effort the viewer may have felt at the beginning of the film is undermined by this narrative. This is a war that must be close, and it intertwines with a politics that must be equally close. Freddy's words ring with keen insight a scene later when Iraqi officials reject Ahmed Zubaidi (Raad Rawi), the exiled Iraqi who has been handpicked by the Americans to lead the country. Technology and distance both fail and undermine America's will to control Iraq. An isolationist narrative emerges as American officials are portrayed as corrupt and incompetent fools for assuming that their narratives of technology can justify war and execute it cleanly in the service of their political interests. The viewer who has identified primarily with Damon throughout the film finds her-or-himself equally lacking control in the end. Unlike in the response to Vietnam films, however, viewers do not feel pity or shame for the male lead or for what the war has done to him. Instead, the film vindicates U.S. soldiers and the shame is not for making them victims of violence but for exploiting them for political gain. This is a collective shame that preserves the soldiers' dignity by blaming the Bush Administration for lying to the American people and attempting to control a foreign people Americans do not understand. In short, the American people are to be ashamed because they are still a colonial power that treats *the other* and its own soldiers as pawns in a political game. However, engaged spectators are also able to distance themselves from this critique by identifying with Miller and Freddy, much the way viewers of *Born on the Fourth of July* may distance themselves from blame for the Vietnam War by identifying with its victims.

Conclusion: Shameless Responses

As Helen B. Lewis suggests, one response to shame is to perform a "distancing maneuver" that allows the shamed person to "save face" and deny the emotional component of the shame. Such a response can take the form of "shame rage" or "humiliated fury," which allows the individual to fend off the shame with hostility toward the judging other. At the individual level, this may resemble the actions of the veteran in *Born on the Fourth of July* who assaults a prostitute for laughing at his inability to get an erection. In the collective shame over the Iraq War, defensive hostility exacerbates the division between the critics of the war and those who defend it. This explains why films such as *Redacted* and *Green Zone* have been met with furious accusations of the filmmakers' supposed anti-American agendas. Hostile reviewers of *Green Zone* bring up Matt Damon's liberal political views to support claims that the film presents lies and propaganda designed to undermine the military and the government.[46] In "New Damon Flick Slanders America," *New York Post* columnist Kyle Smith wrote, "After all of Hollywood's Iraq movies have flopped (even the Oscar-garlanded 'The Hurt Locker' earned only $15 million at the box office), one studio thinks it has the following secret to success: The previous films didn't insult the United States enough."[47] He goes on to call the film a "slime job," "preposterous," "a daydream," "dumbfoundingly brazen in its effort to rewrite the facts," "a fantasy film," and "one of the most egregiously anti-American movies ever released by a major studio." This review was shared and reposted widely on conservative blogs and echoed in online forums, including the *Internet Movie Database* discussion board dedicated to *Green Zone*, where, for example, one user described the film as a "Pathetic attempt by this runt actor to impugn the objective of the Iraq War" and added sarcastically, "I guess, RUNT Damon, Hanoi Jane Fonda, BJ Clinton and cop-killers are the true heroes of American society and our noble military are the evil-doers."[48] Such responses have been common for all of the post-Iraq-invasion films that critique the Bush Administration and highlight the shame of America's role in Iraq. Whereas the critical voices of the filmmakers offer critical viewing publics an opportunity to distance themselves from the portion of the American people that is seen as responsible for militaristic rhetoric, the conservative publics they are shaming in the process respond in kind: they distance themselves from "anti-American liberals" whose citizenship and legitimacy they disclaim.

Of course, the polarization over Iraq characterizes both sides no less than it did during the Vietnam and post-Vietnam eras when conservatives could blame liberals for betraying U.S. soldiers and liberals could blame conservatives for supporting an unjust war. In both cases, the soldier was portrayed as the brutalized victim of betrayal but the citizens of Vietnam were often neglected or dehumanized, especially in the films of the era. *Green Zone* and other films compensate for this neglect by refusing to portray the soldier as a pitiful, emasculated victim of war and refusing to erase or dehumanize the suffering civilian. Miller is a victim of politics who presumably will escape from Iraq not only unscathed but energized by a political mission to expose the lies of the Bush Administration. Freddy is left behind to fight for his country. Meanwhile, the innocent civilians of *Battle for Haditha, In the Valley of Elah,* and *Redacted* are either dead or left to mourn and to find an explanation for why their family and friends died. The shame of the Iraq War stems from the discordance between American myth and the reality on the ground. After Vietnam, the myths of American moral superiority bolstered by the memory of World War II could no longer be assumed unquestionably true.[49] Pride in the nation's military past was now infected by shame.

The Iraq War proved to be "another Vietnam" in the sense that it renewed many of the critiques of that war. As Iraq War films make clear, the truth of war remains the misery and suffering the people came to know through representations of Vietnam, not the sanitized images of bloodless victory the American people were shown during the Persian Gulf War. The technologies of war are designed to destroy the human body, and the goal of war, as Elaine Scarry argues, is always directed at injuring the enemy, disarming and disabling the enemy soldier to ensure that one's country clearly holds the advantage in its ability to strike.[50] In short, the myth of a clean war amounts to a contradiction in terms, not a cure for the shame of Vietnam or a renewed source of pride. The shame of the American people is that they were willing to forget about the human costs of war and allow themselves to be swept up in post-9/11 hysteria and the Bush Administration's rhetoric.

Although films are only one part of the discourse on the war, analysis of narrative Iraq War films offers a chance to understand how critics evoke shame in order to mobilize moral judgments over intense issues of collective identity and politics. They also offer a chance to better understand how this shame and these moral judgments inspire "distancing maneuvers" that deepen the political divide.

Notes

1. Erika Lee Doss, *Memorial Mania: Public Feeling in America* (Chicago: University of Chicago Press, 2010), 56.

2. Alison Landsberg, *Prosthetic Memory: The Transformation of American Remembrance in the Age of Mass Culture* (New York: Columbia University Press, 2004); Angus Calder, *Disasters and Heroes: On War, Memory and Representation* (Cardiff: University of Wales Press, 2004). 23; Paul Grainge, "Introduction: Memory and Popular Film," in *Memory and Popular Film*, ed. Paul Grainge (Manchester, U.K.: Manchester University Press, 2003), 4; Miriam Bratu Hansen, "*Schindler's List* is not Shoah: Second Commandment, Popular Modernism, and Public Memory," in *Visual Culture and the Holocaust*, ed. Barbie Zelizer (London: Continuum International, 2001), 147; Anton Kaes, "History and film: Public Memory in the Age of Electronic Dissemination," *History and Memory* 2, no. 1 (1990): 309; John Storey, "The Articulation of Memory and Desire: From Vietnam to the War in the Persian Gulf," in *Memory and Popular Film*, ed. Paul Grainge (Manchester, U.K.: Manchester University Press, 2003), 101; Marita Sturken, *Tangled Memories: The Vietnam War, the AIDS Epidemic, and the Politics of Remembering* (Berkeley: University of California Press, 1997), 23.

3. Robert Hariman and John Louis Lucaites, *No Caption Needed: Iconic Photographs, Public Culture, and Liberal Democracy* (Chicago: University of Chicago Press, 2007); Barbie Zelizer, "The Voice of the Visual in Memory," in *Framing Public Memory*, ed. Kendall R. Phillips (Tuscaloosa: University of Alabama Press, 2004); Janis L. Edwards, "Echoes of Camelot: How Images Construct Cultural Memory through Rhetorical Framing," in *Defining Visual Rhetorics*, ed. Charles A. Hill and Marguerite H. Helmers (Mahwah, NJ: Lawrence Erlbaum, 2004).

4. A. Susan Owen, "Memory, War and American Identity: *Saving Private Ryan* as Cinematic Jeremiad," *Critical Studies in Media Communication* 19, no. 3 (2002); Peter Ehrenhaus, "Why We Fought: Holocaust Memory in Spielberg's *Saving Private Ryan,*" *Critical Studies in Media Communication* 18, no. 3 (2001); Aaron Hess, "'You Don't Play, You Volunteer': Narrative Public Memory Construction in *Medal of Honor: Rising Sun,*" *Critical Studies in Media Communication* 24, no. 4 (2007); Jeffrey K Olick and Daniel Levy, "Collective Memory and Cultural Constraint: Holocaust Myth and Rationality in German Politics," *American Sociological Review* (1997); Tony Judt, "The Past Is Another Country: Myth and Memory in Postwar Europe," *Daedalus* (1992).

5. Doss, *Memorial Mania*; Cheryl R. Jorgensen-Earp and Lori A. Lanzilotti, "Public Memory and Private Grief: The Construction of Shrines at the Sites of Public Tragedy," *Quarterly Journal of Speech* 84, no. 2 (1998); Geoffrey M White, "Emotional Remembering: The Pragmatics of National Memory," *Ethos* 27, no. 4 (1999).

6. Jesse J. Prinz, *The Emotional Construction of Morals* (Oxford, U.K.:Oxford University Press, 2007), 18.

7. John Hellmann, *American Myth and the Legacy of Vietnam* (Columbia University Press, 2013); Susan Jeffords, *The Remasculinization of America: Gender and the Vietnam War* (Bloomington: Indiana University Press, 1989); Harry W. Haines, "The Pride Is Back: Rambo, Magnum, P.I., and the Return Trip to Vietnam," in *Cultural Legacies of Vietnam: Uses of the Past in the Present*, ed. Richard Morris and Peter Charles Ehrenhaus (Norwood, NJ: Ablex Publishing, 1990); George N. Dionisopoulos, "Images of the Warrior Returned: Vietnam Veterans in Popular American Film," in *Cultural Legacies of Vietnam: Uses of the Past in the Present*, ed. Richard Morris and Peter Charles Ehrenhaus (Norwood, NJ: Ablex Publishing, 1990); Gaylyn Studlar and David Desser, "Never Having to Say You're Sorry: Rambo's Rewriting of the Vietnam War," *Film Quarterly* 42, no. 1 (1988), 9–10; Sturken, *Tangled Memories*, 85–89.

8. Hellmann, *American Myth and the Legacy of Vietnam*.

9. Jeffords, *The Remasculinization of America*; Sturken, *Tangled Memories*, 51–58; Adi Wimmer, "The American Idea of National Identity: Patriotism and Poetic Sensibility before and after Vietnam," in *Cultural Legacies of Vietnam: Uses of the Past in the Present*, ed. Richard Morris and Peter Charles Ehrenhaus (Norwood, NJ: Ablex Publishing, 1990); Blema S. Steinberg, *Shame and Humiliation: Presidential Decision Making on Vietnam* (Cambridge University Press, 1996).

10. Albert Auster, "*Saving Private Ryan* and American Triumphalism," *Journal of Popular Film & Television* 30, no. 2 (2002); John Bodnar, "*Saving Private Ryan* and Postwar Memory in America," *The American Historical Review* 106, no. 3 (2001); Ehrenhaus, "Why We Fought"; Marouf Hasian, "Nostalgic Longings: Memories of the 'Good War,' and Cinematic Representations in *Saving Private Ryan*," *Critical Studies in Media Communication* 18, no. 3 (2001); Owen, "Memory, War and American Identity."

11. Greg M. Smith, *Film Structure and the Emotion System* (Cambridge: Cambridge University Press, 2004), 44.

12. Evelin Gerda Lindner, *Making Enemies: Humiliation and International Conflict*, (Westport, CT: Praeger Security International, 2006), 21.

13. Brian Lickel, Toni Schmader, and Marchelle Barquissau, "The Distinction between Collective Guilt and Collective Shame," in *Collective Guilt: International Perspectives*, ed. Nyla R. Branscombe and Bertjan Doosje (Cambridge: Cambridge University Press, 2004).

14. Helen B Lewis, "Shame and Guilt in Neurosis," *Psychoanalytic Review* 58, no. 3 (1971): 38.

15. Ibid., 39.

16. Michael C. McGee, "In Search of the People: A Rhetorical Alternative," *Quarterly Journal of Speech* 61, no. 3 (1975): 242.

17. Barbie Zelizer, "Reading the Past against the Grain: The Shape of Memory Studies," *Critical Studies in Mass Communication* 12, no. 2 (1999); Carole Blair, Greg Dickinson, and Brian L. Ott, "Rhetoric/Memory/Place," in *Places of Public Memory: The Rhetoric of Museums and Memorials*, ed. Greg Dickinson, Carole Blair, and Brian L. Ott (Tuscaloosa: University of Alabama Press, 2010).

18. Wimmer, "The American Idea of National Identity," 58.

19. Hellmann, *American Myth and the Legacy of Vietnam*, 221.

20. G. Thomas Goodnight, "Reagan, Vietnam, and Central America: Public Memory and the Politics of Fragmentation," in *Beyond the Rhetorical Presidency*, ed. Martin J. Medhurst (College Station: Texas A&M University Press, 1996); Patrick Hagopian, *The Vietnam War in American Memory: Veterans, Memorials, and the Politics of Healing* (Amherst: University of Massachusetts Press, 2009); Hellmann, *American Myth and the Legacy of Vietnam*, 99; Robert L. Ivie, "AIM's Vietnam and the Rhetoric of Cold War Orthodoxy," in *Cultural Legacies of Vietnam: Uses of the Past in the Present*, ed. Richard Joseph Morris and Peter Charles Ehrenhaus (Norwood, NJ: Ablex Publishing, 1990); Jerry Lembcke, *The Spitting Image: Myth, Memory, and the Legacy of Vietnam* (New York: New York University Press, 1998); Richard Morris and Peter Charles Ehrenhaus, eds., *Cultural Legacies of Vietnam: Uses of the Past in the Present* (Norwood, NJ: Ablex Publishing, 1990); Studlar and Desser, "Never Having to Say You're Sorry," 11–14.

21. Myra Mendible, "Post Vietnam Syndrome: National Identity, War, and the Politics of Humiliation," *Radical Psychology* 7 (2008): 4.

22. Ronald Reagan, "Peace: Restoring the Margin of Safety," address to the Veterans of Foreign Wars Convention, Chicago, August 18, 1980.

23. Sturken, *Tangled Memories*, 123.

24. Ibid., 86.

25. Smith, *Film Structure and the Emotion System*, 42.

26. Sturken, *Tangled Memories*, 110.

27. Jeffords, *The Remasculinization of America*, 146.

28. Russell Meeuf, "John Wayne as "Supercrip": Disabled Bodies and the Construction of "Hard" Masculinity in *The Wings of Eagles*," *Cinema Journal* 48, no. 2 (2009): 89.

29. Ibid., 96.

30. Laura Mulvey, "Visual Pleasure and Narrative Cinema," *Screen* 16, no. 3 (1975): 12.

31. Sturken, *Tangled Memories*, 111.

32. Lewis, "Shame and Guilt in Neurosis," 41.

33. Thomas D. Beamish, Harvey Molotch, and Richard Flacks, "Who Supports the Troops? Vietnam, the Gulf War, and the Making of Collective Memory," *Social Problems* 42, no. 3 (1995): 345–346.

34. Daniel C. Hallin, "Images of the Vietnam and the Persian Gulf Wars in U.S. Television," in *Seeing Through the Media: the Persian Gulf War*, ed. Susan Jeffords and Lauren Rabinovitz (New Brunwick, NJ: Rutgers University Press, 1994); Victor J. Caldarola, "Time and the Television War," in *Seeing Through the Media : the Persian Gulf War*, ed. Susan Jeffords and Lauren Rabinovitz (New Brunswick, NJ: Rutgers University Press, 1994).

35. Roger Stahl, *Militainment, Inc.: War, Media, and Popular Culture* (New York: Taylor and Francis, 2009), 27.

36. Christina S Jarvis, *The Male Body at War: American Masculinity during World War II* (DeKalb, IL: Northern Illinois University Press, 2004), 86.

37. Elaine Scarry, *The Body in Pain: The Making and Unmaking of the World* (New York: Oxford University Press, 1985), 67.

38. Stahl, *Militainment*, 27; Slavoj Žižek, "Passion: Regular or Decaf?" *In These Times* 24 (2001), http://inthesetimes.com/article/146/passion_regular_or_decaf.

39. Ann Scott Tyson, "A Top General's Thoughts on Iraq," *Christian Science Monitor*, March 5, 2003.

40. Brad Knickerbocker, "Can New Arms Cut Casualties?" *Christian Science Monitor*, March 11, 2003; Bradley Graham, "Military Turns to Software to Cut Civilian Casualties," *Washington Post*, February 21, 2003; Brad Knickerbocker, "War Aim: Quest to Reduce Accidental Casualties," *Christian Science Monitor*, March 14, 2003.

41. *Washington Post/ABC News* Poll, 25 February, 2003, http://www.washingtonpost.com/wp-srv/politics/polls/vault/stories/data022503.htm.

42. Deepa Kumar, "Media, War, and Propaganda: Strategies of Information Management during the 2003 Iraq War," *Communication and Critical/Cultural Studies* 3, no. 1 (2006): 51.

43. Michael Griffin, "Picturing America's 'War on Terrorism' in Afghanistan and Iraq: Photographic Motifs as News Frames," *Journalism* 5, no. 4 (2004); Cynthia King and Paul Martin Lester, "Photographic Coverage during the Persian Gulf and Iraqi Wars in three US Newspapers," *Journalism & Mass Communication Quarterly* 82, no. 3 (2005); B. William Silcock, Carol B. Schwalbe, and Susan Keith, "'Secret' Casualties: Images of Injury and Death in the Iraq War across Media Platforms," *Journal of Mass Media Ethics* 23, no. 1 (2008); Sean Aday, "The Real War Will Never Get on Television," speech to the Annual Meeting of the International Studies Association, Montreal, March 18, 2004.

44. Anthony Kaufman, "Brian De Palma Explains Himself," *Village Voice* September 25, 2007; Nick Broomfield Discusses *Battle for Haditha,* October 30, 2008, http://www.channel4.com/programmes/battle-for-haditha/articles/nick-broomfield-discusses-battle-for-haditha; Sumi, Glenn. "Life after Crash." In *Now.* Toronto, September, 20, 2007, http://www.nowtoronto.com/stage/story.cfm?content=159898.

45. Lindner, *Making Enemies: Humiliation and International Conflict*, 3.

46. Joe Piazza, "Critics Decry Matt Damon Movie 'The Green Zone,' Calling It 'Anti-American,'" *Fox411,* March 11, 2010, http://www.foxnews.com/entertainment/2010/03/11/new-matt-damon-movie-green-zone-called-appallingly-anti-american/.

47. Kyle Smith, "New Damon Flick Slanders America," *New York Post*, March 9, 2010.

48. Jake-ryan1968, "Damon's Pathetic political lie," *Board: Green Zone* (IMDb, 2011).

49. Wimmer, "The American Idea of National Identity," 56–57; Hellmann, *American Myth and the Legacy of Vietnam*, 72–95.

50. Scarry, *The Body in Pain*, 67–68.

TEN

Deinstitutionalization of the Mentally Ill, Shame, and the Rise of the "Slasher" Trope in *Halloween*

Anthony Carlton Cooke

In his study, *Projected Fears: Horror Films and American Culture* (2005), Kendall R. Phillips acknowledges his debt to early critical works on American horror films and, in particular, the "slasher" movie *Halloween* (1978).[1] Granting Phillips's claim that he chooses only "those horror films that made such an impression on American culture that they became instantly recognizable and, indeed, redefined the notion of what a horror film is," the slasher film, epitomized by *Halloween,* seems to possess the highest degree of cultural resonance.[2] Indeed, in terms of sheer numbers, over time the slasher film has come to define horror, mainly, I argue, because of its intimacy with postwar cultural fears over mental illness and criminality. In fact, the major slasher critical texts cited by Phillips—*Games of Terror* by Vera Dika (1990), *Men, Women, and Chainsaws* by Carol Clover (1992), and *Hollywood from Vietnam to Reagan . . . and Beyond* by Robin Wood (2003)—all use a psychoanalytic methodology to analyze these films, in which a mentally ill male antagonist pursues and murders random victims.[3]

Yet Phillips goes on to claim that psychoanalysis falls short when one investigates "why this particular version of the horror formula became so prominent at the end of the 1970s."[4] Then, after he asserts the superiority of his project due to his utilization of a "historical perspective [in order to place] these [psychoanalytic] elements . . . into the broader cultural contexts with which they resonate," he organizes his argument around what he believes are three pivotal concerns of the period: "paranoid apocalyptic thinking, the general decline in the American family, and a growing hedonism," all of which fall under the purview of psychoanalysis.[5] However, the depth with which psychoanalysis has confronted these issues since its inception remains such a truism as to remind one of its essential role in understanding the "historical perspective" and "broader cultural contexts" expressed through slasher films, especially *Halloween.*

Nevertheless, a simple re-reversal of dominating methods means little without a binding (and so guiding) focus. Therefore, this essay draws on both psychoanalytic as well as historico-cultural criticism via an urgent concern of the seventies in America: the deinstitutionalization of the mentally ill. This movement, based on the belief that mentally ill persons stand a better chance of recovery when treated in communal settings and sustained by the invention of psychotropic drugs in the fifties, led to massive influxes of patients into the public sphere during the sixties and into the present.[6] However, lack of adequate outpatient infrastructures, a conservative backlash in the seventies against the counterculture movement of the previous decade, and the public's lack of education regarding mental illness (leading to stigmatization of ex-patients)—all contributed to cultural panic over communal safety.[7] Indeed, anxiety over the return of the chronic mentally ill to public life, as well as concern over community safety, occupies a central place in *Halloween*.

Although *Halloween* is not the first slasher film—*The Texas Chain Saw Massacre* (1974) precedes it by four years—film scholars generally refer to it as the first "true" slasher film, that is to say, the first film of its type to achieve financial and critical success. It also sets the formulaic parameters for subsequent slasher horror. Future films all follow *Halloween*'s basic structure and use its core elements. Vera Dika notes that, while *Halloween* cost only $320,000 to make, it returned $80,000,000 across the world, thus earning reviews in respected periodicals such as the *New York Times* and the *New Yorker*.[8] Film critics generally agree that *Halloween* and its imitators (*Friday the 13th, Prom Night,* and others) all descend from Alfred Hitchcock's *Psycho* (1960).[9] Carol J. Clover comments on the achievements of *Halloween*, yet also points out important differences setting the film apart from *Psycho* and *The Texas Chain Saw Massacre*. In *Psycho*, the slasher, Norman Bates, occupies a place however tentative in the social order until his exposure; in *The Texas Chain Saw Massacre*, the violence takes place in a secluded area and is perpetrated by a cannibalistic family who avoid large populations; in *Halloween*, the murderer comes from a suburban community, is locked in a mental institution, and escapes to commit more murders.[10] The return of Michael Myers, the antagonist, after his escape from the asylum at age twenty-one to the town where he committed the original crime at age six, plays on cultural paranoia over the return of the mentally ill who, prior to incarceration, lived undetected in the social order. Indeed, one of the reasons that ex-patients remain hidden is a sense of personal shame regarding their condition that is fostered in the asylum as well as a fear that any untoward behavior may, at any moment, result in readmission, a phenomenon Erving Goffman terms the trajectory of a patient's "moral career."[11] Within these contexts, then, issues of deinstitutionalization that, for the American public, previously concerned only the mental health community, begin to concern everyone. As the mad gain access to the public sphere through the ongoing process of deinstitutional-ization, *Halloween* articulates this process as an eruptive event leading inevitably to the mad's violent rending of the social sphere.

Halloween takes place in the fictional town of Haddonfield, Illinois, on two nights: "Halloween 1963," the night Myers, at age six, murders his sister Judith, and "Halloween 1978," when Myers, at age twenty-one, returns to the town of his birth and murders two teenage girls and one teenage boy.[12] The film excludes audience members from access to any sections of the town except for the suburbs, creating the illusion of Haddonfield as comprising only suburban areas, the ideal all-American town: little to no crime of note, quiet, and neighborly—a phantasy place. Indeed, such a device seems designed to arouse in the audience a level of narcotic desire for the image. Haddonfield is presented as temporally and spatially distant (on screen before an audience as well as on prerecorded film) yet also as, at least temporarily, accessible.[13] Indeed, during an interview John Carpenter, the film's director, said, "Suburbia is supposed to be safe . . . Your house is supposed to be a sanctuary."[14] The opening scene, however, contains a hidden signifier within the signifier "Illinois." According to Vera Dika, "The choice of Illinois . . . introduces the concept of 'illness,' or 'ill,' which it incorporates within its spelling. In short, Haddonfield is a normal American community, but illness is a part of it" (p. 35).[15] This "illness" is so interlocked with "Illinois" that to separate it out undermines the sign. In *Halloween*, the asylum housing Michael Myers is located in Smith's Grove, Illinois, and thus stands at a remove from the placid area of Haddonfield.[16] Yet, as evidenced by the all-American "Smith's" (and its associations with the normative family unit) and "Grove" (with its implications of idyll or pastoral), the asylum, as well as Myers, remains a part of Haddonfield just as Haddonfield remains a part of Smith's Grove, just as both remain apart as well as on a continuum. Moreover, through its material distance and its social presence-absence, Smith's Grove provides the illusion of safety and peacefulness that Haddonfield requires to maintain its cohesion. Thus, the physical return of Myers to Haddonfield once he escapes from the asylum provides the film's tension because it disrupts the suburban communal phantasy and rewrites communal history regarding a past that has allegedly been discursively purged.

In this context, it is significant that Myers, whether voluntarily or involuntarily, does not use language; he never speaks throughout the entire film. His lack of participation in discourse, more so than his incarceration, strips him of any humanity, especially for those whom society charges with the task of rehabilitation. As Sam Loomis, Myers's doctor, and Marion, a nurse, drive a station wagon toward Smith's Grove, their conversation reveals their true feelings toward Myers and the mentally ill in general.[17] Marion asks Loomis if he has any "special instructions" regarding how to handle Myers; Loomis cryptically warns her to maintain awareness of Myers's potential for violence and not to "underestimate it"; Marion curtly reminds the doctor that "we should refer to 'it' as 'him.'"[18] However, her chiding of Loomis for insensitivity soon reveals her own true feelings toward asylum patients: "The only thing that bothers me is their *gibberish*. When they start *raving* on and on," she confesses. Loomis responds by assuring her that "[she does not] have anything to worry about. *He hasn't spoken a word* in 15 years" (emphasis added).[19] This exchange between Marion and Loomis occasions a number of linguistic complexities, most prominently the method by which Marion and Loomis exchange discourses of mental illness in order to reify their sense of normalcy, of the stability of their place in the cultural order.

The strength of shared discourses of desire for social inclusion and the demand that such discourses constantly be rejuvenated via mutual identification of the other overrides Marion's individual desire to articulate her humanistic charity toward the mentally ill as well as her desire that Loomis, as a doctor, act according to the humanistic ethics of the medical profession. Paradoxically, Marion appears to persuade Loomis to refer to Myers as a person, a "he," through an interpersonal shaming ritual (reminding him of his duty of consideration to his patient) and so attribute to him a modicum of humanity at the same time that her own statements about the mentally ill remove any trace of humanity from her speech through verb choice as opposed to pronoun use. Her description of patients' language as "gibberish" and "raving" suggests that, while the mentally ill do speak, their language remains outside of comprehension by the sane. And so, while "they" may seem human subjects to Marion, their "inability" to use language exiles them from normal discourse. What is at stake in situations such as these is not the ability to speak but rather the circumscriptions around which the speakable and the nonspeakable are permissible.[20] "Gibberish," "raving," or even silence take on different valances when considered as expressions not so much beyond language as excised from it in order to determine who may or may not attain the status of subjecthood with all the considerations such status entails on even the most basic interpersonal level.

Indeed, the desired effect is achieved. Loomis and Marion subtly bond in their assessment of the mentally ill when Loomis uses the subjectivity-acknowledging pronoun "he," thus appealing to Marion's belief at least in the biological humanity of the mentally ill. In turn, Loomis assures Marion of her normalcy (and so her own corporeal safety) by calling attention to Myers's unwillingness or inability to participate in "humanity" via discourse, thus strengthening the assumed distance between the "sane" and the "ill." Moreover, this "weeding out" process operates via a stigmatizing mechanism that "determines who will be a subject depending on whether the speech of such a candidate for subjecthood obeys certain norms governing what is speakable and what is not"; yet such a process is always "haunted" by "the ramblings of the asocial [or] the rantings of the 'psychotic' that [this process] produce[s]."[21] Or, perhaps more important, the process remains "haunted" by the utter silence of the "psychotic." Silence keeps Myers further from subjecthood than his fellow asylum patients. Not only because of his "lack" of language, however, but more so because his silence overtakes any question of muteness or simple refusal. Silence, like bodily stillness, does not require the same level of discursive or physical policing as speech or motion, and it is for this reason that silence remains further away from discourse, further than "gibberish" and "raving," which demand more attention from discursive circumscription practices.

Although Loomis also labels Myers as "evil," implying a thoughtless engine of murder, the scene in the film in which Myers escapes the asylum attests to a greater level of understanding and purpose on Myers's part.[22] Myers attacks Loomis and Marion not to kill them but rather to secure their station wagon and drive back to Haddonfield; also, he does no harm to any fellow patients who wander about the asylum lawn. Within the filmic narrative, both of these facts remain obfuscated by Loomis and Marion's dialogic insistence on the potential threat to the suburban community. To the audience, Myers thus becomes "the violent and unstoppable predator who stalks the community's teenagers . . . the escaped mental patient. Simultaneously, though, he is also the boy next door gone terribly wrong, the ultimate juvenile delinquent."[23] Yet Myers's dual role as "escaped mental patient" and "juvenile delinquent" also figures into seventies-era conflations of a growing number of released mental patients with violent crime.

Released in 1978, *Halloween* should not be critiqued without looking at the deinstitutionalization movement, one of the major cultural and political changes taking place prior to and contemporaneous with the film. As mentioned previously, deinstitutionalization began in the mid-fifties as a result of the invention of psychotropic medication as well as a growing sense of sympathy for patients on the part of doctors and the public. However, as public policy, deinstitutionalization officially began with John F. Kennedy's Community Mental Health Centers (CMHC) Act of 1963, which aimed at combating abuse, neglect, and misdiagnoses in asylums by releasing patients into more personalized, community-based care facilities, a move that led to a 62 percent reduction in the number of asylum residents between 1963 and 1975.[24] Concurrent with the deinstitutionalization movement for the mentally ill, deinstitutionalization of juvenile offenders and prison inmates, prompted by similar calls for reform and community-centered rehabilitation, led to population reductions of "98 to 69 per 100, 000 [in] 1970–1977," and a 70 percent rise in the prison parolee population during the 1960s and 1970s.[25]

Statistics only provide generalizations through raw data, however; they do not reveal the individual circumstances of each case. And this is precisely the point. Public knowledge of high numbers of the mentally ill, juvenile offenders, and prison inmates, as typically reported through the media, gives no perspective on the number of violent or "at-risk" individuals within the percentages; they could be low, medium, or high. The media, then, do not so much produce public knowledge as provide "the starting point for communication . . . a huge, but nonetheless limited, range of possibilities from which communication can select when it is temporarily deciding on particular topics."[26] Indeed, even the academic journal from which the statistics are taken fails to provide such crucial information needed for properly accessing the nuances of the debate and framing an informed position.

Deinstitutionalization also participates in the conflicts between psychoanalysts, psychiatrists, pharmaceutical companies, and federal and state governments. During the seventies, as more patients were administered antipsychotics and subsequently found their way back into community settings, the authority of psychiatry and psychoanalysis diminished, partly because of scientific medicine's growing influence and its assault on psychiatry's more person-centered approach, which stressed "the failure of the suffering individual to adapt to his or her environment" as expressed in the American Psychiatric Association's (APA) treatment guidebook, *Diagnostic and Statistical Manual of Mental Disorders (DSM I and II)*.[27] Insurance companies, bolstered by a growing scientism that stressed experiential causality and backed by a budget-conscious federal government in search of itemized accounts of treatment, began agitating for exclusively biological classifications for mental illness; some providers even set restrictions on the amount of annual treatment they would cover.[28] In contrast, psychoanalytic psychiatry, according to psychiatrist Karl Menninger, "a leading dynamic psychiatrist of the time," held that "the mentally ill person [is] not an exception," and that "almost everyone has some degree of mental illness at some point in their life."[29] Such leveling of the "normal" and the "pathological" was intolerable not only to scientific medicine (and the potential profits from strict categorization procedures) but to the general culture as well because ossified categories provided the discursive structures on which normativity rested. And so in *Halloween*, when Loomis says to Marion, "You can calm down. The evil's gone," he is only assuring her that her life is no longer in danger; the threat to Haddonfield that the film builds up, both in its narrative and for the audience, stills exists in the cinematic narrative and in the public sphere from which the audience seeks a temporary escape.[30]

From a cinematic standpoint, Loomis's major role in the film is that of the "redeemed panic figure," the lone person who attempts to warn the larger populace of impending danger. Regarded as unstable or at least as an alarmist by most, the "panic figure" performs the aesthetic work of providing a film's necessary tension and suspense, and she or he performs the cultural work of reminding audiences that fissures in the social order must be contained and expunged.[31] As a panic figure, Loomis's first stop in his pursuit of Myers leads him to Taylor, owner of a local cemetery and the only person besides Loomis who, according to the film and the script, seems to remember any details about Myers, his family, or his crime. Loomis and Taylor make their way among the graves until they reach the place where Judith Myers, Michael's sister, is buried. When the two men reach the gravesite, however, they find the headstone missing, a fact Taylor attributes to kids playing a Halloween prank but that Loomis reads as proof of Myers's intent to return to Haddonfield.[32]

Loomis correctly guesses that responsibility for the stolen headstone rests with Myers, yet never questions the act itself. Carrying off a physical marker of the sister he murdered represents Myers as more complex than the "simply, purely evil" entity Loomis later describes to the Haddonfield sheriff.[33] Although the robbery could read as a sadistic act (the ritualistic need to keep "trophies" from murders attributed to all serial killers) or as a repetition of his murder of Judith by removing her memorialized body (the headstone) from living discourse, I believe a more satisfactory interpretation is possible with the application of object relations psychoanalysis as articulated by Melanie Klein.[34] While Myers's theft of his sister's headstone is undeniably an aggressive act, it is also an act of grieving. Judith Myers stands in for the two siblings' absent parents, especially the mother, or breast figure. In having the breast figure forcibly transferred from the mother to the irresponsible and absent sister, the young Myers undergoes a harmful imbalance between positive and negative interactions with those closest to him, most important the sister-breast, leading to "increase[d] ambivalence, diminish[ed] trust and hope and confirm[ed] anxieties about inner annihilation and external persecution."[35] Klein writes that, when such an event occurs in children, neurosis begins to develop, overtaking positive experiences that contribute to forging a healthy relationship between a child and her or his inner and outer worlds.[36] Thus, the stunting of personal growth and the retaining of infantile neurosis and psychosis into adulthood become more and more likely.[37] The sister-breast becomes, through Kleinian "splitting" by Myers, both a "bad object" and a "good object."[38] Myers grieves over the loss of the "good" sister-breast, but he also remains trapped in a struggle against the "bad" sister-breast. The material presence of Judith's headstone serves as a source of reality testing; that is to say, it serves as a reminder of irreplaceable loss of a good object, irredeemable shame and guilt over participation in that loss, and thus his phantasy of unending persecution by the remaining, seemingly indestructible bad object. Indeed, Myers' theft of the headstone constitutes a taking of a "sadistic souvenir" but one that acts as a tormenting, shaming force against Myers himself. This sense of persecution manifests itself as a repetition compulsion in Myers because, throughout the film, the "bad" sister-breast continually returns.

Loomis's first order of business when he reaches Haddonfield in pursuit of Myers is to enlist the aid of Leigh Brackett, the local sheriff. He approaches Brackett just as the latter is conducting an investigation into a robbery at a hardware store, where the only items stolen are "some Halloween masks, rope, a set of knives." Like Taylor before him, the sheriff brushes off this crime as "probably kids."[39] The arrival of Loomis—the panic figure—at just such a moment reflects *Halloween*'s narrative insistence on the extent to which Haddonfield is an ideal (idyll) community while also serving to alert the audience to the magnitude of threat Myers poses to local order. That Sheriff Brackett finds no cause for alarm in the stolen items as a possibility of future crime or at least harmful intent, considering the upcoming holiday, seems troubling at the very least. He seems unconcerned that, right before Halloween, children of an unknown age want a mask, rope, and knives badly enough to steal the items from a hardware store instead of from their own families. Either Brackett is incompetent or Haddonfield is such a peaceful community that nothing short of homicide can induce him to use his inductive reasoning. However, the narrative does not allow for representation of Brackett as incompetent because that would imply two things: first, Haddonfield's familiarity with violent crime; second the inability of law enforcement to control it. If this were the case, the magnitude of Myers's original crime would lessen (and perhaps would remain in communal discourse instead of relegated to social and discursive outskirts like graveyards) and so undermine the high level of dread the film self-consciously attempts to invoke regarding Myers's impending return. Therefore, Haddonfield must be a space if not of innocence then of tranquility, with Brackett as a figurehead holding his office simply out of adherence to convention, as a symbol of the law's potential power.

Two scenes demonstrate Brackett's relationship to Haddonfield. The first occurs when Loomis resorts to coercing the skeptical sheriff into investigating the old Myers house with him. The second occurs when, inside the house, they find the corpse of a mutilated animal. Loomis uses the occasion to drive home how dangerous Myers is, which also serves to play on narrative dread over communal safety and in turn plays on audience stereotypes of inevitable connections between the mentally ill and violent behavior. Loomis asks Brackett what he has found, to which the latter replies, "A dog. . . . Still warm."[40] The dog's body temperature signifies a strategic heightening of tension in that it suggests not only Myers's former presence but the more terrifying possibility that he is present but unseen. The likelihood of such a scenario plays out via Brackett's quick rejection of Loomis's comment that Myers "got hungry": "Come on . . . a skunk could have killed it."[41] When Brackett protests that "a man wouldn't do that," Loomis rejoins, in a cryptic tone similar to the one he used with Marion: "He isn't a man."[42]

Loomis's allusions to Myers's psychosis do not read as hyperbole in the film, nor do they read as such in the world outside the film. The reason for this is simply that a mentally ill person's "social position on the outside will never again be quite what it was prior to entrance [to the asylum]," because "the total institution bestows an unfavorable status [upon him]."[43] For instance, Loomis and Brackett come upon a mutilated, partially eaten animal. Neither one knows how it arrived there. Loomis, certain that Myers "isn't a man," hints at Myers as the culprit; examining the animal for human teeth marks does not seem necessary. Therefore, because Loomis *alludes* to the *fact* that *he knows* Myers is guilty, Myers eats dogs (a household pet, "man's best friend") and so violates the sanctity of the nuclear-Oedipal family and thus the normal Oedipal social order, represented by Haddonfield.[44] No definitive proof exists yet within the narrative of *Halloween;* the proof is self-evident. However, within the cultural discourse in which the film participates, the fact of a previous institutionalization for any mentally ill person translates into an "inevitable" predilection for violence that the fact of institutionalization proves in advance of any violent act.

The next few minutes of the film serve to justify Loomis's view of Myers and audience perceptions of the mentally ill. The two men walk through the Myers house, ultimately revisiting the 1963 crime scene. The fact that Myers returns to Haddonfield (attested to by the half-eaten dog that Loomis asks Brackett—and the audience—to believe Myers is responsible for) "proves" the "truth" of the perceived connection between mental illness and criminality. At this point, glass breaks, startling Loomis into revealing his hitherto concealed gun and his past association with Myers:

LOOMIS
I met him fifteen years ago. I was told there was nothing left, no conscience, no reason, no understanding, in even the most rudimentary sense, of life or death, or right or wrong. I met this six-year old boy with a blank, cold, emotionless face, and the blackest of eyes, the devil's eyes. I spent eight years trying to reach him and another seven trying to keep him locked away when I realized what was living behind that boy's eyes was purely, simply evil.[45]

Loomis encounters Myers at six years old, just after the child is tried and committed, already diagnosed as a hopeless case. But this is not Loomis's diagnosis; eight years pass before he gives up on rehabilitating Myers, after which, according to his confession to Brackett, an epiphany convinces him that there is nothing within Myers worth reaching.[46]

Loomis's verdict reflects only one possibility. However, because of his authority as Myers's doctor, other options, other methods of reaching Myers through the depths of his silence, remain inconceivable in the film as well as in the cultural discourse in which the film is embedded. Some psychoanalysts suggest that, in cases such as these, when analyst and analysand confront each other from irreconcilably opposite poles or find themselves in a situation of mutual antagonism, doctors should attempt to find a more amenable caretaker for the patient.[47] After eight years, Loomis had failed to consider that perhaps a different doctor, a fresh approach, might help Myers. Indeed, Loomis's hubris is such that, instead of approaching colleagues to take over the case, he simply amends the diagnosis handed to him when he first begins to treat Myers—a diagnosis, it should be noted, that is blatantly contradictory. If Myers has "no conscience, no reasoning, no understanding, even in the rudimentary sense of life and death, or right or wrong," he cannot be "purely, simply evil" because evil depends on an object relation, recognition of, and interrelation with, good. Loomis fails to reach six-year old Myers because he lacks interpretive skills and sensitivity to Myers's condition, which is what Michael Eigen calls "the ego's hate . . . in part, aimed against its needs and love wishes" to the point that it "develops a reproachful attitude towards an apparently ungiving and overwhelming world," at the same time fighting such contradictory affects by "repelling those who venture near."[48] For a childlike Myers, such repulsions push him deeper and deeper into an unreal world populated by hostile entities he must either flee from or attack.[49]

In her essay "The Psychotherapy of the Psychoses," Klein writes about children whose levels of play exhibit traits of an inability to deal with the frustrations of reality.[50] Similar recession and advancement of the ego from and toward reality occur within Myers. It is conceivable that during his confinement Myers fled from Loomis via extreme affective dissociation because of the latter's power over the child's *body*. Within the strictures of the asylum, Myers's physical world (the ego and its link to reality as well as to the unconscious) was controlled by Loomis, so the child resisted by receding further into phantasy. When he escapes the asylum and regains control over his body, Myers uses physical violence against his persecutory phantasies. Although he remains immersed in phantasy at all times, the depth of that immersion and the corresponding strength of his ego's connection to reality increases or recedes because of external triggers or frustrations. A strictly delimited, categorical approach to treating patients leaves no room for overlaps or inconsistencies in its criteria—for instance, the "self-evident" immutable differences between "good" and "evil." As Eigen makes clear, such absences of affect are actually signs of intense reservoirs of emotion and reasoning. Unable to make such a diagnostic leap, to strike a balance between a supportive and antagonistic position, Loomis makes the mistake of hating his charge, which Eigen claims causes a negative narcissistic reaction in the analysand, leading to her or his *retreat*.[51] In other words, what Loomis views as lack of conscience is the paranoid-schizoid position of a child attempting to fight reality-frustration.

One of the ways Myers combats reality-frustration in *Halloween* is through the wearing of masks. Rick Worland, in *The Horror Film: An Introduction*, devotes almost four pages to Myers's murder of Judith during the opening scene in *Halloween* and to the significance of mask wearing. He expands on earlier critical interpretations by concentrating on cinematic strategies of audience identification and the fluidity between points of view ("camera / killer / audience"), correctly noting the sexual significance of the clown mask Judith's boyfriend toys with and Myers wears when he murders her.[52] Yet even before *Halloween*'s narrative begins, the audience is placed behind the camera and thus literally forced to wear the killer's mask. As the credits roll on the right side of the screen during the film's opening, accompanied by ominous piano music, the audience sees a sinister-looking, smiling jack-o-lantern on the left side, set against a black background. The camera slowly zooms in on the jack-o-lantern, in which a flickering light builds on the contrast between the bright orange pumpkin and the screen's deep darkness. When the camera closes in on the jack-o-lantern, however, it zooms to the right, focusing on one eye and the nose. At this point, the light inside the jack-o-lantern has been extinguished and the eye and nose holes remain dark and empty.[53] This opening not only attempts to frighten viewers but also leads them inside Myers's psyche via the jack-o-lantern, whose smile reflects both the clown mask that Myers wears during his first murder and the dark-eyed mask he wears during his return to Haddonfield.

The narrative proper begins with a black screen and the words "Haddonfield, 1963" accompanied by children singing, following with a camera view of the front of the Myers house. Here the camera, moving toward the house, functions as a mask. Yet the camera-mask also views the house as a mask, a reflection of Myers's inner turmoil, presented through the physical nature of the house. The Myers house has two stories, with two windows on the far left and right sides on both floors and a door centered on the ground floor, a design that calls to mind the features of a human face, a mask, and the spatial distribution of features on the jack-o-lantern seen during the credits. Indeed, a jack-o-lantern with a light inside sits on the right side of the Myers porch. Moreover, as the camera zooms in on the house, it becomes apparent that only two lights are on inside: one on the far right of the second floor and one in the foyer as seen through a window in the front door, both of which call to mind the final image of the jack-o-lantern eye and nose during the credits; they also reverse this image in that the dark spaces of the jack-o-lantern are now replaced by the lighted spaces in the Myers home. More than just nice cinematography, the back-and-forth self-consciousness of such visuals serves as a commentary on and demonstration of Myers's psychosis.

The camera pans to the right and moves around the side of the house to observe the living room from outside as Judith's boyfriend playfully puts on the clown mask and makes kissing sounds. "Are we alone?" he asks, to which Judith replies, "Michael's around here somewhere." The couple then moves upstairs to have sex, which, as will be seen later, "underlines the theme of childhood innocence giving way to adolescent sexuality . . . then twisting into murder."[54] Next, the camera does a reverse pan back to the front of the house, where the upstairs window on the right goes dark, before performing another reverse pan back to the rear of the house to enter through the kitchen. Although the pacing of these scenes is neither sped up nor slowed down, the erratic back and forth of the camera suggest a representation of psychosis. As Myers takes a butcher knife from the kitchen, the camera's point of view shows that the (at this point unknown) stalker wears a clown costume.[55] Myers approaches the stairs unseen as Judith's boyfriend comes downstairs, putting on his shirt and hurriedly leaving just as Myers goes upstairs to murder his sister. Worland writes that "the boyfriend is spared and the killer's rage vented exclusively on the helpless girl for reasons we must take, literally, at face value," a claim that does not ring quite true.[56] The audience witnesses Judith's boyfriend wearing the clown mask while he and Judith kiss; moreover, it witnesses the arm of the unknown wearer of the clown costume get a butcher knife from the kitchen. These two scenes imply both incompleteness and identification—a mask without a costume and a costume without a mask.

When one wears a costume, the mask completes or authenticates the costume by hiding the most identifiable aspect of the subject—the facial features that, more so than the body proper, promote intimacy between subjects. As Myers (without a mask) witnesses the masked boyfriend having sex with Judith (the child's breast-object), the primal scene is initiated. Myers sees the authenticating mask and senses incompleteness and an impassable distance between himself and his sister-object, a distance that, to his mind, should not exist. The child's desire for his sister, and his concurrent shame over his desire, becomes expressed as sadism and conflated with a sexuality he experiences voyeuristically when, to him, a physical component (represented by the wearing of the mask) should be present as well. The inexplicable complexity of the situation leads to Myers's splitting his sister-object. However, the good object (desire) vanishes inside Myers, residing within him as a phantasy relation and leaving the bad object (shame) projected into the physical world and onto his sister. Myers's own guilt and shame therefore stare back at him, reminding him of a desire he holds but feels he should not possess. Freud notes this same basic foundation of paranoid psychosis: "The person to whom the delusion ascribes so much power and influence . . . is, if he is definitely named, either identical with someone who played an equally important part in the patient's emotional life before his illness, or else is easily recognizable as a substitute for him."[57] Moreover, "the emotion is projected outwards in the shape of external power, while its quality is changed into its opposite," while "the main purpose of the persecution asserted by the patient's delusion is to justify the change in his emotional attitude."[58] The mask, then, becomes the site of splitting, internalization, and projection, an object that Myers competes with by appropriation, by "reclaiming the discarded mask with its red phallic nose" moments before he murders Judith.[59] Not only does Myers supplant Judith's boyfriend through the wearing of the mask; the camera-mask presents this act through the placement of the clown mask over the lens, leaving only two eyeholes for vision. In other words, the mask wears a mask, an act that pushes Myers backward, further away from integration with reality. More important, Myers, now fully inside the clown costume (body and face), his ego receding further from connection with reality, uses the larger phallic object of the butcher knife, as mentioned earlier, to "enter" the bad sister-object and control her from the inside. This is also an attempt to reintegrate the good sister-object and the bad sister-object; control of the bad sister-object would allow Myers to control and so eliminate his shame over his desires. And this attempt fails precisely because of the nature of psychosis: the bad sister-object is already projected outside the boy's psyche into reality in the form of ever changing persecuting figures.

A brief return to the aforementioned discussion of Myers's relationship with his sister's headstone provides insight into the exact nature of his frustrations. For instance, as previously noted, Myers both grieves the loss of his sister and sees her as a source of shame and persecution. He acts out these contradictions through the theft of Judith's headstone. The headstone serves as a reminder of the physical death of the good sister-object and the ongoing presence of the bad sister-object. However, when Myers, at age twenty-one, returns to Haddonfield, his sense of shame transforms into a need to destroy the bad sister-object, which takes the form of the three female babysitters in the film: Annie, Lynda, and Laurie. Myers's strategy for coping with his psychosis manifests as an outward articulation of lack of affect through the wearing of a white mask that ironically resembles a corpse or a statue: the eyes are cavernous and dark, and the mouth is tightly pursed, suggesting an inability or unwillingness to speak, an inversion of the exaggerated affect of the clown mask.

The script for *Halloween* refers to Myers as "The Shape," a designation that corresponds with the featurelessness of his white mask and the strange anonymity he possesses as he stalks Laurie and her two friends throughout the film. In an early scene, Laurie, Lynda, and Annie encounter Myers while they walk home after school; Myers drives by them in the station wagon he has stolen from Loomis and Marion, but his face remains hidden from view.[60] Lynda asks, "Isn't that

David Graham?" and Laurie replies, "I don't think so," but the most telling aspect of the scene comes from the script: "Laurie stares at the station wagon as it moves past. She looks directly at the shape inside. There is a quick glimpse of him, a strange pale face staring back."[61] This scene indicates that Myers wears the feature-less mask as he moves through Haddonfield. His mask allows him to go unseen, at least at a distance—*unseen* here meaning that the mask's lack of distinguishing features signifies his status as the folk devil of the undetectable sexual psychopath.

Public identification of the mentally ill revolves around four markers: "labels . . . (people who are publically known as mentally ill) . . . bizarre behavior . . . poor social skills . . . and physical appearance."[62] Yet only the first category actually provides enough information for definitive stigma; one of the other three, or any of them in combination, may signify a variety of other conclusions depending on the context: for example, drug or alcohol abuse, grief, fatigue, or preoccupation with private concerns. The instability of categories of stigma make the mask (and the subsequent revelation of what it hides) crucial to public perception of mental illness; the mask mitigates public shaming of mentally ill persons by suggesting that anyone might have a mental illness and so threats to public health may lurk anywhere. Deinstitutionalization problematizes the idea that the "mask" eventu-ally, inevitably, must come off, exposing the "illness" for eventual excision from the body politic. Fascination with hidden psychosis as represented in the media assures the public of the resilience of its zones of normalcy. Because violent psychosis is only definitively identifiable after its physical manifestation, "people fear becoming the next random victim of violent, often grisly crimes."[63] Thus, the most terrify-ing aspect for the public in such cases is the very phenomenon that mentally ill persons depend on to survive in public life: the impossibility of the public defini-tively recognizing mental illness.

Cultural paranoia over the apparent initial normality of the mentally ill be-came a popular topic of debate during deinstitutionalization in the seventies. For example, a 1974 *Boston Globe* article, "Psychologist Warns Public to Prepare for Mental Patients," quoted Dr. Samuel Grob: "Just because the state is kicking pa-tients out of all the mental institutions doesn't mean that they are cured"; it went on to describe one of Grob's past patients as having stabbed two women.[64] Grob stated that many patients released under the deinstitutionalization program were "harmless" unless denied their medication, which could occur because of the reluctance of pharmacies to fill prescriptions for people receiving government aid.[65] Furthermore, a *New York Times* article from 1978, the year of *Halloween*'s re-lease, described growing resistance to state policy by local law enforcement and neighborhood organizations, complaining of "destructive elements" reducing resi-dential areas to "slums," a theme that echoed the narrative of anxiety over com-munal safety in *Halloween*.[66] However, the article did not designate the location and previous condition of the areas that were becoming "slums," suggesting that the neighborhoods in question may have been suburban locations similar to Haddonfield in *Halloween*.[67] It stated that no violence was reported and the only devastation to these locations came from the presence of the mentally ill.[68] Yet this fear of proximity to the mentally ill and potential violence had another dimension; it was further embedded within another concern of the times: the increasingly high profile of the serial murderer.

During the late seventies, David Berkowitz, the Son of Sam, murdered six people and injured seven others before his arrest.[69] Yet he did not fit the image of a "lunatic," "maniac," "psycho," or any other popular epithet used for the mentally ill; described as having a "paunch [a] round and smooth face . . . short, curly hair and [a] calm manner," Berkowitz seemed "an unexceptional figure unlikely to attract attention anywhere."[70] Indeed, only his psychosis connected the horrible murders he had committed to the person authorities apprehended. During questioning, Berkowitz claimed that he murdered at the insistence of "Sam," his neighbor Samuel Carr, whom Berkowitz alleged "lived 6,000 years ago" and communicated to him through Carr's dog.[71] Although the arbitrary nature of the murders as well as Berkowitz's mental illness terrified New Yorkers (and surely must terrify those who come across accounts of them today), arguably the most frightening aspect of the Son of Sam story, and others like it, is the normalcy of the murderer. For instance, Berkowitz's physical appearance, at least as described by *Time* magazine, was that of an unassuming "everyperson," and the manner of his capture was full of banalities: a parking ticket for a "properly registered 1970 Ford Galaxy sedan" led to a man exiting his inconspicuous apartment in Yonkers seemingly going about his uninteresting routine.[72] With the public exposure of the mysterious psychotic Son of Sam as boring David Berkowitz at the same time as public debates were taking place over the effectiveness of deinstitutionalization, it is no wonder that popular opinion regarding policies of releasing the mentally ill into community care met with resistance.

President Jimmy Carter and First Lady Rosalynn Carter, both advocates for mental health reform, entered the White House in 1977, one year after the start of Berkowitz's then ongoing attacks. The following February, Carter created the President's Commission on Mental Health (PCMH) to address definitions, origins, and solutions regarding mental illness.[73] According to Otto F. Wahl and Rachel Roth, the PCMH findings in 1978 showed that media representations shaped public conceptions of the mentally ill; moreover, they cited studies suggesting that during the late seventies television soap operas, dramas, and even films showed a marked preference for less than favorable depictions of mental illness.[74] And yet, while such studies provided useful information, they lacked references to specific television shows, commercials, or other media accounts consulted, resulting in an incomplete representation of the actual images determining public stigma of the mentally ill during the period in question.

One such medium is the televised horror, or "telefright," film, produced exclusively for home viewers over one or two nights.[75] During the seventies, these films enjoyed immense popularity and many catered to popular fears of the mentally ill, using female protagonists as victims. *Are You in the House Alone?* (1978) depicts a high school student, Gail Osborne, who is stalked by an assailant who, once caught, circumvents the courts; *Someone's Watching Me* (1978), directed by John Carpenter, features a young woman menaced by a mysterious stalker.[76] In *Halloween*, Laurie and Tommy watch a rerun of the horror/science fiction movie *The Thing from Another World* (1951), and it is the terror inspired in Tommy by this movie about a breach of normal life by an alien creature that heightens his sensitivity such that, when he looks out the window, he is able to see "the boogeyman" (Myers) stalking them from across the street.[77]

Although Myers stalks Laurie through the first half of *Halloween* once he glimpses her on the front porch of the old Myers house, it is her friend Annie who becomes his first victim. Annie "transforms" into the sister-object when she accidentally spills butter on her clothes while babysitting a neighborhood child, Lindsey Wallace. Annie's half-nakedness recalls the primal scene where young Myers finds Judith half-naked. Unknowingly stalked by Myers, Annie walks to the garage to wash her clothes. Later, wearing an oversized shirt over her underwear, she returns to the garage to get her car, finds the door locked, and goes for her keys. After getting her keys from her purse, she enters the garage again and opens the car door, failing to notice it is unlocked. Once she is inside, Myers emerges from the back seat and strangles her, her face staring out of the car's front windshield, where the rearview mirror hangs down, reminiscent of the mirror Judith sits in front of when young Myers enters to commit murder. Indeed, in the film's final twenty minutes, Laurie, concerned about the whereabouts of her friends, stumbles on Annie's corpse lying in the upstairs bedroom of a neighbor's home underneath Judith Myers's headstone, which Myers, earlier in the film, had stolen from the cemetery.[78]

Previous scenes foreshadow this revelation of the deeper purpose behind Myers's return to Haddonfield. While Lynda, a friend of Laurie, and her boyfriend Bob kiss on the couch of a friend's house in the dark, Myers, now twenty-one and roaming in Haddonfield, watches them. Although this is not made clear in the film, the script calls for Myers to watch the two teenagers "on the stairway," a discrepancy that may account for why Worland assumes that Judith's boyfriend is inexplicably "spared"; Myers's presence on the stairs in a scene repeating the primal scene from his childhood suggests that Judith's boyfriend escaped by chance and that Myers, aware of the similarities of the situations, intends to correct his mistake through reliving that night.[79] In fact, the scene in which Myers lifts Bob inches off the ground before impaling him to the kitchen wall with a butcher knife is arguably the most gruesome in the film, attesting to a certain determination on Myers's part to ensure that "Judith's boyfriend" does not escape. Myers then appears in the bedroom doorway concealed under a sheet and wearing Bob's glasses (a keepsake that, like Judith's headstone, serves as an attempt at reality testing for the boy's death). As Lynda, imagining the figure as Bob playing a prank, engages in conversation, Myers stands in the doorway, exactly as he did at six years old with Judith. Lynda pulls the bed covers down so that her breasts are visible, saying, "See anything you like?" Again, this alludes to the primal scene, when Myers picks up the clown mask off the floor and puts it on before Judith turns toward him and, recognizing him, reproachfully calls his name as she attempts to cover up her breasts in an instinctual gesture of shame. Lynda, on the other hand, gets out of bed, turns away from Myers, and throws on her shirt, making her half-naked from the waist down. Only after she tries to call someone does Myers move in and strangle her.[80]

Myers's murderous actions in *Halloween* not only represent popular conceptions of mentally ill persons as murderous criminals; indeed, in looking back over the historico-cultural construction of mental illness and the deinstitutionalization process, two things emerge: the inevitable stigmatization of the mentally ill because of a social status attached to them both inside and outside the asylum, and a *pattern* of cultural representation of violent criminality by the mentally ill as inevitable. To consider that groups such as the mentally ill may be excluded from the cultural order specifically to be *incompletely* brought back in to live under a mask of shame explains the paradoxical method of their representation. For instance, the narrative of Michael Myers in *Halloween* gives no information on him except what corroborates Dr. Loomis's assertion that he is evil. Myers's return to the Haddonfield suburbs is explained only in terms of a simple lust for murder. As a commentary on the deinstitutionalization movement during the seventies, *Halloween* proposes only one answer to the issue of how to address mental illness, especially the chronic mentally ill and psychotic cases: as criminality.

Notes

1. Kendall R. Phillips, *Projected Fears* (Westport, CT: Praeger, 2005), 128–129.
2. Ibid., 3.
3. Clover defines the "slasher" film through six major elements: "killer"; "locale" or "terrible place, most often a house or tunnel, in which victims sooner or later find themselves"; "weapons"; "victims"; the "Final Girl," a woman who lives through terrifying events by "find[ing] the strength to either stay the killer long enough to be rescued (ending A) or kill him herself (ending B)"; and "shock effects." Dika offers a set of binary oppositions combined with a "past/present event" schema: ". . . valued/devalued . . . in-group/out-group . . .

strong/weak . . . life/death . . . ego/id (controlled/uncontrolled)"; "Past Event: The young community is guilty of a wrongful action; the killer sees an injury, fault, or death; the killer experiences a loss; the killer kills the guilty members of the young community. Present Event: An event commemorates the past action; the killer's destructive force is reactivated; the killer reidentifies the guilty parties; a member from the old community warns the young community; the young community takes no heed, the killer stalks the young community; the killer kills members of the young community; the heroine sees the extent of the murders; the heroine sees the killer; the heroine does battle with the killer; the heroine kills or subdues the killer; the heroine survives; but the heroine is not free." Wood uses Freudian psychoanalysis to argue for horror films in the seventies as a "return of the repressed" regarding the increasing presence of alternative definitions of race and ethnicity, gender, class, and sexual orientation. See Carol J. Clover, *Men, Women, and Chainsaws: Gender in the Modern Horror Film* (Princeton, NJ: Princeton University Press, 1992), 26–42; Vera Dika, *Games of Terror: Halloween, Friday the 13th and the Films of the Stalker Cycle* (Cranbury, NJ: Associated University Presses, 1990), 134–136; and Robin Wood, *Hollywood from Vietnam to Reagan . . . and Beyond* (New York: Columbia University Press, 2003), 63–84.

4. Phillips, *Projected Fears*, 129.

5. Ibid., 129.

6. Michael Madianos, "Deinstitutionalization," In *International Encyclopedia of Rehabilitation* (Center for International Rehabilitation Research Information and Exchange, 2015): 2; David Mechanic and David Rochefort, "Deinstitutionalization: An Appraisal of Reform," *Annual Review of Sociology* 16, no. 1 (1990): 303–304.

7. Ibid., 1–7; Phillips, *Projected Fears*, 132; Wood, *Hollywood*, 25–26.

8. Dika, *Games of Terror*, 30–31.

9. Clover, *Men, Women, and Chainsaws*, 23; Dika, *Games of Terror*, 33–42; Rick Worland, *The Horror Film* (Malden, MO: Blackwell Publishing, 2007), 230–231.

10. Clover, *Men, Women, and Chainsaws*, 23–24, 26, 30.

11. Erving Goffman, *Asylums* (Garden City, NY: Anchor Books, 1961), 151–152, 167.

12. John Carpenter and Debra Hill, *Halloween*, directed by John Carpenter, 1978, DVD.

13. Christian Metz, *The Imaginary Signifier* (Bloomington: Indiana University Press, 1982), 135–136.

14. Joseph Maddrey, *Nightmares in Red, White, and Blue* (Jefferson, NC: McFarland, 2004), 133.

15. Dika, *Games of Terror*, 35.

16. Carpenter and Hill, *Halloween*.

17. Ibid.

18. John Carpenter and Debra Hill, *Halloween: Revised Shooting Script*, 1st ed. (1978), 5, ebook. http://www.dailyscript.com/scripts/halloween.html.

19. Ibid., 6.

20. Judith Butler, *Excitable Speech* (New York: Routledge, 1997), 133.

21. Ibid., 133.

22. Carpenter and Hill, *Halloween Script*, 8–10.

23. Bernice M. Murphy, *The Suburban Gothic in American Popular Culture* (Basingstoke, U.K.: Palgrave Macmillan, 2009), 143.

24. Mechanic and Rochefort, "Deinstitutionalization," 302.

25. Ibid., 312.

26. Niklas Luhmann, *The Reality of the Mass Media* (Stanford, CA: Stanford University Press, 2000), 66.

27. Rick Mayes and Allan V. Horwitz, "DSM-III and the Revolution in the Classification of Mental Illness," *Journal of the History of the Behavioral Sciences* 41, no.3 (2005): 250, doi:10.1002/jhbs.20103.

28. Ibid., 253.

29. Ibid., 250.

30. Carpenter and Hill, *Halloween Script*, 10.

31. The basis for the concept of the "redeemed panic figure" comes from *Madness and Cinema*, in which Patrick Fuery discusses different examples of the "madperson" trope and cites the example of the "wild-eyed doctor who is initially treated as mad" in the science fiction film *Invasion of the Body Snatchers* (1956). Fuery's point is that a relation exists between cinematic representations of madness and the cultural moment that such depictions metaphorically articulate. In *Invasion of the Body Snatchers*, the doctor's insanity, according to Fuery, demonstrates the broad cultural belief held by Americans in Communist infiltration. While many other examples warrant inclusion, perhaps the best literary example is Dr. Van Helsing from Bram Stoker's *Dracula* (1897). Van Helsing, a specialist in rare diseases, is called in by a former student, Dr. Seward, to investigate a mysterious illness afflicting Lucy Westerena. Already in the text, the frequency of inexplicable occurrences is steadily rising. When Van Helsing arrives, examines Lucy, and finds the two small puncture wounds in her throat, he cryptically alludes to a cause of her illness by advising Seward: "You keep watch all night . . . You must not sleep all the night . . . I shall be back soon as possible. And then we may begin." Seward asks the doctor to clarify his remarks, but Van Helsing simply replies, "We shall see!" Over the course of the novel, Van Helsing, referred to by Seward as "a seemingly arbitrary man," an eccentric, gradually reveals his suspicions of vampirism, which ultimately prove correct. See Fuery, *Madness and Cinema* (New York: Palgrave Macmillan, 2004), 18; and Bram Stoker, *Dracula* (Boston: Bedford/St. Martins, 2002), 129, 139–140.

32. Carpenter and Hill, *Halloween Script*, 10.

33. According to an article in an FBI training manual, "Frequently, the murderer will take a 'souvenir,' normally an object or article of clothing belonging to the victim, but occasionally it may be a more personal reminder of the encounter . . . The souvenir is taken to enable the murderer to relive the scene in later fantasies. The killer here is acting out his fantasy, and *complete possession of the victim* is part of that fantasy." Emphasis is added to highlight the similarities between this study and Kleinian psychoanalysis regarding childhood object relations. See Ann W. Burgess et al., "Sexual Homicide: A Motivational Model," *Journal of Interpersonal Violence* 1, no. 3 (1986): 251–272; and U.S. Department of Justice, *Criminal Investigative Analysis: Sexual Homicide* (Washington, DC: Federal Bureau of Investigation National Center for the Analysis of Violent Crime, 1990), Federal Depository Library Program Archive. fdlp.gov.

34. Klein defines splitting as the process whereby the infant mentally separates the breast-figure into two distinct, opposing experiences, one "good," and the other "bad" in an effort to avoid coming to terms with the complexities of the child's growing interaction with reality. While all children undergo splitting, the process can result in the development of neuroses and psychoses such as paranoia and schizophrenia. See Juliet Mitchell, ed., *The Selected Melanie Klein* (New York: Free Press, 1986), 180–186.

35. Melanie Klein, *Love, Guilt, and Reparation & Other Works, 1921–1945* (New York: Delacorte Press/S. Lawrence, 1975), 150.

36. Ibid.

37. Ibid.

38. Ibid.

39. Carpenter and Hill, *Halloween Script*, 33–34.

40. Ibid., 37.

41. Ibid.

42. Ibid., 37–38.

43. B. A. Pescosolido, "The Public Stigma of Mental Illness: What Do We Think; What Do We Know; What Can We Prove?" *Journal of Health and Social Behavior* 54, no. 1(2013): 3, doi: 10.1177/0022146512471197.

44. Although the scene of the mutilated dog appears insignificant within the film's greater narrative, in a historical/contextual sense, it is extremely important. In 1974, four years before *Halloween's* release, the television show *Lassie,* the story of a Collie and its relationships with humans, aired its final episode. Running from 1954 to 1974, *Lassie* articulated such American mythic themes as the bond between males and dogs and the value of the family unit. Regarding the loyalty of dogs to their masters, it is significant that Lassie was female, adding a gendered dimension to the cultural work the show performed of reifying American heteronormative discourses. Another popular dog during this period was Benji, a tiny, shaggy, mixed breed that starred in the successful film *Benji* (1974). Benji participated in the same American mythic tradition as Lassie and also emphasized discourses of romanticized childhood innocence. The young audiences drawn to *Halloween* would have grown up during this period and been connected in these discursive chains. See *IMDb, Benji* (1974), 2015, http://www.imdb.com/title/tt0071206/?ref_=fn_al_tt_1; and *Lassie.com,* 2015, http://www.lassie.com/.

45. Carpenter and Hill, *Halloween Script*, 39.

46. Carpenter and Hill, *Halloween*.

47. Michael Eigen, "On Working with 'Unwanted' Patients," *The International Journal of Psychoanalysis*, no. 58 (1977): 109–110.

48. Ibid., 115.

49. Klein, *Love*, 151.

50. Ibid., 235.

51. Eigen, "Unwanted," 115.

52. Worland, *Horror Film*, 232–233.

53. Carpenter and Hill, *Halloween*.

54. Worland, *Horror Film*, 233.

55. Ibid.

56. Ibid., 233–234.

57. Sigmund Freud, "Psycho-Analytic Notes on an Autobiographical Account of a Case of Paranoia (Dementia Paranoides)," in *The Complete Psychological Works of Sigmund Freud, Standard Edition. Vol. XII: The Case of Schreber, Papers On Technique, and Other Works,* 1st ed. (London: Hogarth Press and the Institute of Psycho-Analysis, 1911), 40. http://www.pep-web.org.proxy.library.emory.edu/document.php?id=se.012.0001a&type=hitlist&num=0&query=zone1%2Cparagraphs|zone2%2Cparagraphs|title%2C%22%E2%80%9CPsycho-Analytic+Notes+on+an+Autobiographical+Account+of+a+Case+of+Paranoia+%28Dementia+Paranoides%29%2C%E2%80%9D%7Cviewperiod%2Cweek|sort%2Cauthor%2Ca#hit1.

58. Freud, "Psycho-Analytic Notes," 40.

59. Worland, *Horror Film,* 233.

60. Carpenter and Hill, *Halloween Script,* 22.

61. Ibid.

62. Matthew Schumacher, Patrick W. Corrigan, and Timothy Dejong, "Examining Cues That Signal Mental Illness Stigma," *Journal of Social and Clinical Psychology* 22, no. 5 (2003): 469, doi:10.1521/jscp.22.5.467.22926.

63. FBI, *Sexual Homicide.*

64. Jean Dietz, "Psychologist Warns Public to Prepare For Mental Patients," *Boston Globe,* April 29, 1974, 5.

65. Ibid.

66. Ronald Sullivan, "Mental Patients Releases Questioned: Background for State's Policy Against State's Policy Outlook." *New York Times,* http://search.proquest.com.proxy.library.emory.edu/hnpnewyorktimes/docview/123780953/abstract/B61F599B13144026PQ/1?accountid=10747.

67. Ibid.

68. Ibid.

69. "Sam Told Me to Do It . . . Sam Is the Devil," *Time,* https://web-a-ebscohost-com.proxy.library.emory.edu/ehost/detail/detail?vid=8&sid=deb52333-0963-49de-a776-91f1a65e05a8%40sessionmgr4005&hid=4104&bdata=JnNpdGU9ZWhvc3QtbGl2ZQ%3d%3d#AN=53520800&db=a9h.

70. Ibid., 26–27.

71. Ibid.

72. Ibid.

73. Gerald N. Grob, "Public Policy and Mental Illnesses: Jimmy Carter's Presidential Commission on Mental Health," *Milbank Quarterly* 83, no. 3 (2005): 429–430, doi:10.1111/j.1468-0009.2005.00408.x.

74. Otto F. Wahl and Rachel Roth, "Television Images oMental Illness: Results of a Metropolitan Washington Media Watch," *Journal of Broadcasting* 26, no. 2 (1982): 601, doi:10.1080/08838158209364028.

75. David Deal, *Television Fright Films of the 1970s* (Jefferson, NC: McFarland, 2007), 3.

76. Ibid., 6–7, 161.
77. Carpenter and Hill, *Halloween Script*, 42–43.
78. Carpenter and Hill, *Halloween*.
79. Carpenter and Hill, *Halloween Script*, 64.
80. Carpenter and Hill, *Halloween*.

ELEVEN

Shaming and Reclaiming Women's Sexuality through Cinematic Depictions of Masturbation

Megan Tagle Adams

American cultural discomfort regarding masturbation is rooted in the rich socio-historical context of sexual policing, particularly with regard to alienating women and children from their own sexuality under the pretense of discipline and well-being. Particularly during the eighteenth and the nineteenth century, the fear mongering aimed at anyone who dared to self-stimulate effectively pathologized any sexual expression that did not fit neatly within the confines of conventional heterosexual intercourse.[1] While mortifying autoerotic misadventures seem to be a common trope in boyhood coming-of-age stories, today masturbation is largely accepted as a central component of men's sexuality and development. Women's masturbation, on the other hand, remains quite a different story. Whereas a man's admission of self-stimulation is rather mundane, a woman's is notable at best and downright scandalous at worst. Although threats of sterility, blindness, and hairy palms are no longer perpetuated with the same fervor as in centuries past, it seems this cultural taboo isn't merely a vestige of more conservative times; there remains an evident investment in effecting a sense of shame around women's masturbation—a stigmatization that suppresses authentic and varied expressions of women's sexual self-actualization and identity formation.

Traditionally in American culture, women's (presumed hetero) sexuality has been conceptualized in contrast to men's more overt libidinous desires; this framework designates that the expectation of feminine passivity first compels resistance and then ultimately acquiescence to masculine dominance. Women have traditionally been positioned as sexual gatekeepers—as bearers of respectability and morality responsible for tempering men's urges until the necessary criteria have been met prior to engaging in proper intercourse, which is to say after marriage and primarily for reasons of either dutiful procreation or men's gratification. The Cult of True Womanhood and its attendant fixation on purity rose to prominence during the nineteenth century, and the influence of this standard for feminine values remains apparent in contemporary gender roles and stereotypes. The prevalent commodity model of sexuality perpetuates early and persistent sexualization of girls and women and at the same time yields a preoccupation with their virginity as an indication of their self-worth and respectability[2]; as a result, girls and women trapped in the double bind of being sexy but not sexual are expected to be desirable and accommodating to men but not independently motivated for their own pleasure.[3] Because this androcentric model is insufficient to capture the complexities of women's sexuality, many women have found themselves unsatisfied and frustrated with their perceived "frigidity" and inadequacy when penile-vaginal intercourse is unsuccessful in bringing them to orgasm.[4] Historically, failure to orgasm properly was internalized as failure to fulfill one of the primary gender roles of traditional womanhood. Queer, sexually immature, or afflicted were the characterizations of women whose libidinous desires could not be sated through socially sanctioned penile-vaginal penetrative intercourse. Women's carnal dissatisfaction was even pathologized as "hysteria," further obscuring fundamental problems with the dominant sexual paradigm and providing another opportunity to discourage women from taking control of their own sexual self-determination.[5] Given these harsh conclusions, while the act of masturbation itself may well be regarded as deviant and shameful, that judgment is as much about the women themselves for even wanting or needing to use alternative means to achieve orgasm.

Rejecting an ahistorical view of the construction of American identity and gender roles, the enduring legacy of the Cult of True Womanhood at the same time reflects both historically and presently relevant patriarchal cultural anxieties about women's agency, respectability, and value. Opposition to women's masturbation as threatening and objectionable is fundamentally grounded in the heterocentric and phallocentric paradigm that continues to reify masculine authority to demarcate the conditions of normative sexual behaviors and desires. There is no space for exploring the wealth of manifestations of women's carnal desires within this prescriptive patriarchal framework without profoundly disrupting the schema of feminine sexuality as controlled by and responsive to the needs and whims of men rather than independently experienced and enacted. Forthright acceptance and representation of autoeroticism as a normal component of sexuality asserts women's autonomy and therefore threatens the very core of ideal American womanhood. The resulting erasure and persistent omission of women as self-determined sexual agents is essentially a matter of symbolic annihilation, an effective strategy of oppression.

Onscreen representations of masturbation offer opportunities to reaffirm the very existence and indeed the complexity of women's autonomous sexual desires and expression. This essay seeks to examine just a snapshot of mainstream and "indie" film portrayals of women's masturbation from the past few decades to unpack how they exist in conversation with larger sociohistorical narratives that enmesh stigma and shame with women's sexuality and selfhood. Because, as bell hooks plainly states, "there is power in looking," it is crucial that feminists interrogate representations and interpretations of women's self-stimulation onscreen in order to initiate a strategy for taking control of cinematic space and deconstructing images of women's bodies as sites and sights of resistance rather than simply spectacles to be consumed.[6]

Theoretical Background: Screening Autoeroticism

Feminist philosopher Marilyn Frye's ruminations on a lesbian gaze provide a theoretical foundation for understanding how the heteropatriarchy maintains the illusion of men's supremacy by perpetuating women's invisibility and queer erasure. In her extended metaphor of lesbians as theater stagehands, Frye contends that they threaten the precariously constructed phallocentric reality simply by focusing their attention on other women and thus making them visible. The men in the foreground, then, find themselves in a quandary because they cannot address the risk presented by this exposure without necessarily acknowledging its existence; in attempting to counter the threat, they must fundamentally concede the fallibility of the heretofore invisible—and ostensibly invincible—heteropatriarchal system.[7] Women who masturbate can be theorized as metaphorical lesbians because of their preoccupation with women's experience and sexual satisfaction, even if only their own, and their attendant disregard for men's needs and desires. Without the negative judgment historically implied, there can indeed be an inherent queerness read in the body of the masturbating woman. Images that displace men's gratification as the driving force behind sexual scripts are met with reactions of anxiety and subjugation, which are evidence of the enduring cultural investment in preventing disruption of the gender(ed) status quo. The "power of looking" is thus the potential to reveal the accepted heteropatriarchal reality as pretense rather than as a logical extension of gender-based sexual relations. In the face of a film industry that often reduces women to passive accessories to the male protagonist, women spectators' oppositional and negotiated readings of depictions of autoeroticism can yield transgressive, empowering, and even feminist interpretations of sexual identity formation despite hegemonic master narratives.[8]

Because women's masturbation is not yet entirely normalized, the creation and reception of these few portrayals as both reflecting and affecting the discursive construction of sexual mores potentially indicate proportionately greater social significance in terms of the de-stigmatization of autoeroticism or otherwise influencing of the American sexual landscape. Rejecting the limitations of a solely text-focused semiotic analysis, a dynamic cultural studies approach applies contextualized and negotiated readings and resists collapsing meaning making into a localized process with conclusive interpretations. By contextualizing and engaging with the following selected depictions of women's self-stimulation, and by interrogating the surrounding discourses, it is possible to carve out spaces for readings oppositional to hegemonic constructions of women's sexuality within the heteropatriarchy. Even in scenes that are primarily composed to titillate straight men and reinforce the power of the male gaze, representations of women's masturbation may still be read as potentially subversive if they provide space to focus on women's genuine sexual desire and gratification independent of men.

Three tropes illustrate common approaches to depicting women's autoeroticism as crossing conventional sexual boundaries: first, a woman whose physical desire and pleasure are emphasized is often shamed or punished later as a cautionary warning to others; second, a woman's foregrounded self-stimulation can be co-opted for the pleasure and possession of the dominant male gaze; and, third, a woman's masturbation can focus on self-discovery in addition to physical pleasure This last perspective is not as easily co-opted or punished and so is the most readily challenging to hegemonic constructions of sexuality; however, it is certainly not invulnerable to concerted efforts to undermine its paradigm-shifting potential. *Black Swan, American Pie, The 40-Year-Old Virgin, She's Gotta Have It, Coming Soon,* and *Pleasantville* vary in the particularities of their framing of women's masturbation, yet each film offers valuable insight into the cultural representation and construction of women's sexual identity. This essay examines how these films reflect and perpetuate society's continued investment in upholding the agenda of the phallocentric sexual paradigm, how shaming tactics are strategically employed to compel submission to the disempowering and sexist standards for American womanhood, and how opportunities for claiming women's erotic power are orchestrated by filmmakers or negotiated by spectators.

Self-Realization and Self-Destruction

In recent memory, perhaps the most prominent portrayal of a woman experimenting with autoeroticism comes from the 2010 dark drama *Black Swan*. The production courted its fair share of publicity when word leaked that the film would feature a masturbation scene and a lesbian sex scene performed by lead actresses Natalie Portman and Mila Kunis. In press interviews, Portman joked that the production team was depending on the predictably broad audience appeal of a lesbian scene to counter the difficulty of marketing a cross-genre ballet thriller.[9] That an art-house film blatantly caters to the more common voyeuristic desires of its spectators as much as any mass-market Hollywood film indicates that sensual scenes can indeed be read with an eye to how they satisfy both the audience and the story. In *Black Swan*, neurotic and repressed ballerina Nina (Portman) competes against rival dancer Lily (Kunis) for the lead in *Swan Lake*. The dynamic between the two characters mirrors the virgin-whore binary as the film explores the well-worn dualism of darkness against light.

The imagery of the white swan's purity juxtaposed against the volatile lust embodied by the black swan is evident in the visual and symbolic contrast between Nina's restrained girlish virtue and Lily's dark passion. Nina's fractured and stunted development is framed as stemming from her unhealthy relationship with her passive-aggressively overbearing mother. This seemingly contradictory relationship is representative of the increasingly common American dynamic of parenting that overemphasizes ambition and achievement with the side effect of undermining the development of children's autonomy. Nina's ensuing sexual repression ultimately impedes her efforts to realize her professional ambitions. After deriding her "frigidity," the lecherous artistic director commands Nina to masturbate in order to get in touch with her carnal desires to better perform the role of the Black Swan. Seeking a bit of self-fulfillment outside of her mother's omnipresent shadow, Nina follows his instructions when she next awakens and first tentatively then vigorously self-stimulates in what is likely her first act of sexual pleasure, either solo or partnered. The floral pink of her bedroom, the conspicuously visible stuffed animals in the background, and her modest white underwear all signify her childlike innocence and inhibited development.

Lost in the sensations, Nina enthusiastically touches herself while rolling around in her bed with her eyes closed; unfortunately, it is only after several moments of self-pleasuring that she opens her eyes to the disturbing sight of her mother asleep in a chair. Horrified by the unexpected parental presence, she quickly hides herself under her bed covers and immediately regresses back into a timid child. The overwhelming shame that accompanies her mortification further underscores the psychosexual damage resulting from her dysfunctional relationship with her domineering mother.

Black Swan maintains the hegemonic double bind and presents women's sexuality as both externally constructive and internally destructive. The worth of women's sexuality is in its significance as determined by others. Nina's sexual development is important because the male artistic director identifies repression as the source of her limitations as a dancer—the significance of her sexuality as it relates to her own self-realization is not valued in and of itself. Although her masturbation is not performed directly for the visual pleasure of the director, his demand nonetheless provides the impetus for the act, which negates much of Nina's agency in her efforts at self-discovery. Throughout the film, Nina is constantly reminded that her body is hers to control with regard to punishment but not pleasure. In patriarchal constructions of gendered sexual and social relations, men and men's interests determine needs and priorities and women are expected to accommodate those needs and priorities, even to their own detriment. Rejecting sexual shaming and infantilization is necessary for Nina's personal and professional coming of age, yet the same sexual power that enables her to actualize her role as the Black Swan also reinforces her descent into schizophrenic madness. Following the directive to unleash her passion, the lines between fantasy and reality are increasingly blurred as her sexual exploration and expression, real or unreal, becomes entangled with psychological trauma. The masturbation scene is quite representative of the film's overall approach to women's sexual self-discovery; it is theoretically important for development and self-realization, but its destructive consequences make it seem inadvisable in practice.

Voyeurism and Exhibitionism

The image of a masturbating woman onscreen, one knowingly or unknowingly being watched, presents an exceptional opportunity to observe the numerous ways in which the power dynamics of the gaze can shape a particular scene, especially given the voyeuristic nature of cinema in general. One film playing with layered meta-voyeurism and sexual surveillance in conjunction with autoeroticism is the 1998 teen comedy *American Pie*, which prominently features scenes of a man and woman each masturbating. However, whereas the man's dessert-oriented masturbation is painted as humorously cringe-worthy, the woman's self-stimulating is designed for the erotic viewing pleasure of the audience. When the sexy foreign exchange student Nadia (Shannon Elizabeth) inexplicably finds herself alone and nude in sexually inept high school student Jim's (Jason Biggs) room, she inadvertently becomes part of a carefully orchestrated peep show. This particular scene exemplifies the traditional concept of the male gaze: not only is the movie marketed toward a male teen audience but Nadia herself unknowingly has a large male teen audience. Unbeknownst to her, Jim has set up a webcam feed for his peers in a desperate attempt to demonstrate his masculinity through sexual possession, supporting the idea that there is a degree of power inherent in the gaze. In her foundational exploration of the male gaze, Laura Mulvey contends that a woman's onscreen presence often slows or even interrupts the narrative because of "moments of erotic contemplation";[10] Nadia's languid exhibition provides ample opportunity for the camera to roam over her body, not only slowing the narrative but actually rendering other characters nearly speechless as they watch her in awe. By interrupting the narrative action to emphasize the spectacle of a sexualized woman's body, Nadia's status as an object to be acted on rather than as a subject who acts is reiterated, undercutting her agency when she "acts" on herself.

This fairly graphic depiction of a woman responding to visual stimuli and submitting to purely physical—and stereotypically masculine—desires offers a convenient opportunity for satisfying public demand for commodified representations of women's sexuality while maintaining the shame-based discourses that delineate the boundaries of acceptable sexual expression. Clearly an experienced self-stimulator like the rebellious bad girl and nerdy sex freak characters, Nadia stands in stark contrast to the all-American girlfriend foil who shyly admits she has never masturbated or had an orgasm—a contrast that recalls the enduring virgin-whore dichotomy. Although she unflinchingly engages in what is perceived as shocking behavior, Nadia's forwardness and lack of sexual inhibition are presented as likely due to her exotic background rather than to any conscious personal or political rejection of conservative sexual mores demanding feminine passivity and modesty. She is constantly othered as the hypersexual "Czechoslovakian chick," as illustrated by everything from her bare pubic region—a couple years ahead of the Brazilian waxing trend that would become all but compulsory—to her keenness to have sex with a nerdy and undesirable virgin. Jim's coming-of-age story is as American as the apple pie he uses to masturbate; Nadia, on the other hand, is distinctly non-American in her behavior as much as in her origin because her actions stand in opposition to those of proper womanhood.

With the all-or-nothing Madonna-whore binary, sexually active is equated with permanently willing and publicly available, a bit of slut-shaming presumption that stresses the extolled value of purity. While her brazen masturbation serves to conflate sexual autonomy with hypersexuality, for Nadia the act ultimately has no climactic payoff. Increased intercutting pulls the focus away from her pleasure and instead centers on strangers' captivated reactions until Jim interrupts to crudely proposition her for sex. Viewers greedily consume her unwitting exhibition of an ostensibly self-focused act, yet Nadia never comes to orgasm; in this instance, the potential power of women's masturbation to counter the phallocentric paradigm is quelled by redirecting the pleasure away from the woman and framing the act for men's gratification and consumption. The intratextual voyeurism in *American Pie* is unapologetically sexist and exploitative, minimizing the violation to imply the film viewers' complicity without culpability. Because Nadia herself unreservedly consumes explicit images of women, her objectification by the young men's predatory voyeurism becomes more justifiable. Extending this projection of acceptable meta-voyeurism further, viewers can enjoyably watch and become aroused by the image of her vulnerable character, who is both watching and nonconsensually being watched.[11]

Although Nadia's unrestrained eroticism easily overpowers Jim with her demand for an awkward striptease, prompting two premature ejaculations, his humiliating inability to physically consummate his possession of her can actually be interpreted as further justification for the earlier violation. Her sexual voraciousness is permissible to the extent that it can be co-opted by patriarchal narratives of sexuality to affirm the primacy of men's arousal and needs. An unwilling participant in the broadcast of the explicit activities, Nadia's shameless pursuit of pleasure and the near constant othering nevertheless sufficiently negate her innocence and necessitate her discipline. The engrossed collective viewing gives way to extensive public shaming that results in Nadia being sent home; essentially, the expression of her sexual identity is but an accessory in Jim's sexual development—to her own detriment. There are undoubtedly redeeming interpretations of *American Pie* that focus on assuaging guilt and encouraging self-reflexivity among women viewers who may feel alienated or conflicted by their response to visual stimuli or their own autoerotic practices. However, the dominant sexist policing customs in American culture dictate that the threatening prospect of a woman's overpowering sexuality and perceived deviance cannot be allowed to go unpunished.

The 2005 box-office hit *The 40-Year-Old Virgin* also depicts a male virgin's encounter with a sexually uninhibited woman and raises similar issues of co-optation and shaming. When sexually inexperienced Andy (Steve Carell) practices awkward flirting with Beth (Elizabeth Banks), his innuendo about whether or not she likes to "do it [her]self" gives her hardly a pause. She coyly replies with a giggle: "Sometimes. If the mood strikes," as her flirty and forthright affirmation subtly furthers the normalization of women's autoeroticism as fulfilling in both solo and partnered sex. A while later, when the two drunkenly return to Beth's apartment for sex, she excitedly, though mistakenly, presumes that Andy is kinky because she has misinterpreted a couple of cues. Her enthusiasm for less conventional sexual proclivities further positions her as experienced and self-assured, in stark contrast to Andy's sexual naïveté. Evidently lacking in any inhibitions, Beth slips into the bath and places the showerhead between her legs, moaning: "This is how I'm going to warm up for you." Although her comment is directed at Andy, the camera angle makes it appear as though she is gazing right into the lens and addressing the viewer in breathless anticipation of audience arousal. Because she intends for Andy to watch her as part of their foreplay, her masturbation can be seen as more of a performance that not only endures but welcomes the male gaze. Although her fervent erotic expression does appear to be authentic and self-possessed, her established lack of internalized shame means that the phallocentric paradigm that dictates women's submission to men's heteropatriarchal dominance must somehow be reasserted through an external element.

Youthful, blonde, and conventionally attractive, Beth well fits the criteria for desirable American womanhood. However, as she goes from demurely obliging a double entendre to actually initiating bold sexual acts, she pushes the bounds of acceptable feminine comportment. More than her explicit actions, it is her unapologetic attitude that puts her in conflict with the social order that stipulates feminine submission. Her wantonness reveals a disregard for public opinion and social values, and this indifference renders impotent the sexual policing that depends on perpetuating self-consciousness through unnecessary preoccupation with "reputation" and valuing restraint over self-direction. Such insidious social surveillance and shaming groom women to internalize the sexist, culturally sanctioned delineations of what is permissibly sexy versus punishably sexual, ultimately leading them to become largely self-policing subjects. Beth's resistance to confined, hegemonic constructions of appropriate sexual expression is evidenced by her adeptness with the showerhead, which suggests that she has no qualms about sating her carnal urges in whatever manner she pleases. With most of her body submerged, the camera shows a close-up of her rapturous face, eyes closed as she squeaks and moans her way toward climax. Visibly uncomfortable, Andy watches her "graphic" exhibition for a few moments before turning to leave, at which point men's collective and individual control and valuation of women's sexuality is confirmed as Andy learns that his three friends have been standing in the doorway watching the private encounter. Like Nadia, Beth remains blissfully unaware of the newly introduced dynamic, yet the unnoticed observers' presence fundamentally shifts the context for interpreting the act of masturbation. Instead of directly focusing on the woman, the viewer's attention is now split between watching her and watching the other characters watch her. The presence of in-text voyeurism certainly facilitates a more self-reflexive consideration of the viewer's complicity in the near constant surveillance and evaluation of women's bodies and sexuality.

More than just theoretical scrutiny, the literal surveillance carried out by the three men has troublesome implications for Beth's safety and well-being. It was theorized previously that the true power of the male gaze lies in its potential to go beyond merely looking to actually possessing the image.[12] Unlike the digital voyeurs and Jim's nonthreatening appearance in *American Pie*, here the physical presence of four grown men emphasizes how Beth's sexual voraciousness does not counteract her vulnerability. The film does not question this aggressive invasion of her space, nor are the men overtly discernible as predatory, which is precisely what is so alarming about the threat they pose. Because she does not demonstrate appropriately feminine hesitance or humility, her body and her sexuality are regarded as available for public consumption on demand, regardless of the presence or absence of consent or boundaries. It is precisely this framing of sexually experienced women as consenting to all things at all times that perpetuates the rape culture endemic in American society through victim-blaming and slut-shaming dismissiveness about the "unrapability" of sex workers or women who are perceived as "promiscuous" or otherwise "asking for it" through dress or behavior.

Even more direct shaming further denotes Beth as an aberration in liberated sexuality, not a model to emulate. As the sound of her moaning Andy's name fills the background, one of the men acknowledges that he had slept with Beth previously and describes her as a "freak." Andy vehemently agrees with the assessment:

"Oh, you think? All I know is that woman scares the shit out of me and I just want to go home." One could easily dismiss Andy's intimidation based on his lack of sexual experience, but his philandering friend is able to authoritatively denigrate Beth's character and presumed licentiousness. There is no need to further clarify precisely why she is designated a "freak," nor does Andy need to justify his fear and revulsion. This stigmatization effectively allows men to access and benefit from women's sexual expressiveness while simultaneously reinforcing sexist rhetoric about proper manifestations of feminine carnal desire. As the other men leave, Cal (Seth Rogen) enters the bathroom and introduces himself, taking off his shirt and implying that he intends to join her; although the audience does not see her response to his presumptuous advance, her approval is deduced when the two are later shown together as a couple. Just as exotic stunner Nadia welcomes dorky Jim's advances, Beth is likewise ready and willing to submit herself to schlubby Cal at a moment's notice because apparently masturbation signifies hypersexuality and a lack of boundaries or standards. *The 40-Year-Old Virgin* is not particularly transgressive in its treatment of women's sexuality, with its association of masturbation with kinkiness and hypersexuality harking back to turn-of-the-century American pathologization of masturbation. That said, portraying a woman's vocal and unapologetic commitment to self-satisfaction does fill a conspicuous gap in representations of women's sexuality in film.

Stigma and Sexual Autonomy

The prudent employment of freak stigma serves to disrupt the perceived alignment of Beth's character with many of the ideals of White American womanhood, but when race is made highly visible the freak stigma compounds existing racist and sexist stereotyping. The White supremacist heteropatriarchy excludes women of color from the model of virtuous feminine purity propagated by the Cult of True Womanhood and instead marks them as inherently promiscuous and perpetually sexually available for conquest. Specifically, Black women's sexuality has been coded as animalistic and excessive—as even a destructive force in need of taming.[13] A powerful stigma persists against Black women who are thought to be claiming any degree of sexual power and autonomy; the jezebel stereotype, one of the central controlling images identified by Patricia Hill Collins, demonstrates that hypersexuality cannot be confused with meaningful sexual liberation. Spike Lee's directorial debut *She's Gotta Have It* (1986) was heralded as an invigorating spotlight on Black women's sexuality, depicting Nola Darling's (Tracy Camilla Johns) sexual exploits with her three male suitors, her flirtation with a queer female friend, and an artfully brief scene of masturbation. Although Nola's opening monologue suggests that the viewer will learn her story from her perspective, the film actually privileges the perspectives of the men around her, many of whom condemn her alleged promiscuity as a divisive force within the Black community. Furthermore, her sexual fluidity signifies a carefree disregard for the boundaries of proper behavior, a liberty that cannot be allowed without heteropatriarchal masculine interference.

After enjoying the affections of her many admirers, Nola finds herself alone in her bed masturbating. The camera travels from her breasts to her hand moving beneath the sheets and then pans up toward her face at the close of the brief scene, which notably does not end in orgasm. Because Nola flagrantly resists hegemonic expectations of respectability and freely engages in various intimacies that bring her pleasure, she too receives the freak stigma. As her current and past lovers pathologize her sexuality, she eventually begins to internalize the stigmatization of hypersexuality and even visits a therapist to address the issue. Watching the seemingly self-assured protagonist second-guess her usual means of intimate and erotic expression underscores the fundamental point that even the most fiercely self-directed woman must continue to grapple with the deeply entrenched cultural scripts that value narrow ideals for good American womanhood and deter any deviation from the traditional paradigm.

There remains a cultural disconnect between White women and women of color regarding sexuality and sexualization as a potential site of power and resistance. The legacy of racism and colonialism in the United States precludes Black women from wholly embracing reclamation narratives that rely on the false equivocation of sexual "liberation" and self-actualization. In her preeminent critical piece "'Whose Pussy Is This': A Feminist Comment," Black feminist theorist and media critic bell hooks argues that Nola commodifies her sexuality as social currency to be used with her lovers, seeking control through "pussy power": "Men do not have to objectify Nola's sexuality because she objectifies it. In doing so, her character becomes the projection of a stereotypical sexist notion of a sexually assertive woman—she is not in fact liberated."[14] Nola's sexual assertiveness does not translate into self-determination because the pleasure she brings to men takes priority over her own fulfillment.[15] She's Gotta Have It tells a story of shame and blame in the construction of—and reactions to—Black women's sexual identity. Given the context of suppression, although negotiated readings celebrating incidents of self-love and assertiveness are understandable, their significance cannot be mistaken for self-actualization.

It's not the masturbation scene itself so much as its juxtaposition with the rape scene that underscores the reactionary position of She's Gotta Have It on Black women's autonomous sexual pleasure in America's racist and sexist system. As one of the most vocal critics of Lee's claim that the film was intended as a revolutionary representation of Black women's sexual emancipation, hooks writes, "Suddenly we are not witnessing a radical questioning of female sexual passivity or a celebration of female sexual self-assertion but a reconstruction of the same old sexist content" meant to excite audiences.[16] As the spectator watches Nola being sexually dominated, any potential rebelliousness in her previous act of masturbation fades away: the sexual autonomy of a Black woman is presented as no match for the dominance of Black men. Though hooks demands too much resistance from a character being raped, the spirit of her criticism rings true for many who are desperate to see complex, self-determined Black women represented onscreen as sexual beings in their own right:

> As Jaime rapes Nola and aggressively demands that she answer the question "whose pussy is this," this is the moment of truth—the moment when she can declare herself independent, sexually liberated, the moment when she can proudly assert through resistance her sexual autonomy. . . . Ironically, she does not resist the physical violence. She does not assert the primacy of her body rights. She is passive. It is ironic because until this moment we have been seduced by the image of her as a forceful woman, a woman who dares to be sexually assertive, demanding, and active. We are seduced and betrayed.[17]

Nola's whimpered response that her pussy is Jaime's certainly does drive home the point that Black women's sex and bodies are objects to be marked and claimed by Black men, which is not much of a departure from the colonization enacted by White supremacy.[18] Although Jaime would seem to be referencing her other paramours with his territorial inquiry, the previous masturbation scene makes the question much weightier. Not only is this rape a cruel reminder that Nola does not ultimately control her sexuality despite outwardly expressing her affections how she chooses, but its juxtaposition seems to frame the violation as punishment for even daring to seek meaningful pleasure apart from the men in her life. Within this sociohistorical context, where Black women are denied the virtuous innocence expected of White womanhood, their presumed sexual availability situates them as impossible to violate. Nola's sexual availability is scorned to such an extent that not only can the rape scene be read as a Black man taming a Black woman, but often it is not even recognized as an actual rape.[19] In her twenty-year anniversary reflection on *She's Gotta Have It*, Thelma Wills Foote argues that the extent to which Nola does or does not resist the rape is beside the point.[20] To her, "Lee's film represents the communal nature of the punishment imposed on Nola by means of the rape scene's barely detectible cuts," which intercut her three lovers as if they are all participating in her rape.[21] That the punishment, shaming, and standards are communally imposed necessitates that the most effective subversion and resistance, too, be communal rather than individual.

Whereas White American constructions of sexuality often focus on heteropatriarchy, leaving Whiteness unnamed and unexamined, *She's Gotta Have It* makes explicit the racialized aspects of the shaming of women as culturally permissible expressions of sexuality, which most certainly do not encourage or allow Black women's self-love. Given the lack of opportunities for women of color to see themselves reflected onscreen, this dearth of images of them as sexually fulfilled and self-aware maintains *She's Gotta Have It*'s resonance even decades after its release. Although Nola is not by any means a perfect example of liberated Black women's sexuality, it is nonetheless possible for viewers to apply media theorist Jacqueline Bobo's idea of engaging in deliberately subversive readings in order to reject hegemonic images of Black womanhood and subsequently identify and isolate redeeming aspects of the film, even if it means simply focusing on the depiction of Black femininity as beautiful and desirable.[22] Feminist film theorist Jane Gaines identifies the cultural anxieties and priorities at work and ruminates on the implications of prominent depictions of authentic and sexually liberated women of color in the face of White supremacist colonization: "If, as feminists have argued, women's sexuality evokes an unconscious terror in men, then black women's sexuality represents a special threat to white patriarchy; the possibility of its eruption stands for the aspirations of the black race as a whole."[23] Again, the shortcomings and limitations of perceived sexual liberation cannot be overlooked; however, women of color taking control of their own orgasms can then be symbolic of their rejection of racist and sexist social limitations and prioritization of their own personal fulfillment and pleasure, thus raising the stakes in shaming or outright punishing of sexual self-determination in order to reassert the dominant order of gender roles.

Black Swan, American Pie, The 40-Year-Old Virgin, and *She's Gotta Have It* are each to some extent troubling in their respective depictions of women's masturbation and the construction of women's sexuality as a whole. Graphic depictions of women's autoeroticism are allowable to a degree because of the male centrality and dominance that is ultimately reasserted through either the gaze or actual possession of a character. Viewers can vicariously enjoy women exploring their sexual freedom as long as their perceived transgressions are condemned or punished unambiguously before the sociopolitical implications of masturbation as an avenue for liberation can be fully realized. However, in navigating the problematic representations of women's sexuality produced in an androcentric culture, women viewers who actively seek feminist or sex-positive images and narratives can develop the film and media literacy to critique and then detach the promising aspects of certain texts. All critical spectators with a similar propensity for oppositional readings can develop subversive interpretations of mainstream and seemingly hegemonic texts by actively engaging with the films and focusing on positive images and messages, multiplying the opportunities for women to identify instances of female masturbation that speak to their own experiences. This critical lens allows problematic representations to be consciously reimagined in ways that make visible certain iterations of desire and sexual being.

Self-Stimulation and Self-Discovery

Films that portray women's masturbation as primarily driven by libido and carnal desire are easy enough to co-opt for the indulgence of male-driven narratives while maintaining the necessary distance to effect varying degrees of discipline against the women who fail to demonstrate the requisite shame and humility that are part and parcel of being a "good woman." Yet there is another motivation for the recurring autoeroticism in recent American cinema that seems torn from the self-help books of the godmother of masturbation, Betty Dodson. In addition to its pleasurable physical attributes, some depictions of women's masturbation emphasize its thematic importance to women's sexual self-discovery. First, masturbation to orgasm is imbued with such meaning that the two become deeply intertwined, unlike in early films, where a woman's climax is of no great concern. And so, interestingly, orgasm may be shown as long as it is not about purely sexual satisfaction but instead is critical to a greater narrative of self-determination and sexual development. The representation of self-stimulation and the significance of self-directed orgasm then become subjected to another degree of patriarchal scrutiny and sexist shaming.

Coming Soon (1999), a rare teen romantic comedy written and directed by a woman, focuses on three wealthy White teenage girls seeking fulfilling sexual relationships. The fact that the main characters are already sexually active sets the film apart from most other teen coming-of-age stories, which often center on a heterocentric ideal of virginity loss as though the first penetrative intercourse marks the most significant initiation into emergent adulthood regardless of personal satisfaction. Director Colette Burson noted the opposition she faced when tackling the project because advocating the idea of teen girls enthusiastically pursuing sex and the empowerment of orgasm did not fit into the predominant narratives of appropriate sexuality for young women.[24] This discomfort is most plainly revealed by a production designer who reportedly admitted: "This movie really gets to me, it's as if these girls think that they have the right to have an orgasm."[25] A producer also expressed his distaste for the protagonist Stream's (Bonnie Root) active and unapologetic search for gratifying sex, saying that it made her character "unlikable."[26]

Even when filmmakers have unambiguously feminist intentions, external factors throughout the production process can restrict the diversity of representations of feminine desire portrayed onscreen. Burson acknowledged the limits of her control as a filmmaker by describing the constant pressure she faced from producers to make the film's overt political message less radical by cutting the line where Stream challenges the sexist double standard point blank: "What's wrong with girls wanting to have sex as much as guys?"[27] The crux of the issue seems to be just that—patriarchal norms dictate that women are not entitled to pursue sexual satisfaction outside the confines of male-initiated heterosexual coitus, and therefore the shaming narratives reasserted throughout the production are directed not just toward the physical act of masturbation itself but toward the very prospect of women controlling their sexuality on the face of it.

Dissatisfied with the inadequacy of partnered sex thus far, Stream sets out in deliberate pursuit of an orgasm despite the discouragement she encounters. Her snobby friend Jenny (Gaby Hoffmann) calls masturbation desperate and pathetic, insinuating that she easily achieves orgasm through vaginal intercourse. Her judgmental reaction and the implication that masturbation to achieve orgasm denotes frigidity recalls the myth of the vaginal orgasm. Jenny's eventual dejected confession that she too has been unsatisfied with her sex life further illustrates the social pressure to adhere to androcentric models of sex. In fact, in her examination of the phallocentric sexual paradigm, Rachel P. Maines is careful to note that "the penetration myth is not a conspiracy perpetuated by men; women too want to believe in the ideal of universal orgasmic mutuality in coitus."[28] This pervasive misconception of women's sexual gratification, and particularly their internalization of these misguided beliefs, has effectively contributed to the continued pathologizing of women's justifiable sexual frustration while also leaving them responsible for the egos of their sex partners. Sexuality is just one sphere in which women face internal and external pressure to deny their lived experiences and realities in favor of preserving the status quo.

In one of the most telling scenes in the film, Stream's selfish boyfriend uses gaslighting tactics to convince her that she has orgasmed during sex when she actually hasn't. His disregard for her pleasure is appalling, but more troubling is the way she begins to doubt her own perception of her experience because of his confident assertion. Again, men are treated as authorities on women's bodies and sexual needs while women are left struggling to reconcile their frustration and confusion with the conventional sexual scripts they have been sold. Shame at failing to meet the normative ideals of White womanhood perpetuates a cognitive dissonance that further distances women from their own embodied sexuality. After being rebuffed by her boyfriend and resigning herself to disappointing sex, Stream inadvertently climaxes with the aid of a well-placed water jet in a hot tub. Rather than roaming her body, the camera's focus on her changing facial expressions of shock, confusion, and ecstasy is a marked departure from a film like *American Pie*. Later Stream confronts her boyfriend about his dismissal of the importance of her orgasm with her newfound self-assurance that she can and should have satisfying sex.

Although they are clearly subject to the standards of proper femininity for their social position, the young women's privileged lives likely influence their assured sense that they are entitled to sexual fulfillment when they grow weary of faking it, contrary to the many women who struggle for years with feelings of shame and inadequacy because vaginal intercourse does not lead to earth-shattering orgasms. Burson says that the girls' social status creates tension between their false sense of maturity and entitlement and their sexual dissatisfaction;[29] nonetheless, it is ultimately Stream's persistence, not her privilege, that results in the orgasm and sexual satisfaction she has been seeking.

Coming Soon can in many respects be read as a gender-flipped version of *American Pie*, and it is a prime example of how moving beyond a textual analysis of a film itself to examine it as the product of an industry can further clarify the cultural investment in restricting depictions of women's masturbation. Film historian Timothy Shary says that the film's cool reception illustrates the industry's attitude toward women's sexuality: "The same double standard that promoted female sexual practice while denying female sexual pleasure in earlier youth films was obviously still a disruptive factor in bringing more realistic and positive depictions of teenage sexuality to American movies."[30] The Motion Picture Association of America (MPAA) repeatedly crippled the film with an NC-17 rating because of its focus on the girls' blatant desire for gratification, citing seventeen areas of issue despite the film's complete lack of violence, nudity, or graphic sex.[31] According to Burson, the MPAA found Stream's orgasm in the hot tub to be "too lurid" and suggested that a scene be cut by 75 percent if it showed a girl coming to orgasm.[32] The director claims that she was told expressly that the MPAA did not like girls and women having orgasms, double standard or not. In fact, a representative from the MPAA stated that, because parents judge movies with a sexist framework, the association was responsible, as the public's moral compass, to do the same.[33]

The low-budget cult favorite *But I'm a Cheerleader* (1999) directed by Jamie Babbit further illustrates the proscriptive politics involved in determining which images of women's masturbation and sexuality are deemed acceptable for distribution and public consumption. The campy comedy tells the story of rebellious queer teens at a "de-gaying" camp and includes a brief scene of a teen girl masturbating but features no nudity, explicit sex, or violence. Like *Coming Soon*, the film was hit with an NC-17 and lacked the influence of major studio backing to push for a more accessible rating.[34] Because their budgets could not adequately support their politics, sexually progressive films like *Coming Soon* and *But I'm a Cheerleader* are doomed to gather dust on a video rental shelf with limited audience reception; meanwhile, other, more male-centered films with graphic sexual and violent content easily earn R ratings and big box-office returns, highlighting the inconsistencies in the industry's attitude toward reflecting ideals of American masculinity and femininity. Director Kevin Smith alleges that his relatively tame 2004 film *Jersey Girl* was given an R rating because during an innocuous conversation the female lead openly proclaims that she masturbates twice a day. Smith recalls the pearl-clutching objections of a woman from the MPAA who said that she would be bothered if her 16-year-old daughter were to see that scene—precisely the sort of morally conservative discomfort that manifests in harsh ratings and limited audiences.[35] Films that reject or otherwise challenge patriarchal constructions of sexuality in favor of woman-centric explorations of pleasure, power, and identity are too often censored precisely because of the socially progressive alternatives they represent. This double standard exposes the circular loop of onscreen depictions of sex, both reflecting and reinforcing real-life cultural disapproval of women's sexual liberation within a patriarchal society.

A strikingly different example of an adult woman whose orgasm is vital to her self-discovery can be found in the film *Pleasantville* (1998). Betty (Joan Allen), a repressed mother living a seemingly perfect White suburban existence, discovers masturbation and in turn discovers herself and her sexuality. Whereas *Coming Soon* depicts orgasm as central to sexual awakening and self-discovery, *Pleasantville* takes a less direct approach and positions climax as just one part of the exploration and development of a woman's sexual identity. Following two teens who have been magically transplanted into a black-and-white 1950s sitcom world, *Pleasantville* offers an opportunity to examine how messages regarding traditional femininity and sexuality stifle women's autonomy. Betty is a June Cleaver-esque housewife who lives only for her husband and children and has quite literally never even heard of sex. The film does have conflicting messages about women's sexual autonomy, which are particularly apparent with the reformation of rebel daughter Mary Sue/Jennifer (Reese Witherspoon). Initially unabashedly promiscuous, her sexual influence corrupts the local boys while she remains personally unfulfilled, lamenting her black-and-white visage despite her extensive sexual experience. Finally, she declares she has outgrown "the slut thing" and dedicates herself to her studies, setting up the typical contrast between the archetypal smart good girl and the unambitious bad girl and entangling sexual activity with integrity and worth. Though nostalgic, the film is reflexively critical of stifling 1950s values and the decade's reinvigoration of the Cult of True Womanhood; however, it remains conservative in its treatment of acceptable sexual exploration and expression.

While Jennifer's sexuality is presented as unsatisfying and inauthentic, perhaps because Betty is older and married her need for sexual exploration is more sympathetic. She appears earnestly puzzled when her daughter explains the concept of sex and intrigued when Jennifer says, "There are other ways to enjoy yourself—without Dad." Soon after, Betty lies in the bath mostly submerged, which limits the camera's access to her body. She tentatively begins to masturbate and looks on in wide-eyed disbelief as the bathroom begins to turn to color. As Betty comes to orgasm for the first time, the spectator sees from her perspective rather than indulging in the spectacle of her body. Unlike the other films, which foregrounded the male gaze and framed women's masturbation as performative, this scene focuses on the authenticity and magnitude of her self-actualization as intimately linked to orgasm. At this moment, the bathroom turns to color and the tree outside the window bursts into flames "as though, enflamed by the profundity of Betty's awakening, the Tree of Knowledge itself seems to be catching fire."[36] This impressive imagery may appear (over) dramatic; however, testimonials from Dodson's *Sex for One* are a reminder of just how powerfully transformative orgasm can be, particularly for women who have been anorgasmic for years.

The holistic and revolutionary nature of Betty's sexual awakening demonstrates that masturbation and climax are just part of her journey toward a self-defined identity. Her burgeoning consciousness clashes with confusion and shame at rejecting the role of wife and mother so clearly outlined for her. When her decision to pose nude for a painting incenses some of the townspeople, who are then moved to vandalism, the film accentuates the perceived threat of autonomous feminine sexuality even in artistic representations. That "it is Betty's emergence that epitomizes the changing tone of the community" highlights the idea that the construction of women's sexual identity is central to the construction of the social order.[37] Although the messages are similar, unlike *Coming Soon*, *Pleasantville* did not face the same criticism from producers or the MPAA. Arguably, this was in large part because it was a bigger-budget film distributed by New Line Cinema and thereby escaped the increased scrutiny that "indie" films often face. However, the lack of opposition is further evidence that masturbation and sexual awakening are more acceptable for certain people and within certain contexts. For a married adult woman in a make-believe world, sexual self-discovery is more poetic than problematic. With teenage girls in the real world, on the other hand, orgasm-centered self-discovery presents a condemnable threat to the patriarchal status quo. Certain bodies and identities are culturally policed more than others because they represent a reality contrary to the dominant narratives of normative gender roles and sexuality. Notably, though, Betty's status as exemplifying the ideals of true American womanhood makes the implications of her personal paradigm shift that much more culturally significant. Particularly when women are positioned as vessels for cultural transmission of values and mores, the image of middle-class White motherhood rejecting hegemonic norms is unsettling on a larger scale.

The American cultural imagination still largely regards sex as primarily a source of pleasure and pride for men whereas for women it has yet to be fully extricated from shame-based narratives of appropriate feminine identity formation. Film functions as a powerful avenue for encouraging or suppressing diverse images of women as multifaceted sexual beings. For this reason, comprehensive feminist film criticism is crucial to identifying and promoting savvy readings of contemporary films—as hooks declares, "the truth that every aesthetic work embodies the political, the ideological as part of its fundamental structure. No aesthetic work transcends politics or ideology."[38] Women's bodies become sites of resistance—the body, of course, always being a function of discourse—when they are marked with possibilities for self-motivated sexual expression. A wealth of varied images would support the complexity of feminine sexuality, a vision in which more women could see themselves and their lives reflected.

Though necessarily limited in scope, this analysis of a selection of films indicates that current cinematic depictions of women's masturbation barely begin to reflect the range of women's experiences in navigating their sexuality in a patriarchal society that overlooks the significance of women's orgasms. Masturbation can be about self-discovery or seduction, or simply about physical gratification; more representations are needed to show the varying roles of autoeroticism in women's sexual identity development. Not every representation is or must be equally feminist or sex-positive on its face, but all depictions offer an opportunity to construct subversive readings and identify redeemable aspects, even if only as reminders that women can and do masturbate at all. By unapologetically embracing masturbation and other forms of sexual expression and rejecting the shame-based limitations of overvaluing penetrative intercourse, it is possible to appreciate the multiplicity of women's sexuality and the power of the erotic.

To revisit Frye's theorization of the implications of lesbians looking past the foreground and instead focusing on the women who help construct representations of reality, the fundamental hypervisibility of a self-stimulating woman can redirect attention to women's needs and desires. Learning that they can be seen, these women then learn to see themselves, recognizing the fragile structure of the patriarchal system that works to maintain women's invisibility. Although it is true that even the most outwardly sexist and hegemonic constructions of women's masturbation in film can yield positive and even radical glimpses of feminine sexuality when read with a generous yet critical feminist lens, that possibility does not mean that women should be satisfied with collecting the scraps of cinematic images of women's holistic personhood. Nor is this to suggest that there is ultimately a truly authentic and comprehensive view of women's sexuality that could be committed to celluloid. Because of this inability to pigeonhole the multiplicities of women's experiences with their own sexualities, a diversity of representations is crucial to reflecting the variations in all women's lived experiences regardless of how they fit into the overarching narratives of either hegemonic or feminist sexuality. The disciplinary impact of shaming with regard to masturbation as a precursor to sexual autonomy and self-determination remains both intra- and extratextually salient in demarcating the standards for American womanhood. However, even though shame is strategically used to prohibit or prescribe certain behaviors, women continue to create their own visions of subversive and empowered sexual identity and expression.

Notes

1. It is worth noting that men and boys were more often directly targeted by these "anti-onanism" warnings, given that the very existence of women and girls' carnal desires removed from procreative relations was largely denied and disregarded. For a more thorough account of the sociohistorical denunciation of masturbation as sexually deviant, see Thomas W. Laqueur, *Solitary Sex: A Cultural History of Masturbation* (New York: Zone, 2003); also see Jean Stengers and Anne Van Neck, *Masturbation: The History of a Great Terror*, trans. Kathryn A. Hoffman (New York: Palgrave, 2001).

2. Thomas M. Millar, "Toward a Performance Model of Sex," in *Yes Means Yes! Visions of Female Sexual Power and a World without Rape*, ed. Jaclyn Friedman and Jessica Valenti (Berkeley, CA: Seal Press, 2008), 30.

3. Marilyn Frye, "Oppression," in *The Politics of Reality: Essays in Feminist Theory* (Trumansburg, NY: Crossing Press, 1983), 3.

4. See Rachel P. Maines, *The Technology of Orgasm: "Hysteria," the Vibrator, and Women's Sexual Satisfaction* (Baltimore, MD: Johns Hopkins University Press, 2001); for more detailed explorations of the construction of women's sexuality within the androcentric model, also see Luce Irigaray, *This Sex Which Is Not One* (New York: Cornell University Press, 1985); and Anne Koedt, "The Myth of the Vaginal Orgasm," in *Notes from the First Year* (New York: New York Radical Feminists, 1968).

5. Maines, *Technology of Orgasm*, 3.

6. bell hooks, "The Oppositional Gaze: Black Female Spectators," in *Black Looks: Race and Representation* (Boston: South End Press, 1992), 115.

7. Marilyn Frye, "To Be and Be Seen: The Politics of Reality," in *The Politics of Reality: Essays in Feminist Theory* (Trumansburg, NY: Crossing Press, 1983), 165–170.

8. For a more extensive analysis of spectator difference and negotiated readings, see hooks, "The Oppositional Gaze" and Jane Gaines, "White Privilege and Looking Relations: Race and Gender in Feminist Film Theory," in *Hollywood: Cultural Dimensions: Ideology, Identity and Cultural Industry Studies*, ed. Thomas Schatz (London: Routledge, 2004).

9. Adam Markovitz, "Natalie's Dark Victory," *Entertainment Weekly*, January 7, 2011, 32–36.

10. Laura Mulvey, "Visual Pleasure and Narrative Cinema," in *Feminist Film Theory: A Reader*, ed. Sue Thornham (New York: New York University Press, 1999), 63.

11. Linda R. Williams, *The Erotic Thriller in Contemporary Cinema* (Bloomington, IN: Indiana University Press, 2005), 341.

12. E. Ann Kaplan, "Is the Gaze Male?" in *Feminism and Film* (Oxford, U.K.: Oxford University Press, 2000), 121.

13. Patricia H. Collins, *Black Feminist Thought* (New York: Routledge, 2009), 91.

14. bell hooks, "'Whose Pussy Is This': A Feminist Comment," in *Talking Back: Thinking Feminist, Thinking Black* (Boston: South End Press, 1989), 136.

15. Ibid.

16. Ibid., 139.

17. Ibid.

18. Collins, *Black Feminist Thought*, 160.

19. Ibid.

20. Thelma W. Foote, "Happy Birthday, Nola Darling! An Essay Commemorating the Twentieth Anniversary of Spike Lee's *She's Gotta Have It*," *Women's Studies Quarterly* 35, no. 1/2 (2007): 223.

21. Ibid., 223–224.

22. Jacqueline Bobo, "*The Color Purple*: Black Women as Cultural Readers," in *Female Spectators: Looking at Film and Television*, ed. E. Diedre Pribram (London: Verso, 1988), 103.

23. Gaines, "White Privilege and Looking Relations," 260.

24. Rachel Lehmann-Haupt, "Don't You Know That It's Different for Girls?" *Salon*, July 9, 1999, http://www.salon.com/1999/07/09/coming.

25. Ibid.

26. Ibid.

27. Ibid.

28. Maines, *Technology*, 115.

29. Lehmann-Haupt, "Don't You Know?"

30. Timothy Shary, *Teen Movies: American Youth on Screen* (London: Wallflower, 2005), 106–107.

31. Mary Vause, "Doing It Ourselves: Female Masturbation Past and Present," *Iris: A Journal About Women*, no. 48 (2004): 58–62.

32. Lehmann-Haupt, "Don't You Know?"

33. Ibid.

34. Amy Taubin, "Erasure Police," *Village Voice*, August 3, 1999, 57.

35. *This Film Is Not Yet Rated*, directed by Kirby Dick (New York: IFC Films, 2007), DVD.

36. Richard Armstrong, "'Where Am I Going to See colours like That?' Bliss, Desire and the Paintbox in *Pleasantville*," *Screen Education*, no. 52 (2008): 158.

37. Ibid.

38. hooks, "'Whose Pussy Is This,'" 135.

TWELVE

Dieting for the Sake of Art: Eleanor Antin, Rachel Rosenthal, and Faith Ringgold

Emily L. Newman

Oprah Winfrey graced the cover of *People* on January 14, 1991, with a headline proclaiming, "I'LL NEVER DIET AGAIN!" and the statement "Fed up with her 14-year fight for a model figure, OPRAH WINFREY is learning to love the robust shape she's in." Since the national syndication of *The Oprah Winfrey Show* in 1986, Winfrey's body had been a recurring topic of discussion in the media. This was the persona that Winfrey put forth, that she was now, after years of yo-yo dieting and struggling to lose weight—finally at peace with her larger form. But it was not to last. Nominated for a Daytime Emmy Award in 1992, Winfrey went to the ceremony hoping that she would not win and would not have to accept the award on stage. Journaling about that night, she described her feelings: "I felt so much like a loser, like I'd lost control of my life. And the weight was symbolic of how out of control I was. I was the fattest woman in the room."[1] Oprah's personal feelings about her body, her shame and disgust with her weight, conflicted with her public statements about self-acceptance.

As an important and powerful public figure, Oprah Winfrey represents a significant entry point into discussions of American female body image in the 1980s and 1990s. National success had prompted her to seek out weight loss, and in November of 1988 she walked onto the set of her show in her "skinny jeans" pulling sixty-seven pounds of animal fat in a wagon to celebrate her achievement. Winfrey had lost the weight and proclaimed success, but just fourteen months later, she was back to her original size. That her battles with weight resonated with the American public could be seen in the explosion of the U.S. diet and exercise industry evidenced by the success of Weight Watchers (founded in 1963) and Nutrisystem Weight Loss Centers (founded in 1972).[2] Following these successes, Americans embraced aerobic exercise in the 1980s, with programs such as Jazzercise adding to the many influences on the shaping of women's physiques.[3] To strengthen their muscles, an estimated 25 million Americans enrolled in aerobic dance classes between 1981 and 1985.[4]

Health and fitness were the ultimate goals of these programs, but something alarming was affecting women instead. In 1984 it was estimated that 1 in every 200 to 250 women between the ages of thirteen and twenty-two was suffering from anorexia and as many as 33 percent of college women were controlling their weight through vomiting, diuretics, and laxatives.[5] Around 90 to 95 percent of all anorexics are women, and many experts agree that this disease is closely linked to women's body issues.[6] The extensive media coverage of Karen Carpenter's 1983 death, Gilda Radner's revelations about her struggles with eating disorders in her 1989 autobiography *It's Always Something*, and even Meredith Baxter Birney's turn in the television movie *Kate's Secret* (1986), in which she portrayed a successful lawyer and mother wrestling with bulimia, were among the many instances where the media attempted to deal with eating disorders.[7] The plight of women with disordered eating became a strange fascination for a broader public.

In the 1970s and 1980s, women's bodies were being publicly examined in terms of shape and size, especially in America. In evaluating the work of Eleanor Antin, Rachel Rosenthal, and Faith Ringgold, we can begin to examine how these artists were attempting to challenge societal expectations of their physiques while simultaneously encouraging discussion of *their* bodies because they did *actually* desire to lose weight and become healthier and/or more attractive.[8] It was not just body size that these artists were confronting; it was also society's judgment of women's bodies. Amy Erdman Farrell insightfully discusses this issue: "Fatness in the United States 'means' excess of desire, of bodily urges not controlled, of immoral, lazy, and sinful habits. Much more than a neutral description of a type of flesh, fatness carries with it such stigma that it propels us to take drastic, extreme measures to remove it."[9] While drawing attention to the unfortunate and unfair ways that the U.S. media has always dissected the female form, these artists, for a variety of reasons, many including their own body shame, attempted to lose weight to conform to ideal body size. Their artworks were bound in contradiction because the artists wanted to critique the privileging of thin female bodies while appearing to simultaneously support this position by trying to make their bodies thinner.

Eleanor Antin

By consistently using her short body and dark brown hair in her work, Eleanor Antin (b. 1935) was countering the tall, blonde ideal of the moment. Born and raised in New York, Antin was enmeshed in the contemporary art scene of New York in the late 1960s, befriending Vito Acconci, Joan Jonas, Robert Morris, Yvonne Rainer, and John Perrault, among others, who were interested in exploring the relationship of performance to art.[10] Antin was profoundly influenced not only by the rise of performance art but by the development of conceptual art, which privileged the idea and the process over the final object. In 1969, Antin and her husband David, a poet, moved to San Diego, which immediately affected Antin's work as she began reading feminist texts and eventually formed a women artists' group at the University of California, San Diego.[11]

Inspired by these exposures to feminism, Antin created *Carving: A Traditional Sculpture* in 1972. This piece is composed of 148 photographs of Antin's nude body taken from July 15 to August 21 as she followed a strict dieting regimen. Each morning for thirty-six days, Antin had her picture taken from the front, back, left, and right.[12] Viewed from left to right and from earliest to latest, the pictures chronicled the small changes in Antin's shape as she gradually lost eleven pounds.

There is a documentary aspect to the photos; arranged sequentially they seem like a police lineup or possibly Eadweard Muybridge's photographic experiments. The pseudo-clinical treatment of her body made the weight loss scientific in a way that distanced Antin the artist from Antin the person. As curator Howard Fox observed, "With great deadpan skill, the piece gently satirizes much of the humorless monotony, ponderously presented under a veneer of pseudoscience and alleged clinical objectivity that characterized much of the conceptual art of the day."[13] The scientific documentation of Antin's body and weight loss clearly objectified her body. While the clinical treatment of the body and the scientific documentation of the diet distanced Antin the person from the photographs, the work's success depended on Antin's presence and the fact that she lost weight.[14]

Carving was originally created in response to an invitation to show in the Annual of the Whitney Museum of American Art, which was featuring sculpture that year.[15] Antin explained: "I thought it was a sculptural Annual and since I figured the Whitney was academically oriented, I decided to make an academic sculpture. I got out a book on Greek sculpture, which is the most academic of all. (How could they refuse a Greek sculpture?)"[16] Yet she did not choose to make a conventional three-dimensional object; rather, she treated her body as her medium. Melissa Thompson sees Antin as toying with gender in her use of the term *sculpture*, in recognizing that as a female "sculptress" she was an anomaly in the field. Thompson notes the continued return of artists to the ideal sculptural form epitomized by the female Venus de Milo. The fleshy female body must be constructed and trimmed. Antin's "fat" had to be lost through her dieting, in the process reinforcing the idea that she could become ideal and therefore an appropriate subject for conventionally male sculptors to depict[17]

Carving, then, can be viewed as a performance piece of her dieting with secondary photographic documentation.[18] The work exists today as photographs and wall text, but for Antin in 1972 it was a thirty-six day performance endeavor that involved a strict system of dieting and documentation. She explained her actions in the label that she created to accompany the photographs: "This artist may have a different aesthetic for the female body than Greek sculpture exhibited for the Korai but it should be kept in mind that two considerations determine the conclusion of a work: (1) the ideal image toward which the artist aspires, and (2) the limitations of the material." Antin then paraphrased Michelangelo: "Not even the greatest sculptor can make anything that isn't already inside the marble."[19]

Antin struggled against the increasing popularization of the ideal of the slender yet curvy body exemplified by models (and later actresses) Lauren Hutton (b. 1943), Marisa Berenson (b. 1947), and Cybill Shepherd (b. 1950). These tall, strikingly beautiful women obliquely functioned as the desired end result for Antin's dieting.[20] Naomi Wolf discusses the issues surrounding this ideal body in her seminal book *The Beauty Myth: How Images of Beauty Are Used against Women* (1991), articulating the issue that Antin was fighting against. Women are constantly bombarded with images of beautiful women whose putatively "ideal" yet heavily retouched bodies are unattainable. For Wolf, women's aspirations to these ideal standards force them into a battle over power with men:

> "Beauty" is a currency system like the gold standard. Like any economy, it is determined by politics, and in the modern age in the West, it is the last, best belief system that keeps male dominance intact. In assigning value to women in a vertical hierarchy according to a culturally imposed physical standard, it is an expression of power relations in which women must unnaturally compete for resources that men have appropriated for themselves.[21]

Antin, then, was critiquing the way that women have been forced to focus their efforts on how they look instead of on advancing themselves intellectually or otherwise. By showing her body as it changed throughout the process of weight loss, she was not only drawing attention to the pressures that women face but also illustrating her dissatisfaction with her body. While Antin may not have been happy with her body, she repeatedly turned to its form as a starting place for much of her work.[22]

What many historians do not take into account is the ordinariness of what Antin did: over the course of thirty-six days she put herself on an intensive diet. Anne Wagner hints at this in her review of the 1999 retrospective of Antin's work, where *Carving* functioned as a centerpiece in the show: "Yet from what I could tell, the message seemed to strike many viewers less as critical or ironic analysis than as realism pure and simple: testimony to the inevitable order of things. Of course women diet."[23] Antin's use of dieting in *Carving* paralleled the burgeoning of the diet industry and the rise of the exercise movement in the early 1970s. The publishing of *Dr. Atkins' Diet Revolution* in 1972 made history when in just seven months it sold one million copies. In addition, the number of diet essays and books published dramatically increased, with diet articles in *Reader's Guide* quadrupling over the course of the seventies.[24]

Most important to this discussion is the flowering of diet groups such as Weight Watchers and Overeaters Anonymous in the early 1970s. In 1961, Jean Nidetch, who created Weight Watchers based on her own experiences in a weight loss support group, was described in a 1972 *Time* article as "a 214-lb. Queens housewife [transformed] into a trim 142-lb career woman."[25] At that time, Weight Watchers had 101 operations in 49 states and some foreign countries. Along with a bestselling cookbook, a magazine, and prepared foodstuffs, Weight Watchers succeeded as their revenues went from $160,000 in 1964 to a whopping $8 million in 1970.[26]

Weight Watchers bears comparing to Antin's *Carving* because its increasing success and visibility corresponded to the development of her artwork, and the way Weight Watchers members were encouraged to lose weight can be related to the structure of Antin's piece. *Time*'s aptly titled "Fortune from Fat," which reported that 3 million "fatties" paid to attend Weight Watcher meetings, described the program:

> The unique mark of the Weight Watchers operation is the weekly class, which combines the atmospheres of a religious revival meeting and a high school pep rally. As they arrive, members weigh in; their weekly gains or losses are recorded on cards and later read off to the assemblage. Under the guidance of a trained lecturer, those who have taken off pounds are loudly applauded; backsliders are sympathetically counseled to show renewed dieting determination.[27]

Members were held accountable by their fellow dieters, and their weight was recorded each week; menus and food diaries were distributed for the week ahead.

The public process and scrutiny Antin put her body through as displayed in *Carving* was not unlike how a Weight Watchers member confronted her weight publicly each week. The frequency and repetition of the weekly weigh-ins coupled with the encouragement to use food journals, demonstrates the program's dependence on documentation to keep its members aware of their weight. In addition, the public recounting of weight gain and loss could work toward shaming members into losing weight. Daniel Martin, a sociologist who studied the program through research and personal participation, explained how shame played a critical role in its effectiveness:

> As a participating observer, I experienced the anxiety that members later recounted in interviews about "facing the scale," that is, weigh-ins. Because weigh-ins take place in semipublic space, it is possible that queuing members will learn of one's weight, increasing the anxiety

that is already present for some members. Having failed weigh-in several times by gaining weight, I was struck by the capacity for the ritual to evoke, simultaneously, feelings of dependency and embarrassment.[28]

Because this "ritual" actually caused many people to leave the program, it was eventually dropped.[29]

Similarly, through her system of documentation, Antin held herself accountable in much the same way that a Weight Watchers member does. Even in the text that accompanied the work, Antin felt compelled to emphasize the limitations of her body, "The work was originally intended to include a regimen of exercise also, but this proved unacceptable, in practice, to the artist who appears to have lost her skills at this technique."[30] While this was intended as self-deprecating and humorous, it spoke to Antin's challenges with changing her body. Although she was able to succeed at dieting, exercise was problematic. She was acknowledging that there was only so much she could do with her body, as if it were a predetermined shape already formed in the marble. She was not the classical ideal and never would be. She could slightly alter her size, but she could not become a Korai. Antin did not discuss *Carving* in the context of feeling bad about her body or its size; rather, she saw it as an artistic endeavor.[31] Simultaneously, by taking on a project with such scrupulous documentation of her physique where she was visibly trying to change her form to be more ideal, Antin was clearly expressing how her body did not meet societal norms and should be changed, even going so far as to express how she was never ideal enough. The Whitney Museum refused to show *Carving* in their sculptural annual, which can be seen as reinforcing Antin's failed attempt at becoming the desirable thin body that society covets.

Rachel Rosenthal

Similarly, Rachel Rosenthal (b. 1926) also used photographs of her overweight body as compared to her newer, svelter figure in *The Death Show* (1978). Both Antin and Rosenthal used photographic illustrations of the fluctuations of their body size to simultaneously document their weight changes and become the subject of their art and performances. While Antin intended her photographs to demonstrate the "sculptural" changes to her body, Rosenthal's performances entailed a personal revelation about her weight. Even so, both of their artworks were autobiographical, documenting the changes their bodies experienced—for their art, for their health, and/or for their appearance.

Rosenthal is nine years older than Antin, and her art emerged out of experimental theater. Born in France of Russian-Jewish blood, Rosenthal called herself a "DP"—a displaced person—because she shuffled between Paris, New York, and Brazil throughout her early life.[32] In 1955, Rosenthal moved to California and established Instant Theatre (1956–1966), which focused on a combination of improvisation and theater exercises. She did not, however, produce a project conceived of as performance art until the mid-1970s.

Like Antin, Rosenthal had been fundamentally changed by the feminist movement; she was encouraged by fellow feminists to explore performance art and to incorporate in it her life experiences. She explained in 1989: "I was able to do in my performance work what I had never been able to do in my life, which is to reveal myself, to disclose, to air, to put out all this garbage and turn it around and make it into art, and in a sense reveal all the dark secrets that I had kept locked up all these years. It was redemption and exorcism."[33] Rosenthal's performance of *Charm* (1977) was a breakthrough for the artist; in it she began to address issues concerning her troubling childhood and its effect on her body.

Subtitled *A Sonata in Three Movements*, *Charm* was performed at Mount St. Mary's College Art Gallery in Los Angeles on January 28, 1977.[34] The piece was structured in three movements around multiple definitions of "charm," through which Rosenthal wove stories about her parents, her childhood, her first home in Paris, and her relationship with her servants. As the piece progressed, the pace quickened and the environment grew increasingly frantic. On an elevated platform, supporting cast members dressed in black, called "nightmare figures," engaged in acts of sadism and sadomasochism at escalating speeds until they became a mesh of bodies. Meanwhile, on a lower platform, Rosenthal regaled the audience with tales of her aristocratic Parisian life. Throughout the piece, she became increasingly anxious and upset, shouting at intervals, "CAN YOU ALL SEE ME? CAN YOU ALL HEAR ME?"[35] As she spoke, a butler presented her with pastries, which Rosenthal ate rapidly, repeatedly asking for more. As the pastries piled up faster than she could devour them, she frantically shoveled them in her mouth. For the triumphant finish, the butler brought out a large chocolate cake, which Rosenthal plunged into face first.

As these events took place, Rosenthal tied the piece together by relating childhood stories and events. Speaking of how she was forced to go to bed early and was left under the watch of the servants, she noted that she had a particularly contentious relationship with her governess, who openly mocked the six-year old Rosenthal and put her on a diet. As she explained in the piece, "Downstairs I was adulated and loved. Everything I did was wonderful and pretty. Upstairs my hair was pulled, my face was slapped, I was told I was stupid, that I was an idiot and a show-off, and that people were only nice to me because my father was rich . . . ."[36] Then Rosenthal rang a bell to alert the butler for more food, and her stories grew darker and darker, pushing her into a frantic state where she gorged on the sweet pastries.

Charm was the first piece Rosenthal performed where she addressed food, and it marked the first time she discussed her deep-seated self-consciousness about her body. In a 1975 letter to the artist Barbara T. Smith, she spoke of her desire to lose weight and change her body size. Rosenthal traced the origins of her overeating to the Cordon-Bleu chef who worked for her family.[37] She went on to explain how her body was physically hindering her work: "Barbara, needless to say, I am petrified. Here I am, almost fifty, having to have my knees operated on, overweight, ten years older, out of shape and training, trying to resume one of the most difficult and demanding forms art can take."[38] *Charm* was Rosenthal's attempt to come to terms with the issues surrounding her body and food, which she so specifically traced back to her childhood. In a later interview, she said, "My half-sister was obese and was getting a great deal of flack from my mother, so I associated being loved with being thin. That created a lifelong problem and an eating disorder. For example, I can never remain an even weight because it either goes way up or way down. I eat emotionally—and for all of the wrong reasons."[39] Rosenthal struggled with her weight constantly, and after the revelations discovered through the performance of *Charm*, she joined Overeaters Anonymous and successfully shed several pounds.[40]

Rosenthal returned to performance art significantly thinner and healthier, which she addressed in *The Death Show* (1978),[41] in which she recited a text about death, primarily three deaths that "stick out as prototypes of all the others": her beloved Teddy—a childhood toy taken away from her when the "grownups" felt she was too old for him, Defective Kitten—a cat Rosenthal mercy-killed when it was abandoned by its mother, and her treasured cat Dibidi, which she had for eighteen years and which for twelve of those was paraplegic and had to be constantly attended to and supervised.[42] As she told these stories, it became clear that *The Death Show* was about Rosenthal exorcizing these demons of her past as she strove for redemption. Addressing this piece in 1979, Rosenthal explained, "Although our body knows death and stores this knowledge 'in our memory bank at the cellular level,' we must consciously rehearse for the 'Big One' by learning how to die the myriad deaths of our lives, letting go and shedding people, events, parts of ourselves. If this is not done, a 'monster emerges.'"[43] While she dealt with the deaths of others, Rosenthal also had to shed a part of herself.

As part of *The Death Show*, Rosenthal revealed a picture on an easel, called the "Icon of the Fat Vampire." Mounted on plywood was a photograph of Rosenthal before the weight loss, near the time *Charm* was made, surrounded by a funeral wreath composed of pastries, cakes, and doughnuts spray-painted black. Explaining the icon to her audience, Rosenthal said, "The Fat Vampire is fat from the accumulation of countless botched-up deaths not allowed to die, fat from the unrecognized fear of the Big One, fat from the wrong substances ingested for life and sustenance, fat from opaqueness, the refusal to let in the rays of light. Fat from blocked deaths."[44] Emphasizing that the Fat Vampire had taken over her life, she exorcized it by letting out a primal scream.

Then Rosenthal addressed how she rid her life completely of this monster. Initially, she resisted killing the Fat Vampire because she was afraid to let go and leave her comfort zone. Lighting candles at the front of the stage, she defined the "stations of the Fat Vampire" as moments when she could have killed it but was too afraid of dying. The stations began with a year, then a type of food, and then a statement about refusing a death (her virginity, her parents, her identity as an artist, etc.). For example: "6. 1972: Cheesecake. I refuse the death of my feminine role and resist the call to feminist arms. . . . 9. 1978: Häagen-Dazs Ice Cream. I refuse the death of the Fat Vampire, of my marriage, of 51 years of my life. The 10th Station is this performance."[45] The death of the Fat Vampire became an exorcism of all her "deaths," those demons that had haunted her and made her body fat and bloated. She continued, "I want to be a good suicide. I don't want to botch up my death. I want to bury the Fat Vampire, and with it, all my small and medium-sized deaths that were left to decompose without proper burial."[46] Rosenthal then approached the icon and repeatedly slashed it with a knife.

By Rosenthal's account, the Fat Vampire had taken over her life, manifesting itself physically through the size of her body. She claimed to never have been fat but that the Vampire wrapped around her body and encased her: "As for me, I finally lost track of my real boundaries and, amnesiac of my true self, I too mistook this padded shroud for my own skin."[47] This concept of alien fat enveloping the true person resonates with Susie Orbach's arguments in *Fat Is a Feminist Issue* (1978). Published at the same time that Rosenthal was producing her work, Orbach's book pointed to fat as a tool that women use to avoid complex issues: "Fat is a social disease, and fat is a feminist issue. Fat is not about lack of self-control or lack of will power. Fat is about protection, sex, nurturance, strength, boundaries, mothering, substance, assertion and rage."[48] For Orbach, becoming fat could be a way of taking control of one's body and attempting to avoid objectification in the eyes of men. In contrast, Rosenthal claimed that the fat had overtaken her, shifting, shaping, and obscuring her true self. Both Orbach and Rosenthal, then, saw fat as an insidious entity separate from the individual, one that with hard work (dieting, exercising, etc.) could, and should, be exorcized.

As she recounted and demonstrated in *Charm*, Rosenthal was an overeater and specifically an emotional overeater.[49] Orbach constructed overeating as a deliberate act and choice to avoid becoming the ideal woman:

> My fat says "screw you" to all who want me to be the perfect mom,
> sweetheart, maid and whore. Take me for who I am, not for who I'm
> supposed to be. . . . In this way, fat expresses a rebellion against the

powerlessness of the woman, against the pressure to look and act in a certain way and against being evaluated on her ability to create an image of herself.[50]

Such ideas may have been evocative for Rosenthal, who was constantly moving from the ideal thin body that her mother wanted for her (her mother had told her often when she was little, "When you are fat, I don't love you") to an overweight body that delighted in consuming French pastries.[51]

Rosenthal's attempt to gain control of her weight in the late 1970s by joining Overeaters Anonymous, coupled with her own comments about her weight, emphasize that she was preoccupied with and shamed by her appearance. At the same time, she was concerned about her health and physical condition. In 1989 she was experiencing such serious health setbacks due to her weight that her art production was hindered. This was probably the period between *Charm* and *The Death Show*, when Rosenthal ceased performing:

> There was a time in my life when if I'd looked the way I look now I would hide. I would not show myself. I would not perform. I would not go out. I would hide under the sheets and nobody would see me. And I knew, deep in my heart, that I could never be loved or appreciated or even considered as part of the human race if people could see me with these pounds overweight. And now I thank goodness have gotten past that. . . . But it is still a problem, because I know how good I look when I'm thin and I feel so much better too.[52]

The Death Show became particularly powerful when it illustrated Rosenthal's exploration of her heaviness as a hindrance and a destructive force—one that provoked anger and violence. Rather than working to accept her figure at its current weight in the late 1970s, Rosenthal's health and shame pushed her to change her body significantly.

To reiterate, *The Death Show* showcased a picture of the larger Rosenthal in the Icon of the Fat Vampire. The pastries she devoured in *Charm* surrounded the face of the former, fat Rosenthal in *The Death Show*. The two pieces, in their demonstration of her weight loss and physical transformation, recall Antin's comparable, albeit smaller, change as documented in *Carving*. Antin photographed her body and recorded her weight as the changes happened, systematically evaluating the shape and size of her body as she dieted. Her clinical approach was far removed from the dramatic and psychological portrait that Rosenthal presented, yet both artists expressed dissatisfaction with their physiques. When discussed together, the two artists illustrate both the physical and mental experiences one has while undergoing weight loss.

Both also were responding to the ideal L.A. woman, who was generally viewed as healthy because she was thin (if not underweight) and active, participating in the California beach culture. In 1983, Dr. Peter Wood published *The California Diet and Exercise Program*, which postulated that Californians "played" more and ate healthier because most American healthy foods came from the fertile valleys of California.[53] An active lifestyle and beautiful weather permitted the wearing of skimpy bikinis, but also began to be reflected in artists' work in the late sixties and seventies. The icon of the beach-worthy body coupled with proximity to Hollywood led some women artists to incorporate the social anxieties that their location inspired into their artwork.[54]

With regard to Antin, Lisa E. Bloom has argued that her Jewish identity precluded her attainment of the putative ideal: Here, Bloom discusses Antin's ethnicity in relation to *Carving*:

> Antin's project can be seen as her inability to adapt to the ideal and thus to assimilate as an unmarked subject . . . Antin does not offer an easy solution to the dilemma of being both Jewish and female. Instead she points to the limits of fitting in, by presenting a series of anti-aesthetic photographic self-portraits that refuse to offer a neutral and undisturbing aesthetic experience.[55]

The attempts of Jewish women to assimilate and change themselves to look "Whiter" has been well documented. As Melvin Konner articulates, "Hair was straightened and dyed blond, eyebrows trimmed and plucked, skin bleached, and ears tucked back closer to the skull in innovative surgical procedures. And, in the greatest step in the cosmetic surgery of the era, Jewish noses were straightened and 'bobbed'—cut short—to remove this most obvious and 'indestructible' Jewish stigma."[56] By tracing the history of rhinoplasty from its invention by the Jewish doctor Jacques (né Jakob) Joseph to its popularity with celebrities and teenage Jewish girls, Konner emphasizes the lengths Jewish men and women have gone to change their bodies to fit in.

More specifically, Jewish women, arguably including Antin and Rosenthal, have historically tried to resemble a particular figure type—one that is significantly less Jewish. Sander Gilman explores this idea: "The desire for invisibility, to 'look like everyone else,' still shaped the Jew's desire to alter his / her body. . . . The internalization of the negative image of the Jew is one model of response to the sense of being seen as 'too Jewish,' or, indeed, being seen as Jewish at all."[57] By documenting her body in a straightforward and scientific way, Antin drew attention to her Jewish nose and short stature and her differences from the California woman. Similarly, the Jewish refugee Rosenthal, a self-proclaimed displaced person, never felt she fit in with any group. Her body type, with her dark hair, larger frame, and

Dieting for the Sake of Art   *261*

troubled knees, was certainly distinct from the figure of her erstwhile mentor, Barbara T. Smith, who was a quintessential blonde beauty. Changing their bodies and making themselves thinner could serve as a comfort for Antin and Rosenthal, making them more American and, as Gilman says, more "invisible." Furthermore, as Thomas Rees asserts, "Everybody wanted to look like a shiksa."[58]

Derived from the Hebrew verb *shakaytz* (to abominate an unclean object), *shiksa* evolved into an epithet describing the gentile female, one who was desired by men but forbidden.[59] While the term does not necessarily imply a thin body, it does frequently suggest some attractiveness or appeal that the Jewish woman is lacking. Rosenthal and Antin strove to make their bodies look more like that of the shiksa and therefore more conventionally desirable.

Faith Ringgold

Interweaving questions of Jewishness into the struggle about weight certainly complicates Antin's and Rosenthal's relationships with their bodies. Even so, there is something universal about their struggle to fit in as their attempts to change their bodies paralleled the plight of the "average" woman, who was constantly trying to conform to a thin ideal. Faith Ringgold (b. 1930) went through a similar struggle with her weight, and after twenty years of focusing on her career and creating successful work, the African-American artist decided that she, much like Rosenthal, needed to make a change in her body and in 1986 lost one hundred pounds.

Ringgold's art career began in earnest in the 1960s, when she painted large works that confronted issues of race. In the 1980s, she began working in fabric, creating story quilts that used a combination of painting and text to present activist arguments, historical narratives, personal events, and recollections. To celebrate her new, healthier body, she created the first of a series of three quilts, all titled *Change: Faith Ringgold's Over 100 Pound Weight Loss Performance Story Quilt*. The quilts included both photographic and painted portraits of the artist, showing all versions of herself—from young to old and skinny to fat. To make the first and second of these quilts she used a combination of photo etchings on fabric, painted portraits and texts, which were then pieced onto the quilt by assistants whom she had hired. In particular, this first quilt focuses on anecdotes and personal feelings regarding Ringgold's weight by incorporating parts of a text she had been writing for a then unpublished autobiography organized by the decades of Ringgold's life.[60]

The central section is the exception as "January 1, 1986" told of Ringgold's current relationship with her body and her weight-loss goals. Shifting from the first to the second person, the tone of her writing also moved from autobiographical to motivational: "In this year, 1986, I will lose 128 pounds. By January 1, 1987 I will weigh 130 pounds, or I'll eat your hat. Mine I've already eaten. Faith, you have been trying to lose weight since the sixties. For the last twenty, twenty-five years you've been putting yourself on diets, charting your lack of progress and gaining weight."[61] Thus, the quilt became not just a history of her life through photos and text but also an attempt to encourage herself to lose more weight. Ringgold admitted that she wanted to lose weight, not just to become healthier and to increase her agility when working and performing but to look better.[62] Moira Roth astutely articulates the way that Ringgold used her quilt to express her emotional state:

> With this quilt Ringgold visually records the progressive transformation of a woman from what she is expected to be to what she wants to be. The weight gain is part of that struggle and a response to the stress and pressures of conflicting demands and expectations. It becomes a protective shield in Ringgold's denial of her stereotyped image as a sex object (the Black temptress).[63]

Ringgold was articulating the desire to claim her body for herself, but by emphasizing weight loss she was also calling attention to the pressure put on women. Roth claims that Ringgold used her excess weight so that her body would not become a sexual object, an idea that recalls Orbach: "Just as many women first become fat in an attempt to avoid being made into sexual objects at the beginning of their adult lives, so many women remain fat as a way of neutralizing their sexual identity in the eyes of others who are important to them as their life progresses."[64] Ringgold echoed Orbach in the 1970–1979 section of the quilt: "You used to say your husband Burdette made you eat so that no one else would look at you. And then you didn't look at you either."[65] Throughout the narrative, Ringgold vacillated between taking responsibility for her own weight gain (listing all the types of food that tempted her) and blaming others who encouraged her bad habits.

The text was laced with humorous and perceptive moments. For example, the section for 1980–1985 began with this insight: "By the 1980s you had finally eaten yourself into a corner. The only way out was cold turkey without dressing."[66] She went on to tell the story of a political benefit she attended: "You posed with her [the candidate], not realizing you held a greasy bag of nuts. She slapped you on your hand and ordered you to 'put that away' . . . You could have made the front page and the Nightly News that day, 'Fat Woman Goes Nuts,' but you smiled, wiped your mouth, and put your nuts out of sight."[67] Humor, however, could not disguise the hurt that Ringgold was feeling as she chronicled painful moments in her life—the binging, the divorces, even the loss of self-control when faced with good wine or chocolate. The quilt's text was an honest account of one woman's experience, her battle with food, her embarrassments, and her determination to overcome her struggles with weight.

After completing the quilt and losing her one hundred pounds, Ringgold incorporated the ideas and anecdotes of the quilt into a performance piece that she presented when the quilt was shown in exhibitions. Through song, dance, and spoken word, she narrated her life and her struggles with weight. At the end of the performance, she removed an oversized jacket that had the same photographs and text as the quilt to show off her new, thinner body. Additionally, throughout the performance she repeatedly attempted to pull twenty, two-liter soda bottles filled with water and stuffed into two large garbage bags. Collectively symbolizing the weight that she had lost, the bottles did not budge easily; this was a blatant metaphor for the burden of the extra pounds she carried and the difficult of shedding them.[68] She invited the audience to get up and pull the "weight," to experience firsthand the weight of one hundred pounds. In an act anticipating Oprah Winfrey's wagon of fat two years later, Ringgold needed to tangibly represent her lost pounds as a way to visualize the changes to her figure. In her performance, Ringgold repeatedly acknowledged her past weight-loss failures: the fad diets, the doctors' advice, even the pills.[69] In contrast, the separation of the extra fat (as represented by Ringgold's bottles) and her body emphasized her triumphs. Throughout her piece Ringgold repeated the phrase "I can change. I can do it. I can do it. I can CHANGE, I can CHANGE. Now." In an attempt to further motivate herself to lose more pounds as well as to inspire others to join in her quest, she encouraged the audience to chant with her, repeating "CHANGE" over and over.

The quilt itself had a performative element. The last panel recorded the date of its completion as an update to Ringgold's progress since the first panel of January 1, 1986: "It is September 27, 1986, and though I have 40 pounds yet to lose I have lost 88 pounds. Today I am thinner than I have been in the last twenty years. I eat fresh fruit and vegetables instead of pasta and pork chops, and I exercise almost every day. I am out to prove something right here and now."[70] What exactly did she prove? The numbers on the scale had changed, and she admitted that her diet had also become healthier—but this change was not enough. Ringgold's quilt articulated her feelings of insecurity and disappointment tinged with hopefulness. The stories expressed in the quilt repeatedly emphasized her anxieties regarding her body. This omnipresent discomfort led Ringgold to keep the series going as she continued to lose weight and attempted to come to terms with her physical presence.

A second quilt dealing with her weight loss, *Change 2: Faith Ringgold's Over 100 Pound Weight Loss Performance Quilt* (1988), was originally intended as a celebration of losing another thirty pounds,[71] but, as she noted in her 2005 autobiography, "I must admit I failed to do that, but I was still fortunate because I didn't gain back the weight I lost."[72] The focal point of this quilt was a painting in the center panel that depicted Ringgold's ideal svelte figure in a simple bathing suit. Behind the figure was the larger shadow of her current, imperfect self. Again, Ringgold had created a performance that matched the quilt in which she wore a costume that worked to accentuate her waist and her successful maintenance of her 100-pound weight loss. Rather than recite the stories of the first quilt, for the second performance piece Ringgold sang the *Change Song*, which included motivational lyrics like the text in the first quilt: "I just got to change / I just got to change / I can't stand the pain / It's like a fire in my brain / Everyday it's the same Never mind who's to blame / It's me that's got to change / Eatin' all that food is so insane / I just got to change / I just got to change."[73] Ringgold made very clear that she was dissatisfied with her body and that its size caused both physical and emotional pain.

Audience participation was critical in Ringgold's *Change* performances because a communal spirit was said to emerge as people sang and danced alongside her, bonding over their commonalities of weight loss, body image, and general insecurities concerning body size. Indeed, the audience, in its support of Ringgold and her project, did not challenge their assigned role in Ringgold's weight loss. Rather, Ringgold used her viewers as a support structure to help her maintain her lower weight. Their complicity also reinforced the need for change in Ringgold's body and perhaps in their own weight loss.

Ringgold's performances captured the desire she felt to fit in and to find others who were experiencing the same challenges. Even Winfrey, reaching out to her audience, sought solace by sharing her experiences. Echoing the strategy used successfully in Weight Watchers and Overeaters Anonymous, Ringgold, Rosenthal, and Winfrey found support through group participation, which recognizes that the struggle with weight or to be comfortable with body size is something that many, many women are working through.

By trying to achieve a putatively ideal body, Ringgold and Winfrey could also be said, in effect, to have tried to achieve the ideal *White* body, as Sidonie Smith argues:

> "Faith's" identity as a subject of disordered eating and disordered self-restraint is a social identity, one manifesting the psychic formations of her specific history as an African American woman. The ironic self-analysis of the narrative points to a profound psychic wound, the internalization of the phantasm of the idealized "feminine" body, raced as "white," and the degraded African American female body stereotyped as unconstrained and excessive.[74]

Traditionally, African Americans have been more accepting than other ethnic groups of a heavier body type.[75] Since the 1980s, however, the African American magazines *Ebony* and *Jet* have shown a marked increase in attention to diet, exercise, and body image issues. According to Becky W. Thompson, only in the last two decades have Black women been able to communicate their struggles with weight, breaking from the mammy stereotype (large, desexualized Black women) that has haunted them.[76] Winfrey's and Ringgold's open discussions about their weight drew attention to the fact that, like Whites, people of color could have issues with their bodies and even struggle with eating disorders.[77] The desire for slenderness so associated with Western White women is no longer specific to them as women of other ethnic groups have generally come to adhere to the same ideals. On some level, Ringgold's and Winfrey's battles with weight demonstrate that their Black bodies could not fit into society the way they were—they had to be modified, slimmed down, to be accepted. Furthermore, their desire to be thin points to something frequently missing in the literature on anorexia, bulimia, and weight issues: the Black body.

Ringgold had started to put weight back on by the time she began making *Change 3: Faith Ringgold's Over 100 Pound Weight Loss Performance Quilt* (1991). Weight gain is not uncommon after dieting. Both Ringgold and Winfrey used a liquid diet, specifically Optifast, to quickly lose pounds. Originally Ringgold lost 100 pounds and kept them off in part through the exercise entailed in the performances and dancing for the first *Change* and for *Change 2*. A trip to France and a pause from her performances prompted a weight gain of about twenty-five pounds.[78] Basically, as soon as Winfrey and Ringgold began to eat solid food, the weight returned. Neither woman was alone, however: more than 95 percent of women reportedly cannot maintain their weight loss after a diet.[79]

For Ringgold, this weight gain served as the impetus to create her *Change 3* quilt, which "contain[ed] no photographs but rather a painted 'group' self-portrait in the nude, showing me at my various different weights over the years—a testament to the continuing struggle I have had with food. The text for this quilt is about the eating habits of different 'women' (all of them, of course, are just me) who are portrayed on this quilt."[80] These nude Ringgolds, while of varying sizes, were much closer to a thin woman than to the heavier woman she once was and could become again.

Because the third quilt did not contain pictures or anecdotes from Ringgold's life, it relied on a fictional event and painted (often idealized) portraits of the artist. Creating this image of her world allowed Ringgold to express these alter egos, some of whom were past versions of herself and others were fictitious. There were the skinny and the overweight Ringgolds, the emotional eaters, and the ones who starved. Ringgold's point was that all of these people were in her and probably in most people. Nonetheless, the text made clear that she was clinging to the idea that one day she could be as thin as the skinniest women in the quilt. For Ringgold at the time of *Change 3*, the goal was still to lose more weight.

The text panel in *Change 3* is illuminating, explaining the central image—a party where everyone invited was actually various versions of Ringgold. "At my party everyone invited is actually me and therefore knows me so there is no need to posture and pretend. . . . The extreme manifestations of me showed up at the party uninvited, and were snubbed. One was eating a fried pork chop sandwich from a greasy bag. When she left in a huff, she got stuck in the door."[81] The text made clear that, as much as Ringgold wanted to be open to all versions of her body, she was not able to accept them and remained uncomfortable with her fat self.

The brief text on the quilt ended with the note that two larger women had showed up at the party, eaten all the appetizers, and then invited Ringgold for "coffee-cake and ice cream after dinner. Really?" Ringgold questioned these two women, perhaps because she identified with them. Sweets were among her weaknesses, and it was as if these two women were perpetuating Ringgold's bigger body. She didn't want to go out with them, but instead wanted to associate with the thinner women, who either show restraint or have disordered eating habits. With those women, her body was safer and more desirable in society.

What had begun as a celebration of her weight loss morphed into a hopeful wish of what her body could be and ended with a reluctant acceptance of her fluctuating weight. The *Change* series tracked her mindset regarding body image, but also provided for the hope that maybe one day she could achieve her desired weight while reinforcing the inadequacy of her current figure. Susan Bordo has argued that the slender body becomes a symbol of the "correct attitude . . . it means that one 'cares' about oneself and how one appears to others, suggesting willpower, energy, control over infantile impulse, the ability to shape your life."[82] A fat person can thus be seen as weak because fatness can "be seen as reflecting moral or personal inadequacy, or lack of will."[83]

Conclusion

Antin's, Rosenthal's, and Ringgold's pieces were ostensibly for creating art, and yet they are intimately personal, reflecting each maker's potentially unsettling dissatisfaction with her body. Discussing Americans' preoccupation with body image, W. Charisse Goodman states:

> Possessed by countless images of perfection always beyond her reach, forever measured and compared with other bodies, trapped in a world where only one size fits in, she is truly haunted by our society's grand obsession. Even when she is acutely aware of the political and social coercion involved in weight prejudice, she nevertheless finds herself apologizing for her "less-than-perfect" figure.[84]

The artists' relationships with their bodies all reinforce the belief that the size of one's body can determine the way one is perceived by society. There is something universal about the struggles of these women to fit in—their attempts to change their bodies paralleling the plight of the "average" woman who is constantly trying to conform to a thin ideal that has the potential to bring about a happier, more fulfilling, and more successful life.

In her work, each artist walked a fine line, wanting to articulate the problematic view of women's bodies in society but also reinforcing the need to have a body that meets an "acceptable" standard. In the process of creating their works or on reflection afterward, the artists expressed a certain discontent or disappointment with their bodies. By making works that forcefully confronted viewers with the size of women's bodies and the physical effects of dieting, they also pushed viewers to consider their own complicity in the shaming of women's bodies. It becomes impossible not to look at these works and think of popular magazine covers and advertisements that "instruct" women on ways to look. The strength of the pieces is in the contradiction they depict. While showing that the dieting industry and the media have effectively determined the way women's figures should look, the artists attempted to challenge these ideas but also succumb to them.

The artists' persistent practices of incorporating their bodies in ways central to their projects demonstrate that their work in the 1970s and 1980s did not resolve any of the issues concerning their weight. The decision to showcase their bodies allowed their work to prompt further examination of body size and its role in art and society by future generations of artists.[85] Professionally, they did not incorporate their weight issues or insecurities concerning their bodies in their art again. This is not to say that dissatisfaction with their bodies dissipated; rather, it persisted but did not continue as a subject for their art.[86] In an interview in 1998, discussing her work and her desire for change, Eleanor Antin explained one of the key reasons that she moved away from her dissatisfaction with her body: because nothing could really be done about it. "But can you really win? Have you ever seen a revolution that didn't swallow itself? Isn't defeat built into the world, as basic as carbon? Aren't we all doomed? We got out in the morning and we're going to be defeated at night. If we have really bad luck, we'll be defeated by noon."[87]

Notes

1. Quoted in Ella Howard, "From Fasting toward Self-Acceptance: Oprah Winfrey and Weight Loss in American Culture," in *The Oprah Phenomenon*, ed. Jennifer Harris and Elwood Watson (Lexington, KY: The University Press of Kentucky, 2007), 110.

2. Roberta Pollack Seid, *Never Too Thin: Why Women Are at War with Their Bodies* (New York: Prentice Hall, 1989), 167.

3. Seid, *Never Too Thin*, 235.

4. Seid, *Never Too Thin*, 236.

5. Susan Bordo, *Unbearable Weight: Feminism, Western Culture and the Body* (1994; repr., Berkeley,: University of California Press, 2004), 140.

6. Joan Jacobs Brumberg, *Fasting Girls: The History of Anorexia Nervosa*, rev. ed. (New York: Vintage Books, 2000), 15.

7. Gilda Radner discussed how she lost weight through dieting, attributing her success to sugarless chewing gum and throwing up after meals; see Cherie Burns, "Radner's Ready," *People*, December 5, 1977, 92–99. On Karen Carpenter, see Randy L. Schmidt, *Little Girl Blue: The Life of Karen Carpenter* (Chicago: Chicago Review Press, 2010).

8. In this essay, I address the artists' work and biography because the two are intimately intertwined during this period. I do recognize that historically women and people of color who are artists are often discussed in connection with their biography, in part because their work is discussed *only* in the context of their gender or race. Regarding the work of Antin and Rosenthal in the 1970s and Ringgold in the 1980s, the biographies of these artists *must* be discussed because of the nature of their projects. Additionally, the importance of including their experiences recalls the arguments of Anna Chave, "'Normal Ills': On Embodiment, Victimization and the Origins of Feminist Art," in *Trauma and Visuality in Modernity*, ed. Lisa Saltzaman and Eric Rosenberg (Lebanon, NH: Dartmouth College Press, 2006), 132–157.

9. Amy Erdman Farrell, *Fat Shame: Stigma and the Fat Body in American Culture* (New York: New York University Press, 2011), 10.

10. Howard Fox, *Eleanor Antin* (Los Angeles: Los Angeles County Museum of Art, 1999), 16–24.

11. Ibid., 204–207.

12. Technically, the project took place over a thirty-seven-day period because she missed photographing herself on a morning that she was not at home in San Diego. Eleanor Antin, personal communication, June 28, 2009.

13. Fox, *Eleanor Antin*, 44.

14. For a more detailed analysis of the conceptual nature of *Carving*, see Jayne Wark, "Conceptual Art and Feminism: Martha Rosler, Adrian Piper, Eleanor Antin, and Martha Wilson," *Woman's Art Journal* 22, no. 1 (2001): 44–50; and Fox, *Eleanor Antin*, 20–46.

15. The Whitney Museum requested a piece from Antin, expecting something in line with her *100 Boots*. When Antin sent them *Carving: A Traditional Sculpture*, which was composed of photographs and text, the museum rejected it, only to show it twenty-five years later in "The American Century: Art and Culture, 1900–2000." Antin, personal communication.

16. Cindy Nemser, *Art Talk: Conversations with Fifteen Women Artists*, rev. ed. (New York: Harper Collins, 1995), 243.

17. See Melissa C. Thompson, "Size on Display": The Dynamics of Female Fat in Contemporary Performance Art" (Ph.D. diss., University of Wisconsin-Madison, 2006), 44–46.

18. Ellen Zweig provides one example of this type of reading: "The performance, of course, was the actual dieting, but the artwork was the row upon row of photographs, attesting to the fact that Antin could at least strive to 'carve' the perfect sculptural form of

her own body." Zweig, "Constructing Loss: Film and Presence in the Work of Eleanor Antin," *Millennium Film Journal*, no. 29 (Fall 1996): 36.

19. Eleanor Antin, *Carving: A Traditional Sculpture*, black-and-white photographs and text panel (; Art Institute of Chicago, 1972). In her text panel, Antin quoted Carl Bluemel, *Greek Sculptors at Work* (London: Phaidon Press, 1969), 12.

20. The feminist reading is proposed by Howard Fox, who sees Antin as comparing her body to popular models of the day. See Fox, *Eleanor Antin*, 44. For example, Twiggy, one of the most popular models of her time, emerged on the scene in 1967, standing at five feet, seven inches and weighing only ninety-one pounds; see Seid, *Never Too Thin*, 148–149.

21. Naomi Wolf, *The Beauty Myth: How Images of Beauty are Used against Women* (1991; repr., New York: Perennial, 2002), 12.

22. Antin has written more about the use of her body in her artistic creations in the often cited "Autobiography of the Artist as Autobiographer," *LAICA Journal*, no. 2 (October 1974): 18–20.

23. Anne Wagner, "Eleanor Antin," *Artforum* 38, no. 2 (1999): 141.

24. Seid, *Never Too Thin*, 166.

25. "Fortune from Fat," *Time*, February 21, 1972.

26. Ibid.; Seid, *Never Too Thin*, 138.

27. "Fortune from Fat."

28. Daniel Martin, "Organizational Approaches to Shame: Avowal, Management, and Contestation," *Sociological Quarterly* 41, no. 1 (2000): 129.

29. That being said, the organization continues to recognize members in the meetings who have reached a milestone in their weight loss. See Martin, "Organizational Approaches to Shame," 138–139.

30. Antin, *Carving: A Traditional Sculpture*.

31. Antin said in an interview, "When I was smoking I couldn't [sing]. So I stopped. For art you see. For art I could lose weight. For art I could do anything." See Eleanor Munro, *Originals: American Women Artists*, rev. ed. (New York: Da Capo Press, 2000), 417.

32. "Oral History Interview with Rachel Rosenthal," Los Angeles, September 2–3, 1989, transcript, Archives of American Art, Smithsonian Institution, Washington, D.C.

33. Quoted in Moira Roth, *Rachel Rosenthal* (Baltimore: Johns Hopkins University Press, 1997), 14, originally discussed in "Oral History Interview with Rachel Rosenthal."

34. The full script and stage explanations for *Charm* and *The Death Show* have been printed in Una Chaudhuri, ed., *Rachel's Brain and Other Storms—Rachel Rosenthal: Performance Texts* (London: Continuum, 2001). Rosenthal also performed and recorded *Charm* for "Soundings" on KPFC Pacifica Radio almost ten years after its original production, although the performance was strictly aural and performed with a full cast. The piece was also altered for the radio, including more music as well as a performer who wrote and performed new selections that functioned as the voices in Rosenthal's head. See Rosenthal, *Charm: KPFC Pacifica Radio* (Los Angeles: High Performance Audio, 1987), audiocassette.

35. She did this four times throughout the performance, becoming increasingly agitated and louder; see Chaudhuri, *Rachel's Brain*, 20, 23, 24, 30.

36. Ibid., 28.

37. This exchange with Barbara T. Smith, from the summer of 1975, took place when Rosenthal bought "times" in Smith's auction, *A Week in the Life of . . . .,* one of which included a correspondence exchange. She admired Smith's performances and looked up to her as a mentor. See Roth, *Rachel Rosenthal,* 158.

38. Ibid., 166.

39. Linda Montano, *Performance Artists Talking in the Eighties* (Berkeley: University of California Press, 2000), 198.

40. Overeaters Anonymous was founded by Rozanne S. in Los Angeles in 1960 and was modeled after a Gamblers Anonymous meeting she had attended with a friend the previous year. Following a twelve-step program like that of Alcoholics Anonymous and Gamblers Anonymous, the group provides members with a safe place to come together and share not only their struggles with overeating but also coping mechanisms. For a fuller history, see: Overeaters Anonymous, *Beyond Our Wildest Dreams: A History of Overeaters Anonymous as Seen by a Cofounder* (Rio Rancho, NM: Overeaters Anonymous, 1996).

41. Performed only once at Space Gallery in Los Angeles on October 21, 1978, *The Death Show* was part of a larger performance and exhibition event, *Thanathopsis: Contemplations on Death,* which involved a variety of media and thirty-two artists.

42. Chaudhuri, *Rachel's Brain,* 34–35.

43. Rachel Rosenthal, *"The Death Show," High Performance* 2, no. 5 (1979): 44.

44. Chaudhuri, *Rachel's Brain,* 36.

45. Ibid., 38–39.

46. Here, Rosenthal first refers to the "Bardo of the Fat Vampire"; the bardo is defined as the position of the soul between life and death. Chaudhuri, *Rachel's Brain,* 39.

47. Ibid., 36.

48. Susie Orbach, *Fat Is a Feminist Issue* (New York: Berkley Books, 1978), 6.

49. "Oral History Interview with Rachel Rosenthal."

50. Orbach, *Fat Is a Feminist Issue,* 9.

51. Rachel Rosenthal, personal communication, Los Angeles, May 29, 2009.

52. "Oral History Interview with Rachel Rosenthal."

53. Peter Wood, *The California Diet and Exercise Program* (Mountain View, CA: Anderson World Books, 1983), 33.

54. Joanna Frueh, "The Body through Women's Eyes" (1994), in *Power of Feminist Art,* ed. Mary D. Garrard and Norma Broude (London: Thames and Hudson, 1994), 190.

55. Lisa E. Bloom, "Ethnic Notions and Feminist Strategies of the 1970s: Some Work by Judy Chicago and Eleanor Antin," in *Jewish Identity in Modern Art History,* ed. Catherine M. Soussloff (Berkeley: University of California Press, 1999), 150.

56. Marvin Konner, *The Jewish Body* (New York: Schocken Books, 2009), 170.

57. Sander Gilman, *Making the Body Beautiful: A Cultural History of Aesthetic Surgery* (Princeton, NJ: Princeton University Press, 1999), 193. These ideas are also explored in Gilman, *The Jew's Body* (New York: Routledge, 1991).

58. Quoted in Jane Gross, "As Ethnic Pride Rises, Rhinoplasty Takes a Nose Dive," *New York Times,* January 3, 1999.

59. Christine Benvenuto, *Shiksa: The Gentile Woman in the Jewish World* (New York: St. Martin's, 2004), xii–xiii.

60. Michele Wallace, "Soul Pictures: Mid 1940s through Early 1950s," *Soul Pictures: Black Feminist Generations blog,* http://mjsoulpictures.blogspot.com/.

61. Faith Ringgold, *Change: Faith Ringgold's Over 100 Pound Weight Loss Performance Story Quilt*, photo etching on silk, 1986 (private collection).

62. Faith Ringgold, *We Flew Over the Bridge: The Memoirs of Faith Ringgold* (Boston: Bulfinch, 1995), 241–250; and Ringgold, personal communication, Englewood, NJ, November 1, 2009.

63. Bernice Steinbaum Gallery, *Faith Ringgold: Change: Painted Story Quilts* (New York: Bernice Steinbaum Gallery, 1987), 15.

64. Orbach, *Fat Is a Feminist Issue*, 13.

65. Faith Ringgold, "1970–1979," in *Change: Faith Ringgold's Over 100 Pound Weight Loss Performance Story Quilt*, photo etching on silk, 1986 (private collection).

66. Faith Ringgold, "1980–1985," in *Change: Faith Ringgold's Over 100 Pound Weight Loss Performance Story Quilt*, photo etching on silk, 1986 (private collection).

67. Faith Ringgold, "1970–1979," in *Change: Faith Ringgold's Over 100 Pound Weight Loss Performance Story Quilt*, photo etching on silk, 1986 (private collection).

68. Ringgold, *We Flew Over the Bridge*, 249.

69. Lori Ann Beaudoin read the materials in this performance as particularly feminine because the shapes of the two-liter bottles might be reminiscent of Ringgold's curvy form. "Since Ringgold has expressed her frustration with her weight, she may be articulating the pressures of the 'American dream' to be thin, and therefore, feminine. By enclosing the bottles in opaque garbage bags, Ringgold may be in fact denouncing the feminine practice and ideal by covering the hour-glass shape of the bottle-female form. Despite the cultural demands to be thin and Ringgold's struggle with her eating problem, the performance signifies a positive change towards self-acceptance. Moreover, securing the bags with heavy cord connotes the notion of the umbilical cord, and that there is no escaping from your body, yourself, and who you are in the world." See Beaudoin, "A Cultural Illness: Women, Identity, and Eating Problems in Faith Ringgold's Change Series" (master's thesis, Concordia University, Montreal, 1999), 41.

70. Faith Ringgold, "January–October 1986," in *Change: Faith Ringgold's Over 100 Pound Weight Loss Performance Story Quilt*, photo etching on silk, 1986 (private collection).

71. Like the first quilt, *Change 2* included lithographed photographs: five recent photos of Ringgold posing in front of her first *Change* quilt and other works (each photo appears twice for a total of ten); they are accompanied by eight text panels that provide the lyrics to her *Change Song*.

72. Ringgold, *We Flew Over the Bridge*, 247.

73. Faith Ringgold, *Change Song*, in *Change 2: Faith Ringgold's Over 100 Pound Weight Loss Performance Story Quilt*, photo etching on silk, 1988 (artist's collection).

74. Sidonie Smith, "Bodies of Evidence: Jenny Saville, Faith Ringgold, and Janine Antoni Weigh In," in *Interfaces: Women/Autobiography/Image/Performance*, ed. Sidonie Smith and Julia Watson (Ann Arbor: University of Michigan Press, 2005), 145.

75. Meg Lovejoy, "Disturbances in the Social Body: Differences in Body Image and Eating Problems among African American and White Women," *Gender and Society* 15, no. 2 (2001): 240.

76. Becky W. Thompson, *A Hunger So Wide and So Deep* (Minneapolis: University of Minnesota Press, 1994), 109–111.

77. Doris Witt, "What (N)ever Happened to Aunt Jemima: Eating Disorders, Fetal Rights, and Black Female Appetite in Contemporary American Culture," in *Skin Deep, Spirit Strong: The Black Female Body in American Culture*, ed. Kimberly Wallace-Sanders (Ann Arbor: University of Michigan Press, 2002), 99–127.

78. Osteoarthritic knees also contributed to her weight gain by discouraging her from exercising. Eventually she underwent knee surgery, which improved her mobility and her ability to exercise; See Ringgold, *We Flew Over the Bridge*, 248.

79. F. Kramer et al., "Long-Term Follow-up of Behavioral Treatment for Obesity: Patterns of Weight Regain Among Men and Women," *International Journal of Obesity* 13, no. 2 (1989): 123–126.

80. Ringgold, *We Flew Over the Bridge*, 248.

81. Faith Ringgold, *Change 3: Faith Ringgold's Over 100 Pound Weight Loss Performance Story Quilt*, photo etching on silk, 1991 (artist's collection).

82. Bordo, *Unbearable Weight*, 195.

83. Ibid., 192.

84. W. Charisse Goodman, *The Invisible Woman: Confronting Weight Prejudice in America* (Carlsbad, CA: Gürze Books, 1995), 12.

85. Other artists inspired by their example include Vanalyne Green (b. 1948) and Faith Ringgold (b. 1930).

86. Rosenthal, personal communication; Antin, personal communication.

87. Quoted in Fox, *Eleanor Antin*, 219.

CONTRIBUTORS

Megan Tagle Adams holds an M.A. in American Culture Studies from Bowling Green State University. Her recent research examines gender and race play through drag, mimicry, and cultural appropriation in beauty blogging. She currently organizes feminist and social justice programming as Coordinator of the Women's Center at the University of Maryland, Baltimore County.

Anthony Carlton Cooke is Visiting Professor of English at Emory University. His areas of specialization are twentieth-century American literature, African American literature, cinema and media studies, cultural studies, popular culture, and psychoanalysis. He has presented papers and published on these topics in the *Journal of Black Studies* and *Psychoanalysis, Culture, and Society*. His current research explores links between the closure of asylums in favor of community-based care in the mental health professions, the corresponding shift in the horror, crime, and thriller genres toward representations of the "psychopath," and the spread of stigmatization of mentally ill persons in the public sphere.

Renee Lee Gardner received her Ph.D. in English at Western Michigan University. A former American Association of University Women (AAUW) fellow, she specializes in postcolonial and transatlantic contemporary literature as well as queer, gender, and sexuality theories. With a focus on trauma, failure, and submission, she is revising a manuscript that reads female self-abnegation not as evidence of weakness but as a source of power with the potential to undermine nationalist aggression. She also currently serves as Formation Minister at St. Luke's Episcopal Church in Kalamazoo, Michigan.

Noel Glover is a Ph.D. student in the Faculty of Education–Language, Culture, and Teaching at York University in Toronto. His research explores the relationship between psychoanalysis, deconstruction, and education as a human condition.

Meghan Griffin holds a Ph.D. in Texts and Technology from the University of Central Florida and is Associate Professor of Business Communications at Daytona State College in Daytona Beach, Florida. Her research interests include life writing, embodiment philosophy, and gender in the workplace.

Daniel McNeil is Associate Professor of History at Carleton University, where he is also affiliated with the Institute of African Studies and the Migration and Diaspora Studies Initiative. He previously held the Ida B. Wells-Barnett Professorship in African and Black

Diaspora Studies at DePaul University, and taught media and cultural studies in the United Kingdom. His publications include *Sex and Race in the Black Atlantic: Mulatto Devils and Multiracial Messiahs* (2010) and *A Tale of Two Critics: Structures of Feeling in the Black Atlantic* (forthcoming).

Myra Mendible is Professor and Honors Fellow at Florida Gulf Coast University in Fort Myers, where she served as founding university faculty and co-founder of the English program. Dr. Mendible's scholarship and teaching engage diverse theoretical, disciplinary, and cultural perspectives, with primary interests in critical theory, literature and politics, and American studies. She has published widely in national and international peer-reviewed journals and is the editor of two previous collections: *From Bananas to Buttocks: The Latina Body in Popular Culture* (University of Texas Press, 2007) and *Race 2008: Critical Reflections on an Historic Campaign* (Brown/Walker Press, 2010).

Frances Negrón-Muntaner is a filmmaker, writer, curator, scholar, and professor at Columbia University, where she is founding curator of the Latino Arts and Activism Archive as well as Director of the Center for the Study of Ethnicity and Race and the Media and Idea Lab. Among her writings are *Boricua Pop: Puerto Ricans and the Latinization of American Culture* (2004), *The Latino Media Gap* (2014), and *Sovereign Acts* (forthcoming). Her films include *Brincando el charco: Portrait of a Puerto Rican* (1995) and *War for Guam*, broadcast on PBS stations in May and June 2015. In 2005, she was named one of the most influential Hispanics by *Hispanic Business Magazine* and in 2008 the United Nations' Rapid Response Media Mechanism recognized her as a global expert in the areas of mass media and Latino American studies. In 2012, she received Columbia University's "Most Distinguished Faculty Award."

Emily L. Newman holds a Ph.D. from The Graduate Center, City University of New York, and is currently Assistant Professor of Art History at Texas A&M University–Commerce. Often exploring the intersections of popular culture, feminism, and art, her research focuses on the way contemporary artists have addressed female body image. She has presented at national and international conferences and published on a wide variety of topics, including food and performance, rape in contemporary art, Lady Gaga and meat as clothing, and photographs confronting anorexia and eating disorders.

Leah Perry is Assistant Professor of Cultural Studies at SUNY-Empire State College. She received her Ph.D. from George Mason University's Cultural Studies program, one M.A. from New York University in Humanities and Social Thought, and a second M.A. in Religion from Yale Divinity School. Her teaching and research interests encompass gender and sexuality, American studies, immigration, race and ethnicity, religion, and media and popular culture. Her book manuscript about the role of U.S. immigration discourses, gender, and media in the rise of neoliberalism, entitled *Neoliberal Crossings: U.S. Immigration, Gender, and Media, 1981–2001,* is forthcoming from New York University Press. Her work can also be seen in national and international scholarly journals, most recently in a special issue of *Cultural Studies and/of the Law* (2014).

Michael Rancourt earned a Ph.D. in Communication and Rhetoric from Rensselaer Polytechnic Institute in New York. He teaches courses in communication and media at Washington State University, Vancouver. His research focuses on rhetoric and public culture, especially issues of citizenship, public memory, and collective identity in the mass media.

Madeline Walker holds a Ph.D. in twentieth-century American literature. She is the author of *The Trouble with Sauling Around, Conversion in Ethnic American Autobiography, 1965–2002* (University of Iowa Press, 2011) and a book of poems, *birth of the uncool* (Demeter Press, 2014). After distance-teaching academic writing to nursing students for five years, Madeline started her current career as instructional designer and education technology support specialist at the University of Victoria.

Karen Weingarten is Assistant Professor of English at Queens College, City University of New York. She is the author of *Abortion in the American Imagination: Before Life and Choice, 1880–1940* (Rutgers University Press, 2014). Her research encompasses late nineteenth- and early twentieth-century American literature, feminist theories and reproductive justice, and abortion rhetoric.

INDEX

feminism (*continued*)
Eleanor Antin and, 253; *Fat Is a Feminist Issue* (Orbach), 259; film and, 169, 172, 173, 181, 242, 243, 248 (*see also individual films*); masturbation and, 232, 248; power and, 119 (*see also* empowerment: of women); Rachel Rosenthal and, 257, 259; second-wave, 168, 172–174, 179–180; shadow, 110–111, 119. *See also* postfeminism

feminists, shaming shameless, 181

feminized soldiers and veterans, 189, 193–194. *See also* emasculated soldiers and veterans

Ferré, Luis A., 99

Flanders, Chad, 13

Fleming, Ian, 46–48

Flores, Ana, 75

Fontanez, Gloria, 101

food, nature of, 129–133

Foote, Thelma Wills, 241

40-Year-Old Virgin, The (film), 233, 237, 239, 242

Foucault, Michel, 33, 41n18, 41n20, 86, 127, 128, 133; *Birth of the Clinic*, 125–126; *The History of Sexuality*, 113–114

Fox, Howard, 253

Frank, Lisa, 62

freedom: to become shameless, 152. *See also* liberty

Freind, Christopher, 7, 20n30

Freud, Sigmund, 168, 184, 219–220; on anal eroticism, anal stage, anal character, 170–172; *Civilization and Its Discontents*, 169–171

Frye, Marilyn, 232, 248

FTO (fat mass and obesity) gene, 135–136

Fuery, Patrick, 226n31

Gaines, Jane, 242

Gallen, Joel, 182

Gang of Eight (immigration), 77

Garbage Offensive, 96–98

gay men, 6. *See also* homosexuality

Genesis (band), 78n1; "Illegal Alien," 57–59, 78n1

genocide, 68, 113

Gill, Rosalind, 172–174, 181

Gilroy, Paul, 3, 14–15, 53

Gingrich, Newt, 15

Giroux, Susan Searls, 114, 120

Goffman, Erving, 10–11

Gonzalez, Gloria, 100

González, Juan, 92, 102

Goodman, W. Charisse, 267

Greengrass, Paul, 199–202

Green Zone (film), 198–203

guilt, 190; vs. shame, 40n6, 52, 53, 190

Gulf War, 196, 197, 203

Guzmán, Pablo "Yoruba," 84, 85, 89, 94–98, 102

Halberstam, J., 110–111

Hall, Stuart, 9

Halloween (film): deinstitutionalization, shame, and rise of the "slasher" trope in, 208–224; Michael Myers, 209–221, 223–224; psychoanalytic perspectives on, 208, 213, 214, 217, 225n3

Hamid, Moshin, 109–121

Hartman, Saidiya, 27, 30–31

Hartnell, Anna, 109, 110

health. *See* disease; medicalization and public health

Hellmann, John, 191

Herz, Ansel, 99

Hocquenghem, Guy, 171–172

homosexuality, 6, 48. *See also* lesbianism

hooks, bell, 232, 240–241, 248

horror films, 208, 209, 223. *See also Halloween*

Hughes, Langston, 38–39

humiliated fury, 202

humiliation vs. shame, 190

Huntington, Samuel P., 14, 20n28, 53

Hurt Locker, The (film), 197, 198

"Illegal Alien" (Genesis), 57–59, 78n1

"illegal alien," invention of the, 61–62

Illegal Immigration Reform and Immigrant Responsibility Act of 1996 (IIRIRA), 71, 74–76

Immigrant Marriage Fraud Amendment of 1986 (IMFA), 76
immigrants: criminality and, 57–62, 70–78; racism and, 52, 57–61, 67
immigrant women, abuse of, 70–71, 76
immigration, 57–62; importing colonialism/importing criminals (the 1980s), 62–71; Latino, 14; selling porous borders and border security, 71–78
Immigration Act of 1990, 71
Immigration Emergency Act, 63
immigration enforcement, mission of, 75
Immigration Reform and Control Act of 1986 (IRCA), 58, 62–64; amnesty offered under, 59, 62; and border militarization, 65, 69, 72; employer sanctions, 65–69; and the media, 70; ramifications and aftermath, 63, 71, 72, 76
imported colonialism, 61, 62
in-group/out-group, 190
integration (of the disabled), 154, 158, 159; vs. interaction, 160
interdependence, 150, 153–155, 157–161
In the Valley of Elah (film), 197, 198
Invasion of the Body Snatchers (film), 226n31
Iraq War films, 188, 202–204; emotion and closeness in, 188–189, 197–204

Jaeger, Paul T., 158
James Bond, 46–50, 52, 53; and BDSM, 48–49
Jersey Girl (film), 246
Jewish women, 36, 37, 261–262
Jews, 67, 261
Jiménez, José "Cha Cha," 84
John Birch Society, 44, 47
Johnson, Joyce, 32–33, 41nn13–14
Jolles, Marjorie, 169
Jones, LeRoi, 93
Joseph, Nathan, 92
Joyce, James: *Ulysses*, 167
Juno (film), 31
Junod, Tom, 4

Kennedy, Anthony, 39n2
Klein, Melanie, 214, 217, 226–227nn33–34
Koffler, Keith, 3
Konner, Melvin, 261
Kovic, Ron, 192–195
Kratina, Karin, 134
Kristeva, Julia, 156
Kundera, Milan, 167

Lacot, Antero, 98
Lait, Jack, 96
Larsen, Nella, 51
Latimer, Heather, 31
Latinos, 13–14; racism and, 11, 57–61, 66–70, 87–89, 96. *See also* immigration; Puerto Ricans; Young Lords
Latino Threat Narrative, 14, 70
Lazarus, Emma, 65
Leigh, Mike, 28–29
lesbianism, 232–235, 248
Leverenz, David, 53
Levinas, Emmanuel, 4
Lewis, Helen B., 190
Lewis, M., 175
Lewis, Sinclair, 36–37
liberalism, education, and the interpersonal self, 145–148
liberty, 116
life, 119–120
Luciano, Felipe, 86, 93, 99, 102
Lupton, Deborah, 132–133

Madonna-whore binary, 236. *See also* virgin-whore binary
mainstreaming. *See* integration
Mallory, Carol, 176
Mariel boatlift, 62–63
Martin, Daniel, 255–256
Martinot, Steve, 60
masculinity, 46, 88, 192–194. *See also* emasculated soldiers and veterans
masturbation, women's, 230–233; in film, 232–248; self-realization, self-destruction, and, 233–235; self-stimulation, self-discovery, and, 233–235, 243–249; stigma, sexual autonomy, and, 230, 232, 239–243; voyeurism,

masterbation, women's (*continued*)
exhibitionism, and, 235–239. *See also*
autoeroticism

McGee, Michael C., 191

McRobbie, Angela, 170, 173

medicalization and public health,
125–128

Meeuf, Russell, 193

Meléndez, Miguel "Mickey," 85, 87, 91,
92, 96

Memorial Mania (Doss), 187, 188

Mendez, Mervin, 85

Menninger, Karl, 213

mental illness, 213, 217, 221; and criminality, 209, 212, 214–216, 221, 224;
in film, 223 (see also *Halloween*); and
stigma, 209, 211, 221, 223, 224. *See
also* deinstitutionalization

Merleau-Ponty, Maurice, 150, 154, 160

Mexican Americans. *See* immigration

Mexico-U.S. border: border militarization,
65, 69, 72; Border Patrol, 69–71; selling porous borders and border security, 71–78

Milbank, John, 115–116

Miller, Teresa, 60

Minor Characters (Johnson), 32–33

Monterro, Felipa, 44

Morales, Iris, 90, 93, 101, 102

Mortimer, Lee, 96

Mudry, Jessica, 131, 132–133

Mulvey, Laura, 235

Mumolo, Annie, 168

narcissism: and shame, 150, 155. *See also*
autoeroticism

national identity, 87, 90, 187, 191

national memorials, 187, 188

Nealon, Jeffrey, 114, 120

neofeminism, 173

neoliberal crimmigration, 58–62, 70, 73,
75–78

neoliberalism, 53, 58–61, 65, 68

New York Lords, 84–85, 90, 100, 101. *See
also* Young Lords

Nidetch, Jean, 255

Nin, Anaïs, 45–46

9/11 terrorist attacks, 18, 109–113, 116–
120

North American Free Trade Agreement
(NAFTA), 71–72

Not Another Teen Movie (*NATM*), 182–184

notions, 9

nude paintings, 247, 266

nude photographs, 253

Nussbaum, Martha, 146, 147, 155, 158, 160

Obama, Barack, 14–15, 53, 77

*Obama's America: Unmaking the American
Dream* (D'Souza), 15

obesity. *See* fat/obesity

Oboler, Suzanne, 13

obscenity, 175, 176

O'Hara, Lily, 136

Oliver, Denise, 89, 93–94

Oprah Winfrey Show, The, 251

Orbach, Susie, 259–260, 263

orgasms, women's, 231, 238, 243–248

Ortiz, Juan "Fi," 85

other-regarding shame, 147, 152–157,
159–161

Overeaters Anonymous, 258, 260, 265,
271n40

pain, sociality of, 3–4

Pakistan. *See Reluctant Fundamentalist*

Perez, Richie, 93

Persian Gulf War, 196, 197, 203

Petchesky, Rosalind, 33

Phillips, Kendall R., 208

Piepmeier, Alison, 41n16

Pleasantville (film), 246–247

Poovey, Mary, 33

postcolonial melancholia, 112

postfeminism, 169–170, 172–174; contradictory character of, 174; as double
entanglement, 179; Freud and, 169,
174; postfeminist episodes in contemporary Hollywood films, 167–184

postfeminist sensibility, 168–169, 172–174,
179, 181, 184

post-traumatic stress disorder (PTSD),
191

Pothier, Dianne, 145, 158

self-consciousness, 4, 11, 215, 218, 238, 258
self-control, 5; lack of (*see* women: out of control); need for women to have, 170–172, 176
self-deprecating humor, 171, 256
self-destruction, 116, 118–120, 233–235
self-determination: Black, 88; Puerto Rican, 99, 100; sexual, 231, 240–243, 248–249
self-discovery, sexual, 233–235, 243–249
self-realization, masturbation and, 233–235
self-regarding shame, 147, 151–153, 157–161; vs. other-regarding shame, 161
self-regulation, 168, 169, 174
self-reliance, 7–8
self-stimulation, women's, 230, 232–235, 243, 248. *See also* masturbation
self-sufficiency, 146, 155, 158, 159
self-surveillance, 138, 172, 174, 179, 180, 184
September 11 attacks, 18, 109–113, 116–120
sexual autonomy, 93, 236, 246, 248; masturbation, stigma, and, 239–243
sexual intercourse, 230, 231, 243–245, 248
sexuality, female, 182, 230–231; and power, 16, 18, 236, 239, 240, 248; racism and, 239, 240, 242. *See also* anal eroticism; masturbation
sexual self-actualization, female, 230, 240, 247
sexual self-determination, 231, 240–243, 248–249
sexual self-discovery, 233–235, 243–249
shadow feminism, 110–111, 119
Shakespeare, William, 169
shame: and the breakdown of civilization, 182–184; contingent role as cultural practice, 9; defined, 8, 32, 52, 175, 190; vs. guilt, 40n6, 52, 53, 190; vs. humiliation, 190; nature of, 149–153; omnipresence of, 148–149; representational power of, 9; that binds, 9–18; two kinds of, 151–152 (*see also* other-regarding shame; self-regarding shame). *See also individual topics*
shameful sharing. *See* education, liberalism, and the interpersonal self

shameless feminists, 181
shamelessness, 5, 202–204; becoming shameless, 150, 152; in "Cora Unashamed" (Hughes), 38; and depiction of women's bodily functions, 167, 168, 173, 175, 176, 179, 181, 184; merchandising of, 6; shame and, 148, 150, 179
"shameless times," 6
"shameless" women, shaming of, 176, 181, 184
shame rage, 202
shame revivalism, 16; and the politics of virtue, 4–8
shaming, ashamed, 155
shaming rituals, 10, 11, 13, 31, 211
She's All That (film), 182–183
She's Gotta Have It (film), 239–242
"shock and awe," 199
Simpson, Alan, 65–66
slasher films, 208, 209, 224n3. See also *Halloween*
slavery, 30–31
slut shaming, 16
Smith, Greg M., 188–189, 192
Smith, Kyle, 202
Smith, Paul, 62
Smith, Sidonie, 265
Smith, William French, 63
sociality of pain, 3–4
socially inferiorized bodies, 16
Solinger, Ricki, 40n3
Son of Sam (David Berkowitz), 222
spectacle, shame as, 1–4
Spielberg, Steven, 188
splitting (defense mechanism), 214, 219, 220, 227n34; defined, 227n34
Stahl, Roger, 196
Statue of Liberty, 65–66
stigma, 6; abortion and, 35, 39; disabilities and, 153, 156–158; masturbation, sexual autonomy, and, 230, 232, 239–243; of the mentally ill, 209, 211, 221, 223, 224; Mexican Americans, immigration, and, 58, 60–61, 70, 71, 74, 77–78; and the politics of

Myra Mendible is Professor in the Languages and Literature Department at Florida Gulf Coast University in Ft. Myers, where she served as founding university faculty and co-founder of the English program. Dr. Mendible's scholarship and teaching engages diverse theoretical, disciplinary, and cultural perspectives, with primary interests in politics and literature, media culture, ethnicity, and gender. She has presented her research at national and international conferences, published widely in a variety of peer-reviewed journals, and is the editor of *From Bananas to Buttocks: The Latina Body in Popular Culture* (2007) and *Race 2008: Critical Reflections on an Historic Campaign* (2010).

www.ingramcontent.com/pod-product-compliance
Lightning Source LLC
Chambersburg PA
CBHW020830270326
41928CB00006B/481